CONTENTS

Part 1

	Introduction	5
1	The Glasgow Critique	15
2	Contours of Coverage	26
3	'Figures' − and Facts	47
4	Trade Unions and the Media	71
5	Case Studies I: The Glasgow Dustcart Drivers' Strike	83
6	Case Studies II: The Problems of the Car Industry	93
7	More Case Studies	108
	The Westminster Hospital Pay-Beds Dispute	
	The Imperial Tyepwriter Sit-In	
	Demonstrations over Closures at Ebbw Vale	
	Trouble at British Airways	
8	'Framing' the News	119
9	Conclusion	133

Part 2
News Scripts

	Introduction	149
1	The Hospital Consultants' Work-to-Contract	154
2	The Problems of the Car Industry	174
3	The National Graphical Association − Newspaper Publishers' Association Dispute and the Daily Mirror/ NATSOPA Dispute	245
4	The Glasgow Dustcart Drivers' Strike	262
5	Scottish Ambulance Controllers' Strike	288
6	The Imperial Typewriter Sit-In	294
7	The London Bus Strike	301
8	British Airways	305
9	The Avon Computer Strike	314
10	The British Rail Signalmen's Strikes	315
11	The Ebbw Vale Demonstration	332
12	The Morriston Hospital Strike	334

13	The British Aircraft Corporation Sit-In	338
14	The London Docks Containerisation Strike	339
15	Industrial Civil Servants' Strike	369
16	The Westminster Hospital Dispute	371
17	Liverpool Dustcart Drivers' Strike	380
18	Sealink Ferry Strike	383
19	Daily Mirror/SOGAT Dispute	384
20	Electricians' Strikes	390
21	British Rail Workshop Supervisors' Work to Rule	392
22	The Hull Dock Strike	399
23	The Newmarket Stable Lads' Strike	400
	Appendix: Harold Wilson's speech on the car industry, 3 January 1975	403
	Index	406

INTRODUCTION

'Pure bias'. Succinct, to the point, this was Arthur Scargill's characterisation of the two main evening television programmes' coverage of the 1984 coal strike.{1} Blunter still, the leader of the Nottinghamshire miners roared at the cameras, 'It's all being distorted. Take the bloody thing away'.{2} Both Scargill and Chadburn were of course fighting their corner in the gravest industrial confrontation ever covered by television in Britain. Arthur Scargill at least may have been lacing his attack on television journalism with a measure of calculation. Nevertheless he, Ray Chadburn and the band of sympathisers who maintained an intermittent enfilade fire against TV news throughout that strike were refuelling a genuine sense of grievance and a controversy reaching back more than a decade — the recurring complaint that despite its commitment to 'due impartiality' television news is consistently biased against the unions.

Not that the unions have had a monopoly of complaint. The Confederation of British Industry, the Association of British Chambers of Commerce, the Institute of Directors and Aims of Industry all complained to the Annan Committee on the Future of Broadcasting in the mid-1970s about incomplete, under-informed, superficial and unduly negative reporting. The most outspoken, Aims of Industry, contended that:

> 'The majority of businessmen, however, do believe that television is biased against industry, and that this is constantly illustrated in a number of ways, not least in an imbalance in the over-large number of militants of left-wing anti-capitalist views invited to appear.'{3}

At one time Aims of Industry even ran a series of 'Bent Microphone Awards' for unbalanced presentations of industrial or business subjects. But management's unhappiness was most frequently voiced privately or expressed in unwillingess to appear in interviews. Even the Aims of

Industry campaign petered out without marshalling more than sporadic and anecdotal evidence for its contention that newsrooms contained too many people whose attitudes were unsympathetic to private industry. If some of the unions' criticisms ran parallel to those of the the employers, they were more comprehensive and tenaciously voiced, and they were to develop in more substantial form.

The reasons for these discontents were as numerous as their relative importance was elusive. To put the matter adequately would require little less than a recapitulation of the history of industrial relations and the development of the media in Britain since the second world war. Painting with strokes that are bold to the point of caricature, since both these stories have been amply told elsewhere, one of the salient elements was clearly the rise of television itself. Only recently a minority outlet that was still not taken altogether seriously, it had established itself as the most pervasive of all news media, and among the most trusted. It was now a force to be reckoned with, even feared.

As it happened, the new medium was displaying a growing interest in economic affairs. For this was also the period of deepening awareness of Britain's flagging economic performance, of the search for a cure for 'the English disease' – and for the culprits. Other considerations also combined to push the trade unions into greater public prominence: their pivotal involvement in the internal politics of the Labour Party; and attempts by governments of either hue to discover how best to respond to the unions' enhanced power and status – for these were the days when they were treated as a new 'estate of the realm'. At one moment they were wooed into a variety of partnerships with government in the recurring quest for that secular grail of the 1960s and 1970s, a workable prices-and-incomes policy. At other times the carrot gave way to the stick, as Labour and Conservative Governments in turn sought to impose unwelcome changes on the unions. Whether courted or coerced, the unions repeatedly found themselves on centre stage. One may question whether their power for either good or ill was as great as many in the media – and some within the unions themselves – imagined. Nevertheless, they were widely seen as powerful organisations with a role to play in respect of a host of important and controversial public issues. The ensuing media attention was not in fact confined to the darker or more aggressive face of unionism, as some trade unionists came to feel. Day by day microphones and cameras hung on the words of union secretaries as they emerged from Congress House or a conclave with Ministers to air their views on some weighty issue of the moment. In the mid-1970s Jack Jones of the Transport & General Workers' Union and Hugh Scanlon of the Amalgamated Union of Engineering Workers were to be presented as among the most important figures in the country, perceived by the public as more powerful than many Ministers. As, perhaps, for a moment they were.

Yet this enhanced attention was a mixed blessing. In most respects the unions conduct their affairs more openly than many other power-holding groups in Britain. Their internal arguments and tensions are more readily accessible to reporters than those in the board room, where more discreet forms of carnage are the norm. If industrial relations deteriorated it was usually the unions which, by striking, provided the hard news event that caught the media's attention, however great the underlying responsibility of management. And that attention was caught with increasing frequency at the end of the 1960s and in the early 1970s. As industrial unrest grew, groups which had hitherto been inhibited about 'industrial action' were more ready to use such 'muscle' as they might have, or to employ more aggressive tactics, not least in such celebrated episodes as the mass flying pickets of the 1974 coal strike. And when Governments riposted with legislation to curb union power, there was a greater readiness to frustrate or flout the new laws. In 1974 the confrontation between the miners and the Heath Government over pay precipitated a general election, a change in government and Edward Heath's fall from party leadership. With the intense politicisation of industrial relations that characterised those years the unions inescapably made news. Their misfortune was that this was often in highly controversial settings, and at times in ways that gave rise to vivid pictures that left a mark on the memory out of all proportion to the time they occupied the screen.

It would be an oversimplification to say that the unions became unpopular. Healthy majorities continued to tell Gallup that trade unions were 'a good thing', and apart from periods when a major strike was in progress the public attached only modest priority to industrial relations reform. On several notable occasions the workers' case was shown to enjoy more public sympathy than the Government's or the employers'.

The polls even found more people to blame the Common Market and decimalisation for inflation than the unions. However, increasing numbers saw them as unduly powerful, and sympathy with workers' demands rarely extended to backing for strike action. Most seriously, the strong support for most of the Wilson and Heath Governments' proposals for limiting union power included many union members.{4}

Aware of the changing climate of opinion at both governmental and popular level, many in the unions were convinced that the problem was not one of substance but of image. Inured to the hostility of much of Fleet Street, they became increasingly frustrated with the way television coverage underplayed their quieter and constructive activities to concentrate on controversial and negative matters. Some alleged that reporting of the 'activist' strand of trade unionism fell short of the broadcasters' commitment to impartiality. These resentments found expression in a report by the Association of Cine & Television Technicians in 1971, which surveyed the handling of industrial relations by radio and television over the course of the week. It was highly critical of the 'erratic' and 'superficial' nature of part of the coverage, and of imbalance in the reporting of several stories.{5} For all its acknowledged limitations the ACTT report deepened convictions in the trade union movement that declining public sympathy and the widespread support for industrial relations legislation owed much to the 'bad press' they were receiving nightly from television.

They were not alone in questioning the way television behaved. As academic interest in the medium grew in the wake of its expansion some researchers were not prepared to take the broadcasters' claim that coverage was balanced and fair at face value. Nowhere was this sceptical, radical mood stronger than with the Glasgow University Media Group. This was an eight-strong research team, mostly of sociologists, funded by the Social Science Research Council, and initially based on the University of Glasgow. Its senior member was John Eldridge, Professor of Sociology at Glasgow, although Greg Philo was to become its most active public spokesman and advocate. The Group's analysis of the way television reported industrial affairs during the first five months of 1975 was to become the most detailed and influential study of television news yet published in Britain. Running to over eight hundred pages, Bad News, published in 1976, and More Bad News, which appeared in 1980, drew on traditional textual analysis, 'critical' insights and the newer techniques of semiology and sociolinguistics to reach a damning conclusion. Television, they held, constructs a 'picture of society in general and industrial society in particular' which includes the

'laying of blame for society's industrial and economic problems at the door of the workforce. This is done in the face of contradictory evidence which, when it appears, is either ignored, smothered, or at worst is treated as if it supports the inferential frameworks utilised by the producers of news' (Bad News 267-8).

Though initially arising from television's treatment of the unions, their indictment subsequently broadened to include its handling of the working class generally. It was to be amplified and reiterated at union conferences, summer schools and seminars, in video presentations and later works such as Peter Beharrell and Greg Philo's Trade Unions and the Media (1977) and Really Bad News, published by four members of the Glasgow Group in 1981. BBC-TV twice devoted 50-minute programmes to their criticisms — although on neither occasion were the Group satisfied with the way their case was dealt with.

Most academic social science enjoys, at most, a mayfly moment of public attention, followed, at best, by the obscure immortality of a thousand footnotes. This did not happen to the Glasgow volumes. A decade later they were still the only large-scale studies of British television news. And they were influential. For all the anger and contempt with which they were greeted by such senior broadcasters as Sir Geoffrey Cox, one of the great formative influences on the development of Independent Television News, and Paul Fox, a former head of BBC-TV Current Affairs, they laid their mark on thinking about the media by politicians, trade unionists, academics and even broadcasters.{6} As the BBC's assistant director-general ruefully acknowledged some years later:

'Despite the BBC's misgivings about the methods employed in their research, the BBC recognises that it would be unwise to overlook the influence their work may have had in some circles.'{7}

Those circles extended to substantial sections of the trade union movement and the Labour Party. There were strong overtones of the Glasgow volumes in the passage on the media in Labour's Programme, 1982, and they featured prominently in a party broadcast that was highly critical of existing media structures and practices. Many trade unionists saw the Glasgow studies as weighty academic confirmation that their anger or unease over the way television reported their affairs was only too well founded. The work of the TUC's Media Working Group strongly reflected the impact of their findings.{8} The Campaign for Press & Broadcasting Freedom hailed them as a 'devastating indictment of the broadcasters' claims that they were impartial', strengthening the case for a 'right of reply' for groups and individuals aggrieved by television coverage – just one of a number of schemes for reforms of media structures or practices that drew sustenance from the Glasgow work.{9} Tony Benn also found ammunition in them for his longer-standing campaign for changes in the media.{10} The Group's influence was also evident in a complaint to the BBC and Independent Broadcasting Authority in 1981 by over a hundred Labour MPs, academics and trade union officials alleging 'bias against the trade union and Labour movement in public broadcasting'.{11}

But the impact was not confined to the Left, although for understandable reasons the criticisms found a readier home there. The Committee on the Future of Broadcasting, under the chairmanship of Lord Annan, 'detected an initial bias' in the Group's work, but seems nevertheless to have been influenced by it in arriving at its conclusion that television 'coverage of industrial affairs is in some respects inadequate and unsatisfactory'.{12} And despite a cool initial reception in professional reviews, the Group's work has over the years been absorbed into the mainstream of academic media studies on both sides of the Atlantic.{13} The findings have been treated as a major empirical contribution to the debate within sociology about the role of the media in society. There can be few courses in media studies or journalism which do not give a prominent – though not necessarily uncritical – place to the Glasgow studies. They have even established their place on A-level reading lists. Even within broadcasting, although the immediate effect was to generate a furious hostility to media sociology which was very slow to dissipate, and which hampered access for researchers for years after, some were receptive to at least part of the Bad News argument. This was to be seen most clearly in The Friday Alternative, which offered an 'alternative' view of the news during the early months of Channel Four, and less directly in such programmes as Trade Union

World and Diverse Reports.

Politically, academically and within broadcasting, then, the Glasgow studies have undoubtedly left their mark. Even after a decade they retain their initial importance. For they are not merely a discussion of five months' TV news; they amount to a standing critique of the values and operating principles which have governed first radio, and later television, news practically since the birth of broadcasting in Britain. For their contention is not simply that television is biased against the trade unions. It is that the routine practices of newsgathering and reporting, which the broadcasters have seen as ensuring the balance and impartiality to which they are committed by law or convention and professional ethics, in reality constitute a form of ideology which is consistently prejudicial to the trade unions, and indeed to the working class and Labour movement generally. The conclusions appear as pessimistic as they are fundamental. For it is hard to come away from the two principal volumes other than convinced that there is no way of eradicating or even attenuating the engrained biases they identify within anything like the present structures and techniques of broadcasting.

But are the Glasgow criticisms founded? Four years after the publication of Bad News the Group felt entitled to claim:

'The response from both broadcasters and critics to the first volume of our study, included arguments mounted against the overall strategy of our work: but, significantly, not against its evidential detail' (More Bad News 398).

And again:

'It is significant that little attention has been paid thus far to the evidence on which we based these conclusions' (More Bad News 402).

Or, as Greg Philo, wrote several years later:

'We can only repeat, yet again, that our work stands or falls as detailed empirical evidence. If we are shown to be wrong or to have counted or measured incorrectly then we will retract what we have said. But we cannot answer the vague accusations of 'bias' and 'selectivity' which are constantly made about us by those at the top of the TV tree.'{14}

If it is implied that the absence of challenge was a tacit acceptance of the solidity of the evidence, this was a trifle disingenuous. For their main sample amounted to 5,942 items, with no fewer than 2,065 reports on 261 different stories being classified as 'industrial news' (Bad News 131-133 and 143). The latter were analysed both in terms of verbal content and of a range of technical and presentational features. Even the broadcasters would have found it difficult, if not impossible, to reconstitute their sample for a comprehensive re-scrutiny, for at that time master tapes of programme output were not systematically preserved. Much of the evidence had vanished. The further task of reassessing this material would also make the stoutest heart quail. The Glasgow project at one time or other occupied eight authors and a support staff, and stretched over several years. Small wonder that few contemplated retracing their footsteps in detail.

Yet the Glasgow findings constitute a fundamental challenge to the values and practices of British television news. If they are valid, the case for a comprehensive reconsideration of both processes and structures would seem as hard to resist now as when they first wrote. Our purpose here, therefore, is to give those findings that closer attention the importance of the issues warrants, and which the Group itself invites. Accordingly, we will consider the 'evidential detail' on which the Glasgow findings rest. For reasons of practicality we will sample that evidence, just as the original volumes did, concentrating on coverage of industrial disputes by Independent Television News between January and April 1975. Even so, the material amounts to some 1,700 pages of running orders, scripts and transcripts from ITN's microfilm record. The discussion is of necessity confined almost entirely to the verbal record, though a partial indication of the vision output is available. Regrettable though this limitation so obviously is, it is rather less of a disability in reviewing the Glasgow critique than might be imagined, because the main elements of that critique rest wholly or mainly on verbal analysis. Indeed, this was one of the grounds on which reviewers justifiably criticised the first volume – although, as Bad News notes, a high proportion of coverage in fact consisted of newsreaders or journalists speaking to camera. These months produced little striking visual material. To some extent More Bad News rectified these omissions, but the sample selected for vision analysis was small, and the findings did not greatly modify or extend the first volume's criticisms of strike coverage. Since our concern lies essentially with the Glasgow

Group's treatment of strike reporting, the sad absence of the visual record has fewer consequences for the chapters that follow than perhaps it should.

1   The Guardian, The Daily Telegraph, 28 August 1984.
2   The Nine o'Clock News, BBC1, ?30 May 1984.
3   Evidence for the Committee on the Future of Broadcasting, Aims of Industry, 1974, p.1.
4   Cf. The Gallup Political Index for the period.
5   One Week: A Survey of Television Coverage of Union and Industrial Affairs in the Week Jan. 8-14, 1971, ACTT, 1971.
6   Cf. Sir Geoffrey Cox, 'Bad News – or Poor Scholarship?', Independent Broadcasting, December 1976; Paul Fox, 'Getting it Wrong', The Listener, 9 September 1976.
7   A. Protheroe, Holding the Balance in Current Affairs Programmes, BBC, May 1983, 10-11.
8   Cf. Reports of the Trades Union Congress, 1974-1981; Media Coverage of Industrial Disputes, January and February 1979: A Cause for Concern, TUC, 1979; How to Handle the Media, TUC, 1979; Guide to Critical View and Listening, TUC, 1981.
9   'Why Their News is Bad News', 'Open Door', BBC2, 1982.
10 In Arguments for Democracy (Cape, 1981), he refers to the Group's 'careful monitoring' of broadcasts (103), and their 'carefully researched analysis' (118). Arguing that 'there has been a sustained media campaign against the trade union movement, its members, its industrial role, and its political aspirations – a campaign centering on the thesis that the trade unions, and the working people they represent, are mainly responsible for virtually all our economic difficulties – he notes:
    'The methods used by the BBC and ITN newscasters to achieve this are, at last, being monitored and studied scientifically, and the results of some of these studies have been published, for instance in two Glasgow University Media Group studies...'(160).
    See also a letter from Michael Meacher, MP, another advocate of media reform, suggesting that 'The overall weight of the total Glasgow evidence cannot be impuned' (The Guardian, 2 September 1982), and his remarks in 'The Man Alive Debate', BBC2, 28 July 1982.
11 The Times, 6 April 1981. For a fuller discussion of the influence of the Group's work on the Left see C. Gardner and J. Sheppard, 'Transforming Television', Part 1, 'The Limits of Left Policy', Screen, 25(2), March-April 1984, 26-38. Their assessment is that 'The repercussions ... were enormous'.
12 Report of the Committee on the Future of Broadcasting, Cmnd. 6753, HMSO, 1977, 272.

13 See, for example, to cite only books, T. Burns, The BBC: Public Institution and Private World, Macmillan, 1977; A. Piepe, S. Crouch and M. Emerson, Mass Media and Cultural Relationships, Saxon House, 1978; J. Fiske and J. Hartley, Reading Television, Methuen, 1978; P. Golding and P. Elliott, Making the News, Longman, 1979; D.L. Altheide and R.P. Snow, Media Logic, Sage Publications, 1979; H.J. Gans, Deciding What's News, Constable, 1980; C. Gardner, Media, Politics and Culture: A Socialist View, Macmillan, 1979; T. Gitlin, The Whole World is Watching, California U.P., 1980; P. Golding, 'The Missing Dimensions – News Media and the Management of Social Change' in E. Katz and T. Scecsko, Mass Media and Social Change, Sage Publications, 1981; R. Clutterbuck, The Media and Political Violence, Macmillan 1981; G. Tuchman, 'Myth and the Consciousness Industry: A New Look at the Effects of the Mass Media' in Katz and Scecsko, op.cit.; R. Silverstone, The Message of Television, Heinemann, 1981; J. Curran and J. Seaton, Power Without Responsibility, Fontana, 1981; J. Seaton, 'Trade Unions and the Media' in B. Pimlott and C. Cook, Trade Unions in British Politics, Longman, 1982, 272-290; J. Hartley, Understanding the News, Methuen, 1982; D. McQuail, Mass Communication Theory: An Introduction, Sage Publications, 1983; P. Schlesinger, G. Murdock and P. Elliott, Televising Terrorism: Political Violence and Popular Culture, Comedia Publishing Group, 1983; J. Tunstall, The Media in Britain, Constable, 1983.

14 The Guardian, 1 June 1982.

THE GLASGOW CRITIQUE

In essence the Glasgow studies see television news as 'a manufactured product based on a coherent set of professional and ideological beliefs and expressed in a rigid formula of presentation' (Bad News 31). It 'conveys many of the culturally dominant assumptions of our society' (Bad News 1). They argue that 'routine news practices led to the production of bad news' (More Bad News xiii). There was a 'consistent failure to cover the area thoroughly' and the reporting of strikes was 'clearly skewed against the interest of the working class and organised labour' and 'in favour of the managers of industry' (More Bad News 400). Indeed, the news presented 'an entirely coherent view of the world at a deep level', so that 'the attentive viewer of the TV bulletins would have found *nothing in the period of our sample...which did other than confirm this belief system*' (Bad News 37, 31 emphasis mine).

The Glasgow volumes are not just about news: they are also about power. As Bad News puts it:

'Communicative power is about the right to define and demarcate situations. When we look at cultural power in this context we mean the power to typify, transmit, and define the 'normal', to set agendas. The power is used to reproduce highly selected events, and to manufacture news as if these events were the centrally important events of that day. In short, one must see news as reflecting not the events in the world 'out there', but as the manifestation of the collective cultural codes of those employed to do this selective and judgmental work for society' (13-14).

It further argues:

'There is much that is intrinsic in the social and normative coding of those messages we call 'news', which prevents the realisation of the aims of neutral communication of information.

The code works at all levels: in the notion of 'the story' itself, in the selection of stories, in the way material is gathered and prepared for transmission, in the dominant style of language used, in the permitted and limited range of visual presentation, in the overall duration of bulletins, in the duration of items within bulletins, in the real technological limitations placed on the presentation, in the finances of the news services, and above all, in the underpinning processes of professionalisation which turn men and women into television journalists' (10-11).

In general terms the proposition that the mass media are involved not only with reflecting reality but in some sense defining and creating it would be accepted by many communications researchers. But the Glasgow argument goes further. The processes of news production are neither neutral nor pluralist. Instead, they result in certain meanings or perceptions of reality being preferred while others are rendered marginal or illegitimate. In the words of Bachrach and Baratz, the media appear to underwrite systematically 'a set of predominant values, beliefs, rituals and institutional procedures ('rules of the game') that operate systematically and consistently to the benefit of certain persons and groups at the expense of others'.{1}

This is not to suggest television news was mere ruling class propaganda (More Bad News 124). Nor was it packed with anything so crude as conscious, deliberate bias — despite references to evidence being 'ignored' or 'smothered' (Bad News 19; Trade Unions and the Media 128, 133) — though this is the impression many readers take away from the Glasgow study.{2} Rather, the distortions .are attributed to the concealed ideological implications of the conventions of television news, and the routine practices of the newsrooms. Stuart Hall puts the issue in these terms: 'Unwittingly, unconsciously, the broadcaster has served as a support for the reproduction of a dominant ideological discursive field.'{3} In short, 'communicative power' is a form of political power. Television's functions in society include 'the cultural legitimation of the consensus and the status quo'. It is 'a front-runner medium of cultural legitimation' (Bad News 15). The Group quotes with apparent approval Gerbner's contention that mass communications 'are the cultural arm of the industrial order from which they spring', adding that 'they reflect and reinforce the power structure of the society in which they operate. Thus they are *in all ways political*' (15, their emphasis).

As a piece of social and political analysis this obviously leaves a number of important issues unexplored or unresolved. How can so many hundreds of journalists have been totally unaware that their output was so massively and consistently biased in so many ways that were so transparently obvious to the Glasgow team? This is never directly explained. Just what is the 'consensus' the news is said to reflect and create — if indeed it exists? If it is taken to be some very broad form of commitment to the underlying values of 'parliamentary democracy', then there is no issue, for the broadcasters readily acknowledge that to be their position.{4} But some critics at least conceive 'the consensus' in much narrower terms, suggesting that it encompasses a span of opinion ranging no wider than from Denis Healey to Jim Prior by way of David Steel. Or, as a Campaign for Press & Broadcasting Freedom pamphlet argued:

> 'To put it at its crudest, achieving 'balance' within this scheme of things means airing the Tory and Labour views, whilst the 'consensus' is seen as lying somewhere within the ambit of the Tory Left, Labour Right and the Alliance.'{5}

There is clearly a substantial difference between those two positions, with a wide range of possible intermediate points between them. Just which 'consensus' Bad News believes television to be defending never becomes clear. And much the same can be said of 'legitimating the status quo'; we need to know just what balance of forces or set of ideas are in mind, not simply in the interests of clarity but because the point is fundamental and is by no means agreed even among 'critical' students of the media.{6} A scattering of quotations and foggy references to 'some taken for granted consensus' and 'this hidden consensus' are hardly sufficient. Really the notion that television unwittingly propagates a hidden consensus strains credulity to breaking point. The failure to define such basic points in their analysis does nothing to facilitate assessment of the extent to which the Glasgow Group establish their case.

Not only is Bad News imprecise about basic terms, it is also reticent about the wider implications of its findings, though the authors were clearly aware of the wider context of media studies and sociological theory. Their piecemeal remarks give the impression they have at least some sympathy for the view that the media play a central role in the creation and maintenance of popular political consent — that they perform the crucial function of so shaping perceptions of reality the interests of a particular class come to be seen as the general interest of a popular majority. And so it is that the dominant class in capitalist society continues to rule despite being in a tiny numerical minority. This is a debate which stretches back to Marx and Engels' classic observation that, 'The ideas of the ruling classes are in every epoch the ruling ideas', and which in recent years has come to turn on the role of the media in conveying and sustaining 'cultural hegemony' or 'the dominant ideology'. Where Bad News stands in relation to these issues is never entirely clear. However, the Group seem closer to Stuart Hall (whose work seems at many points a sophisticated working through of ideas the Group no more than hint at), rather than to either those who depict media institutions as simple arms of the government or ruling economic interests, or the rather stark 'economism' of some other analyses. As Hall sees it, the media enjoy a certain autonomy, and in dealing with contentious public issues they do not systematically adopt the viewpoint of any particular party or section of capitalist interests. But they do have a central role in achieving 'hegemony', which in a society such as Britain is seen as being accomplished less by compulsion than by 'cultural leadership' - a process which entails the media becoming

> 'part and parcel of that dialectical process of the 'production of consent' — shaping the consensus while reflecting it — which orientates them within the field of force of the dominant social interests represented within the state.'

And so it is that 'the consensus of the majority can be so shaped that it squares with the will of the powerful'.{7} Whether or not this approximates to the Group's view, it is a notable example of a line of analysis their work has been held to sustain, though one that is debated almost as fiercely within 'critical' theory as by its critics. For the moment at least there is no need to plunge into the thicket of passionate scholasticism these issues have stirred. Suffice to note that both the concepts of 'dominance' and 'hegemony' and their empirical underpinning have been subjected to serious challenge.{8}

As we have seen, the Glasgow verdict on television is unwaveringly negative. Their contention is not that television is sometimes, often, or even usually slanted against the unions. When they say that *nothing* during their sample period diverged from a hostile belief system, they mean just that. Of the 261 industrial stories the BBC and ITN reported during the period, not one seems to have met the Group's approval. Out of 2,065 news items the merest handful are acknowledged as passing muster — and when one does, this is more often than not by way of highlighting the deficiencies of another item (eg, Bad News 239, 251). If the Glasgow analysis is to be believed, the BBC and ITN did almost nothing right in their coverage of industry over the entire 22 weeks. Some have suggested that such totally negative findings reflect some element of subjectivity in the Glasgow Group itself. This they briskly dismiss:

> 'Having argued that the ideology of neutrality is impossible of performance [by the broadcasters] we would not claim to exercise it ourselves...Our very interest in this area of broadcasting might be seen by some as clear evidence of a host of other attitudes and beliefs which can be attributed to us. But although we would deny little of this, the facts still remain. We did not anticipate the possible production of 'neutral' news, and still less would we in some way welcome such production; on the contrary we are arguing and demonstrating that the ideology of news which requires it to be neutral, unbiased, impartial and balanced merely leads to a 'naturalism' on the level of stylistics which hides its ideological components. How we stand as regards that ideological component is irrelevant, given the weight of our findings' (More Bad News 402).

By its style, syntax, logic and epistemological implications alone that passage could give rise to an extended commentary. It provides a typical illustration of the difficulties one meets in attempting to grasp and discuss the Group's argument and evidence. Firstly, there is the quality of the writing, about which one reviewer of Bad News commented: 'It is

> astoundingly badly written...The serious parts — which needed, and failed to get, the ruthless and grammatical pen of a literate editor — suffer from a simple lack of understanding of verbal communication...'{9}

It is ironic that while the Group are quite prepared to castigate the broadcasters for an ill-chosen 'and' or 'but', many of their own key passages are so unclear or inconsistent as to preclude rigorous analysis.

The authors criticise the broadcasters for falling short of professional standards (More Bad News xv), while making it clear they themselves have little time for those standards. They distance themselves from 'the ideology of neutrality' — whatever that may be — but never spell out their own 'ideology of news'. They clearly believe 'neutrality' to be impossible, and they seem to say that it would in any case be undesirable. If this is in fact their view, they would of course be casting aside that commitment to impartiality that both the BBC and ITN are committed to observing, and which Robert Hargreaves has described as 'the central creed of most broadcast journalists'.

At the risk of labouring the point — but it is fundamental to what follows — Bad News is not the simple study of anti-union bias so many readers have quite clearly taken it to be. It operates on a plane where the 'fairness', 'balance' and 'objectivity' that are the common currency of customary debate appear not to apply, though occasional diversions are made in that direction. In short, the Glasgow Group appear to be knocking away the principle on which news and current affairs claims to rest, and the terms in which they have customarily been discussed. But what they are replacing it with is far from clear.{10} The authors acknowledge their own absence of neutrality while insisting that the weight of their findings is so commanding as to make their 'personal attitudes and beliefs' irrelevant to any assessment of their work. The detailed content of their personal 'attitudes and beliefs' is indeed of no particular interest. What is of interest is whether their findings are in any sense the product of their personal 'ideological component', whatever that might be. And that is what remains to be seen.

However, it is clear enough that Bad News presents itself not as a political tract but as a 'scientific critique of contemporary news output' (Bad News 15). In calling themselves The Glasgow University Media Group the members doubtless saw this as no mere geographical expression, but as a legitimating invocation of the highest academic standards. The Annan Committee detect an 'initial bias' in their work; such well-disposed critics as Gardner and Sheppard refer to the 'thin veil of professional detachment and respectability' of the first two volumes, but the Group itself insists its work is not to be assessed as mere partisan polemic; it is to be judged by the traditional canons of scholarship. As Greg Philo put it:

'If political views were creeping into our work and affecting our

analysis there are any number of people who would jump on us and say, 'Look, you know you've said this, and it doesn't measure. You haven't assessed the evidence properly'.'{12}
He added, as if emphasising their detachment:
'As scientists, it was our job to simply measure what was going out on television.'{11}
So this is work which proclaims its scholarly integrity, and which, though remaining controversial, has in considerable measure been assimilated into the corpus of scholarly knowledge. But how secure are their conclusions? That is the central question throughout the ensuing discussion. It is consequently directed to the case the Group actually makes rather than the case others have wished it had made, or with developing a comprehensive alternative analysis of the way television reports industry. Not will it be concerned with the Group's personal 'attitudes and beliefs', though there may be cause to wonder as the analysis progresses whether its 'ideological component' is as irrelevant as we are asked to believe.

What is our concern is the nature of the Glasgow Group's evidence and their handling of the evidence. It may as well be said from the beginning that this is the most problematic element in their work. Consider, for example, this item from the Early News on 5 February 1975. It was led in by the newsreader:
'At a coal mine in Scotland, pit workers have been celebrating a new British record for coal production. In one working week, the men produced 25,260 tons of coal – over three thousand tons more than the previous record.
Trevor McDonald reports from the Solsgirth Colliery in Fife:'
McDonald was initially heard over film of underground scenes of coal being mined at Solsgirth, his report closely following the images on film:
'Further north than any other mine in Britain, and in country so unlike that around any other coal pit, is Solsgirth colliery where, in five days, miners have set a new national record in British coal production. The Solsgirth is one of three collieries which make up the multi-million pound Longannet mining complex. And it is by far one of the most modern mines in Europe. The descent, between 700 and a thousand feet into the heavily vaulted depths, is gradual. And

the 58 miners who have broken the national production record work in three integrated shifts. Half an hour's walk from the record-breaking coal face, 03, tons of machinery chug noisily away, in preparation for the coal soon to be mined. Along the coal face itself, 600 feet long, two spiral-veined discs cut into the solid wall of coal like a giant ham slicer. There's not a pick or shovel in sight. From the face, the coal, some 500 tons of it every hour, is disgorged on to the longest underground conveyor belt in any coal mine anywhere. The conveyor belt which links three mines in the complex to the power station is 5 1/2 miles long and never once does the coal come above ground.'

The film now moved above ground with McDonald interviewing a burly and begrimed miner who had just emerged from the pit, against the background of the pithead winding gear:

'MCDONALD: The leader of the 58-man record breaking team told me about the secret of the men's success.

ADAMSON: Cooperation. I...really it's cooperation between the men and the management. And a good relationship, good relationships.

MCDONALD: It all works very smoothly, does it?

ADAMSON: Oh, ah, well, there's times it disna', but it usually does, usually does.

MCDONALD: There's a national target of 120 million tons which seems quite a lot. With efforts like these, do you think the NCB will make it?

ADAMSON: Oh, well, the men's right behind them. The men and the officials are right behind them. Ah, we're really trying.

MCDONALD That target of 120 million tons of coal is now a national drive, and the unions say that in their drive, Scotland must do its share.'

Such good-news stories are of course very much the exception. Yet if Bad News claims to be a scientific critique it is hard to see how the contention that television conveyed an 'undeviating frame' that was prejudicial to the unions, and that 'nothing' departed from the dominant belief system, can resist that single example. But that is not all. ITN ran that item on the day when the National Coal Board was due to announce its pay offer to the miners. More Bad News devotes a full chapter to a blow-by-blow commentary on the treatment of the miners' pay claim which devotes almost two pages to coverage on 5 February. Trevor McDonald's report is not so much as mentioned. One wonders why.

Discouraging though that foretaste is, the issues call for systematic investigation rather than the singling out of an individual instance, however damaging. Through the following chapters the discussion will broadly follow the pattern of Bad News itself, to the extent of adopting some of the same chapter headings of the first volume. Not that Bad News will be followed through systematically. Its early chapters describe the conception and conduct of the project and offer sketches of the BBC and ITN news operations. While the sketches caused considerable offence among the broadcasters, those sections need not detain us here as they shed little direct light on the coverage of strikes. These sections are followed by a detailed analysis of the structure of television news during the period. Although particular points will be drawn from this chapter in later analysis, the actual data is largely unproblematical. Consequently we pick up the discussion here with 'Contours of Coverage', where the crux of the Glasgow argument is that a comparison between the pattern of industrial disputes provided by official statistics and the pattern of television reporting shows that TV offered a severely distorted representation of reality. The next chapter considers the criticism that the news failed consistently to provide viewers with basic facts and explanations about stoppages. From there we will move to 'Trade Unions and the Media', which considers the way in which the unions responded to television and their criticisms of media behaviour. This leads in turn to a reconsideration of the two main case studies in Bad News, one a protracted stoppage by dustcart drivers in Glasgow which led eventually to the Army's being called in; the other the way in which television covered the problems of the car industry. But since Bad News considers only two cases in any detail, a further chapter looks more closely at a number of other stoppages which raised a range of rather different issues. This leads to a concluding assessment of where the Glasgow critique stands in the light of this reappraisal, and some reflections on the implications for media studies and for broadcasting. But finally, recognising the difficulty of deciding between competing versions of events without access to the original material, the lengthy second section sets out ITN's coverage of industrial disputes during the period in full. In the last analysis, the reader can reach an independent judgment about where the balance of fact and argument may lie — and the ground is laid for that continuing informed debate the issues so amply merit.

1 Quoted in S. Hall, 'The Rediscovery of 'Ideology': Return of the Repressed in Media Studies', in M. Gurevitch (ed.), Culture, Society and the Media, Methuen, 1982, 64.

2 The Group complain that 'Stuart Hall and his group' identify them with a 'simplistic notion of television 'bias' (still to be found residually in Bad News) as though simply directed by 'the ruling class'' (More Bad News citing Screen, Winter 1977/8).

3 S. Hall, op.cit., 89.

4 In his first speech as chairman of the BBC Stuart Young argued that to suggest that because the BBC believed in balance it had no biases was 'absurd':
'Of course we are biased. We are biased in favour of the truth. We are biased in favour of the rule of law. And we are biased in favour of parliamentary democracy — because without that parliamentary democracy there would be no BBC...We are biased against those who use violence to further their aims and we are biased against racism...We believe the best way to further the values of a tolerant and civilised democracy is practising the values which define the BBC — fairness, impartiality and balance' (BBC Record, October 1983).
In similar vein see a speech by Sir Charles Curran, then director-general of the BBC, 'BBC Journalism: The Relevance of Structures', BBC Press Service, 1 March 1977, and discussion of the so-called 'Hugh Greene doctrine' enunciated by another director-general, The Guardian, 2 March 1982.

5 D. Jones et al, Media Hits the Pits, Campaign for Press & Broadcasting Freedom, 1985, 19.

6 Thus Golding and Murdock see broadcast news as portraying 'a world which is unchanging and unchangeable. The key elements of any ruling ideology are the undesirability of change, and its impossibility; all is for the best and change would do more harm than good, even if it were possible. Broadcast news substantiates this philosophy...' P. Golding and G. Murdock, 'Ideology and the Mass Media: A Question of Determination', M. Barrett and others, Ideology and Cultural Reproduction, Croom Helm, 1979, 218-219. S. Cohen and J. Young are among critics who see the dominant class in a more directly manipulative role. See their edited volume, The Manufacture of News, Constable, 1973, 16-17.

7 S. Hall, op.cit., 85, 87.

8 On which see, M. Barrett and others, Ideology and Cultural Production, Croom Helm, 1979; N. Abercrombie and others, The Dominant Ideology Thesis, George Allen & Unwin, 1980 and their associated bibliographies; also D.L. Altheide, 'Media Hegemony: A Failure of Perspective', Public Opinion Quarterly, 48, Fall 1984, 476-490.

9 Broadcast, 12 October 1976.

10   'Coverage of Controversial Issues', Airwaves, Spring 1985, 12. Words like 'neutral', 'unbiased', 'balanced' and 'impartial' are of course not precisely interchangeable. The Broadcasting Act, 1981 (superceding the IBA Act, 1973 which was in force at the time of the Glasgow survey) imposes on the Independent Broadcasting Authority the duty of ensuring that programmes maintain 'a proper balance', and of satisfying itself that 'all news…is presented with due accuracy and impartiality.' Programmes must maintain 'due impartiality as respects matters of political or industrial policy or relating to current public policy.'
Although the BBC is not under the same statutory obligations as the IBA, in 1964 its chairman gave the Postmaster General undertakings modelled on them. These were reaffirmed by the Board of Governors in 1981 when a new charter and licence were granted. Cf. C. Munro, 'Legal Controls on Election Broadcasting', duplicated, Conference on Political Communication in the 1983 general election, University of Essex, 1984.
11   'Does Television Tell The Truth?', BBC-TV, 13 November 1981.
12   Ibid.

How much attention does television news pay to strikes? Is it too preoccupied with them — or not enough? Although these are commonsensical rather than 'scientific' questions they make a reasonable starting point for assessing both television's behaviour and the Glasgow analysis of it. The basis for one of Bad News' principal lines of attacks is laid in their sections exploring the 'Contours of Coverage' — outlining the volume of industrial news, the relative attention paid to strikes within that, and the distortions in the pattern of coverage as compared with the 'real' distribution of unrest across the various sectors of industry.

There is no reason to challenge their general picture of the level of coverage. Over their 22-week survey period the two BBC channels and ITN together carried 2,065 *reports* about industry, relating to 261 different *stories* (Bad News 143). This accounted for 18.8 per cent of *items* on BBC1, amounting to 17.4 per cent of running time, and 16.1 per cent of those on ITN — 16.6 per cent of duration (Bad News 101). Within these totals, the three channels carried 805 reports on 54 stories about 'stoppages, strikes and lockouts' amounting to 39.7 per cent of reports about industry on BBC1 and ITN, and 39.5 per cent on BBC2.

Clear though these figures seem, they must be treated with caution. Firstly because the assessment of what constitutes coverage of an industrial dispute inevitably cannot be entirely precise. Accordingly it is probably wise not to treat anything that comes after a decimal point in those figures or any that follow with indue reverence. Secondly, the Glasgow figures are clouded by counting sometimes in 'stories', sometimes 'reports' and sometimes 'items'.{1} As these are differing units they cannot be aggregated or compared — or checked for either accuracy or consistency.

But while so much is reasonably clear, curiously enough Bad News never actually provides a figure for the share of news time given to industrial disputes, and the inconsistencies in their presentation mean the figure cannot be directly inferred from their other data. Fortunately it can be calculated for ITN from the original scripts and programme running orders. Output was classed as 'dispute coverage' if 'industrial action' was undertaken. Thus a work-to-contract by hospital consultants was included but reporting of the miners' pay claim was not because, despite threats and speculation about the possibility of a strike, the matter was finally resolved without one. Obviously there are arguments for shifting the dividing line slightly to one side or the other, but the criterion seems as sound as any other.

Working to that definition, reporting of all forms of industrial action took 8.0 per cent of the editorial content of the lunchtime news, 8.8 per cent in the early evening and 6.3 per cent for the main evening news, giving an overall average of 7.4 per cent. (If industrial action not entailing any stoppage of work is excluded the average falls to 6.7 per cent.) News of industrial disputes accounted for approximately 9.6 per cent of ITN's output in January, 5.4 per cent in February, 8.5 per cent in March and 5.7 per cent in April. So dispute coverage accounted for somewhere in the region of 7 per cent of ITN news, perhaps a little more, perhaps a little less. This was much less than the attention given to foreign affairs or politics, about the same as was devoted to home affairs, and a little more than was received by finance and business, sport and crime (Bad News 100).{2}

That is of course not the whole story. 'Disputes' formed the largest single sub-category of industrial coverage. They featured in 58 of the 104 editions of the lunchtime news, 78 of the 120 early news bulletins and 84 of the 120 late news programmes. Items wholly or partly about industrial action led eight lunchtime programmes, thirteen in the early evening and seven later in the evening. (Since some of these reports were tagged on to other essentially peaceful industrial stories this somewhat overstates their prominence.) Viewers were rarely far away from news about strikes, but this usually came some way down the running order. The median placing of the top dispute item was fourth at lunchtime and in the early evening and sixth on News at Ten. Moreover, the mean duration of items was no more than seventy seconds — a consideration which will be discussed at greater length later.

Whether this adds up to excessive or insufficient coverage is a matter on which opinions may reasonably differ. What is clear is that disputes were a very small proportion of ITN output, albeit a highly persistent one, and that industrial coverage was predominently *not* about strikes. And almost certainly the level of coverage was less than most readers of the Glasgow studies would be likely to imagine – if only because their figures are not sufficiently clear or consistent.

Moreover, the findings are obviously affected by the choice of period. While sampling is almost inevitable in content analysis research, because of the torrential volume of media output, the field is strewn with sweeping conclusions based on a few days or weeks. The Glasgow sample is more substantial than many. Nevertheless it may not have been entirely representative of either industrial relations experience or television news behaviour. As table 1 shows, their survey came after several years of relatively high strike activity. Although 1975 showed a decline from the particularly high level of the previous year, over the five months of their survey the number of days lost ran at an annual rate of more than 7,000,000 – a fairly severe rate of disturbance. The 'contours of coverage' might have been markedly different if they had chosen 1976, which was much quieter, or 1984, when the coal strike featured in almost every news broadcast for months on end, accounting for over 20 per cent of output.{3} They might even had differed had the survey fallen later in the same year, for not only was strike activity down, but this included the conference season when the unions were seen relatively more in debate and relatively less in industrial action. At all events the Glasgow Group happened on a period when disputes received more than average attention.{4} But with *any* period as brief as 22 weeks – and many of the Glasgow findings rest on considerably less than that – it would be as well to present the results with diffidence.

So much for the overall level of attention to industrial unrest; what of the ways in which that attention may have varied between different sectors of industry? One of the central arguments in Bad News is that comparison between news coverage and the actual occurrence of stoppages recorded in the Department of Employment statistics shows that there was no consistent relationship between the pattern of disputes and the pattern of reporting. The motor industry accounted for 17.7 per cent of working days lost but 28.0 per cent of dispute reports. But

Table 1: Stoppages, Strikes and LockOuts, 1961-1984

	Stoppages beginning in year	Days lost		Stoppages beginning in year	Days lost
	no.s	000s		no.s	000s
1961	2,686	3,046	1973	2,873*	7,197
1962	2,449	5,798	1974	2,922*	14,750
1963	2,068	1,755	1975	2,282	6,012
1964	2,524	2,277	1976	2,016	3,284
1965	2,354	2,925	1977	2,703	10,142
1966	1,937	2,398	1978	2,471	9,405
1967	2,116	2,787	1979	2,080	29,474
1968	2,378	4,690	1980	1,330	11,964
1969	3,116	6,846	1981	1,338	4,266
1970	3,906	10,980	1982	1,528	5,276
1971	2,228	13,551	1983	1,352	3,754
1972	2,497	23,909	1984	1,154	26,564

*Excluding coal mining for Dec. 73 – March 74 except the national stoppage.
Source: Department of Employment Gazette

engineering, which had 24.9 per cent of days lost, got only 5.3 per cent of the reports. Nothing was heard of stoppages in mining; the manufacture of food, drink and tobacco; coal and petroleum products; chemicals; 'other manufacturing'; gas, electricity and water; and the construction industry – although these sectors together accounted for 17 per cent of recorded days lost and 37 per cent of stoppages (Bad News 167-172). Comparison of the coverage with the Department of Employment's list of principal disputes gives rise to similar findings (Bad News 172-180). Moreover, the flow of coverage failed to reflect other indices of strike activity – whether the number of workers involved, the number of stoppages per worker, or the numbers of days lost per worker.

For the Glasgow Group the conclusion is clear: 'This reveals a highly distorted picture of UK disputes during the period of the study' (Bad News 20). There is a 'rather arbitrary relationship between strike severity and news coverage' (Bad News 188). 'The information given by television on these events is, in a statistical sense at least, unrepresentative. This itself is an important conclusion about the skewed nature of industrial reporting in relation to specified criteria' (Bad News 202). Having noted 'the non-representative nature of reporting in this area of industrial news' (Bad News 168), and an 'overall skewing of the picture given of disputes in industry', the authors comment that the relatively greater duration of disputes compared with many other stories means that they are reported more often; 'The skewed nature of reporting of strikes is correspondingly amplified by the repetition of reports that the nature of disputes demands' (Bad News 169). Later More Bad News asserts flatly that 'viewers were given a misleading portrayal of industrial disputes in the UK when measured against the independent reality of events' (xiii). Noting these 'distortions', Trade Unions and the Media warns that 'the average viewer must therefore suffer serious perceptual inaccuracies if he regards the industrial news as a guide to what is actually happening' (38).

These are clearly serious criticisms rather than incidental sideswipes. Indeed they constitute one of the main pillars supporting the Glasgow Group's case. They also received close attention from the Annan Committee, though it did not endorse them in its conclusions.{5} But is the Group's verdict warranted? The argument turns on the validity of comparing television coverage with the Department of Employment's statistical presentation of the pattern of industrial unrest. One of the recurring aims of media researchers is to establish some objective standard of reality against which output can be tested for bias. But the difficulty, as Bad News at one point recognises (296), is that the Department of Employment figures are as much a 'social construct' as TV news. They are not, and do not claim to be, unerring reflections of reality. They are simply a useful statistical series whose limitations have long been recognised, not least by the Department, which draws attention to these with proper professional regularity. They relate only to days lost directly and indirectly at the establishment where the strike occurs. They take no account of consequential lay-offs or short-time working at 'establishments other than those at which the disputes occurred.'{6} There are many disputes where the knock-on consequences excluded by this definition are considerably more extensive than those logged in the official count of days lost. Whether knock-on effects are statistically reckonable consequently depends to a considerable extent on how industry is organised, and may vary from one sector to another and even between firms in the same sector. Thus, statistically, a strike by 500 British Leyland workers will be identical to one by 500 Swan Hunter workers, although the former may rapidly halt other car assembly plants employing thousands of workers, while the shipyard dispute might remain essentially self-contained for weeks. A series of one-day stoppages by a few hundred railway signalmen made only a minimal impact on the official statistics, but disrupted a high proportion of the railway network and affected hundreds of thousands of travellers and deliveries of freight. As the authors of an exhaustive study of the 'stoppages data' concluded, they constitute 'valid but heavily incomplete indicators of industrial relations'; 'Information on stoppages, however sophisticated, can never yield an adequate representation of industrial relations'.{7}

Testing Against Reality
Nevertheless, a comparison between the official statistics and the 'contours' of television news could reasonably be used to raise questions about why the news took a particular form. At one point the Glasgow analysis declares that:

'Our use of the Department of Employment statistics in this chapter has one main purpose: to demonstrate the existence of an independently derived and publicly available alternative description to that of the news' (Bad News 296).

But having stated this modest and unexceptionable aim, and fleetingly recognised the appropriate caveats about the limitations of the statistics, the Group for ever after treat them as a definitive, objective yardstick by which the broadcasters can be assessed and condemned. True, there are occasional oblique acknowledgements of the shaky nature of the exercise, as when it is noted that coverage was 'in a statistical sense at least, unrepresentative, or 'skewed...in relation to specified criteria'. But it would take a very attentive reader to realise the significance of such 'small-print' caveats, and elsewhere even such indirect pointers are abandoned in favour of judgments like: 'highly distorted picture', 'arbitrary relationship', 'skewing', 'misleading portrayal...when measured against the independent reality of events'. This final accusation was levelled by More Bad News after there had been ample time to consider reviewers' criticism of the use of these statistics in the first volume. Far more weight is put on the Department's figures than they can possibly bear and the enterprise collapses under the strain.

Much the same kind of comment can be made about the use of the Department's data on major strikes. Here is how the authors put it: 'A useful review of the performance of television news covering the 'big story' amongst industrial disputes is provided by the Department of Employment survey of 'Principal Disputes' in 1975. The Department of Employment analysis selects those disputes which resulted in the most serious stoppages of work, recording a high number of working days lost, causing noteworthy disruption of production' (Bad News 172-4). They then discuss coverage of the '20 strikes selected by the Department of Employment analysis as 'principal disputes'' (Bad News 173). Elsewhere members of the Group state:

'Of the twenty principal disputes (those singled out by the Department of Employment analysis as being particularly significant for the economy) nine were not mentioned at all on television news' (Trade Unions and the Media 128).{8}

But the complaint that 'television news did not even cover all the disputes deemed to be of real significance by the Department of Employment' (Bad News 20) is remarkably disingenuous. In fact the Department of Employment's term is 'prominent stoppages of work', not 'principal disputes'; its 1975 survey shows 101 such stoppages starting in the first five months of the year, rather than twenty, and the criterion for inclusion is not some arcanely expert professional judgment that they were 'particularly significant for the economy', but simply 'the loss of 5,000 or more working days'.{9} Despite references to the '1975 survey' the Group seem not to have consulted it but to have relied on the thumbnail reports on a much smaller number of disputes, selected by less clearly defined criteria, and published month by month in the Department of Employment Gazette. At all events, Bad News once again employs a far from definitive bureaucratic artefact as a yardstick to 'review' the performance of the broadcasters and condemn them. Yet the very fact that the Department publishes quite different monthly and annual listings of 'prominent stoppages' emphasises how precarious the enterprise is. The underpinning to the Group's conclusions collapses as irretrievably here as in the previous instance.

By implication ITN is held at fault for not covering all the 'prominent stoppages'. Yet within anything like the time available there was no way in which they could have reported all 101 — for on the Glasgow reckoning they covered only 36 stoppages in all, up to the point where they became strikebound themselves in May (Bad News 166). Unless of course it is suggested that ITN should have given far more attention to strikes than it did. But taking only the more modest group of 20 stoppages, rather than the impossibly demanding 101, the nine ITN passed over were by:

- 1,600 production workers at a machine tool factory in protest over a suspension following restrictive practices in pursuance of a pay claim.
- 70 crane drivers at a Birkenhead shipbuilding yard over a claim for wage parity with boilermakers; 1,200 other workers were progressively laid off;
- 800 car warehouse selectors at Oxford in protest over methods used in security checks;
- 165 testers and other male workers at a telephone cable factory at East Kilbride over rates of pay and equal pay issues; 450 female production workers were laid off;
- 600 maintenance electricians and engineers at a tyre and rubber plant over a compensatory pay increase and discontinuance of weekend working. 3,900 production workers were laid off;
- 4,600 workers at an agricultural machinery company over pay;
- 118 testers at GEC's Stafford works over pay and differentials, leading to 1,200 production workers being laid off;
- 96 electricians and pipefitters at a truck and tractor assembly plant at Bathgate over pay and differentials, causing the progressive layoff of 3,800 other workers;
- 25 platers in a dispute over the grading within the pay structure of a new automatic plating process occupation; 1705 production workers were laid off progressively

Some of these strikes appear to have been covered in regional news. But why did they fail to make the national bulletins? Some of the classic discussions of news values have drawn on accounts by copy-tasters and sub-editors of their 'gate-keeping' activities. Unfortunately such explanations were not gathered at the time and are lost, and any attempt to 'read them back' from news output can only be speculative. But it is noteworthy that six of the nine strikes began in an extremely small way, leaving editors no reason to recognise a 'prominent stoppage' in the making. And other things being equal editors apparently preferred to cover a strike from the beginning – though there were exceptions, such as the London docks containerisation strike, whose spread eventually forced a belated appearance on the screen. Most of these strikes also seemed to have had limited knock-on consequences beyond the plants directly involved. While ITN would not have been at fault if it had reported any of these stories, it is not easy to see on what grounds it is to be criticised for not doing so – and Bad News offers no argument beyond the implication that scale should command coverage. The stoppage which possibly had the greatest claim for attention was the one at East Kilbride. Not because it was the biggest – though it lost some 18,000 working days – but because of the tensions over equal pay that made it so bitter and protracted. That particular issue was, however, covered by ITN on other occasions.

The Glasgow analysis criticises a number of further omissions:
'we find no instance in the sample period which refers to employers' action which are the equivalent of strikes, such as lock-outs, witholding pay or refusing overtime money' (More Bad News 129).{10}

Now, having invoked the yardstick of 'reality' the Glasgow analysis offers no evidence that 'reality' actually provided significant instances of such management behaviour going unreported. (Lock-outs at the Bank of England printers and in independent television fell outside the January-April sample they were using at this point). As it happens, ITN *did* run ten items which referred to the attempt by the Newspaper Publishers' Association (NPA) to dismiss members of the National Graphical Association and to the resulting court action. In the course of an interview with the general secretary of the NGA an ITN reporter specifically put it to him that, 'The NPA have threatened what amounts to a lock-out' (E,L 16 Jan.){11}. When the Daily Mirror management gave notice to 7,000 employees this was reported several times on 18-20 January. In March the Mirror dismissed all 1,750 London-based members of the Society of Graphic & Allied Trades in response to unofficial action (25-28 March and 2-4 April). This was referred to in at least seven ITN bulletins. The Group also appear not to have noticed either ITN's report that the London port employers had sent the Tilbury dockers home during the container handling dispute (L 27 Feb.), or the allegation by workers at Morriston Hospital that the management had locked them out (F 19 Feb.). Again, on 9 April, all bulletins attributed a strike by Hull dockers to the failure of the employers to honour an agreement to make a pay rise based on the retail price index, while a sit-in at Ford's Swansea plant was explained as a protest against suspensions (F 23 April). Strangely, not one of these caught the Group's eye.

Bad News also makes much of the fact that there were substantial variations in the level of strike coverage between different sectors of the economy and at different periods within particular sectors, notably the car industry. This is not surprising, given that the official statistics are a very imperfect indicator of strike severity. Moreover, the critique at this point rests on data from only two months (180-193) – a quite unnecessarily slender basis on which to convict ITN of skewed reporting and 'inconsistency in the application of news values' (191). It is even more remarkable when we consider some of the examples provided. Thus:

'The number of working days lost through disputes, although an indicator of strike severity, does not necessarily have any effect on 'newsworthiness' for television...In the case of the construction industry, where the Department of Employment recorded 8 major stoppages involving a total of 900 workers and 5,000 days lost in January, there was no coverage in either the National Press or TV' (Bad News 187).

Or again:

'In the distributive trades, 5 major disputes began in January involving 2,000 workers, resulting in 29,000 working days lost. Whilst The Times and Guardian covered only one such dispute on one day, neither the [Press Association] nor the television carried any reports. Disputes in this sector accounted for 9.5 per cent of the total working days lost in January' (Bad News 187).

To describe as 'major disputes' stoppages which, in the construction industry, averaged 111 workers and 625 days lost strains credulity – especially as the Department of Employment reserves 'major' for stoppages costing over 100,000 working days. The entire construction sector accounted for only 1.9 per cent of the January total of workers involved and 1.6 per cent of days lost. Strikes in distribution were more substantial, accounting for 2.6 per cent of workers and 9.5 per cent of days lost in January – but even here the averages per strike were no more than 0.5 and 1.9 per cent of the monthly totals. This scarcely seems adequate grounds for castigating ITN.

Another reason why some sectors may have received relatively little coverage in relation to the incidence of strikes is that they were characterised by relatively frequent short, scattered strikes which may have built up a bad record in penny packets. Thus there was no national coverage of stoppages in coal mining in January or February 1975 although no fewer than 34 were recorded as beginning during that period – but only 9,000 working days were lost. This is a typical pattern for the industry, but the example underlines the extent to which the Glasgow results reflect the choice of period. Had they studied 1972 or 1974, let alone 1984-85, under-representation of the coal industry would have been just about their least likely finding. Strikes in shipbuilding and marine engineering were more serious in terms of the official statistics, with 17 accounting for 109,000 days lost over the two months. As noted earlier, the lack of national coverage compared with the car industry probably reflects the differing speed and scale of knock-on effects in the two industries, but there may also be an implied assessment of their relative importance to the national economy.

Another consideration is that the very limited time available in television news almost guarantees that output will look 'lumpy' over a period as short as eight weeks. Bad News comments that 60.5 per cent of the February dispute items related to transport. The ITN figure was 52.5 per cent – less if the consultants' work-to-contract is included – and related to just two strikes: by British Airways clerical staff and British Rail signalmen. The latter was a classic instance of a strike which did not meet the official criterion for a 'prominent stoppage' because so few men were involved, but it received extensive coverage partly because the stoppages recurred weekly and had such widespread effects. Essentially though, television can report such a small proportion of strikes that it is quite unrealistic to expect the pattern of coverage to correspond even approximately to the industry by industry variation over periods as brief as a month or so.

Given the importance Bad News attaches to the 'representative' character of the news, it is worth noting one further criticism in passing. According to Bad News television tends to exaggerate the importance of pay issues as a cause of strikes. It complains that

'basically, for television, the explanation is usually assumed to be about money. Again, this is strange, for a glance at the Government statistics...would reveal that between one quarter and one third of industrial disputes are about matters other than money' (20-21).

These issues will be examined at considerably greater length in the next chapter. However, a glance at table 2 shows that fifteen of the twenty prominent stoppages were labelled by the Department of the Employment as wholly about pay or pay-related. Seven of these were reported and eight not. Of the five disputes where pay was apparently not the major factor ITN reported four and the BBC three. So in the batch of strikes the Glasgow Group themselves chose as comparators those that were not about pay were in fact more likely to be reported than those that were.

Towards the end of their discussion the authors ask, 'if there are no clear relationships between indicators of real activity and industrial news

Table 2: Causes and Coverage of 'Prominent Stoppages'

Main issues	Total	Not Reported	Reported
Total	20	11	9
Pay (including parity and differentials)	12	6	6
Pay + weekend working	1		1
Pay + suspensions	1		1
Grading (with pay implications)	1	1	
Manning levels	1	1	-
Safety of LT bus crews	1	1	
Activities of security staff	1		1
Job protection in docks	1	1	
Short-time working	1	1★	

★ITN only

coverage, what light does this throw on news values?' (Bad News 202). What ensues is already fatally flawed from the outset by the false premise that the official statistics reflect 'the independent reality of events'. Nevertheless, although that particular argument is doomed, the wider issues of why some stories are covered and others not remains unresolved.

Identifying Journalistic Criteria

The authors claim to have identified 'two of the essential journalistic criteria [for selection] in the industrial area, which are embedded into, and structure, the news on television' (Bad News 2). The first is 'concern for the inconvenienced consumer of goods and services' (Bad News 2). While recognising that strikes can cause inconvenience, and sometimes worse to other members of the community, they view such a 'consumerist' approach with manifest suspicion. More Bad News accuses television of over-concentration on 'the consequences, effects and inconvenience of any dispute' (182) and is echoed by Trade Unions and the Media's criticism of 'overconcentration on effects or consequences' (129). But how much attention constitutes 'overcon-centration'? The Glasgow discussion produces little apposite argument or illustration. Yet – as they acknowledge in More Bad News (181-2) – the 'innocent bystanders' affected by a strike can be far more numerous than the strikers themselves, and may even suffer more serious consequences. Thus the overtime ban and work-to-rule by British Rail workshop supervisors in pursuit of a fairly routine pay claim might not have merited coverage in sixteen national bulletins, had it not led to reductions of up to 50 per cent in services in some regions, altering the travel plans of many times their numbers of travellers (News Scripts 21). Similarly with the coverage of the strike by Sealink crews over the Easter holiday over closure of the Heysham-Belfast service (News Scripts 18).

But by no means every story which might have emphasised effects did so. Coverage of a stoppage by British Airways clerks opposing in-flight sales of tickets (News Scripts 8) might have made much of the resulting inconvenience, but did not. And while reporting of disputes between the Newspaper Publishers' Association and the National Graphical Association, and between the Daily Mirror and the Society of Graphic and Allied Trades (News Scripts 3) may have sprung partly from the thought that viewers might be wondering why they were not receiving their daily paper, the reporting laid little emphasis on their 'deprivation'.

The Glasgow analysis refers particularly to the handling of a series of one-day strikes by British Rail signalmen over a claim for adequate pay recognition for their skills. The extended discussion of the ideological implications of the 'lexical system' contained in a News at Ten report on the dispute on 10 February (News Scripts 10) needs to be read in the original (More Bad News 171-2, 181-3), since its own 'lexical system' renders paraphrase hazardous. Conceeding that there 'might be a case for ordering the sequence in such a way as to give the consequences of the strike priority', they emphasise the 'dubiousness' of ITN's presentation of the strike. But it was surely legitimate to give priority to effects when those affected outnumbered strikers by upwards of one thousand to one. Nevertheless, these items cannot fairly be reduced to mere preoccupation with 'disruption'. They also warned prospective travellers of what might await them — and ITN would surely have been at fault had it not done so. But ITN also made clear the nature of the men's grievance and laid bare the longstanding feud between the National Union of Railwaymen and the unrecognised Union of Railway Signalmen which was an important part of the background to the strikes. It is reasonable to single out some particular item in the coverage of a story for particularly detailed criticism, but it is equally reasonable to expect that the item will be set in a wider context. Fortunately the full record published here now makes independent assessment possible.

The second 'criterion of selection' is expressed thus:

'Recall the dominant coverage allocated to the car industry, transport and communication and public administration. The first of these is the pre-eminent example of mass production industry. It may be used to summarise what are held to be the problems of production in an advanced industrial society: strike-prone workers who, despite high wages, are not content; the cycle of prosperity and depression always more dramatic with a consumer product in a mass market; the competitiveness of the international market and the relevance of this for the balance of payments; the relation of Government to industry as it pertains to financial aid, control structure and the promotion of industrial efficiency. In a phrase, the car industry may be said to embody a concern with the principle of industrial (even social) survival in a society exposed to the stiff winds of competition and inflation' (Bad News 2).

Whatever else this farrago may be, it is certainly not a criterion for news selection any working journalist would recognise — nor is it accurately summarised in the subsequent reformulation as having 'to do with unscheduled interruptions to production processes' (Bad News 204).

The confused impenetrability of that second 'criterion' inhibits discussion, but two points can be made. Firstly, that the attention given to strikes in the car industry was not simply or mainly because it had acquired some kind of exemplary status (191), but because its industrial relations record was deplorable. The short-term figures given in Bad News were bad enough in all conscience, showing the industry third in both stoppages per worker and days lost per worker. But the Glasgow survey happened to fall at a time when stoppages and days lost were lower than they had been for several years At the beginning of 1975 journalists' understandings of the situation reflected not just their perceptions of the immediate events but their awareness of the persistently high levels of unrest in the industry over a number of years.{12}

But the prominence achieved by the British Leyland Motor Corporation (BLMC) was not solely a matter of days lost in strikes, nor was it, as the Glasgow account suggests, because the company's troubles were presented as emblematic of 'the English disease'. In those early months of 1975 Leyland's affairs took a dramatic turn for the worse. The market for cars had fallen in the wake of the 1973 oil crisis, and their share was flagging as import penetration rose inexorably. By April BLMC was effectively bankrupt, and the Wilson Government took it over to prevent the last British-owned mass producer of cars going out of business. It was not only BLMC that was at stake; so were a large number of suppliers, distributors and their employees, whole towns and even regions, the balance of payments and the exchange rate. Leyland had no need to be seen as a mere exemplar — which in some respects it sadly was; there were all too many reasons why it was a major story in its own right.

So the Glasgow account goes only part of the way towards elucidating why one strike was covered and another passed over. The scale of a strike was obviously an important 'news factor' — but scale was not simply a matter of the numbers directly and indirectly involved. It also reflected perceptions of the importance of the firm or industry in the national economy. The London containerisation strike certainly qualified on grounds of scale — it involved over 10,000 workers and eventually cost 258,000 working days. But it also attracted attention because of the importance of the issue — narrowly who should pack containers, more broadly the preservation of jobs in the face of technical change — and because the union itself was deeply divided. It also happened in London, and news organisations have something of a weakness for stories on their own doorstep.

Strikes were also more likely to be covered where they had a political dimension. Ministers were inescapably involved in the negotiations over the consultants' contracts and the controversy over pay-beds in National Health Service hospitals. They were involved in the Imperial Typewriter sit-in because the unions sought Government help, and in the signalmen's strike because the Opposition began making a political issue of it. The Ebbw Vale demonstrations against steel closures were clearly more newsworthy because they occurred in the constituency of the Secretary of State for Employment. The Government was also closely involved in the issues that gave rise to the London dock strike. It is doubtful whether the otherwise minor strike by industrial civil servants would have been picked up had it not affected the House of Commons and given rise to parliamentary questions (News Scripts 15).

As we have seen, effects were frequently an important news factor, especially when public services were involved. Novelty also seemed to count for a lot. The consultants' work-to-contract received a lot of coverage not just because of the issues and possible effects, and the political controversy these generated, but because it was unusual to find a quintessentially professional group resorting to such behaviour. The strike by Newmarket stable lads attracted attention partly because it was their first (News Scripts 23). The Glasgow dustcart drivers' strike was lifted from being just another dispute over differentials not just because it eventually posed a threat to public health but because the Army was called in to break a strike for the first time in quarter of a century (News Scripts 4).

A London Transport strike also offered the tragically novel feature of springing from the death of a conductor following an assault, highlighting wider issues of safety for bus crews (News Scripts 7). The sit-in by Imperial Typewriter workers in protest at factory closures was also an unorthodox form of action at that time — but the coverage did not overlook the central issue (News Scripts 6). A sit-in at British Aircraft Corporation over disciplinary matters, and the brief occupation of Vauxhall's plant at Ellesmere Port over short-time working were again unusual forms of protest at that period (News Scripts 13). The demonstrations over the closure of Ebbw Vale steelworks also attracted attention not just because such events were as yet still uncommon, but because of the effects of the closure on the town, and the stormy encounter it engendered between Michael Foot and some of his constituents (News Scripts 11). And one strike — by Avon County Council workers protesting at the havoc a wayward computer was wreaking on their pay packets — was reported in essentially 'human interest' terms (News Scripts 9). It was also the latest in a tradition of 'computer error' stories, to which the news media showed considerable attachment.

This listing of the kind of news factors that led ITN to cover particular disputes has obviously been speculative and makes no pretence at being definitive. Most strikes achieving coverage do so for a variety of reasons that could not be satisfactorily quantified. What does seem clear is that the reductionism of the Glasgow analysis is inappropriate; the factors governing news selection are broader and more varied than they suggest. Specifically they include a number of elements which cannot readily be said to work necessarily either for the trade unions or against them.

Strike coverage cannot of course be considered in isolation. Time is always the scarcest resource in television news. Consequently strike competes for inclusion with strike and strikes compete with all other news. Around this time television was also reporting 'the fall (liberation?) of Saigon', as the Group put it (Bad News 76), the fighting in Cambodia, the Labour Government's continuing struggle to operate the Social Contract, the resignation of Edward Heath and the subsequent Conservative leadership contest, the Moorgate tube disaster, the Budget, the controversy over Britain's membership of the European Community in the run-up to the national referendum, and a sensational kidnapping and murder hunt — to mention just a varied few of the major stories of the time. One likely reason why some strikes at BLMC received more coverage than others was the variability of this pressure from other events (Bad News 191-2). The ITN running orders show numerous occasions when items about strikes were crowded out or cut at the last moment — not forgetting all those that never even came up to the starting post. Conversely some strikes appear to have been covered because they began on a slack news day. The Glasgow dustcart drivers' strike is a case in point. It crept in sixth story down on a quiet Saturday teatime. More generally, similar considerations probably explain why there is a higher proportion of industrial news in weekend bulletins (Bad News 106).

In short, the factors taken into account by television journalists in deciding which strikes are covered, and to what extent, are necessarily wider than those determining the Department of Employment's statistical series. It is futile to look for it to conform to the reality of official statistics, both because the statistics themselves are by no means a pure distillation of reality, and because despite its naturalistic style television news is neither a sample survey nor a cross-section of reality. Its very name proclaims it to be otherwise. To put the matter bluntly, if the 'contours of coverage' and the Department's figures had coincided, the news editors concerned would have been more likely to have merited dismissal than congratulation.

Television does not set a mirror to reality. It is the product of a process that has been variously defined as 'creating', 'defining' or 'signifying' reality — or putting reality together, to use Schlesinger's term.{13} This process is undeniably steeped in values — judgments about what is unusual, tragic, important, exciting, funny, significant and so on. It also implies understandings about the nature of the world and our current situation, some structure of explanation, however elementary and commonsensical, about 'how things are', quite possibly taking the form of the 'explanatory frameworks' classically explored by Irving Goffman.{14} The training and teamwork inherent in network news production both depend on and promote 'routinised' understandings of what constitutes news and how it is to be presented. But these perceptions are perhaps best seen as fluid, changing, and constantly influenced by wider changes in social attitudes, rather than uniform, static or peculiar to the professional world of journalism. The greater attention paid to trade union affairs in the 1970s than even a decade or so earlier — and the reduced attention paid to the views of the Trades Union Congress in the early 1980s — are products of just such changes in perception. On this score there would probably be little disagreement with the Glasgow Group. Where our analysis parts company with theirs is in maintaining that there is no evidence that these perceptions can properly be lumped together as 'ideological' in any useful sense of that highly slippery term — whether in the sense that defines it as any systematically structured theory of man and society, or in the more Marxian definition preferred by the Glasgow Group:

'Our use of ideology...throughout refers to sets of ideas which represent or serve the interests of social groups or classes' (More Bad News 402).

To put the matter in other words, the Glasgow analysis rests on remarkably limited perceptions of what makes strikes newsworthy, and on a totally inappropriate yardstick of assessment. The criteria for a story that will 'run' on television are diverse. They are of course open to criticism, whether because they are incomplete, superficial, wayward or even capricious — and the present analysis will have reason to challenge them more than once in subsequent discussion. But what the Glasgow study ultimately fails to do is to demonstrate that the very selection of items and the resulting 'contours of coverage' are in fact prejudicial to the trade unions specifically or the working class more generally. And that, after all, was what they had to do.

1   For statistical purposes the present study will reckon in 'stories' and 'items'. 'Story'
     refers to the entire coverage of an affair — say the strike of Scottish ambulance
     controllers or the dispute between railway workshop supervisors and British Rail
     management. 'Item' refers to coverage within a particular bulletin, assuming this to be
     uninterrupted by material on other stories. (A separate report at the end of a bulletin
     would count a second time.) So an 'item' could be anything from a 15-second update
     to the 10½ multi-segmented handling of the Government's decision to take a
     controlling interest in the British Leyland Motor Corporation. An occasional story
     might consist of a single item, as when the havoc wrought by a wayward computer
     provoked a strike by Avon County Council workers (News Scripts 9), but most were
     reported several times. So the tally of 'items' runs well ahead of the number of
     'stories'. 'Report' will be used here in a loose sense, although within ITN it indicates
     news input by a correspondent or a reporter rather than a newsreader. Some Glasgow
     figures tabulated as 'reports' appear to refer to 'items'. Generally, though, the
     Glasgow analysis appears to have worked to broadly similar definitions.
2   The point cannot be made more precisely because Bad News presents the information
     in the form of a histogram without stating the precise figures.
3   A. Hetherington, 'Miners and Media: is TV news impartial?', The Listener, 17
     January 1985.
4   Denis McQuail's analysis of the main topics in newspaper coverage of industrial
     relations in 1975 shows that 'reporting of strikes and 'other disputes' was relatively
     prominent in the first two quarters of the year, while reporting of 'union/TUC
     actions' was highest in the third quarter, as were references to 'inter- and intra-union
     affairs" (Analysis of Newspaper Content, Cmnd. 6810-4, HMSO, 1977, 115).
         McQuail found that 'industrial relations' accounted for around three per cent of
     editorial space in quality dailies, and about two per cent in popular tabloids like the
     Daily Mirror and the Sun (102). A 1973 study found that the main BBC evening news
     on television devoted six per cent of time to 'industrial relations', and ITN's main
     news four per cent. Cf. P. Hartmann, 'Industrial Relations in the News Media',
     Industrial Relations Journal, Winter 1975, 5-6, and J. Tunstall in O. Boyd-Barrett et
     al, 'Studies on the Press', Royal Commission on the Press Working Paper No. 3,
     HMSO, 1977, 367-371.
5   Report of the Committee on Broadcasting, Cmnd. 6753, HMSO, 1977, p.272.
6   Department of Employment Gazette, May 1976.
7   C.T.B. Smith et al, 'Strikes in Britain: A Research Study of Stoppages in the United
     Kingdom', Department of Employment Manpower Paper No. 15, HMSO, 1978, 13
     and 89.
8   The Glasgow sample related solely to national news; this criticism goes beyond the
     evidence. Sir Geoffrey Cox argues that judging the news organisations by their
     national output 'is like judging a newspaper only by its front page.' He contends that
     had the Group 'looked at the regional news for this period they would have found
     much to qualify their findings. They make a great deal, for instance, of the almost
     complete lack of [coverage of] strikes in shipbuilding.... But in Tyne-Tees, to take
     only one region, these stoppages were constantly reported.' 'Bad News — Or Poor
     Scholarship?', Independent Broadcasting, December 1976.
9   Department of Employment Gazette, May 1976.
10   This remark cross-references to a table on p.180 listing the frequency of terms
     denoting 'industrial action' in the main evening news. But 'lock-out' is not among the

23 terms included, and nor are 'dismissal', 'sacking', 'suspension' or 'disciplining', though all were employed by ITN. Yet it is argued that 'the structure of news talk often serves to obscure managerial responsibility for the antagonisms in social relationships which at times explode into the disputes reported' (More Bad News 179).

11 The following abbreviations are used throughout: F = First Report, transmitted at lunchtime Monday to Friday, and the Saturday 'Lunchbox' bulletin; E = Early Evening News; L = News at Ten, normally broadcast on Monday to Friday, and the Late News at weekends and on public holidays.

When Bad News and More Bad News are quoted their transcription of news output is invariably followed. When ITN scripts are quoted these are followed exactly, except when square brackets indicate the contrary. When unscripted output is quoted the same procedure is followed, but there has been some rearrangement of punctuation and correction of spelling errors from the transcription made by ITN's audio typists. Occasional discrepancies between the ITN and Bad News texts are not significant.

12 The manner in which lags can develop in the way the news media perceive and present situations is classically explored in J. D. Halloran, P. Elliott and G. Murdock, Demonstrations and Communication: A Case Study, Penguin Books, 1970.

13 P. Schlesinger, Putting 'Reality' Together, Constable, 1978. See also H.J. Gans, Deciding What's News, Constable, 1980, D.L. Altheide, Creating Reality, Sage Publications, 1976, and G. Tuchman, 'Making News by Doing Work: Routinizing the Unexpected', American Journal of Sociology, 1973, 110-131.

14 E. Goffman, Frame Analysis, Harper and Row, 1974.

3

One of the more serious charges levied at television news is that it consistently failed to provide viewers with the most basic and elementary information about the disputes it covered:

- 'which trades unions are involved in a dispute is...not *normally given*' (Bad News 20);
- 'routine facts as to whether disputes are official or unofficial are *rarely given*' (Bad News 20);
- 'causal explanations for industrial disputes...*rarely appear* on the screen' (Bad News 20); 'even the use of "pay" to qualify "dispute" is uncommon' (More Bad News 172);
- 'if the strike is not an official one...then the shop floor view *may not surface at all*' (Trade Unions and the Media 129; here and above emphasis is mine).

Drawing these criticisms together during a later discussion of information theory the Glasgow Group maintain that:

'[When] the news moves on to some industrial coverage with its common forms of introduction, such as 'And now some industrial news', culturally attuned viewers should know that well over 50 per cent of the time they are about to hear news in which strikes and disputes will figure. Indeed, as the only likely information which follows will be time, location, number involved and place, the industrial stories are a highly redundant form of communication which can be said to be conveying very little that is new or unpredictable.

'One way of interpreting this high degree of predictability in news talk is to assume that it refers to a high degree of factuality; that the bare essentials of the news are conveyed by unambiguous, factual categories and vocabulary. But, as we have shown in Volume 1, essential facts are frequently not given; information regarding causes, which unions are involved, whether the strike is official or unofficial, amongst other central facts, are rarely given' (More Bad News 129).

From this and the allegation about the failure to mention lock-outs that was analysed in the last chapter they conclude that:

'In short, the coding of industrial news is heavily weighted against the trade union and labour point of view; for its lexical and syntactical performance in our sample excluded much of the information that is needed to convey such an interpretation. The ideology of its producers thus far reflects a management and anti-strike bias, and this manifests itself even in its apparently neutral language.' (129-30)

Television's failure to give the most basic facts is also seen as helping to make the behaviour of the workforce appear incomprehensible or irrational (Bad News 223, More Bad News 172).

The difficulty in assessing these charges is that while their general drift is clear, words like 'rarely' or 'not normally' lack the precision one expects in a 'scientific' critique. Bad News nowhere sets out the criteria that were used to decide whether or not a particular bit of information was supplied. In short, the charges are so casually levelled and fitfully documented as to make verification difficult. In these circumstances the validity of the allegations is perhaps best assessed by taking all the disputes that received a substantial degree of attention – there were sixteen on which ITN reported five times or more – and seeing how many items included each of the elements that Bad News singled out for comment.

Which Trade Unions?

Information about which unions were involved is said to be 'not normally given'. Table 3 shows that ITN in fact reported this in 37 per cent of the items. There was, of course, considerable variation from one dispute to another. In some the union was named almost every time, in others rarely or not at all. The instances where the union was not identified or was mentioned infrequently seem to fall into two categories. The first group were unofficial stoppages, such as those involving the Liverpool and Glasgow dustcart drivers and industrial civil servants, where the role of the unions seems to have been secondary.

Table 3: Identification of Unions

Dispute	News items total	naming union
British Leyland tuners	44	15
NHS consultants	24	11
Fleet Street/NGA	20	18
Glasgow dustcart drivers	44	5
Scots ambulance controllers	9	4
Daily Mirror/NATSOPA	10	10
Railway signalmen	24	10
Morriston Hospital	8	2
British Airways clerks	15	6
London docks	42	12
Industrial civil servants	6	0
Westminster Hospital	11	7
Liverpool dustcart drivers	8	0
Daily Mirror/SOGAT	9	8
Railway workshop supervisors	16	0
Imperial Typewriters	5	1

(They were identified more often in coverage of the London docks containerisation strike and the stoppages by railway signalmen, where tension between the official and unofficial leaderships was so obviously central to the whole affair.) The second group most notably included the overtime ban by railway maintenance supervisors, which involved three unions. Sometimes – particularly in the car industry – the number of unions involved was even larger. There is a simple practical point here about whether listing several unions repeatedly, or even once, within relatively brief news reports is the most sensible use of scarce air time.

Official or Unofficial?

It is also alleged that the routine facts about whether or not a dispute is official are rarely provided. Yet in the real world the situation is often far from simple. Strikes may begin unofficially and be made official retroactively – as with the British Leyland tuners at Cowley. Early in the strike, when it was technically not official, Keith Hatfield nevertheless reported that:

> 'The District Secretary of the Engineering Union has warned that if British Leyland want to continue producing cars, they must come up with what he calls positive proposals tomorrow. If they don't, he says that it's very likely that the 250 engine tuners will walk out again...' (F,E 7 Jan.).

So although the strike was still unofficial – and remained so for another fortnight – the only reported comment from the union was supportive and local officials would appear to have been promoting the tuners' claims. Some strikes may end before the process of official recognition can be completed, as seems to have happened during the paybeds dispute at Westminster Hospital. Others may be declared official by some unions but not by others. They may even achieve official status and then lose it. Sometimes a union may feel unable to bless a strike with official standing, but will turn a blind eye of complicity. At other times there may be deep internal divisions, as with the London dock strike. So the distinction between 'official' and 'unofficial' action may be central to understanding what a dispute is about, or may be unclear, uncertain or simply not particularly germane to reporting what is happening.

For what it is worth table 4 shows how many ITN items gave a reasonably clear indication of the status of the action in progress. This came about in a variety of ways. Usually the words 'official' or 'unofficial' were used directly. Sometimes a union official was shown or quoted as supporting the strikers or opposing them. On other occasions there was unequivocal evidence of a rank and file challenge to the official leadership. For example, although First Report did not actually use the word 'unofficial' in covering the London dock strike on 3 March, the reality of the situation was made clear enough in all conscience:

> 'Despite an appeal from their union leader, Mr Jack Jones, a mass meeting of about 2,000 dockers in London voted this morning to carry on blacking lorries...'

Similarly, on 26 March, News at Ten did not say in as many words that the strike was unofficial but reported that:

> 'They've been on strike for four weeks during which the main dockers' union, the Transport & General Workers', has repeatedly urged them to go back.'

Table 4: Official or Unofficial Status

Dispute	News items total	giving status
British Leyland tuners	44	5
NHS consultants	24	8
Fleet Street/NGA	20	20
Glasgow dustcart drivers	44	10
Scots ambulance controllers	9	0
Daily Mirror/NATSOPA	10	6
Railway signalmen	24	21
Morriston Hospital	8	0
British Airways clerks	15	4
London docks	42	19
Industrial civil servants	6	5
Westminster Hospital	11	1
Liverpool dustcart drivers	8	1
Daily Mirror/SOGAT	9	3
Railway workshop supervisors	16	1
Imperial Typewriters	5	0

What could be clearer than that? Or take another News at Ten report on the unofficial action by a number of British Rail signalmen:

'A 24-hour rail strike which could disrupt services in London and other parts of the country may still go ahead on Thursday, even though the executive of the National Union of Railwaymen have accepted a new pay deal for signalmen. The union say the new offer will give pay rises of up to £5.35 a week to more than 2,000 of Britain's 8,000 signalmen. But a leading member of the signalmen's committee, Mr Theedon, claims only 500 men will get more than £3 a week out of the latest offer.' (L 11 Feb.).

Once more it seems hard to tax ITN with failing to provide the 'routine facts'.

When action was unofficial ITN tended not to emphasise the fact. Thus the Cowley tuners' application for their strike to be made official was reported in two bulletins and the decision by the executive of the Amalgamated Union of Engineering Workers (AUEW) to endorse it was reported on three occasions at the time but then not subsequently stated directly – but several reports did refer to the union acting on the strikers' behalf, both through the Advisory, Conciliation & Arbitration Service (ACAS), and in direct talks with British Leyland management. During the strike by Scottish ambulance controllers there was no direct reference to its status, but the strikers were reported as meeting at the Glasgow headquarters of the Transport & General Workers' Union (TGWU), and on no fewer than three occasions TGWU officials were seen speaking on their behalf (L 12 Jan.; E,L 13 Jan.). In the coverage of the work-to-rule by hospital consultants the fact that their action had the support of both the British Medical Association and the Hospital Consultants' & Specialists' Association was made amply clear, although – perhaps because of the somewhat unusual context – the word 'unofficial' was never actually used. In short, there were at times good reasons for either not applying an 'official'/'unofficial' label or not insisting on it too frequently. Nevertheless, at a conservative estimate, this 'rarely given' information was conveyed in 35 per cent of all the reports.

It is worth noting that at around this period about 95 per cent of recorded strikes were eventually classed as unofficial. Not surprisingly – since many unofficial strikes are very short and localised – official strikes bulked relatively large in the ITN coverage. Nevertheless, the proportion that were at some point unofficial was high enough that if their status had been reported systematically ITN might well have been criticised for 'delegitimising' the workers' action – or worse, since both Labour and Conservative Governments had recently been minded to tackle 'unconstitutional' strikes through legislative action.{1}

Causal Explanations

The Glasgow studies are also highly critical of the handling of the causes of industrial action. That much at least is clear. The exact nature of television's supposed failings is less so. They allege that causal explanations are 'rarely given' (Bad News 20), and that 'even the use of 'pay' to qualify 'dispute' is uncommon' (More Bad News 172). On the other hand, they assert that, 'basically, for television, the explanation is usually assumed to be about money' (Bad News 20-21), that the news encouraged the assumption that 'disputes are always about pay' (More Bad News 172), and that it was guilty of 'the routine reduction of workers' aspirations to cash "demands" (More Bad News 189). So we are led to believe that the news, while failing to mention causes, systematically conveyed the view that strikes were invariably about pay – a remarkable allegation implying an equally remarkable achievement by the broadcasters. Its validity will be examined in a moment. However, the wider conclusions that are drawn from television's failure to provide causal explanation must also be noted. More Bad News contends that this leaves room for 'the kind of interpretation that suggests that industrial action is unnecessary, non-rational activity…'(172).

It also contends that:

> 'The causes ascribed or inferred are rarely given in a balanced manner, so that the workers involved in any dispute can come to be regarded by many viewers as essentially the trouble-makers' (189).

Moreover,

> 'the labour force is often painted in a manner which gives it the appearance of being a group of people with apparently suspect motives precipitating unnecessary action against organisations whose legitimacy is taken for granted' (178).

Where does the truth of the matter lie? The Glasgow studies never say what they consider to be a 'causal explanation', although their reference to 'dispute' being qualified by such a simple word as 'pay' implies a fairly elementary yardstick. For present purposes the criterion followed will be the basic one of whether or not the coverage provided some unambiguous indication of what the action was 'about'. The analysis set out in table 5 immediately puts the Glasgow criticisms in perspective. In all, seven out of ten items referred in some way to the reasons for industrial action. The amount of detail varied considerably. Sometimes the reference was as bald as 'pay' or 'restoring differentials'; at other times it was quite detailed:

> 'The Hull dockers say this [action] will go on until employers honour an agreement to make a pay rise based on the Retail Price Index. Talks broke down on Monday when the employers offered a 7 1/2 per cent increase. The dockers want between 11 and 12 per

---

Table 5: Indication of Causes

Dispute	News items total	indicating cause
British Leyland tuners	44	27
NHS consultants	24	17
Fleet Street/NGA	20	13
Glasgow dustcart drivers	44	22
Scots ambulance controllers	9	9
Daily Mirror/NATSOPA	10	4
Railway signalmen	24	17
Morriston Hospital	8	8
British Airways clerks	15	14
London docks	42	26
Industrial civil servants	6	6
Westminster Hospital	11	10
Liverpool dustcart drivers	8	6
Daily Mirror/SOGAT	9	7
Railway workshop supervisors	16	14
Imperial Typewriters	5	5

---

cent' (F 9 April).

Again, Michael Green's first report on the London dock strike said that:
'The dockers are trying to force the container depots to employ registered dockers. They argue that these depots do work which traditionally belongs to them.

But the haulage workers have retaliated by picketing some dock gates — to bring the issue to a head.

The fear is that the dispute could erupt into a repeat of the 1972 dock strike....At that time the inland container depots were urged to employ dockers. But not many followed the advice.

Now the dockers want the Government to legislate that all container handling in a five-mile corridor round the main ports has to be done by dockers' (L 24 Feb.).

And as the strike drew towards an end six weeks later Michael Green's report added further detail:

'The Number One Docks Group demands on which the dispute has been fought were again reiterated: payment for the first two days of the dispute, when the dockers claim they were locked out; that diverted ships should be returned to their port of origin, and, most important, that dockers should not be disciplined and therefore allowed to picket container bases, and to black certain container cargoes coming into the docks' (F 4 April).

Early in the consultants' action ITN reported:

'11,000 hospital consultants throughout Britain began their work to rule or work to contract today to protest about the new contract offered to them by the government...

The consultants say the contract they've been offered will put an end to the independence of the medical profession...' (F 2 Jan.).

Keith Able of the Hospital Consultants' & Specialists' Association was subsequently given an opportunity to explain their grievance at some length:

'Well, the move to change the consultants' contract was initiated by the profession some time ago, and during the course of last year, the Owen Working Party discussed with the Government all aspects of the consultants' contract, and at the government's request, on the agenda for discussion was the question of private practice. In fact, that question of private practice had virtually no more than ten minutes discussion throughout the whole of these negotiations, so that the profession, who agreed to work the health service when it was instituted 25 years ago, and at that time the Government agreed that private practice should continue, has had no means of discussing with the Government how private practice should be phased out, and our view is that it isn't up to a militant minority within the health service, because this is what these people are at [the] Westminster, to determine the policy in regard to private beds throughout the country' (F 18 March).

If viewers were still not entirely clear what the issue was after this, perhaps the fault did not entirely lie with ITN. However, the situation became a little clearer in the course of exchanges between Robert Kee and the Minister, Barbara Castle:

'CASTLE: ...I am giving them something they have asked my

Conservative predecessors for in vain – namely a contract which is a closed contract. That is to say they get paid for a defined number of hours, and if they do extra sessions, or if they do emergency calls at weekends and at nights, they will get paid extra...

KEE: Yes, but their answer to this of course is that... you've given it to them on terms which totally undermine the independence of their profession...because they are now penalised if they take on private medecine....Surely now by giving a differential of 18 per cent to people who work full time in the National Health Service, and don't have any private medicine, you are really trying to implement a political dogma...' (F 2 Jan.).

And there was considerably more in similar vein.

Or take the issue between the National Graphical Association and the Newspaper Publishers' Association; ITN summarised the bone of contention succinctly:

'The dispute is over the erosion of a traditional wage differential between the NGA and the other five print unions' (L 15 Jan.).

A later programme came back to the causes in more detail in an interview between Leonard Parkin and Tom Baistow. To a somewhat tendentious suggestion that the strikes looked 'suicidal' Baistow replied:

'BAISTOW: ...the National Graphical Association is in fact in dispute not really for much more money, but for 40p for about 1,000 – that is about 15 per cent of their strength on the national papers, and they say that they must have this because traditionally they have 12 1/2 per cent more than any other union in the newspaper industry. It's all about craft, skills and recognition.

PARKIN: Isn't there a lot of nervousness in the newspaper unions about changes which they feel are going to be forced on them, and which are there for the taking if the newspapers could persuade the Union to accept them?

BAISTOW: Very much so. This is really at the bottom of this differential row, because the National Graphical [Association], which claims to be and I think is, the most skilled of the unions, does in fact face within the next two or three years, a big switch over to a completely new system, doing away with the old fashioned hot lead type system, [to] photocomposition, which means retraining and means in effect a row between the unions about who will do which job. This [has] set up a deep feeling of insecurity which is now expressing itself in terms of this 40p claim' (F 17 Jan.).

Relatively detailed explanation was not confined to heavily reported stoppages. The very precise terms in which the grievance of the Hull dockers was presented was noted earlier. Nor was that exceptional. Similar detail was provided in respect of the strike at Westminster Hospital, the occupation of the Imperial Typewriter works and the steelworkers' demonstration at Ebbw Vale, as later case studies will show. When seamen on British Rail ferries went on a 48-hour strike ITN reported that

'services...have been cancelled...as a protest against the withdrawal of the Heysham-Belfast ferry service next month' (E 27 March).

The one-day strike by London busmen in January was explained at some length and with some emotion:

'The action is simultaneously a protest against the general increase in such urban violence which is making their working life a real personal hazard.

Mr Jack Jones, general secretary of the Transport & General Workers' Union, who led thousands of busmen on the funeral march said: 'This is a symbol of the problems we've been trying to impress on successive Governments about assaults, attacks and abuse of the men and women carrying out essential public service" (F 29 Jan.).

When ambulance controllers in Scotland came out on strike ITN reported:

'They are demanding a pay rise, believed to be £10 a week, back-dated to November, to restore the differential with ambulance crews who had an increase in November. The strikers also claim that they were left out of an overtime agreement which was part of the settlement of the last strike by all 1,100 ambulancemen almost exactly a year ago' (L 12 Jan.).

The strike by Ford workers at Swansea was reported in these terms:

'Workers at the firm's plant in Swansea are staging a sit-in as a protest against the management and its methods – and this morning they locked out the members of that management.

Stuart Leyshon of HTV reports:

The sit-in began early this morning after the suspension of two men. Their workmates on the night shift decided to lock out the management and staff. Then hundreds of men on the morning shift arrived, and blocked the main gates with lorries and other vehicles. The men are demanding the reinstatement of the suspended workers...'(F 23 April).

Events at another car plant were said to be 'in protest against the company's plan to reintroduce short-time working' (E 4 April). Later that evening News at Ten returned to the story in more detail:

'Workers at the Vauxhall plant at Ellesmere Port in Cheshire took over in a 'token' demonstration which lasted for more than eight hours. They were protesting against the company's plan to re-introduce short-time working.

Martyn Lewis reports:

It was a takeover designed with publicity rather than disruption in mind. At eight o'clock this morning, after a mass march among the production lines, 200 shop stewards moved in to commandeer all main gates, telephone and tannoy systems, and the administration offices with their reception area. The men were shocked and annoyed at Vauxhall's announcement that short-time working was to return to the Ellesmere plant. 8,000 workers here were only able to go back to a full five-day week a fortnight ago, after two and a half thousand of their colleagues had responded to a management appeal for voluntary redundancies...

[AUEW CONVENOR]: We was at a meeting for the JNC on wage negotiations yesterday, when this dropped like a bombshell. Works did not give the membership in the plant any warning whatsoever after coming off the short working week back on to a five-day system.

[LEWIS]: The shop stewards were careful not to let their takeover interfere with the running of the plant. Supplies flowed in as usual, and full production was maintained throughout the day....The plant manager, who called the news extremely regrettable, said tonight he found the men's reaction understandable' (L 4 April).

Or again, when Newmarket stable lads struck for more pay it was reported that:

'At the moment, lads average £35 for a seven day week. The dispute is over an extra £4.70 claimed by the Transport & General Workers' Union which represents over half of the lads. The trainers have offered £3, and I asked picket Ian Ramidge for his opinion...' (L 30 April).

The Avon computer strike was hardly the most momentous of industrial conflicts, but the issue mattered to those involved, and ITN conveyed the essence of the problem:

'[The computer] belongs to Avon County Council and works out wages for council employees. Recently it's [been] giving some people thousands of pounds too much in their pay packets and others nothing at all.

...The 200 strikers who picketed Avon County Hall today weren't asking for more money – they just want the cash they've already earned. Since the new Avon county took over, they say they never know from one week to the next how much they'll have in their pay packets, or even if it'll arrive at all. So today, 5,000 workers, from canteen cooks to caretakers, joined the walk-out... Council officials blame the teething troubles of a new authority for this chaos at County Hall' (L 3 Feb.).{2}

As summaries of the underlying reasons for strikes these brief accounts may well be open to criticism, but it cannot reasonably be contended that causal explanation was systematically omitted or that in general 'industrial action and the breakdown of 'normal' relationships in industry are not seen as needing causal elaboration' (More Bad News 182). Neither was it the case, as the quotations demonstrate, that ITN paid 'little but lip-service to the framework which renders any fact or set of facts intelligible' (More Bad News 157). Nor can it be fairly contended that all the 'explanatory frameworks' employed were directly or indirectly unsympathetic to the workers. In asserting that causes were given 'only rarely', the Glasgow Group go beyond exaggeration to the further shores of imaginative hyperbole. The extracts also enable at least a first judgment to be reached on whether ITN presented the workforce as 'essentially the trouble-makers', acting from 'apparently suspect motives', concerned only with pay and creating trouble without themselves experiencing it.

The quotations also put in perspective the assertion that

'the highly dubious practice of emphasising effects rather than causes and other aspects occurs in as much as 40 per cent of reports of industrial action; that is, in two out of every five reports in our sample' (More Bad News 159).

The Group further comment that:

'In certain areas, especially, when direct inconvenience to the public looms large in the reporting, the consequences of industrial action are emphasised, thus serving, ideologically or unwittingly, to avoid the question WHY' (More Bad News 160).

More generally, they see this as one more example of the way

'journalistic values work to buttress the basic inferential framework of the broadcasters, which has broader ideological components' (More Bad News 160).

Yet except where a strike call is disregarded, reports about industrial action are almost bound to convey something about effects, whether directly or by implication. (And if they did not they might well find themselves being criticised for implying that the action was futile or ineffectual.) At times the effects of a strike quite properly bulk larger in coverage than its causes (though 'emphasis' on effects does not of course imply 'avoidance' of the question WHY). This is particularly likely to occur when action by a small number of workers affects large numbers of actual or potential consumers (the strikes by signalmen and Scottish ambulance controllers), or where much larger groups of workers are consequentially laid off (as with the Cowley tuners). Such circumstances quite obviously do not relieve broadcasters of responsibility to report what gave rise to the stoppage, but they legitimately affect the balance of attention within the coverage. That balance cannot be discredited by branding reference to effects as a 'highly dubious practice' or brushing it aside as a mere 'professional defence' (More Bad News 159). Moreover, the allegation that 'as much as 40 per cent of reports' were guilty of 'emphasising effects rather than causes' is of little analytical value in the absence of illustrations or indications of what is held to constitute 'emphasis'. The extracts have presented some of the evidence on which the allegations can be weighed; more is available in the transcripts.

This is not to suggest ITN's reporting was beyond reproach. Although by no means all strikes have multiple causes some do, and the underlying reasons may differ markedly from the immediately apparent ones. While the need for explanation was never forgotten, like the official statistics news reports usually identified only one cause, and occasionally two. Consequently some disputes were under-explained rather than flatly unexplained. There were also occasional errors or inconsistencies. The issue between the management of the Daily Mirror and SOGAT was initially reported as being about pay (E,L 25 March; L 26 March), then — correctly — as about the Mirror Group's insistence that, 'as part of a new pay deal...the long standing practice that any worker who leaves is automatically replaced should be abolished' (L 28 March), then as about 'manning' (E 1 April) and later as about 'manning and pay' (L 1 April). But such hesitation and variation was rare.

So the Glasgow Group's flat contentions that television 'rarely' provided causal explanations, and that workers were presented as behaving in a 'non-rational' manner therefore cannot stand. What of the alternative allegation that it encouraged the assumption that 'disputes are always about pay', and that TV news was guilty of 'the routine reduction of workers' aspirations to cash 'demands'' (More Bad News 189)? ITN covered 39 instances of industrial action beginning between January and April 1975. As table 6 shows, not one was left totally unexplained. 'Pay' was indeed the most frequently identified issue, but this is scarcely surprising because, if official statistics are to be believed, 530 of the 852 strikes that began during this period (62 per cent) were in fact about pay.{3} Pay-related conflicts were 59 per cent of the disputes reported by

Table 6: Identifying the Issues

Total instances of industrial action	39

Pay and/or differentials	19
Pay/grading	1
Pay/manning	1
Pay and other conditions	1
Closures/job security	6
Private beds in NHS hospitals	4
Manning levels	2
Disciplinary/management methods	1
Job transfers	1
Safety at work	1
Short-time working	1
'Computer error'	1

Table 7: To-Camera Statements

Dispute	Status of Participant			
	manage-ment	full-time official	shop steward/ worker	other
Totals	19	28	28	13
British Leyland tuners	1	5	6	1
NHS consultants	5★	8	4	1★
Fleet Street/NGA	2	4	0	1
Glasgow dustcart drivers	2	2	4	3
Scots ambulance controllers	3	3	0	0
Daily Mirror/NATSOPA	1	0	0	0
British Rail signalmen	0	3	2	1
Morriston Hospital	0	0	0	0
British Airways clerks	0	1	0	0
London docks	1	2	7	4
Industrial civil servants	0	0	0	0
Westminster Hospital	2	0	3	1+
Liverpool dustcart drivers	0	0	0	0
Daily Mirror/SOGAT	1	0	0	1
British Rail workshop supervisors	0	0	0	0
Imperial Typewriters	1	0	2	0

★The Minister is included with 'management', while the 'other' is Bernard Dix of NUPE, who criticised the consultants during an interview on the paybeds dispute.
+ A consultant who criticised the unions in an interview on the consultants' action.

ITN. Our table covers all forms of industrial action while the Department's statistics record only those entailing stoppages of work. Nevertheless, by the sort of yardstick of 'reality' that is so often invoked in the Glasgow studies, there is really no basis for chiding ITN for paying exaggerated attention to pay disputes. Conflicts over pay were relatively numerous among the stories receiving extensive coverage, but since stoppages about pay accounted for some 82 per cent of the days officially recorded as lost around this time, this is scarcely surprising either.{4} But the London dock strike was not about pay, and that was covered at greater length than any other during the survey period. Like the assertion that the news failed to provide causal explanations, the allegation that it assumed strikes to be about money cannot stand – even though most of them were in fact about pay.

The Shop-Floor View

What of the contention that in unofficial strikes 'the shop-floor view may not surface at all'? The assumption that one can safely speak of 'the' shop-floor view is itself interesting, especially in light of the Group's criticism of TV news for tending to oversimplify relationships which 'involve not just two but three or more "sides" (More Bad News 185). This seems to be yet another case of the pot calling the kettle black. The classic warning of the dangers of speaking of 'the' shop floor view will long remain the 1984 coal strike, where the news carried a considerable range of contrasting views by rank-and-file miners and their families which were crucial to understanding the character and course of the dispute. But even in 1975 the evidence that the 'shop floor' does not invariably speak with a single voice was apparent in several disputes, not least in the London dock strike.

Table 7 lists all the interviews and statements to camera relating to the sixteen most-reported disputes. In the period January to April 1975, contributors from the unions and the workforce comfortably outstripped all others. In nine disputes the unions outnumbered management; only twice did management spokesmen outnumber those from the unions. There were three stories where none of the participants was quoted directly (Morriston Hospital, Liverpool dustcart drivers and the industrial civil servants). Coverage of the Glasgow dustcart drivers' strike contained four 'grass-roots' statements (not counting a jaundiced comment on the drivers from a non-striking dustman which was run twice), to two from an official union spokesman who could scarcely be said to have spoken out against them. However, as Bad News points out, the rank-and-file statements were not screened until after the decision to return to work. (This point will be considered in more detail in the next chapter.) At Westminster Hospital, where action was at least partly unofficial, the rank-and-file leadership was heard but not the full-time officials. Coverage of the Imperial Typewriter sit-in, which seems to have been unofficial, included shop-floor vox pops and a supportive statement from the TGWU steward.

In any case it cannot be assumed that if a strike is unofficial the union and the 'shop floor' will necessarily be entirely at odds. For example, during the series of stoppages by railway signalmen Robert Kee interviewed the secretary of the Union of Railway Signalmen. He explained that the URS had not organised the strikes, but contended that the men had had 'a very bad deal'. Kee asked:

'Are you then, as leader of the Union of Railway Signalmen, against the strike?'

HOLLOWAY: I wouldn't like to comment on that. It doesn't affect me at all in as much as this union never authorised the strike.

KEE: But Mr Holloway, you say it doesn't affect you at all, and therefore you are not particularly interested in whether the strike's right or not. It affects thousands, hundreds of thousands of people today. You must be either for the strike or against it.

HOLLOWAY: Well, the attitude of the men I'm in sympathy with because they've had such a raw deal. In short I could say that I condone their actions in making a fight against this award.

KEE: But not perhaps this particular form of fight?

HOLLOWAY: No, I would sooner it be done by negotiation round the Board's table' (F 13 Feb.).

There were also two appearances by members of the unofficial strike committee. In the London docks dispute, by far the most important instance of unofficial action during the period, where there was *very* serious tension within the TGWU, unofficial spokesmen featured much more prominently than the union's officials.

Statements to camera are of course not the only valid source of information about shop-floor views. ITN also carried a significant number of reported statements, mostly attributed to convenors, shop-stewards or members of rank-and-file committees. Workers who held no elective position featured much less prominently, though they were seen briefly in coverage of the Cowley tuners' strike, the Glasgow rubbish dispute and the Imperial sit-in. Several reports touched on tension between stewards and other activists and the shop floor, and occasional shots of strike meetings showed members voting for or against their stewards' advice. But over these four months, when there was dissent between stewards and workers the rank-and-file workers were offered few direct opportunities to challenge them. In the coverage of the London containerisation strike the most conspicuous absentees were the haulage workers whose jobs the dockers were attempting to take. In that sense Bad News' assertion that in unofficial disputes 'the voice of the shop floor' was not always heard had some validity. Somehow one suspects that these were not exactly the kind of shop-floor views the Group had in mind.

The Group also criticize the manner in which workers were heard. Trade Unions and the Media comments:

'Although in the news as a whole there is the semblance of balance between 'the two sides', they appear in different context. Workers are more likely to be interviewed in groups, in the streets, in noisy surroundings, etc., while management are more likely to be filmed in surroundings which help to lend authority to their statements' (129).

The Annan Committee was clearly impressed. It chided the broadcasters with failing to think their reporting through:

'They too often forget that to represent management at their desks, apparently the calm and collected representatives of order, and to represent shop stewards and picket lines stopping production, apparently the agents of disruption, gives a false picture of what strikes are about.'{5}

In view of the Committee's identification of an 'initial bias' in the Group's work, not for the first time they gave the Group's submission a remarkably credulous reception. As the present review is based on scripts a conclusive check on the allegation is not possible, though it is clear that there were many exceptions. But to the extent that it was the case that managers were more often interviewed in their offices and workers outdoors, we must bear in mind that news interviews are usually conducted where people are to be found. Senior managers are on the whole more likely to be in their offices – junior management being seen only rarely in any case. Union officials, and particularly shop stewards, are on the other hand more likely to be accessible during a strike either on the picket line or at the close of a mass meeting. If the stewards have an office at the workplace, they or the camera crew might well not have access to it while the dispute is in progress.

Neither Bad News nor the Annan Committee pauses to consider such practicalities, or to reflect on whether what they take to be the obvious implications necessarily follow. For while managers may gain authority from being filmed in comfortable, prestigious surroundings, it is at least possible that these trappings of power will brand them in the eyes of some of those watching as 'bosses' or 'fat cats', isolated and alienating figures. Conversely, if stewards are indeed rarely shown alone, this could well confirm their representativity and convey a feeling of working-class solidarity to at least some viewers. Many of the interviews with the President of the National Union of Mineworkers during the 1984-85 coal strike, which showed him almost submerged by rank-and-file miners, sometimes literally singing his praises, powerfully conveyed such feelings. Far from resenting being interviewed in such circumstances Arthur Scargill, who has never been slow to criticise the media, seemed to revel in this tacit rebuttal to allegations that he did not truly represent his members. He was also interviewed frequently in more formal settings.{6} In other words, such images can reasonably be read along lines quite different from those asserted in the Glasgow studies and accepted so remarkably uncritically by the Annan Committee.

It seems, then, from this reconsideration of the evidence, that television regularly provided the sort of information that the Glasgow Group maintains it usually omitted. Certainly some disputes were covered more systematically than others, and there were a number of inconsistencies that more knowledgeable or attentive sub-editing should have avoided. There appeared to be particular difficulties in achieving a satisfactory level of recapitulation in some of the disputes that dragged on for a considerable time. But the detailed criticism that has been made during the point by point review above is very different from the root-and-branch condemnation noted at the start of the chapter.

But can television's handling of disputes be assessed in terms of the number of times specific types of information are provided, as the Bad News criticisms imply? Some of the things that are declared to be 'central' or 'basic' facts, such as the names of the unions involved and the status of a strike, may not in fact be central to reporting any particular dispute, or to answering the truly basic news questions – who?, what?, where?, how? and why? Nor are newsmen necessarily discharging their responsibilities most effectively if they repeat all the basic facts in every report. That would become wearisome, and at times even ludicrous. Consider this item on the London dock strike:

'50 London dockers who've been on strike for 12 days have agreed to unload and re-load a supply ship from the Falkland Islands. The ship, which arrived on the first day of the strike, at Gravesend, has been waiting to unload a cargo of wool and to pick up supplies for 2,000 Falkland Islanders' (E 13 March).

Here is a report which does not tell us who is on strike, or why, or what the status of the action was. Accordingly it has counted 'against' ITN in terms of the Glasgow criticisms in the various tables above. But does it really merit condemnation as 'bad news'? Does it really offer a picture of an unreasonable and irrational workforce? Is it really convincing as a piece in the mosaic of relentlessly anti-working-class coverage?

It is a mere commonplace to recall that television news in Britain is a hurried and compressed medium. The average item on industrial disputes ran roughly 70 seconds – around 200 words at conventional newsreading speeds. (A few lasted less than 15 seconds; some ran for over four minutes.) Even with the greatest verbal and visual economy, this implies severe constraints on what can be conveyed – in particular, the range of actors and viewpoints, the detail in which information can be provided and the frequency with which it can be repeated if the dispute continues. Since almost any strike is a complex event, it was probably the case that for every dispute ITN reported much more could have been said by way of fact, argument or analysis even though ITN made clear (and by no means unsuccessful) attempts to present more than the bare bones of the situation during most major disputes. This was even true of the 'why?', which is perhaps the most difficult of the basic news questions to answer within very brief compass, and where answers were the most likely to be over-compressed. Even so, as we have seen, material on the strikes by London dockers and British Airways clerks or on the consultants' work-to-contract, for example, included one or more relatively long items which went well beyond the basic facts. Similarly, a long interview with the industrial relations director of British Leyland offered some insight into the reasons for shop-floor unrest:

'[Some] of the reforms which British Leyland has been trying to introduce into its industrial relations in the last two or three years...were almost bound to generate friction, and so if the criticism was that we had been responsible for causing strikes but the results of these strikes were going to lead to better long-term industrial relations, well then I'm not ashamed to admit the charge...

...[We] still have in the company what I regard as a highly unsatisfactory basis of collective bargaining. We have something like 400 different bargaining units for our 160,000 employees, and we're bargaining every day of the year...[We and the unions] jointly inherited a hotch-potch of bargaining arrangements, and jointly we have got to try and introduce a better basis of bargaining in the future'.

However, some of the less prominent disputes, such as those involving railway workshop supervisors and industrial civil servants, were much less well explained, and reporting of them cannot be said to have risen above the most basic, routine level.

So there was always more we might have been told: what was the outcome of the Avon computer strike and the BAC sit-in? What led up to the disciplining of a worker which triggered the Ford sit-in? Why were Litton's British typewriter works the least cost-effective in the group? Why did the Hull port employers refuse to honour a pay agreement? What did Glasgow dustmen and residents of the city think about the dustcart drivers' strike? These were just a few of the questions on which ITN coverage said little or nothing.

But what is one to make of this? One of the worst difficulties in assessing the Glasgow critique is the repeated condemnation of television in relation to standards that are never clearly specified. Thus when the news is accused of 'a consistent failure to cover the area thoroughly' (More Bad News 400), there is no way of knowing what the yardstick is – unless it is the 'reality' discussed in the previous chapter – or how thorough is 'thoroughly'? Within the mean item length of under two minutes that was characteristic of British television news at that period, the coverage of any strike was inevitably far from exhaustive. If that is the standard, then the Group's criticism becomes self-evidently cogent. However, if one asks what can reasonably be expected of a popular medium attempting to give some account of a wide range of happenings within quite severe time constraints, the answer might well be rather different. If coverage on something like the scale presented by ITN is accepted as a reasonable compromise in the face of a range of resource constraints, then one might well feel both that the coverage was less than adequate in a number of respects and that it made a workmanlike use of scarce resources. It is one thing to find the brief, thumbnail style of reporting that characterised the period inadequate – especially in view of the triviality and extreme partisanship with which many viewers would find industrial stories discussed in their morning papers. It is quite a different matter to conclude either that the high compression ratio is 'ideological', or that it is inherently prejudicial to working people as such, or to them more than any other group or interest. The examples provided in this section have by no means shown ITN to be faultless, but they have consistently demonstrated that, within time constraints that will be queried in later discussion, ITN did a sounder and more adequate professional job than any reader of the Glasgow studies would ever imagine. Indeed we have seen once again that they are far stronger on assertion than on sound scholarly demonstration.

1   Although figures are not available for the survey period, Smith and others report that
     the annual average of stoppages known to be official over the years 1966-1973 was 5.4
     per cent in manufacturing and 3.4 per cent in non-manufacturing. Cf.'Strikes in
     Britain: A Research Study of Strikes in the United Kingdom', Department of
     Employment Manpower Paper No. 15, HMSO, 1978, 25 and 115.
2   More Bad News comments that this was carried as a closing 'human interest item',
     remarks that the cause was assigned to the computer rather than to the responsible and
     accountable authorities:
          'Thus it is written within the referential framework of autonomous technology
          getting out of hand or 'going off the rails'. This treatment of the story in human
          interest terms provides not so much a counter-example as confirmation of our
          general conclusion that the language of industrial reporting as structured at
          present cannot cope with multicausality and, whether by ignorance or default,
          almost invariably lays responsibility at labour's door' (182-3).
     All this makes rather heavy weather of a very modest story, which it is hard to see as
     contributing to laying responsibility at labour's door. 'Computer error' almost always
     means human error, but it is hard to see on what basis the blame is wholly assigned to
     the 'authorities'.
3   Department of Employment Gazette, May 1975. For January-May 1975, the period
     covered by the Glasgow analysis, the figures were 683 out of 1,086 stoppages, or 63
     per cent. (Ibid. June 1975).
4   This was a longstanding phenomenon. Over the period 1925-1974, Smith and his
     colleagues report, 'pay has been cited by those closely involved as the main reason for
     half the stoppages recorded in the United Kingdom and for three quarters of the
     working days lost in them.' 'Strikes in Britain: A Research Study of Stoppages in the
     United Kingdom', Department of Employment Manpower Paper No. 15, HMSO,
     1978, 44.
5   Report of the Committee on Broadcasting, Cmnd. 6753, HMSO, 1978, 272.
6   According to Alastair Hetherington's sample of the first eight months' news
     coverage, two-thirds of interviews with NUM officials were in studios or offices and
     one third in public settings. The figures for National Coal Board officials were 31 1/2
     minutes in studios or offices and 5 minutes in public settings. 'Miners and the Media',
     The Listener, 17 January 1985.

TRADE UNIONS AND THE MEDIA

4

When the Annan Committee was reviewing the broadcasters' performance in the mid-1970s, its attention was forcefully drawn to their handling of industry. The Trades Union Congress, the Confederation of British Industry, the Association of British Chambers of Commerce and Aims of Industry all made sharply critical submissions. Although, as we have seen, Annan found the broadcasters 'not guilty of deliberate and calculated bias', it concluded that 'the coverage of industrial affairs is in some respects inadequate and unsatisfactory'.{1} In the light of such criticism there was a case for examining not only what television said, but how unions and managements responded to its demands, how they organised themselves to influence it, and how they assessed the reporting of situations in which they were directly involved. Such an enquiry might have thrown up a crop of grievances that could have been judged as mutually cancelling. But, as the BBC's assistant director-general, Alan Protheroe, has acknowledged, although at one time the broadcasters may have taken criticism from both ends of the spectrum as an indication that they were occupying 'the proper ground', '[such] complacency no longer serves as a defence in a society which is increasingly complex.'{2}

So the Glasgow Group's readiness to complement their content analysis with fieldwork offered the welcome possibility of shedding light on the behaviour and attitudes of various participants in the news process. But although they offer in Bad News a chapter on 'The Trade Unions and the Media', there is no corresponding section on 'Management and the Media'. Yet the requirement to examine the evidence from both (or all) sides is as fundamental to 'scientific' enquiry as to journalism. The nearest the Glasgow study comes to explaining why it looks at coverage from the union angle alone comes when it notes that, late in the first phase of the project, it was realised that theories of the news production process ignored the 'attitudes and strategies' of

those the producers were dealing with – in itself a remarkable admission:
'[It] was not then possible to establish contact with the total range of all parties used by and using the medium in connection with industrial life. Faced with a choice, but knowing that within broadcasting the hostility of trade unions was known to be regarded as a real constraint on coverage, we decided to concentrate on the unions' formal relations with the medium' (Bad News 205).
This scarcely accounts for the continuing absence of detailed discussion of management experience and behaviour in More Bad News, which appeared some four years later. It also bears little relation to the way their subsequent enquiry was conducted.

It seems generally agreed among broadcasters and industrialists that it is harder to persuade management to appear on television news than the unions. The CBI admitted as much in its evidence to Annan.{3} A decade later the industrial editor of BBC-TV News could still report that companies as important as ICI, Dunlop and Cunard had refused news interviews or filming facilities, commenting that, 'In my ex-perience...the major difficulty in an industrial dispute involving a company is to get any interview with management at all', and '[for] all the talk of British industry being misunderstood, it still expects us to understand it without explaining itself.'{4} And Protheroe notes the willingness of chief executives to appear in specialist programmes like Money Box but remarks that

'they remain coy when approached by current affairs programmes to comment on, for example, the broad implications for industry of the level of the minimum lending rate or the Government's economic policy. Many hold the view that politics are public but business is private. More surprising, perhaps, is the reluctance of employers to appear in the studio with trade unionists, apparently because they fear they will be less articulate than the latter.'{5}

The problem is not peculiar to television. McQuail's analysis of industrial relations in the national press, taken about the same time as the Glasgow survey, found that only 13 per cent of the 'participants' quoted were managers or employers and 1 per cent were CBI spokesmen, while no fewer than 54 per cent were union officials or shop stewards. Management sources were heavily outnumbered even in newspapers with strongly anti-union reputations.{6} Also in 1975, unpublished material in the writer's possession shows that union spokesmen outnumbered employers 105 to 87 in interviews on BBC Radio's 'The World at One'. Such figures obviously tell us nothing about either the quality of the coverage or any 'slant' it may have had, but they tend to confirm television's complaints that management tends to be reluctant to make its case, and they suggest that allegations of bias against the unions cannot be sustained in simple terms of volume.

The situation is easily overstated. Some managements are very willing to meet the news cameras. During a strike at a large engineering factory in the North-West a radio journalist commented:

'Throughout the strike [name of company] gave us full co-operation. They never refused an interview. And if their press office didn't have information we wanted, they were always very quick to come back with it.'

During a protracted national strike another broadcaster commented:

'[The Area Manager] is extremely likeable, honest and co-operative and he never dodges a question no matter how difficult. The press office in [town] is also very cooperative.'

That manager was promoted soon afterwards. Not all his peers were as forthcoming:

'Our relationship with [company name] was strained right from the start...[They] wanted to give nothing away...Our frequent requests for interviews with [local management] were invariably turned down.'

And in another part of the country it was said that:

'[The Area Manager] was on a phone-in early in the strike but he has hardly ever been made available for interview. It is perhaps a measure of [their] confidence that [recently] they've rung us several times offering [him] for interview on any subject.'

When a large transnational company was in dispute with its workforce radio and television journalists found its reputation for secrecy well founded. When asked why coverage had not put certain tough questions to the management, the editor responsible replied:

'Not for want of trying. We made several approaches for an interview, but we could not get them to put anyone up to talk for the record.'

These are of course mere anecdotal snatches, gathered on a not-for-attribution basis. But they serve to illustrate how greatly the picture can vary between companies, between branches of the same concern, and at different stages of a strike, according to accidents of personality or differing assessments of the value of an appearance to a particular individual or his company. This was very obvious in the 1984-85 coal strike. In its early phase the National Coal Board opted — with erratic exceptions — for a 'low profile'. By contrast, the president of the National Union of Mineworkers was as indefatigable as he was enterprising in promoting the union's cause through any available camera and microphone. As a result, the time given to pro-strike NUM officials, miners and their families outstripped that given to NCB spokesmen by 89 minutes to 35.5 in a sample of television news coverage of the first eight months of the dispute.{7} Later, when the tide was running in the Board's favour, and after it had changed its spokesman, it displayed far greater energy and initiative, and its technique of rushing the daily tally of 'new faces' returning to work to newsrooms within the hour drove home its advantage relentlessly. Such reticences about appearing as there were now seemed to come more from the miners' camp.{8} One of the perennial problems of dispute reporting is maintaining even-handed coverage in the face of the varying competence and dispositions of the participants.

The reasons for management's under-representation are varied. They range from the lack of articulacy cited by Protheroe, which is surely a minor consideration, to outright suspicion and fear. Whatever the view of the Glasgow University Media Group might be, many senior managers remain firmly convinced that many journalists are ideologically unsympathetic to them. Others think television is only interested in industry when things are going badly, never when there is an achievement to report. Still others resent the imperious urgency with which journalists sometimes make their requirements known. The hierarchical character of some firms can render them incapable of responding to requests for information or interviews within programme deadlines. Some managers have had unhappy experiences with reporters whose knowledge of industry was very superficial or patchy — a problem the broadcasters have acknowledged and worked to rectify over the past decade, but have by no means entirely resolved. And, as the Annan Committee noted, during a strike

'management are often unwilling to say anything in their own defence for fear that it will be seized on by the strike-leaders as provocation and thereby prolong the dispute.'{9}
Many line managers still feel that even a good performance on television will do little to help their prospects within their companies, but a bad one could damage the firm, their career or both. The judgment of a former director-general of the National Economic Development Office, Sir Geoffrey Chandler, was at least as true in 1975 as when he made it in 1984:

'Industry itself has got to learn to articulate what it is about better than it does at the moment.'{10}

Whatever the underlying reasons, the results are clear enough in Bad News. Between January and March 1975, the two networks' industrial news coverage included 58 interviews with union spokesmen but only 33 with management (138-9). In reporting the social contract between January and April of the same year the main evening news carried 25 interviews with union spokesmen and 15 with management.{11} Additionally there appear to have been 46 reported statements from trade unions or workers to 17 from management. The Group argue reasonably enough that the unions' preponderance reflected the nature of the news rather than any bias in their favour (Bad News 138-9, More Bad News 106-9). However, they confirm that there was 'an insignificant number of management spokesmen at the individual factory or plant level', and note that their figures 'confirm a commonly held business view of coverage' (Bad News 138). Nevertheless they press on to their conclusion that the premises on which industrial news rests are skewed in favour of management:

'This is without prejudice to the charges laid at the broadcasters' door by those managers. The level and range of industrial reporting on television does not give them access or allow proper explanatory material to be laid before the public as they might wish. But it is our finding that what news there is is based on premises (inferential frames) sympathetic to their point of view' (More Bad News 400).

Earlier the authors were castigating the broadcasters for discrepancies between coverage and 'reality'. Now, while accepting that some managers at least have a legitimate grievance, they brush the problem aside with an imperious non sequitur.

Yet what we have here is obviously a 'bias' of sorts, however innocent, and it may well have wider implications. Certainly Annan realised there was a problem here, even if its judgment is ultimately questionable:

'[The] broadcasters, in an attempt to redress the balance, make management's case themselves and give the union leaders the impression that the union is being pilloried.'{12}

In fact the imbalance may be unsatisfactory at more than one level. The most obvious danger is that the 'side' which is less frequently represented may be disadvantaged. Less obviously, if one 'side's' case is more frequently delivered directly by its own spokesmen and the other's is more often given through journalists or newsreaders, the imbalance in presentation may not only be a source of unfairness to one or the other, but it can also be more difficult for the broadcasters to be perceived as acting fairly in such circumstances. To put the matter in slightly caricatured form, employers may take umbrage at the relatively high visibility of union spokesmen while trade unionists may object to the bosses' case apparently being put by newsreaders or interviewers. The point is obvious but speculative, and it would merit further exploration. That lies beyond the scope of this review, but it is surely remarkable that in more than 800 pages the Glasgow studies offer no sustained investigation or discussion of them. This suggests something about both their own inferential frames and their approach to scholarship.

In embarking on their section on trade unions and the media the Group declare that 'within broadcasting the hostility of trades unions was known to be regarded as a real constraint on coverage'(Bad News 205). If such a view was indeed widely held 'within broadcasting' it merited investigation. Newsmen could have been asked whether their coverage had been limited by such hostility, and any accusations could have been investigated to discover how far they were true or whether they rested on misunderstanding, mendacity or mere surmise. No such investigation is reported. Bad News mentions a union tradition of hostility towards the media going back to at least 1839 without actually showing whether, or how far, this actually affected the unions' behaviour towards television.

This is odd because there was at least one instance of coverage being affected during the Glasgow survey period. Journalists were barred from a meeting of London dockers which ended in a controversial vote to continue the strike over container handling (News Scripts 14). Such incidents are by no menas rare. For example, during the 1984–85 coal strike BBC Radio's Labour correspondent, Nicholas Jones, reported an occasion when a 'group of television technicians and radio reporters were ejected' from a miners' rally. He commented that:

'This animosity towards the journalists is having an impact on news coverage. Local union officials often decline to be interviewed. The distrust is so great that reporters visiting local strike headquarters are often refused permission and find it difficult to get information.'{13} Shortly afterwards the Transport & General Workers' Union refused to allow 'Newsnight' cameras to cover the result of its re-run ballot for the post of general secretary, following the programme's reporting of irregularities in the previous election.

However, coverage is probably more often affected by the unions' relative neglect of public relations work and lack of understanding of its needs than by active obstruction. It was certainly the case that when the Glasgow survey was taken many unions had still to come to terms with the needs of the electronic media. Such limited public relations efforts as they undertook were largely geared to the press. Although a few unions were quite active, Bad News reports that typically there was 'a fairly low level of input to the media' in the National Union of General & Municipal Workers (now GMBATU, 212). The largest union, the TGWU, had no public relations department at the time. The AUEW's single press officer was said to issue 'occasional press statements' (213).{14} Whatever the failings of the broadcasters, few unions could at that time have claimed honestly to have made any sustained or concerted effort to meet the needs of television. And change was to be painfully slow. Although a few unions, such as NALGO and NUPE, maintained adequately staffed press offices, a TUC survey in 1984 showed that in many unions internal and external relations remained a low priority. The TGWU had only just appointed its first press officer, who was gingerly trying to establish himself in the face of the suspicion of other officials that their authority would be undermined. During the 1984–85 coal strike NUM national headquarters had a single press officer, who doubled as personal assistant to the union's president. The union's move to Sheffield from London created considerable logistical difficulties for television; in the view of some journalists arrangements for press liaison there were inadequate, information about even mundane matters was difficult to obtain, and although Arthur Scargill made frequent appearances on television, the union never had any coherent public relations strategy. Nor was it alone in this. After a pay strike at Austin-Rover in 1984, which was of major importance to the TGWU, and indeed the trade union movement in general, John Torode commented in The Guardian:

'Although the Transport Union was prepared to invest £200,000 in the strike by refusing to comply with a court injunction, the union failed to put out a single coherent and detailed statement justifying the pay claim or attempting to shape some of the media coverage.'{15}

But successful public relations does not necessarily turn on the establishing of a properly-staffed press office. Some industrial correspondents would argue that the unions are now often quicker on their feet than they used to be. Although Arthur Scargill's grasp of the needs and weaknesses of television news during the coal strike was exceptional, a growing number of first- and second-rank union spokesmen have learned how to put their views across effectively.{16} BBC Television News' industrial editor, Martin Adeney, even goes so far as to say that:

'[Labour] and industrial correspondents have little trouble in obtaining economic and social comment from any one of half a dozen general secretaries of unions at the drop of a note-book...[However] much trade unionists complain about the quality or content of coverage, they have, in recent years, become very proficient in achieving large quantities of it. It is a lesson which business in general and companies in particular have still to learn. In a phrase which union activists use to complain about their treatment, they have learnt how to 'set the agenda'.'{17}

Adeney's view would be widely challenged within the trade union movement, and it contrasts with Wintour's criticism that the unions often fail to make their case through disorganisation and indifference. Nevertheless, for all the distrust, amounting at times to overt hostility, of some trade unions to television journalists, there were and still are fewer difficulties of access to the unions than to management. Doubtless in consequence, union statements are more frequent and prominent than those from the employers. This despite the fact that management usually has larger and more professional public relations teams at its disposal. Or, some might say, because of that.

The Glasgow account is sceptical whether greater or better-directed efforts by the unions would have secured more favourable coverage. Unfortunately their discussion is long on sentiment and strikingly short on hard evidence, although the point was and is of crucial importance to the unions' policies for external and internal communications. Yet there were plenty of union sources they could have interviewed. Prime among these was the TUC, which had the most extensive experience both of responding to the demands of television news and attempting to influence it in turn. It is quite astonishing that the Glasgow study says nothing whatsoever about the TUC's view of relations with television during the period; it does not even seem aware of the magnitude of the omission. Similarly with the TGWU. At the time the union's general secretary, Jack Jones, was being reported more often in the national press than any other participant in industrial relations − including the general secretary of the TUC, Len Murray − and his exposure on television was probably comparable.{18} The union was also deeply involved in two of the most widely reported strikes of the period, by London dockers and Glasgow dustcart drivers. It would have been most interesting to know how it saw television's handling of these and other stoppages in which it was involved. But again the Glasgow studies are silent. Instead, most of the complaints recorded in 'Trade Unions and the Media' prove to be directed at the press or at 'the media' generally, or to relate to incidents outside the survey period, and there is no way in which they can be followed through here.

Indeed, 'Trade Unions and the Media' comments at length on only two disputes within the survey period − which explains why this section is in turn so brief. One is the dispute at Westminster Hospital over pay-beds, which is discussed more fully in the case studies section. Although Bad News reports that the National Union of Public Employees was generally unhappy about media coverage of this dispute, all it says about NUPE's behaviour is:

'In the case of the Westminster dispute, the activities of their publicity department were unable seriously to affect or modify the picture which was given of them in much of the popular press and by the BBC' (239).

How did NUPE try to influence television coverage? Why did it fail? We are not told — and opinion is no substitute for hard evidence.

The other case quoted was the threat by branches of NALGO in South Wales to strike on the day of the referendum on British membership of the European Community (Bad News 223-7). This is presented as an example of coverage concentrating on effects rather than causes. But such an emphasis was scarcely surprising, for the NALGO official who was interviewed asserted that if there was sufficient support

'then it could well be that many polling stations will simply not open in South Wales with the result that the whole Referendum will have to be done all over again' (224).

In consequence the story was presented as part of the referendum coverage rather than as industrial news — a reasonable decision in the circumstances. The threatened strike was a purely local one, which would not have warranted national attention had the possibility not been raised — from within the union itself — of political consequences which were quite disproportionate to the matters at issue.

This example is also interesting because the Bad News commentary shows that in answering a question about 'effects', the NALGO official also took the opportunity to assert a view of the union's character which was a matter of internal discussion at the time. Apparently (though there was more to it than this), his references to 'the union' rather than 'the association' implied a particular set of beliefs about the kind of organisation NALGO should be and the way in which it should act (Bad News 227). Such niceties would obviously be caviar to the general, and this was clearly not a typical case. Nevertheless this was an interesting instance of how the news may communicate different meanings at more than one level simultaneously, and of what can be missed by discussing them in terms of a single inferential frame. Content which may have a very clear meaning or carry an unmistakeable set of overtones for one group or individual may have different, ambiguous or even opposing meaning and implication to others.

This is almost certainly not an isolated example. A study of the leadership of the National Union of Mineworkers has commented that although many people on the Left accuse the media of harmful bias, the union's president, Arthur Scargill, seemed to thrive on media attention and to court it assiduously, even at the expense of becoming 'the man the media love to hate'. Whatever the effect on his wider public, this caught a mood within his own union, helping to authenticate his determination to break with the style and policies of his predecessor, Joe Gormley. The very scale of the coverage signalled that the union's concerns were important and that it was in a mood to assert itself after a period of relative decline and retreat.{19}

But to return to the Glasgow Group; by talking to NALGO they acquainted themselves with a dimension of understanding that would otherwise not have occurred to them from the verbal and visual record. The pity is that they did not go out and discuss the coverage they themselves were actually analysing with those involved while the situations were fresh in their minds, and now of course it is too late. Had they done so they might well have gained further insights into the complexities of the interaction between actors and journalists, between news content and audience perceptions. If they had then taken the implications to heart elsewhere in their analysis, they might well have written a very different book.

As it is, that book remains to be written. For although the broadcasters have worked hard in the years since the Annan Committee to improve the calibre of their industrial reporting and to strengthen the range of programmes dealing with industrial questions outside their news output, the problems Annan underlined are not wholly resolved. Hostility and misunderstanding are still widespread, and coverage of industrial affairs is the poorer. One contribution to understanding could be a study of the ways in which unions, management and television interact. Bad News touched on the problems; unfortunately it produced no solutions.

1   Report of the Committee on the Future of Broadcasting, Cmnd. 6753, HMSO, 1977, 273.
2   A. Protheroe, Holding the Balance in Current Affairs Programmes, BBC, May 1983, 10.
3   Report of the Committee on the Future of Broadcasting, Cmnd. 6753, HMSO, 1977, 273.
4   M. Adeney, 'Why Can't British Managers Be Like Trade Union Leaders?', The Listener, 16 June 1983.

5   A. Protheroe, Holding the Balance in Current Affairs Programmes, BBC, May 1983, 10.
6   D. McQuail, Analysis of Newspaper Content, Cmnd. 6810-4, HMSO, 1977, 139.
7   A. Hetherington, 'Miners and Media', The Listener, 17 January 1985; N. Jones, 'Mrs Thatcher Mounts a Media Cavalry Charge', The Listener 26 July 1984; N. Jones, 'The Toughest Contest is the Propaganda Battle', The Listener, 25 October 1984; N. Jones, 'The Government is Winning the Propaganda War', The Listener, 24 January 1985.
8   N. Jones, 'The Importance of Media Presentation', The Listener, 21 February 1985.
9   Report of the Committee on the Future of Broadcasting, Cmnd. 6753, HMSO, 1977, 273.
10 Quoted in BBC, The BBC And Industry, GAC 666, July 1984, 29.
11 Calculated from table 5.1 (More Bad News 98-1), which presents slightly different figures from those at 106-9. Taking all interviews between January and March 1975, 9.6 per cent were classed as management and 7.9 per cent as labour spokesmen. On the Social Contract 39 of the 59 interviews were with members of the 'Labour movement' at one level or another, as were 125 of the 185 reported statements.
12 Report of the Committee on the Future of Broadcasting, Cmnd. 6753, HMSO, 1977, 273.
13 N. Jones, 'NUM's Relations with the Media and NCB's Objectivity – Two Casualties of the Strike', The Listener, 21 June 1984. But individual journalists reported a helpful response even in 'solid' coalfields like Kent. Generally established industrial correspondents and locally-based journalists had fewer problems, younger reporters from national media who were new to the coalfields had more.
14 Cf. J. Tunstall, in O. Boyd-Barrett et al, 'Studies on the Press, Royal Commission on the Press, Working Paper No. 3, HMSO, 1977, 362-365.
15 P. Wintour, 'How the Unions Spread the Word', The Guardian, 21 January 1984.
16 N. Jones, 'The Importance of Media Presentation', The Listener, 21 February 1985. But see also Patrick Wintour's criticism of the NUM's handling of the media during the strike, 'The Lamp the Miners Failed to Light', The Guardian, 20 May 1985, the response by the union's press officer, N. Myers, 'Mines of Misinformation', The Guardian, 3 June 1985, and Media Hits the Pits, Campaign for Press and Broadcasting Freedom, 1985.
17 M. Adeney, 'Why Can't British Managers Be Like Trade Union Leaders?', The Listener, 16 June 1984.
18 Cf. D. Quail, Analysis of Newspaper Content, Cmnd. 6810-4, HMSO, 1977, 141. The author's data from 'The World at One' show a similar indication.
19 A. Campbell and M. Warner, 'Changes in the Balance of Power in the British Mineworkers' Union: An Analysis of National Top-Office Elections 1974-84', British Journal of Industrial Relations, 23(1), March 1985.

CASE STUDIES I:
THE GLASGOW DUSTCART DRIVERS' STRIKE

The closing chapter of Bad News comes 'Down to Cases'. Given the authors' frequent invocations of their 'findings' and 'evidence', and their damning conclusions, it comes as a surprise to find that they provide extended analysis of the coverage of only two strikes. The first is the Glasgow dustcart drivers' strike (News Scripts 4). This featured in 44 ITN bulletins between 11 January and 14 April — nine times in First Report (totalling 13'35″), 15 in the Early News (13'15″), and 20 on the Late News (27'02″).

In the autumn of 1974 heavy goods vehicle drivers employed by Glasgow Corporation struck in furtherance of a claim for parity with rates that private drivers in Scotland had won that summer. The Corporation argued that it was bound by national agreements, and that the knock-on effects of conceding the claim would be unacceptably high. The men returned to work when the Corporation promised that if national negotiations, then in progress did not produce a settlement, they would be willing to reach a local agreement. With national negotiations still under way, the drivers came out in January. Most were dustcart drivers, though smaller numbers were employed on other duties such as delivering school meals or driving handicapped children to and from school. In March the Army was called in to shift the rubbish. In April, after attempts to spread the strike had met only limited success, the strikers returned to work without winning their demands, though they negotiated bonus payments for clearing the backlog of rubbish.

Such were the bare bones of the affair. Fuller accounts would have to say something about the industrial history of Clydeside, and about the apparent ineptitude of the Corporation in making a pledge (or allowing the drivers to believe it had done so) without adequate reflection on its consequences, and in failing to make clear that it considered the promise nullified when the men came out. More would also need to be said about the failure of local union officials to bring home to the men that London was unlikely to recognise a strike which threatened the whole system of national pay awards, and which also, arguably, contravened the 'social contract'. Again, the drivers undoubtedly had a deep sense of grievance; but whether their case had any great merit, and whether they allowed the Corporation enough time for national negotiations are other matters.

The Bad News commentary on the Glasgow dispute opens with the assertion that

'The characteristic inferential framework, used by television journalists in reporting disputes, is to utilise limited aspects of a dispute to create a dominant view' (244).

In the Glasgow strike 'the focus of the coverage became from the outset a "health hazard"' (245). Acknowledging that a serious problem did come to exist, the authors assert that 'it seems reasonable to question the manner in which this aspect was established as the initial focus of the coverage, even before the dumps had been created' (245). They add, 'The threatened health hazard became the dominant theme of all three news services, being established on the very first day of the coverage' (245, emphases mine). Later they note that the story soon lapsed 'until the Corporation transformed the media's supposed health hazard by declaring one existed nearly two months later' (247).

What really happened? ITN ran the following story in the Early News and News at Ten on 11 January:

'Glasgow's 350 dustcart drivers are to go on indefinite strike from Monday.

'The strike means that Glasgow faces another pile-up of rubbish on the pavements as happened for four weeks last autumn. The drivers have asked the national executive of the Transport & General Workers' Union to make the strike official. They want an extra £3.35 to reduce the differential between their pay and that of heavy-vehicle drivers working for private companies.'{1}

From about the word 'pavements' the report was spoken over library film of the piles of rubbish that accumulated during the earlier strike. Coverage the next day was similar but slightly shorter.

The Bad News comment that these ITN reports were 'not so explicit' in suggesting the hazard as the BBC's (246) is worth savouring as a way of conceding that there was in fact no explicit reference at all. To assert so flatly that ITN coverage established a 'dominant frame' around the health hazard from the very start calls for an unusual blend of fertile imagination linked to sheer audacity.

Richard Hoggart, while not challenging the Group's account of the coverage in his foreword to Bad News, suggests that in using library film the intention was not 'any sinister desire to put the strikers in a bad light; it was much more likely...to have been inspired by the trivial notion that this was a 'good news angle', 'good visual stuff'...' (xii). By contrast, a former editor of ITN, Sir Geoffrey Cox, notes that 'only three months earlier Glasgow had faced a strike of dustmen which had produced piles of uncollected garbage, infected by rats. This film was used by the BBC and ITN to inform viewers that they could be in for another such experience' − and, one might add, to show the rest of the country what Glasgow might be in for.{2} It is also possible that, as a way of providing visual variation on the newsreader's 'talking head', ITN editors took the opportunity to run some relevant recent film. There is no conclusive proof of any of these explanations, and at this date we are unlikely to get one. What *is* clear is that among several possible explanations the Group opted unhesitatingly and without qualification for one which, while most straining credulity, showed television news in the worst light of all.{3}

While BBC coverage is not generally under consideration here, it is worth noting that their report, also over library film, stated that the strike decision brought 'fears of a repeat of the situation last October when rubbish piled up in the streets causing a health hazard' (Bad News 245). Scarcely a 'dominant frame'! Be that as it may, the Group's reference to 'the media's supposed health hazard' implies that this was pure invention. Quite apart from the fact that newsmen were perfectly capable of recalling the previous strike and realising that similar problems could readily recur, it is remarkable that, presumably living and working in the city at the time of the strike, the Group failed to notice that the convenor of the Corporation's establishment committee predicted *at the very outset* that it seemed 'certain to last several weeks at least, with the city facing again the health and fire risks of rubbish stored in plastic bags piled up in the streets'.{4} Even more interesting is the fact that on 4 March one of the strikers' stewards said that they had been 'warning for weeks about the potential health risks in the city'.{5} So much for 'the media's supposed health hazard' (247).

The BBC's initial reference to a potential hazard (not an actual one) seems fully vindicated. When ITN did mention the health risk for the first time in the Early News on 23 February they were scarcely rushing in prematurely. Their report featured a warning by Professor Stewart of the Department of Community Medicine at the University of Glasgow that the strike was creating a serious health hazard. He did not criticise the strikers but accused 'the local health authorities of playing down the seriousness of the situation 'for political reasons".{6} The Group make no reference to this report. Indeed, they seem to have missed it completely, since in commenting on the handling of the story by First Report on 10 March they say that 'When ITN ran the story for the *first time since 25 January*, they too were confused as to who was actually on strike' (Bad News 247; emphasis mine). Later they refer again to a 'confusion of nomenclature' (249). The 'confusion' lay in the fact that Robert Kee opened the item with the words, 'In Glasgow where the dustmen's strike, or rather the strike by dustcart drivers...' Having worked through the reports on the dispute the Group should have been aware that this was the only time ITN described the strikers in these terms on the air, and they should also have recognised that the phrasing was not in normal news style. The most likely explanation is that Kee, who often worked without a script, made a slip of the tongue. At all events, he corrected himself in the next breath. Clearly the Group are prepared to seize on the most trivial slip to make an adverse point – and ironically their correction itself contained an error.

As we have seen, Bad News considers the Glasgow dispute as a particularly bad example of television's failure to provide basic information and to report the strikers' case. Yet the initial ITN reports stated clearly who was on strike, and mentioned the TGWU, the application for the strike to be made official, and the essence of the men's demands. In all, 37 reports identified the strikers as dustcart drivers, and where the number on strike was mentioned it was in every case given as 350. Only three mentioned the other services provided by the drivers (thereby passing up the chance of reporting the 'effects' of the strike on handicapped children!). Five reports named the TGWU; ten indicated that the strike was unofficial. Eight mentioned the parity issue in some form, two referred to a 'review of pay grading', and eleven simply identified the issue as 'pay' or 'extra pay for men with HGV licences'. The sums at stake were variously stated as £3.35 twice, £2.50 twice, 14 per cent twice and £5 once. The differing versions of the claim look untidy, but in this case reality itself was untidy. Initially the men were said to be £2.50 behind private drivers of vehicles of between five and ten tons. TGWU regrading proposals would have been worth between £1.27 and £2.16. Later the leader of the city's ruling Labour group, Councillor Dynes, said that the men were seeking '£5 outwith the NJC agreement and outwith the TGWU demand'. At the National Joint Industrial Council the TGWU called for improvements of from 38 pence to £3.29. Later the gap between the drivers and the corporation contractors was put at £5 per week.{7} One possible way of achieving the parity the men were seeking was through regrading rather than a straight pay increase. So it was not surprising that ITN put varying figures on a demand which itself appears to have varied, and which meant different amounts to different people.

The Group contend that there was 'a lack of reference to the unofficial nature of the strike' (Bad News 249). Yet although ITN can be criticised for insufficient recapitulation, ten indications that the strike was unofficial scarcely amounted to an unqualified 'lack of reference'. How much happier would the Group have been if the status of the strike had been carried in all 44 reports? Notwithstanding the status of the strike, the drivers were throughout supported by local TGWU officials, who continued to act on their behalf.{8}

'The essential question', says the Group, was a 'claimed promise made by the Corporation to the dustcart drivers to make a local HGV parity agreement' (Bad News 250). They omit to mention the condition attached to the promise, and therefore any consideration of whether the men allowed the Corporation enough time for the national negotiations. Certainly the feeling that the Corporation had broken its word fuelled the drivers' sense of grievance. Whether this was therefore 'the essential question' is debateable; what about the merit of the men's claim or the integrity of national wage agreements? As the authors say, ITN alluded to the pledge only twice and then indirectly in an interview with Alex Kitson of the TGWU (E,L 14 March), and again at the end of the strike (F 9 April). But then, the few references to the national negotiations (E,L 3 April) and to the problem of the National Joint Industrial Council agreement were not very revealing. ('Glasgow says it can't pay until new national negotiations are complete'; E,L 24 Feb.) ITN also said nothing about the City's fears of a knock-on effect if it conceded the claim, about the refusal of the dustmen to support the drivers, the unwillingness of the TGWU to back a strike in breach of a national agreement, the attempt by the Scottish Trades Union Congress to get the strike called off, or the appeal from the city's eleven Labour MPs for the strikers to return to work.{9}

At one point the Group question the 'adequacy' of television coverage (Bad News 252), only to revert immediately to their narrower concern with the presentation of the strikers' case. But the two are not necessarily interchangeable. ITN's treatment of the strike left many details unreported, but as the examples just cited show these included developments which told against the strikers and not just material which might be thought to favour them. ITN is open to criticism for failing to explore the complicated background to this exceptionally protracted strike more thoroughly, and for not recalling the basic information about the dispute sufficiently frequently. The extent to which it should have done this is a matter of legitimate challenge — providing the pressures of time constraints are faced more squarely than in Bad News.

One of the main complaints is that 'during the whole of the strike not one of the strikers was interviewed on the national news' (Bad News 250; Trade Unions and the Media 133). The words are carefully chosen. Strikers *were* interviewed at the end of the strike and on regional television. Their appearances on Scotland Today and Reporting Scotland are dismissed as irrelevant to the discussion of national television output (Bad News 56-7) — although in view of the authors' argument that the 'unvarying frame' of coverage tends to exclude such groups, they might have been expected to explain why the frame apparently did not operate in regional coverage by the same broadcasting organisations. Nevertheless, it is true that ITN did not interview any striker until Dan Duffy appeared after the vote to return to work (L 9 April; also quoted F,E 9 April). There was also an interview with a driver on the day work resumed, saying that he would be prepared to do it again for 'a justful cause' (F,E,L 14 April). Although they came at the end of the dispute both interviews contributed something to the understanding of shop-floor opinion, and they cannot therefore be dismissed completely.

But what did the imbalance amount to in practice? Up to the decision to end the strike ITN carried interviews with only five people. One was Professor Stewart on the health hazard; he refused to allocate blame for the situation (F 10 March). Another was a single sentence from the Scottish Secretary, William Ross, on the likely reaction from other trade unionists to the decision to bring in the troops:

'This is an unofficial strike, but I think everyone in Glasgow appreciates that you've got to take into account, and the Government must take into account, the whole question of the health risk involved' (L 15 March).

In a third, 2nd Lt. Milne of the Royal Highland Fusiliers spoke for about eleven seconds on the work of the troops (L 1 April). And there was a decidedly soggy interview with Councillor Dynes. After he had been asked whether there was any alternative to calling in the troops the interviewer put the point to him:

'OK, it's fine if the Army clear it up, but surely the only long-term solution is to get the men back to work.

DYNES: Oh, we're entirely in the hands of the men, but it's coming through to me. I've gained certain knowledge that the men haven't had a mass meeting for the best part of two months now, if my information is correct. But the men have been isolated by everyone – government, Members of Parliament, the public and the Corporation, and by their own union, and we're really in their hands, and I'm sure that at the end of the day, when [ever?] that day is, they'll see sense and return to work. I don't think there's any alternative there either for themselves. They've lost a great deal of money from all of this, and I'm sure that they're quite anxious to return. I would hope so anyway' (L 13 March).

Another unhappy man, the Lord Provost, who had earlier been reported as 'appalled and distressed' by the decision to ask for the troops to be sent in, gave the impression of being overtaken by events (E,L 14 March). He said nothing about either the strikers or the issues apart from passing responsibility for finding a solution to the government or the National Board for Prices & Incomes. On the same programme Alex Kitson commented in terms which appeared as embarrassed as they were ambiguous:

'What's got to happen now is that either Glasgow Corporation, and ourselves as a union, have got to pressurise for this situation to be cleared up at a national level, or they go back and fulfil the promise that if it wasn't satisfactorily dealt with at national level, they'll negotiate locally, and I think they've got a responsibility to the citizens of Glasgow, and in the light of the circumstances they should get off this hobby-horse and take into consideration the problems that the citizens of Glasgow are going through' (L 14 March).

However, ITN also reported his earlier, more trenchant warning that to bring in the troops would be an 'act of folly' (F,L 14 March), criticism by the Scottish Trades Union Congress (L 17 March) and the Glasgow Trades Council (L 17 March; L 19 March), and the reaction of the drivers' convenor, Archie Hood:

'It is a pretty shocking thing when a Labour Government is using troops for strike-breaking in this way. I have never known a Labour Government to act like this. I think they are trying to starve us out' (L 15 March).

It also carried an assurance by a drivers' shop steward, Fergus Hilton, that they would not interfere with the Army (F 19 March), and specifically mentioned the pickets' good-humoured behaviour when the Army did move in (F,L 19 March).

The strikers' case did not go unreported, as the Annan Committee was led to believe, and examination of the content of the various interviews shows the imbalance to be less culpable than the crude figures suggest.{10} Nevertheless, it would have been appropriate to have interviewed the strikers, and ITN's failure to do so can fairly be criticised. What the Committee apparently did not know was that the strikers were not the only interested parties whose position received little direct attention. Apart from the inconclusive Dynes interview, ITN carried no statements about the merits of the dispute from the Corporation either, and its position never emerged as clearly as that of the strikers'. Nor were there interviews with the more numerous dustmen who refused to support the drivers, or from ordinary Glaswegians troubled by the smells, rats, fires and general squalor of the dumps.{11} It would seem more profitable to consider the absence of the strikers as part of a wider discussion of the general adequacy of the coverage rather than as an example of specific discrimination against labour. One may well feel that neither Glasgow City Council, nor the strikers, nor the TGWU and the National Joint Industrial Council came out of the dispute with credit. More enquiring coverage might have shed fuller light on their failure.

Initially the Glasgow strike was reported briefly and routinely as one of a clutch of disputes on Clydeside; eight of the first nine reports ran less than 40 seconds. Nevertheless they presented the essentials of the dispute clearly, competently and fairly. A claim for 'parity' has a legitimate sound to it; certainly workers striking for parity are not being taxed with 'irrational' or 'futile' behaviour. Coverage might well have stayed on that very modest scale, as it did with a comparable stoppage in Liverpool around the same time (News Scripts 17). What lifted the Glasgow strike to prominence was the decision to send for the Army. As the first occasion on which troops had been used as strike-breakers for a quarter of a century, this obviously warranted extensive reporting. But ITN's preoccupation with the military angle led to the substance of the strike's being pushed into the background during the later stages. It may be no coincidence that at least ten different people appear to have 'subbed' the story at one time or other, and it was covered from Glasgow by five different journalists, four of them general reporters on brief visits to the city. None was a member of ITN's industrial staff. While the individual reports were competent and fair, the overall handling of the story could have been more coherent, more comprehensive and more inquisitive. Few strikes drag on as long as this one, and the very tenacity of the two sides merited more investigation and explanation. ITN creditably reported what happened; the 'why' was handled less satisfactorily. All the same, there was a greater professionalism to ITN's coverage than to the Glasgow critique of it.

1   According to Bad News, TV10'emphasised the fact that this was the second strike in three months.' Whether reports such as this amounted to 'emphasis' is a matter of judgment; technically the reference was probably inserted to explain the library film.

2   Sir Geoffrey Cox, 'Bad News — Or Poor Scholarship?', Independent Broadcasting, December 1976.

3   Where use of the library film seems more open to criticism is in introducing a 'vision track' which may have distracted viewers and therefore impeded assimilation of the spoken text.

4   Glasgow Herald, 13 January 1975.

5   Glasgow Herald, 5 March 1975.

6   See also Glasgow Herald, 24 February 1975. On 1 March the Herald reported the city's director of environmental health as saying that 'come the breeding season I cannot be responsible for anything that might happen.' On 3 March the Herald said that sanitary officials had warned of the danger of a plague of rats, and there had been increasing claims of a health hazard by medical officials. On 5 March, in addition to the shop steward's warning, it carried a report that the city's corporate policy committee had been told that the potential health hazard could become an actual one in two to three weeks if action was not taken. Reports from council officers referred to rats breeding and the possibility of a plague of flies, with the consequential danger of dysentery and food poisoning. On 7 March the Minister of State at the Scottish Office, Bruce Millan, was reported as appealing to the strikers to return to work because of the very serious potential health hazard. With the exception noted ITN reported none of these.

7   Glasgow Herald, 10 January 1975, 4 and 11 March 1975, 4 and 10 April 1975.

8   Glasgow Herald, 22 January, 28 February 1975.

9   Glasgow Herald, 1, 3, 4, 18 March 1975; 3, 4 February 1975; 27 January, 8 March, 4 April 1975; 10, 11 March 1975.

10 Report of the Committee on the Future of Broadcasting, Cmnd. 6753, HMSO, 1977, 272.

11 Glasgow Herald, 3,4 February 1975.

CASE STUDIES II:
THE PROBLEMS OF THE CAR INDUSTRY

The second Glasgow case study dealt with the car industry (News Scripts 2). Criticism concentrated on the reporting of a speech by the Prime Minister about the problems of the industry, the manner in which television applied his remarks to a subsequent strike by engine tuners at Cowley, and the prominence given to strikes in explaining the difficulties of the British Leyland Motor Corporation (BLMC), and indeed of the industry as a whole (Bad News 256-268).

The way television handled Wilson's speech was singled out for adverse comment not only in the first Glasgow volume, but also in Really Bad News and Greg Philo's presentation of the Group's case in 'The Man Alive Debate'. There were two main lines of complaint. The first was that although the Prime Minister had admonished management and workers alike, television reported his speech as if it had been directed solely at the workers. The second was that:

'This speech covered many areas, notably government policy on industry and investment, but the section of it which received most attention from television news was a reference by Mr Wilson to 'manifestly avoidable stoppages of production' in the car industry. This reference was interpreted by all three channels in such a way that they presented strikes as the main problem facing the car industry in general and British Leyland Motor Corporation in particular' (Bad News 256-7).

To assess the validity of these complaints the Prime Minister's speech should be read as a whole and in context. The full text is consequently provided in the Appendix. Essentially, however, it was a wide-ranging defence of the Government's attempt to maintain employment through selective aid to industry. Its central thrust was that whatever may have been the case when private capital was involved, once public money was put into industry, most notably into BLMC, the

Government 'could not justify to Parliament or to the taxpayer the subsidising of large factories, involving thousands of jobs which could pay their way, but are failing to do so because of manifestly avoidable stoppages of production'. Even if excessive wage demands were attained by a show of strength, they would be won at the expense of the less well off, and possibly of the workers' own jobs:

'In a very real sense, the success of public intervention...means a full contribution, a fair day's work for a fair day's pay by everyone for whose security we are fighting...This means, against the acknowledged background of established collective bargaining and safeguards, efficient working methods and steady week-in, week-out production...An important contribution to this unacceptable failure to compete by our home factories was lack of continuity of production due to strikes.'

The Prime Minister dwelt on the bad strike record of Austin-Morris, particularly the Cowley plant, and of the industry generally: while having just over 2 per cent of total employees it was responsible for one eighth of days lost in 1974 (which included the miners' strike) and nearly one third in 1973. After referring to 'manifestly avoidable stoppages', he appealed for the 'wholehearted cooperation of all whose future, and whose families' future, depend on the course the Government have taken'.

The Glasgow critique makes much of the fact that the first reports on both BBC1 and BBC2 described the speech as an appeal to both management and unions, but later bulletins treated it as applying only to the workers. BBC reporting did indeed vary in this way, apparently because the newsroom recognised on reflection that the emphasis in the first reports was not correct.{1} ITN showed no such hesitation. Throughout it maintained that Wilson's message was directed at the workforce. While the speech made passing references to management and the problems of private capital, major sections were unequivocally directed solely at the workers, even if formally his criticism of the strike record did not apply to them alone. In politics, where delicate problems are being aired, formal and political meanings may diverge. In assessing the speech one must not only see it as text but note his choice of venue — a Labour club in his Huyton consituency — and his known attitudes on wage claims and strikes ever since the controversy over 'In Place of

Strife' in the late sixties. The manner in which ITN covered the speech seems not simply to be defensible but to be correct. Certainly it was understood in the same sense by the next day's Times, which reported it under the headline, 'Mr Wilson Warns Workers that State Will Not Bail Out Strike-Hit Firms'. And it was also the perception of the Guardian which ran the story under the heading, 'Wilson Issues Ultimatum to Car Strikers'. It seems also to have been the understanding of at least two left-wing Labour MPs. Leslie Huckfield was reported as saying that 'the Prime Minister clearly knew very little about the car industry. The real cause of the trouble was the chronic failure of management to invest' (L 3 Jan, but cf. More Bad News 163). Dennis Skinner retorted that 'Mr Wilson should look around him and see precisely who are the real wreckers' (E 4 Jan.).{2} Whether or not Wilson's criticisms were founded, ITN seems to have read him correctly.

The second Glasgow complaint was that, having established a particular interpretation of Wilson's speech, television imposed that interpretation on coverage of a strike by engine tuners at Cowley. In the week following the Huyton speech ITN referred back to it in some fifteen bulletins in the course of reporting the tuners' strike, sometimes recalling that Wilson had singled out Cowley for particular criticism, sometimes citing his words about manifestly avoidable stoppages. Although the Glasgow analysis considers the linking of the speech and the strike reprehensible, the conjunction of yet another stoppage at Cowley which had apparently failed to 'go through procedures' and the Prime Minister's warning a few hours later surely formed a legitimate reporting angle. Moreover, Wilson's speech seems actually to have impinged on the course of the dispute (6 Jan. E,L). Where ITN may reasonably be found at fault is in misquoting Wilson on several occasions. Sometimes the mistake was trivial, as when 'manifestly avoidable stoppages' became 'unnecessary strikes' (E 6 Jan.). On one occasion the error was considerably more serious, as when Giles Smith referred in a report from Cowley to 'this strike which Mr Wilson called manifestly avoidable' (F,E,L 9 Jan.).{3} While charges of 'rewriting' the Prime Minister's speech seem a trifle excessive, Glasgow objections here seem fully justified. Indeed, ITN's coverage of the strike could more generally be taxed with lacking curiosity. Was this indeed another of those 'manifestly avoidable stoppages' the Prime Minister had condemned? And if it was, why had it not been avoided? So strongly cued by the Huyton speech, the question was never directly asked, even though the strike dragged on for four weeks.

These points apart, Bad News offers no general assessment of how the tuners' strike was reported. It involved 250 engine tuners, initially on 6 January, then continuously from 9 January to 2 February. Classed as production workers, the tuners were demanding skilled status which could benefit them in forthcoming pay negotiations in which higher differentials for skilled workers would be an issue. About 12,000 other Cowley workers were laid off on 6 January, but subsequently worked normally, although there were repeated fears that the plant would have to close for lack of storage space. The tuners returned to work on union instructions on 3 February, pending the outcome of an ACAS enquiry into the grading issue (Bad News 174).{3}

ITN reported this protracted strike frequently, though usually at no great length. Only a dozen of the 44 reports exceeded one minute.{4} Twenty-seven gave some indication of the tuners' claim; a couple referred simply to 'upgrading', but most were along such lines as, 'claim to be reclassified as skilled workers'. Longer forms were, 'to be regraded as skilled workers rather than production workers' and 'to be upgraded to the top skilled rate, which could eventually mean higher pay'. (This was one of the few direct references to pay.) A tuner was shown saying, 'we have a very just case — we are not engine tuners, we are motor mechanics' (F,E,L 9 Jan.). By contrast, there was almost no explanation why the management insisted on sticking to a single production workers' rate (L 4 Jan.).

Initially the tuners' action was unofficial but — after some hesitation — it was subsequently endorsed by the AUEW, whose officials were active on the tuners' behalf throughout (eg F 7 Jan.; E,L 9 Jan.). ITN reported both the call for the strike to be made official (E,L, 11 Jan.) and the union's decision (E,L 21 Jan). The involvement of the AUEW or 'the engineering union' was indicated at least fifteen times. There were several direct statements by union officials (F 7 Jan.; E,L 9 Jan.), and reported statements from Reg Birch and Hugh Scanlon of the AUEW and Jack Jones of the TGWU (L 21 Jan.; E,L 24 Jan.). (The AUEW decision to make the strike official was also criticised by James Prior, L 21 Jan.) ITN carried an interview with one of the 12,000 workers threatened with short time, describing the tuners' decision as 'disgusting' (F,E,L 9 Jan.). Giles Smith reported their resentment (F 9 Jan.) and said that the company was relying on their pressure to end the strike (L 9 Jan.). But, given that the Cowley plant continued in production throughout the remaining four weeks of the stoppage, shop floor hostility to the tuners was if anything under-reported.{6} So although coverage was highly compressed, ITN reported the basic facts more accurately and comprehensively than could be guessed from the Glasgow account.{5} Where it missed a trick was in failing to dig more deeply for the 'why?'.

The other big car industry story during the Bad News survey period was the report on BLMC by the Government's chief industrial adviser, Sir Don Ryder. Following considerable pre-publication speculation about Sir Don's findings, News at Ten led on 22 April with a report that owing to Leyland's rapidly deepening cashflow crisis his report was being rushed out. Peter Sissons predicted that it would be

'scathingly critical of British Leyland as it stands, accusing the company of having more out-of-date equipment than any car firm in the world, of needless and wasteful duplication of components, and of actually competing with itself by having too many models'.

The report, he said, also criticised Leyland's management structure, and some of the top management would have 'no alternative but to resign'. There was no reference to industrial relations either then or in the Early News next day, which concentrated on the suspension of share dealings in Leyland, but included an interview with Eddie McGarry, the shop stewards' leader. He noted that Ryder seemed to have

'hallmarked the representation that we made to him − for example the antiquated machinery that we've got, because nowhere here, nowhere in this country, are people required to work with such antiquated machinery as we are, and maintain the work of high levels of production that we do with the machinery that we've got'.

Post-publication coverage of Ryder began with the Early News on 24 April. Noting the scale of the proposed rescue Peter Sissons said that an important condition of government financing would be 'proven stage by stage progress towards reducing industrial disputes and improving productivity'. Leyland's organisation was heavily criticised and would be radically changed. There would also have to be changes in top management. He continued:

'The report really does indict the way British Leyland has been managed. On industrial relations, the Ryder team says it does not subscribe to the view that the ills of British Leyland can be laid at the door of a strike-prone, work-shy labour force. In proposing progress towards the new system of industrial democracy, the report says, "means must be found to take advantage of the ideas, enthusiasm and energy of British Leyland's workers in planning the future of the business on which their livelihood depends"'.

The story led that evening's extended News at Ten at some length — at 10'11" it took up about 30 per cent of the programme. It began by summarising the main lines of the report: the need to inject a vast sum of public money, to reorganise the company's structure and to reshuffle its top management, mentioning the financial terms suggested and the Prime Minister's announcement that talks on implementation had begun. Changes in top management were set out. Peter Sissons gave more details of the scale of the operation, interviewed Sir Don Ryder, and listed further recommendations: that the company should produce new and fewer models, stop competing against itself and cut down duplication of components; and that there should be a massive programme to modernise factories, where a large proportion of the machinery was 'old, outdated and inefficient'. He continued along lines similar to his Early News report:

'And there's to be a completely new system of worker consultation — seen by the Government, certainly, as one of the most important recommendations. Ryder says his team does not subscribe to the view that all the ills of British Leyland can be laid at the door of a strike-prone and work-shy labour force. And the Prime Minister emphasised that unless there were fewer stoppages and higher productivity, the Government would not feel obliged to keep putting money in. Accordingly, a new system of industrial participation has been recommended with joint management/union councils and committees. I asked the Secretary of State for Industry, Mr Benn, if this meant the workers would have a management role in the company...'

Benn replied that the proposals were a little ahead of Government thinking but

'It is part of our belief that the people who invest their lives in industry are entitled to as much account as those who've invested their money, and that will be reflected, I hope, in the new arrangements...I think the people who build the cars are the people in whom really we are investing. The old plant and equipment, much of it will go out the window. So we've got to build on our belief in them and try to draw from new arrangements the best from them and for them...'

Sissons also reported the proposals for restructuring BLMC and likely management changes. BLMC stewards were said to welcome the plan, though some were critical of the lack of detail about worker participation or disappointed that there was not to be full nationalisation. Trevor McDonald asked Eddie McGarry whether there would be an improvement in industrial relations. After briefly defending the record McGarry was asked about the company's potential. He replied:

'...we've been hampered by antiquated machinery and insufficient supplies for longer than we care to remember, and no chance at all to compete with competitors abroad...but if we're given the right sort of tools, the right sort of equipment, as this very welcome money by the public will give us the opportunity to justify their confidence in us, the government's confidence in us, and our confidence in the future.'

Finally, David Rose reported Parliamentary reaction to the Prime Minister's announcement.

From all this the Glasgow Group picked a single sentence from the middle of the story for comment:

'Ryder says his team does not subscribe to the view that all the ills of British Leyland can be laid at the door of a work-shy labour force, and the Prime Minister emphasised in the Commons that unless there were fewer stoppages and higher productivity the government would not feel obliged to keep putting money in' (Bad News 267).

The Group contend that, by inserting 'and' before 'the Prime Minister' despite Ryder's rejection of the view that strikes were the sole or indeed a major cause of BLMC's difficulties, ITN 'actually reversed the sense of the report'. The way Sissons spatched the reference to the Prime Minister's remarks into his report was certainly clumsy. But when the sentence is seen in the context not just of his report as a whole but also of the corresponding passage in his piece for the Early News, quoted above, it seems clear that the intention to stand Ryder on its head was, to say the least, not proven.{7} That sentence and a brief passage in the McGarry interview were in fact the only points in an exceptionally long treatment of the story that evening that made more than a passing reference to strikes. Next day Ryder featured prominently in all three bulletins with no mention of strikes. In all, references to disputes amounted to under 5 per cent of the reporting of Ryder.

More generally, members of the Group complain of television news' 'extraordinary propensity to report the car industry', describing this as 'the most noticeable of the distortions in the early months of 1974' (TUM 128). They note that the '2.1 per cent of Britain's workforce who make cars and other vehicles got 24.4 per cent of the television news' general industrial coverage'. It was of course the industry as a whole rather than its 'workforce' that received the coverage, and it is unclear why this concentration should be considered 'extraordinary' or 'distorted'. The gravity of the strike record can of course be exaggerated, but, as table 8 shows, it gave legitimate cause for concern. In fact, the industry accounted for 5.7 per cent of all days lost in 1972, 28.9 per cent in 1973, 11.9 per cent in 1974 and 13.8 per cent in 1975.

Here was one of Britain's main manufacturing industries, manifestly deep in crisis; it would have been far more extraordinary if its problems had received only 2.1 per cent of the coverage! The Glasgow Group would probably accept that point, but they give no indication of what level of coverage — presumably between 2.1 per cent and 24.4 per cent — they think would have been about right. This is consistent with their general readiness to stigmatise television news without clarifying the standards they are applying.

The Glasgow studies' other major criticism of the coverage is that it focused on only one interpretation of the problems of Leyland's and the industry generally — that strikes were their root cause (Bad News 256-7). They contend that ITN carried 33 references to the strike theme, 8 to management and none to investment. This leads to the conclusion that the ills of Leyland were laid at the door of the workforce (Bad News 266, Trade Unions and the Media 130-1). The accusation can be answered along three different lines. First, for all the apparent precision of the data the form of presentation makes verification impossible, and the terms are

Table 8: Days Lost Per Thousand Employees,
1970-1975

	All workers	Motor vehicle manufacturing
1970	489	2,114
1971	613	6,201
1972	1,081	2,753
1973	318	4,132
1974	647	3,528
1975	265	1,804
Average 1970-75	569	3,422

Source: Smith et al, Strikes in Britain, 98-111.

highly selective. Quite clearly the reckoning takes no account of the references to 'antiquated plant' already noted, while references to the parlous state of the market have not been counted as an explanatory factor at all. Moreover, just as strikes are not necessarily attributable to labour, so under-investment is not necessarily the fault of management alone. A second element of the answer lies in a comment they make elsewhere:

'The coverage of the car industry could be justified by the extent of the stoppages...In all indicators there is no doubt that, coupled with the importance of the industry, the period in question was by no means peaceful and television coverage was therefore appropriate' (Bad News 169).

Yet although disputes legitimately constituted a recurrent news theme, the charge that ITN focused on them as the root cause of the industry's problems does not accord with the facts. For not only did ITN cover only six of the fourteen 'prominent stoppages' in the industry during the period, it ran over fifty items which pointed to other sources of the industry's difficulties.{8} As British Leyland's industrial relations director, Pat Lowry, said in the course of one interview that was, as it happens, devoted to industrial relations: 'Our problem at the moment in a very substantially contracting market is to hold what share of the market we have and, if possible, to increase it' (F 6 Jan.).

Or take two further passages from stories which also dealt with industrial relations. The evening after Harold Wilson's speech a report from Keith Hatfield at Cowley included the following statement by a union official:

'I would say that with the car industry in the state that it is in now, if you abolish the strikes, all you would be heading for is an automatic three days a week anyway, because you could be overproducing in the same way as you did before the war, so that the whole of the industry's got to be looked at from top to bottom — and I don't mean vice versa. From the top, first of all, to the bottom' (L 4 Jan.).

In an interview with Robert Kee, mainly concerned with following up Cowley's problems in the wake of the Prime Minister's speech, Maurice Edelman MP referred to the problems of the industry in the wake of the oil crisis and the mounting stocks of cars, continuing:

'...and I think that until the workers in the industry — and management too for that matter, because they are at least as much to blame as the workers, but until they realise that the crisis which threatens their companies, and threatens the name of very famous companies, until that time, you'll have this running sore inside the industry' (F 9 Jan.).

Later he said:

'I think that Mr Wilson must come back to the argument, and he must give a proper shake-up to the management and to workers in the industry, and explain to them the terrible danger which is threatening companies like Chryslers, Leyland and so on. But the danger isn't only local in Britain. It's a danger to the whole of the western motor industry, and what we are on the eve of now is really cut-throat competition between the motor companies of western Europe, which is going to be a direct threat, not only to the jobs of the few workers, but indeed to the companies themselves in this country.'

Edelman urged 'full public accountability...not only for managements but for workers as well', and advocated nationalisation. He, at least, broke out of the 'dominant frame'.

When workers at Chrysler's Linwood plant were put on short time

ITN ran a report from Martyn Lewis, backed by a sea of unsold cars, which made no reference to strikes:

'9,000 reasons for the four-day week can be found in yards outside the factory and on the Glasgow dockside. For that's the number of unsold cars which Chrysler in Scotland alone have already put into mothballs. Deliveries are at a fraction of a year ago. Chrysler see little point in churning out more products at a high price just to see them stand in the rain' (E 6 Jan.; slightly condensed in L 6 Jan.).

And even while the news was echoing Harold Wilson's criticism of avoidable stoppages, it was reporting that car production for 1974 was 12 per cent down on the previous year, with a particularly sharp decline in the last few weeks of the year:

'There was an even bigger slump in sales of both British and foreign cars in this country — 25 per cent down — which helps to explain the backlog at factories like Ford's Halewood plant' (L 9 Jan.).

It is curious that Bad News found no space to mention a long report on the industry by Joan Thirkettle:

'Strikes — avoidable or otherwise — are not the only problem facing the British car industry at the moment. Sales last year were down by nearly a quarter' (F 10 Jan.).

Her catalogue of the industry's difficulties made only a passing mention of strikes. In addition to a short interview with the general secretary of the AUEW, John Boyd, the item included an interview with a Datsun dealer commenting on the outdated design of British cars, and her warning that unless sales improved cutbacks in production and massive layoffs were inevitable.

ITN coverage of a meeting between the Leyland management and 400 shop stewards reported, without laying blame, Lord Stokes' call for a 'fundamental change in the way in which the company's management and unions work together', the emphasis being on the need to improve Leyland's industrial relations. Pat Lowry, industrial relations director, promised 'an open and participative style of management, if possible, more information for, and greater communication with employees, and what he called the highest possible level of managerial honesty' (E 10 Jan.).

Reporting that Chrysler plants were to remain on a three-day week, ITN attributed this to 'falling sales' (L 13 Jan.). Later Vauxhall also went on a three-day week at Ellesmere Port due to 'the general down-trend in car markets' (E 17 Jan.). On 22 January ITN ran a long item on the industry's problems in News at Ten. Bad News takes legitimate exception to the opening:

'On the day it's been announced by the Government that new car sales were down by 25 per cent, the director of British Leyland's Cowley plant has warned of a "calamity" if the strike situation there gets worse.'

This is a copybook instance of how not to lead a story. Not only because it may be taken to link falling sales and strikes, but because it clutters and weakens the 'intro'; it is poor journalistic writing. However, the Group fail to mention a substantial concluding section which discussed the slump in the market which was affecting all major producers, without mentioning strikes:

'Meanwhile, the problems of the industry as a whole have been highlighted by today's figures showing tens of thousands of the industry's half a million workforce going on short time, and unsold cars piling up in the car parks...All this is the most depressing scenario for an industry whose exports last year totalled nearly £2,000 million — nearly a fifth of the country's overseas sales. If Britain is to make any sort of attempt at clearing the present staggering balance of payments problem, it can certainly not do without a healthy motor industry, with the investment, the manpower and the will to defy the energy crisis and step up sales.'

The next day coverage of BLMC's annual report quoted Lord Stokes as attributing the disastrous decline in Leyland's fortunes mainly to inflation (E,L 23 Jan.). News at Ten also reported briefly the Leyland stewards' proposal that the company be nationalised (3 Feb.). When 11,000 Ford workers were notified of short-time working, ITN noted that their leaders had urged them to keep cool and not take industrial action: 'Mr Moss Evans, national organiser of the Transport Workers, said destructive action wouldn't persuade people to buy cars' (E 19 Feb.). When Vauxhall announced redundancies at Ellesmere Port, ITN's industrial correspondent noted that all the major companies were now on short time. However, Linwood might return to a five day week 'if the car market doesn't get any worse' (L 24 Feb.). Next day it became clear that Chrysler was suffering from more than a temporary bad patch. ITN reported that the company's president had told the Government that the UK subsidiary had 'too much production capacity for the size of the market', and asked for Government support for a cut in vehicle taxes and a relaxation of hire purchase restrictions (E 25 Feb.). Apart from Moss Evans' appeal none of these reports mentioned strikes.

On 6 March News at Ten carried a long report disclosing that BLMC executives had warned that the Budget needed to give a substantial boost to sales:

'if the market for cars continues to decline, the company will be forced to shed between 20 and 30 thousand workers over the next 18 months'.

The remainder of the report enlarged on this theme: a market which had shrunk by a quarter inside a year with no recovery in prospect; Marina production lines turning out 3,500 cars a week, of which only 3,000 were being sold: 400,000 new unsold cars in the country as a whole. BLMC wanted hire purchase relaxed and 'there's also a strong feeling that there should be import controls, particularly against the Japanese'. The one crumb of comfort seemed to be when BLMC captured nearly 45 per cent of the UK market in February (L 10 March). But this was momentary. On 4 April News at Ten reported a token takeover by workers at Chrysler's Ellesmere Port plant in protest at the management's abrupt announcement of short-time working, which was attributed to 'sales folding and a stockpile of unsold Vauxhalls growing'. Including an interview with the AUEW Convenor, the report took a sympathetic view of the men's action. As Chrysler's troubles deepened the British division reported losing £m18 in 1974, for which it blamed 'inflation and removal of the Conservative Government's wage controls' (E,L 9 April).

Perhaps the most serious weakness in the Bad News analysis is the failure to recognise that coverage of the car industry differed from other stories under review. Most of those related to events wholly or mainly within the survey period, even though they may have built up during the preceding months or years − as at Glasgow and in the London docks. Accordingly we have the whole of the television record available for assessment. But the problems of the car industry ran on for years. Only the tiniest fraction of the coverage fell within the Glasgow survey period. Bad News repeatedly reaches categorical, sweeping conclusions, with no allowance for, say, the reports of Leyland's mounting financial problems the previous December, or of Chrysler's struggle for survival in the spring and summer. Yet having commented on the inadequacies of television news when covering protracted processes rather than specific events, Bad News might reasonably have been expected to recognise the same problem in its own analysis.

As it happened, even within their chosen period, as the preceding examples have shown, ITN by no means focused on the single aspect of dispute. Its portrayal of an industry in crisis can be faulted, but it quite clearly returned repeatedly to other dimensions of the problem than labour relations. But in Bad News such 'non-conformist' material is hastily skirted around or referred to in the briefest of snippets.

1   David Holmes, who was among the BBC journalists covering the story, later took the view that the initial emphasis was not correct ('The Man Alive Debate', BBC2, 28 July 1982).

2   In a comment ITN did not report, Ray Carter, Labour MP for Birmingham Northfield, told a meeting of shop stewards at Leyland's Longbridge plant that the remarks 'were directed primarily to Leyland's plant at Cowley 'where no one but the blind or prejudiced could deny there has been an appalling record of disputes and lost production" (The Times, 7 January 1975).

    Barbara Castle commented in her Diary: 'Harold has made one of his great showdown speeches on strikes.' She later remarked, 'Jack Jones's response to Harold's weekend speech on strikes...has been surprisingly mild. The Castle Diaries 1974-1976, Weidenfield & Nicholson, 1980, 267 and 269-70.

3   Wilson's remarks were recalled as referring to 'manifestly avoidable strikes' (F,E,L 4 Jan.; F 6 Jan.); 'unnecessary strikes' (E 6 Jan., F 9 Jan.) and 'avoidable disruption' (L 6 Jan.). A possible explanation for these variations may be that sub-editors handling the story changed frequently.

4   Bad News' final comment is that 'it should also be remembered that the government Arbitration & Conciliation Service vindicated the tuners' basic claim for regrading when eventually they reported' (267). But that was not the whole story. ACAS did recommend that the tuners should be put in a separate category taking account of the skills of their job, but did *not* agree they should be reclassified as 'skilled' rather than 'production workers'. ACAS also noted possible knock-on claims from other groups of workers, which was what management feared. The Times, 25 March 1975.

5   There were 10 in First Report, 17 in the Early News and 17 in the Late News.

6   Cf. The Daily Telegraph, 7 January 1975.

7   More Bad News alleges that there were discrepancies in the number of tuners reported to be on strike (136). Most ITN reports gave the number as 250; a few said 'more than 200'.

    National newspaper coverage of this strike in issues dated 7 January 1975 is also discussed in D. McQuail, Analysis of Newspaper Content, Cmnd. 6810-4, HMSO, 1977, 155-162. McQuail identifies 11 'news points' which were covered by at least six of the nine papers investigated; ITN's reports gave 10 of these. Of 43 points covered in all nine papers ITN reported 23 – more than any newspaper except the Daily Telegraph, which also reported 23.

8   'Newstalk' is rather inclined to treat 'and' and 'but' as interchangeable. Compare this report on the Nine o'Clock News on 31 January 1985: 'The Employment Secretary, Tom King, accepted that unemployment is too high. But Labour's spokesman, John Prescott, said that the latest rise showed the government's arrogant indifference to the unemployed.'

The Westminster Hospital Dispute

The strike of ancillary workers at Westminster Hospital was one engagement in a long campaign over pay beds in National Health Service hospitals. The management planned to close 38 NHS beds while bathrooms were being improved and nurses were on holiday. The union argued that 10 of the 38 beds should come from the private list. There were said to be 20 private beds and over 100 NHS beds unoccupied at the time. The National Union of Public Employees first withdrew non-medical services from private patients, then initiated a general work-to-rule after volunteers had served meals, and finally called brief lightning strikes. The union advised a return to normal working after a promise that in an emergency private beds would be made available to NHS patients.

Bad News's criticism concentrates on the BBC and the press, with ITN on this occasion figuring, relatively, as the 'good guys' — not that their coverage received any word of commendation (Bad News 235-240).{1} Indeed, since the episode is cited 'by many of the trade unionists we interviewed' as a 'prime example of *media* bias' (Bad News 237, emphasis mine), ITN is in the end lumped in with the global condemnations. ITN ran eleven reports over five days (three in First Report, five in the early evening and three in the late news — see News Scripts 16). NUPE was named fifteen times in six reports, excluding supercaptions.{2} ITN's first report, which ran only sixteen seconds, was mutilated in subbing and stated baldly that, negotiations between NUPE and the hospital having broken down, the union would cut off non-medical services to private patients from midnight. No indication was given of the nature of the dispute (E 16 March). However subsequent reports made it clear what the issue was (eg L 16 March), why it extended firstly into a work to rule (F 17; F 18 March), then into lightning strikes (F 19 March), and finally the ground on which work was resumed (L 21 March). Moreover, it is fair to note that just before the Westminster dispute First Report had carried a longish interview with Bernard Dix of NUPE in which he situated his union's campaign in the context of a general commitment by the TUC and the Labour Party to 'get private practice out of the National Health Service because we think it distorts the social purpose' (F 14 March). Having acknowledged that this might lead to the emergence of a parallel private health service he continued:

> 'The immediate issue is that by having inside the National Health Service both a public and a private sector, it means if anybody has the money, they can jump the queue. Let me just — we were talking about Moorfields [Hospital] on your film there. At Moorfields there are empty National Health Service beds, empty beds waiting there for National Health patients, but there's an 18-month waiting list for cataract operations, because the operating theatre facilities and the surgeon's time are overloaded with private patients. So there are beds, and there are patients waiting 18 months, but the surgeons are very busy with their private patients, so the National Health Service patients are way down the bottom of the list.'

Most reports were briefly factual, but four were longer. The NUPE branch chairman was interviewed in four successive bulletins (L 16 March; F,E,L 17 March) receiving considerably more attention than spokesmen for the hospital. Acknowledging this imbalance, Bad News sees this as a cautionary tale for anyone who thinks this might have given the union an advantage. Yet if the outcome was less than a triumph for NUPE this was largely attributable to the branch chairman, Jamie Morris. Asked what would happen to the private patients he replied:

> 'Well, if you come back at midnight and ask me the same question, I'll answer you, 'What private patients?' — because as far as we're concerned, there will be no private patients after midnight. We will just not recognise that they're there.'

Asked, 'But in fact they are going to be there in reality, so what's to happen to them?', he answered that they would not get the services they expected such as food. What if the hospital should make alternative arrangements? The work would be blacked; there might be picket lines. Could they strike?

'No, never. No National Health Service patient will suffer because of what we're doing. That I promise you.'

After volunteers had helped serve breakfast next day Morris said that while feeling was running high he would oppose coming out. By the Early News he was conceding that NHS patients would 'probably be affected very slightly' by a decision to work to rule. 'But isn't this a nonsense?', he was asked. 'This is a dispute about private beds, and yet here you are in fact affecting National Health Service patients.' He replied:

'It could also be argued that management affected National Health Service patients the minute they decided to take the steps they did. We are very sorry about the action we've been forced into taking...'

That evening he was asked whether the strike was an attempt to bring pressure on the pay beds issue. He said:

'Obviously we hope it would help but that is not what the dispute is about. The dispute is simply because the hospital management refuse to close private beds while they're closing NHS beds. We also asked them to transfer the private beds or at least some to the NHS. They point blankly refused. In our view they put people's bank balances before their health.'

Was not the action 'all a bit pointless?'

'No, it's not a pointless dispute. The dispute is also about an issue that my members feel very strongly about. But we are not paid skivvies, we are National Health Service workers. We work for the National Health Service, and we are fed up of being insulted, pushed around and dictated to by a few people who have got money.'

On 19 March Morris was reported to have said that the ancillary workers were ready to 'starve out' the private patients.

In the light of all this it is understandable that members of the NALGO publicity department argued that 'all publicity was very definitely not good publicity' (Bad News 240). Yet ITN's questions were fair and cogent. If the suggestion that 'it's all a bit pointless' is thought rather too aggressive, an equally pointed question was put to a hospital administrator:

'It would surely be very simple just to designate 10 private beds for National Health Service use over the next 3 months. Why don't you do that?' (L 17 March).

The real problem was not one of 'inferential frames' but that Jamie Morris expressed himself in terms which some other trade unionists found embarrassing. Yet the transcript shows that these were very much 'unforced errors'.

The wider course of relations between Morris and the media lies outside this study. However, it is far too simple to present him as a devil-figure created by the media *pour épater les bourgeois*. A man with a considerable faculty for turning a striking phrase, working a stone's throw from the news studios, he seems to be one of those people who can turn the weakness of news editors for colourful characters to their own purposes — along with Arthur Scargill, Tony Benn, Enoch Powell, Ken Livingstone, Ian Paisley and Brian Clough, to mention just a varied few. Whether, in doing so, they also best serve their cause can be quite another matter.

The Imperial Sit-In

The sit-in at the Imperial Typewriter works at Hull received substantial coverage (News Scripts 6). ITN carried a brief report of the decision by Litton Industries to close plant at Leicester and Hull with a loss of 3,200 jobs on 17 January (L). There were five more reports on 21 and 22 February. The first, which ran at some length (3' 11″), reported that 300 workers had taken over the Hull factory, 600 more having accepted redundancy terms and left. The workers had appealed to the Secretary of State for Industry, Tony Benn, to save their jobs. He was awaiting a consultants' report. Meanwhile he accused the firm of 'behaving irresponsibly'.

Michael Green reported that Litton had lost £9,000,000 trying to revive Imperial, attributing failure to 'a rapid increase in costs — particularly wages — and a slump in sales'. The workers had little hope of finding jobs in Hull — as vox pop comments from several of them confirmed. Green reported that the unions were urging the consultants to recommend a £3,000,000 grant to keep the factory going. The company, which planned to concentrate production in Germany, were convinced that the union proposals were impracticable. It denied that it had left it too late to mount a rescue. A management spokesman claimed that in the face of a falling market the least cost-effective unit had to go. But, Green reiterated, the workers did not accept this view. They had been to lobby Tony Benn. Green saw this as one of the few instances of an American firm closing its UK operations with the intention of selling here from abroad:

'It's bound to make the Government more sceptical about foreign takeovers in the future, and will increase its determination to exert closer control over the multinationals here in the future.'

On 22 February the Early News briefly reported the occupation of the factory, along with the appeal to the Secretary of State and his accusation of 'irresponsible behaviour' on the part of the firm. There was 'some hope' in the consultants' report, which suggested ways of resuming production. This would be the subject of talks between the Government and union leaders. News at Ten covered the takeover and Tony Benn's comment and carried a further report from Michael Green. This noted that, to avoid trouble, the management had closed the plant a day early, but militant workers had climbed the gate to begin the sit-in. Through the bars of the padlocked factory gate Claire Tate, TGWU shop steward, described what happened:

'After we had all left, the management sent us all a special delivery letter, at a fee of 44½p, not forgetting this company is telling us all along the line they have no money. After receiving that letter, the stewards gathered round, and we decided what we was going to do. As we have said all along, there's two roads, and we know which road we're on. The factory belongs to us. Littons have disowned us.'

This report mentioned Litton's losses and the Government's promise of discussions on the consultants' report, and reiterated the assessment of the likely impact of the affair on official attitudes towards multinationals.

Next day's lunchtime bulletin reported that the strike was continuing, and that a union official would be reporting on talks with Tony Benn. By the Early News this official was quoted as saying that it would be wrong to raise false hopes. Prophetic words: after determined efforts to negotiate a rescue the union's proposals were eventually rejected by the Government, and after the issuing of a High Court writ the workers had to admit defeat and end their five-month sit-in in July. ITN covered these later developments in five more reports. While these fell outside the survey period, part of the final item is worth quoting.

'Nearly eighty men and women were led out from the plant by

union officials. The sit-in lasted one hundred and forty-six days.
They marked the length of their vigil by a coffin draped with the
Union Jack.
Many were in tears as they passed through the factory gates.
They'd all been clinging to one last hope. A new enterprise had
been promised for the factory. But the firm interested finally
dropped out of the deal' (L 16 July).
ITN's film showed the scene: the strikers' 'scoreboard' marked 'Day
146', the flag-draped coffin, and the sad — yet undiminished — line of
workers exchanging farewells with the stewards as they left the factory
for the last time. Here is how Bad News discusses the coverage:
'One other engineering story received a fairly extensive coverage in
the period of our sample. This was the announcement of the closure
of Imperial Typewriters in January and the subsequent story ran to
sixteen bulletins on both channels, and in only two of these was a
statement from the union included. In both instances the name of the
union was not given. In one other bulletin a TGWU shop steward
was interviewed and named as such' (Bad News 241).
As far as ITN is concerned nothing in that passage is factually
incorrect. What is missing is any acknowledgement that although the
TGWU was named only once, the union's active involvement was
apparent in all five items on the sit-in. Nor is there the least recognition
that the workers' reasons were made amply clear, that they featured
more prominently than management or that they were handled with
noticeable sympathy, particularly in the last, moving report. ITN
reported the management's reasons for closure, but also cited Benn's
condemnation several times and pointedly mentioned the company's
multinational status. It would have been interesting to see how the
Group reconciles all this with the assertion that the 'contours of coverage
never deviate' from a set frame for industrial reporting. But all they offer
is a trivial, misleading point about the naming of the TGWU and an
unwarranted innuendo about coverage of the workers' case.{3}

Protest at Ebbw Vale
Another protest over closures was the 24-hour strike at the Ebbw Vale
steel works over the British Steel Corporation's decision to shut the
plant, and Government readiness to let it do so (News Scripts 11). First

Report explained on 7 February why the strike was occurring, adding that workers were to march through the town, reaching the civic centre at the same time as the local MP (and Employment Minister), Michael Foot, and the Welsh Secretary, John Morris, who was expected to announce a £12,000,000 scheme to offset the unemployment caused by the closure. A short report in the Early News covered the number of jobs to be lost, the likely phasing of the run-down, and the broad outline of the Government's scheme, together with a brief clip of Michael Foot's rough reception with angry steelworkers shouting 'resign' and 'betrayal'.

There was fuller coverage of the noisy confrontation between Foot and the workers in News at Ten. Trevor McDonald reported that although the demonstrators were good-natured enough at first, on hearing of the Government's proposals their anger was directed at Michael Foot. There was some colourful and poignant footage of Foot, once the local political hero, fighting against angry barracking at the site of some of his earlier triumphs, to get across his determination to save the valley towns. More could of course have been said. Some of this wider context was provided in a News at Ten report of a visit to Scotland by the Prime Minister on 28 February, in which he spoke optimistically of the future of the Hunterstone steelworks project and of the industry generally in Scotland — hopes that were to be cruelly falsified within a few years. A harsher and more accurate vision of the future for steel was provided in long reports in all three editions of the news on 23 April of the British Steel Corporation's plans to cut 20,000 jobs by the autumn, with the workforce falling from 220,000 to 180,000 by 1980, and eventually to only 50,000. First Report followed this news with an interview with the general secretary of the Iron & Steel Trades Confederation (but not the BSC chairman, Sir Monty Finniston), and in News at Ten Keith Hatfield reported from Ebbw Vale on prospects for those who would be made redundant:

> 'Since the 18th century, Ebbw Vale has earned its living from making iron and steel, but now the works are out of date, and half the site that dominates the valley is being scrapped. Half the men who work there will lose their jobs. No-one knows more about redundancy in the industry than the steel workers of Ebbw Vale. 4,000 of them have been told that they will lose their jobs when iron

and steel making closes down in the valley. But in Ebbw Vale, redundancy does not automatically lead to the dole queue. Some of the jobs will be saved by a £70 million scheme to convert what is left of the site into a modern plant for galvanising and tinplating steel....'
With hindsight the ensuing interview with a BSC employment counsellor looks cruelly over-optimistic from the workers' point of view; it was in a sense as unduly optimistic from Finniston's viewpoint. For if many of the displaced workers would find jobs far harder to come by than the report suggested, implementation of the Finniston plan was to prove much more difficult and protracted than viewers might have imagined from these initial reports – though two days later ITN reported a speech by the Industry Secretary, Tony Benn, which made clear that the BSC chairman would not have matters all his own way (E 25 April). Nevertheless ITN must be credited with reporting the industry's wider problems as well as the demonstration itself. Even within its coverage of the demonstration, ITN did convey something of what the industrial action was about and the strength of shop-floor feeling.

Trouble at British Airways

At the end of January British Airways faced two industrial relations problems (News Scripts 8). News at Ten reported on the 30th that British Airways shop stewards were advising engineering and maintenance staff to strike because of failure to agree a new pay deal. The deal, which had been accepted by nearly 20,000 other staff, consolidated threshold payments into basic pay and gave an extra 15 per cent in two stages. The engineers wanted 23 per cent. Next day's Early News and News at Ten carried a report from Giles Smith that a mass meeting at Heathrow had voted almost unanimously to accept the pay offer, averting a strike. This was 'a major blow to the authority of the shop stewards'. Smith asked one of them why the men had overturned their recommendation. He answered:

'I suppose they don't want to go on strike. It's as simple as that, isn't it? The majority of people came to the decision because they don't want to stay [sc. strike?], for the simple reason that it's quite a good offer.'

Noting that the airline welcomed the decision, Smith commented that they now had to face the threat of a walk-out if they went ahead with their plans for cabin staff to take fares on the new Glasgow shuttle.

Although Smith's description of the decision as a major blow to the stewards might be arguable, it would be hard, within its limited compass, to fault the ITN coverage on other grounds. It did not name the unions (there were probably several), but the issue was clear, the questions to the stewards were fair, and they were given adequate scope to reply in their own terms. By now it will come as no surprise to learn that the Glasgow Group do not quote the steward's reply.

But if the one strike was averted the other was not. On 1 February First Report covered the strike by booking staff against the introduction of in-flight ticket sales on the London-Glasgow shuttle:

> 'The members of APEX fear that the pay-on-board system will spread to more flights and lead to redundancies among their members.'

Some flights were delayed or cancelled, but a makeshift system was getting passengers away. The Early News and News at Ten carried similar reports, with revised information about the impact of the strike.

Coverage resumed on 3 February with a long First Report interview with the general secretary of APEX (The Asociation of Professional, Executive, Clerical and Computer Staff), Tudor Thomas. Robert Kee's first question would be judged tendentious by some and pertinent by others:

> 'Mr Thomas, aren't you really saying, as if it were a matter of principle somehow, that the maintenance of these clerical workers' jobs is really more important than the convenience and efficiency of the service to the public?

Thomas rejected that formulation, pointing out that British Airways should have consulted the union before taking jobs that were traditionally his members'. This was their first strike in civil aviation, and he produced figures to show how they had cooperated in increasing productivity and introducing new systems. APEX wanted tickets to be bought at the counter and checked at the gate. He was ready to meet ACAS and he hoped to contain the dispute. Some might judge Kee to have been unduly aggressive, others might say that he failed to tackle Thomas strongly enough about the inconvenience to travellers. But it seems hard to deny that the interviewee had reasonable opportunity to state his position, and that he was able to put the union's view across.

In the Early News and News at Ten staff in Manchester were reported as coming out in sympathy; the issue was stated a trifle baldly as an objection to stewardesses taking fares on the shuttle. Next day's First Report explained the strike in similar terms, reported delays and cancellations and said that talks were under way between BA and APEX. The Early News on 5 February reported that there had been further delays and cancellations and that the two sides were meeting at ACAS. If these failed all 7,000 APEX members would come out. The dispute was 'in protest against the selling of tickets on board planes on the new shuttle services'. News at Ten reported that talks had broken down and APEX was threatening to call out its 7,000 members; Manchester might close if the TGWU there came out in support of the clerical staff.

By the next day's Early News British Airways had cancelled all flights out of Manchester following the collapse of talks. The cause of the strike was not stated. News at Ten reported that a plan had been worked out to end the strike, and the union side of the National Joint Council for Civil Air Transport was recommending acceptance. The cause was now stated as 'fear there'll be redundancies over British Airways' decision to sell tickets on board the new London to Glasgow shuttle service'. The Early News on the following day reported that a mass meeting had accepted proposals under which inflight sales would end, and passengers would buy their tickets before boarding. The issue was being referred for further consideration to the NJC. The strike was over. News at Ten reported in similar terms.

Here, then, was coverage in which the union was amply identified, the reasons for its actions were stated several times, albeit in slightly varying and occasionally terse terms, and the official character of the dispute was unequivocally implied even though it was not stated in as many words. The union was able to state its case at length, whereas – for whatever reason – nothing was heard from either the management or the inconvenienced travellers. And far from being shown to be 'futile', the workers were ultimately successful in blocking British Airways' plans. None of this squares very readily with the picture of television behaviour presented in Bad News.

1   Although BBC coverage is not under general discussion, one of the Group's criticisms shows their style of argument revealingly. A BBC story is quoted as saying, 'Michael Vestey put it to [the NUPE branch chairman] that the majority of his members were foreign and didn't understand what the dispute was about.' Bad News comments that 'The BBC went so far as to suggest that because the majority of the union membership was 'foreign' they would be *incapable* of understanding the principles in the dispute' (237-8, emphasis mine). Vestey's words of course carried no such suggestion. Examples like this do not encourage confidence in the handling of more delicate issues of linguistic analysis in More Bad News.

2   Bad News says there were only eleven mentions on all three channels combined.

3   This was not the only sit-in covered. First Report on 23 April featured one by Ford workers protesting at suspensions, who locked out management and staff. The men's spokesman was reported as emphasising that it would be a peaceful occupation. 'Earlier today there'd been talk of an all-out strike at the plant, but the men decided against it because, as a shop steward said, it would put them in a bad light.' The men's spokesmen promised 'we will try to conduct ourselves as responsible people.' Management's view was not reported. This item is not discussed in Bad News.

'FRAMING' THE NEWS

8

'Television news', the Glasgow account argues, 'is concerned with the reproduction of information within the realms of a dominant consciousness'; it plays the role of 'front-runner medium of cultural legitimation' of the consensus and the status quo (Bad News 14, 15). Such, it seems, is their general proposition, with industrial news as the particular instance. If so, there appears to be three stages in the argument. First, that there exists a 'dominant consciousness' — presumably arising from a general acceptance of the 'dominant ideology'. Second, that television news encodes and transmits the dominant ideology. Finally, that these ideologically encoded messages are correctly perceived and internalised by substantial sections of the audience.

The Glasgow studies say little about the first stage, and most of what they do say consists of citations and paraphrases. The authors' own standpoint never becomes clear. Accordingly comment must in turn be brief. Suffice it perhaps to point out that the concept of 'dominant consciousness' is problematical, and its existence certainly cannot be taken as established fact. If it does exist, then as Abercrombie and his colleagues observe in their trenchant review of the literature:

'The content, however, remains remarkably elusive in all existing texts, not because it is so self-evident that it need not be spelled out, which is implicit in much discussion, but because it really is difficult to define precisely.'{1}

Referring specifically to the Glasgow Group's approach they comment:

'The elucidation of specific instances of bias...is used as evidence for a more generalised bias which reflects the dominant ideology. The ideology either appears as a set of concrete items which apply in specific circumstances rather than as a more all-embracing set of values, or merely as a generalised conservative bias which supports the status quo against challenge. This latter claim is so vague and

trivial that the concept of ideology loses all utility.'{2}
And they conclude:

> 'These comments show that the dominant ideology lacks internal
> consistency, with the result that many of its constituent elements are
> contradictory. They further suggest that not all of the dominant
> groups believe in all of the elements. Thus we have a dominant
> ideology that is neither coherent nor subscribed to by all its supposed
> proponents.'{3}

The debate, as they say, continues. Nothing in the Glasgow account
gives 'dominant consciousness' any greater substance or credibility.
Stage one in television's 'front-runner' function is in consequence by no
means proven.

Nevertheless, does the news in fact transmit a view of reality that is
consistently prejudicial to the unions and to the labour movement
generally? Since this is really the heart of the Glasgow studies, the second
stage requires more extended consideration. As we have seen, on the
basis of at most twenty-two weeks output, and at times far less, Bad
News concludes that there are 'unvarying frames' in the reporting of
industrial stories, and that 'nothing' during their sample period did other
than confirm the prevailing 'belief system'. With so slender a data base
one might have expected the conclusions to be phrased somewhat
tentatively. In fact, they are invariably as categoric as they are negative.
Yet we have seen that where statements are couched in terms permitting
a reasonably comprehensive quantitative verification they are at best
exaggerated and frequently they are flatly inaccurate. Time and again
sweeping conclusions are drawn from minuscule evidence, news
performance is assessed against inappropriate yardsticks of 'reality',
inconvenient findings (like the under-representation of employers) are
shrugged off without further discussion, or are kept carefully out of view
(as with their handling of coverage of the car industry), while facts are
massaged out of all recognition (as with their dominant health hazard
'frame' for the strike by dustcart drivers). Indeed, the most evident
'dominant frames' are those created and imposed by the Bad News
volumes themselves.

There is of course more to the studies than a critique of strike
coverage. They discuss the reporting of the social contract and the
miners' pay claim, the nature of 'news talk' and the visual components of

the news. It could be that their handling of these themes is of a different order from what we have seen so far. Unfortunately, the remaining sections seem much of a piece with those we have seen in detail. A few examples suffice to show the process of creating a 'dominant frame' at work there too.

For instance, the analysis of 'news talk' offers this characteristic turn of argument:

'In the phrase 'the strikers are demanding a pay rise of £10 per week' the strikers are alien to mankind in general – strikers are not you or me, they are somebody else. Thus when it is our strike, we are cut out of the message' (More Bad News 169).

The words after 'alien to mankind in general', which might have been expected to confirm or illustrate the assertion do not in fact do so; instead they say something different and weaker. Consequently it is not clear just what is being said. Is it suggested that any use of the third person in news reporting treats those concerned as 'alien to mankind in general', or that third person accounts of any event in which we are involved, be it a strike, a traffic jam, a heat wave or a demonstration over a new by-pass 'cut us out of the message' – or are these fates in some mysterious way peculiar to strikers? And what is the evidence for this 'finding' which is so confidently proclaimed?

It would also be interesting to see the underpinning for this assertion: 'Where first person plurals are used or implied they will appeal to commonsense understandings and problems 'about which we are all agreed' – for example 'the cost of just one day's layoff was 1,200 cars worth 1¾ million pounds.' 'The cost' is not specified to anyone in particular. The implication is that it is a cost to us, to the community, to Britain. But here the cost is in fact an estimated cost to the firm. Costs to the workers are not counted, neither are market conditions' (More Bad News 169).

The quotation singled out for comment was the closing sentence of a report from Cowley by Keith Hatfield (L 7 Jan.). Neither here nor in fuller context is it clear that he implied a first person plural or indicated anything 'about which we are all agreed'. It may be the market was in such poor shape that the British Leyland Motor Corporation would have been hard put to sell the cars had they in fact been produced – but that was not demonstrated. The contention that Hatfield assigned the costs

'to us, to the community, to Britain' remains pure assertion – though
there is of course a sense in which any strike which reduces the supply of
goods or services does have a cost for the community at large as well as
for those directly involved. While Hatfield may indeed have thought
along the lines attributed to him, at bottom there is no way in which the
Group or anyone else can be sure either what was in his mind or how
viewers would 'read' his message. And the Glasgow comment overlooks
other occasions when losses were unequivocally attributed to the
company, as in the reports that 'British Leyland's losses mount at the rate
of 1,000 cars a day' during the tuners' strike (L 4 Jan.), and that the
stoppage by Dunlop clerks was 'costing the company £1 1/2 million a
day.' (L 30 April). Or again, it was reported that 'disruption today cost
the Daily Telegraph and the Sun 360,000 and 170,000 copies respectively'
(L 15 Jan.).

At another point ITN's use of 'stoppage' is challenged as 'one of the
most frequent nominal forms used to describe industrial action',
employed interchangeably with 'strike' (More Bad News 154). But their
own count of the terms ITN used to describe industrial action in the
main evening news shows 'stoppage' accounting for only 12 out of 292
instances, compared with 138 for 'strike' (180). So it was plainly not all
that 'frequent'. Moreover, strikes are stoppages even though by no
means all stoppages of production are due to strike action. Finally, for
many years 'stoppage' has been the term used by the Department of
Employment for its statistics of strikes and lock-outs, and the monthly
listings of 'prominent stoppages' on which Bad News places such
weight.{4}

In similar vein the authors bridle at the ideological overtones in the
way words like 'claim', 'demand' and 'offer' are used in industrial
relations stories, alleging a

'fundamental lack of reciprocity in a vocabulary in which the terms
could apply reciprocally to both labour and management...The
language of news is inhibited from using forms like 'labour offer to
work harder' or 'management demand higher output', which are
perfectly possible...The absurdity of applying concepts like 'offer'
and 'demand' to the 'wrong' side shows how this code works to
legitimate the side which responds and makes concessions rather
than the side which makes requests as though of right' (More Bad

News 184-5).

It is interesting that although they find it significant that 'offer' (with its overtones of generosity) was credited to management, they make no comment on the fact that 'threat' was attributed six times to management against three to labour. Would this have been passed over in silence had the ratio been reversed? And one is tempted to reflect on the 'delegitimation' of management implicit in such an imbalance – but there is no point in matching trivia with trivia. 'Claim', 'demand' and 'offer' are not just 'the language of news' but the customary vocabulary of everyone engaged in collective bargaining, including the unions. If the day comes when the unions table something they call an annual 'pay offer' and it is reported as a 'claim' or 'demand' the Group's criticisms might carry some weight. But not before.

More Bad News also takes exception to an ITN report that a strike by clerical workers at a Dunlop factory had 'made about 8,000 car workers idle' (159). Noting that 'idle' is applied to non-striking workers who have had to stop work, they cite Raymond Williams' contention that there is an 'ideological resistance' to the distinction between being laid off (which is a social situation) and idleness (which is a personal characteristic). 'With its strong moral implications, *idle* in this context must have ideological intentions or effects.'

Far from being an everyday word in ITN's industrial relations vocabulary 'idle' appeared as an occasional synonym for 'laid off' about as often as 'put out of work' and 'workers will have to stay off work'. In four months' coverage of the car industry it was employed twice compared with 22 instances of 'laid off' – a slender base on which to identify it as yet another illustration of the media's role in hegemonic signification! It is perhaps no coincidence that More Bad News does not cite this other occasion when 'idle' was used in a car industry context:

'Already the 3 week old strike has led to more than 13,000 other British Leyland workers being laid off, and another 1,200 will now be made idle' (E 27 Feb.).

It is clear both that 'idle' was used simply to avoid repeating 'laid off', and that being *made* idle carries no overtone of prejudice to the workforce. Scrupulous linguistic analysis would surely also have recognised the irrelevance of Williams' observation on 'idleness' (since its connotations are not identical to those of 'idle'), and would have noted that, according to the Oxford English Dictionary, an impersonal sense of 'idle', carrying no moral overtone or ideological signification, has been used in relation to industry for over a century. And when Mick McGahey declared during the 1984 pit strike that 'the whole Scottish coalfield was 'idle', his intentions may have been 'ideological' but it seems unlikely he was casting aspersions on the Scottish miners!

These remarks are not directed generally against sociolinguistics. It can clearly make a valuable contribution to media analysis. As with any specialised field, the untutored are wise to hesitate before venturing. But it does not require a professional eye to discern the tenuous nature of some of the conclusions drawn by the Glasgow team.

A final example comes from More Bad News' long analysis of supercaptions – the lettering superimposed on the bottom of the transmitted picture to identity participants and location (365-374). Among the 216 cases examined were *two* in which an interviewee had his function described in lower-case letters. One was a 'crew member', who later acquired a supercaption with initial capitals. The other was a 'shop steward' who featured only in lower case, though a 'Convenor' received an initial capital. Some might have hesitated to reach any firm conclusion on the basis of such limited and disparate evidence. Not so here: the heading to the ten-page section is 'Lower Case is Lower Class'. All this looks sadly familiar.

Here, as with the earlier analysis of strike coverage, we see a characteristic technique at work. A portion of the output is selected and declared to have some specific meaning. Frequently it could carry that meaning, but it could also as readily be understood in one or more quite different ways. Nevertheless, the authors can be relied on to seize on a reading which puts the unions in a bad light and then proclaim this to be 'the meaning' television conveyed. They are fully aware that 'industrial news talk is usually open to a plurality of interpretations'. They even quote Hall and Conti to the effect that television messages 'never deliver *one* meaning; they are, rather, the site of a plurality of meanings, in which one is preferred and offered to the viewers, over the others, as the most appropriate' (More Bad News 124). But what they present is *their* preferred meaning, without any demonstration that this was actually preferred by either the broadcasters or the viewers. It is the repeated resort to this technique that lays the groundwork for the eventual conclusion that news routines and explanatory frames are consistent, coherent and structured enough to constitute an 'ideology' inimical to the working class.

So the case for unvarying explanatory frames rests on a combination of multiple factual errors and the creation and systematic imposition of the Group's own 'unvarying frame' on the material they review. The outcome is an exercise in systematic reductionism in the name of 'science' reminiscent of the excesses of the oral/anal zealots of earlier years. Far from being scientific the critique is repeatedly and fatally flawed. It is ironic that Bad News accuses ITN of promulgating a view 'in the face of contradictory evidence which, when it appears, is either ignored, smothered, or at worst is treated as if it supports' their inferential frameworks (267-8), for it conspicuously displays every one of those failings — and a few more for good measure.

In short, even with more than 800 pages in which to develop and sustain them, the Glasgow conclusions simply do not stand. Uncomfortably aware of certain weaknesses some sympathisers have argued that nevertheless 'the overall weight of the total Glasgow thinking cannot be impugned'.{5} But this is mere wishful thinking — particularly as several categoric conclusions are so phrased that they are not merely dented by contrary evidence, they collapse completely. Certainly a number of detailed complaints were justified. With over 2,000 news items, often prepared against the clock, it would be surprising if there had been no ground for criticism — though of course not even the tightest schedule excuses inaccurate or careless reporting. But these specific failures did not add up to anything like the pattern of prejudice against the unions the Glasgow studies allege.

Finally, important though the analysis of output is, television's role of 'selling' the existing order and 'legitimating the consensus' only works if the ideological messages it transmits are widely internalised by the audience. And on this point the Glasgow studies can offer no evidence, only the assertion that particular items 'can only' have been understood in certain specified ways by the audience.{6} Yet it is notorious that television communicates uncertainly and unpredictably. Even something as familiar and relevant to viewers' interests as the weather forecast is fully grasped by only a minority of those watching. It is unlikely industrial news communicates any more efficiently.{7} It seems particularly improbable that many of the subtleties of syntax and vocabulary raised in the sociolinguistic analysis were widely assimilated. (This study has met verbal point with verbal point because of the nature of the Glasgow critique, but it is obvious that the verbal and visual components in television news may sometimes reinforce, but they may also mutually cancel or blur the message.) This is an area where, as McQuail puts it, facts are 'scarce, open to dispute and often puny in stature'.{8} Not only is assertion offered in place of evidence about the effects of television news, but the linear notion of communication implicit in the Glasgow studies takes no account of the long-established evidence on selective attention, selective perception and selective retention. In the end we are invited to believe that ideological messages can be encoded so skilfully that skilled and politically diverse journalists are unaware of this, and yet they are decoded and assimilated in something approximating to their original terms by a mass audience.{9} This is not, of course, impossible – but is it likely?

Although the Glasgow volumes devote relatively little time to developing the wider political and social implications of their conclusions, these clearly identify television news in producing 'dominance' or 'hegemony', and in this way contribute to the radical challenge to pluralist theories of liberal-democracy. But, as Stuart Hall acknowledges, 'dominance is critical if the propositions of pluralism are to be put into question'.{10} In the light of our analysis of the Glasgow studies it seems unlikely that the assault on pluralism can draw much sustenance from that quarter.

Indeed, it is hard not to feel in the light of this experience that, far from being the liberating factor in media studies that Hall proclaims it to be, dominance – or rather the quest to verify it empirically – has had a stultifying effect on British media studies, not least in the tendency to selective use of evidence and reductionist argument which it all too readily engenders. It is really not the case that media research has to choose between 'hard-nosed empirical positivism' and a new 'critical' paradigm heavily laced with dominance theory. Television is more productively considered not as essentially one-dimensional but as conveying a range of contradictory contentions and explanations – the site of ideological conflict, rather than simply fostering 'a climate of conformity' (Bad News 15, citing Ralph Miliband). Such a view is consistent with pluralism – without, of course, 'proving' it, and without excluding radical critical perspectives either. A case in point is Douglas Kellner's discussion of American network television, which argues that, 'caught between conservative and progressive segments of American society, Network's programmes are full of contradictions and tensions'. Television, he suggests, is:

> 'caught in the contradictions of American capitalism and reproduces these in its programming. There is no one monolithic ideological strategy discernible today, and television reflects and reinforces this ideological confusion.'{11}

Herbert Gans recognises that if the news contains ideology,

> 'That ideology, however, is an aggregate of only partially thought out values which is neither entirely consistent nor well integrated; and since it changes somewhat over time, it is also flexible on some issues...'{12}

And Alvin Gouldner also argues against

> 'any simple-minded stereotype of media simply as an agency reproducing the existing system of domination...[They are] a complex system of property interests, technologies, professionalising skills, strivings for domination and for autonomy, all swarming with the most profound inner contradictions.'{13}

One need not endorse any of these varying assessments to recognise that, perhaps because they are written from a situation (in North America) in which there is a stronger tradition of conservative critiques of the media than in Britain, they show a greater sensitivity to the diversity of television and analytical approaches to television, and a sharper awareness of the inadequacy of reductionist theories:

> 'Those theories focusing solely on television's hegemonic-legitimating images and homogenising social effects are one-sided and limited, as are those theories primarily seeing 'subversive' effects. Both sorts of theories fail to see the contradictions within television messages and its contradictory social effects; both exaggerate the power of television and assume a passive spectator and manipulation theory. A critical theory of television must attend to contradictory images, messages, and social effects, while also rejecting monolithic theories of advanced capitalism.'{14}

Kellner's sensitivity to the complexities of the situation is surely the beginning of wisdom.

The prime lesson of the Glasgow studies for media research is as simple as it is fundamental: that there can be no substitute for the traditional disciplines and routines of scholarship. Although the Group's design can be faulted technically their approach was basically sound. The blend of qualitative and quantitative techniques, and of verbal and visual analysis, and the readiness to link the study of output with field investigation of the behaviour of the main actors had the makings of a valuable contribution to understanding television behaviour. The failure lay in execution. There is no more room for slovenly scholarship here than anywhere else. If media studies are thought to have anything to say to a wider public, the need for stringent standards is all the greater. Television is constantly threatened with becoming a partisan punchbag, as 'more and more groups with a stake in public affairs claim not to recognise themselves' in the way they are portrayed in the media.{15} Complaints about 'bias' are of course by no means confined to the two sides of industry; they come from every political party, from the young, the old, women, blacks, homosexuals, pro-abortionists, upholders of Christian morality, football fans – to mention just a few. A programme item, a sentence, even a single word can trigger a chorus of complaint, sometimes justified, sometimes in calculated attempts to bully newsmen, and sometimes with little rationality or sense of proportion.{16} It is not the researcher's brief to spring to the broadcasters' defence , or claim godlike impartiality in arbitrating between the contending themes. But regardless of personal sympathies, researchers have some responsibility to encourage reasoned and systematic analysis, blowing away the chaff of complaints to reveal whatever substance may remain.

One thing that is clearly necessary is to re-assert the value in the investigation of bias of terms like 'fairness' and 'impartiality', which are in danger of being swept away by attitudes like the Bad News dismissal of 'neutrality' in the opening chapter, or in the argument reportedly advanced by a commissioning editor for Channel 4 during an Edinburgh TV Festival debate on coverage of the 1984 coal strike:

> 'We cannot work with a model which sees two sides, and between and above them a group of media professionals seeking to report in a balanced an unbiased way. There is no middle ground. Every report, every picture, every word put out necessarily favours one side or the

other.'{17}

Of course a concept like 'impartiality' is problematical, and in the fallible nature of human endeavour it will never be entirely realised in practice. Yet, despite the very real difficulties, the fact that it is prescribed for broadcast news by a mixture of statute and convention means that it cannot reasonably be dismissed from the discussion. And if it were to be dismissed, what is to replace it? Like the insistence on 'unvarying frames', the assertion that every word and image is biased ultimately stultifies reasoned discussion. Television's handling of the coal strike was inevitably controversial, and quite properly it has been subjected to intensive scrutiny. But unless the ensuing analyses are in some way related to notions of fairness or balance, it is difficult to see how a common discourse is possible, or how any assessment of how adequately the broadcasters discharged their commitment to impartiality can be arrived at.

If the Glasgow studies have made nothing else clear, it is the need for media researchers to put their questions with maximum clarity, to define their yardsticks as clearly, and to conduct their measurements with the greatest possible precision. This may be by no means easy in an area as controversial as industrial relations, where even the basic terms of the argument may not always be agreed, and the most important questions may well be those where measurement is the most difficult. If accepted 'objective' yardsticks exist, so much the better. If they do not, this is no necessary bar to scholarly investigation, providing the nature and limitations of the exercise are recognised — including the possible validity of alternative questions, techniques and insights. It was one of the potential strengths of the Glasgow studies that they were prepared to compare news output with yardsticks of 'reality'. Setting aside the deficiencies in execution, the problem was that too much weight was put on a few sets of measures like the comparison with strike statistics, and findings which could at best point to further questions were instead turned into condemnations.{18}

The problem is not a simple one of whether or not the news is 'biased'. If all departures from a strict cross-section of 'reality' are biases of sorts, then news — which by its very essence is a partial presentation of 'reality' — is inherently biased in a myriad ways. But what is the nature and origin of these biases? With 'bias', as with 'impartiality', we must always begin by enquiring 'bias in relation to what?', and looking for a number of dimensions along which the ensuing enquiry can be pursued.{19} The heart of the issue is whether the investigation reveals consistent patterns that are prejudicial to particular individuals, ideas or interests in ways which infringe the broadcasters' commitment to impartiality — or whether there are conflicting strands which amount to no consistent or continuing pattern. After that we still may need to enquire whether bias was avoidable, or for that matter whether it was defensible. With issues as sensitive as industrial relations it is inevitable that researchers will bring their personal insights, intuitions, even prejudices, to the discussion. But the fact that enquiry will not be value-free does not excuse us from the effort to consider how the output might appear to someone of a different persuasion, and how best those contrasting ways of structuring the material might be investigated and assessed. In short, media research calls not simply for the traditional disciplines we summarise as 'scholarship', but for sensitivity, imagination, a sense of proportion, a healthy awareness of the fragility of some of the techniques and the uncertain character of the communication process — and a more than healthy dose of humility.

1   N. Abercrombie, S. Hill and B.S. Turner, The Dominant Ideology Thesis, George Allen & Unwin, 1980, 130.
2   Ibid. 130.
3   Ibid. 140.
4   For further discussion of usage see C.T.B. Smith et al, 'Strikes in Britain: A Research Study of Stoppages in the United Kingdom', Department of Employment Manpower Paper No. 15, HMSO, 1978, 13.
5   Michael Meacher MP, letter, The Guardian, 2 September 1982.
6   The style of demonstration has not a little in common with much of the argument about the relationship between television and violence, another notorious minefield of premature conclusions.
7   See R. Mendel and C. Graham, 'Weather Forecasts on BBC Television', BBC Broadcasting Research Findings, 8, 1981/2, 75-81. And in the same issue, A. Rawcliffe-King and N. Dyer, 'The Knowledge Gap Reconsidered: Learning from 'Ireland: A Television History by Robert Kee', 55-67. Also Opinion Research Centre report 'News and Current Affairs', ORC 1047, 1971. And D. McQuail, 'The Influence and Effects of Mass Media', in J. Curran et al, Mass Communication and Society, Arnold, 1977, 70-94.
8   D. McQuail, op.cit. 87.

9   On the basis of a survey of labour correspondents taken in 1968, Jeremy Tunstall classifies them as a group as 'strongly Labour', and comments that they 'have similar politics to their mainly trade union news sources' (Journalists at Work, Constable, 1971, 124). Writing in 1985, John Torode, a former chairman of the labour and industrial correspondents' group, says that 'It is hard to identify a single Conservative supporter holding a senior labour reporter's job ('Don't Blame the Organ Grinder – Try the Monkey', The Guardian, 11 June 1985). Paul Johnson, in an article severely critical of industrial reporting, complains that
       'the industrial correspondents are heavily dependent on one source of information – the official union machines – and are correspondingly docile and afraid to bite the hand that feeds them copy...[While] purely City affairs are usually well chewed over, industry itself tends to fall into a journalistic black hole except when there are strikes, when the so-called industrial correspondents take over and often report them from a union viewpoint.'
     P. Johnson, 'Fleet Street's Black Hole', The Spectator, 11 May 1985. Although all three assessments refer primarily to Fleet Street, Tunstall's sample included broadcasting journalists, and it is probable that both Torode and Johnson also had broadcasting in mind.
10   S. Hall, 'The Rediscovery of 'Ideology': Return of the Repressed in Media Studies', in M. Gurevitch et al, Culture, Society and the Media, Methuen, 1982, 84.
11   D. Kellner, 'Network Television and American Society', Theory and Society, 10, 1981, 43 and 51. Kellner emphasises that he is not using 'contradictions' in the marxian sense of irreducible oppositions which cannot be resolved without the structural transformation of society.
12   H.J. Gans, Deciding What's News, Constable, 1980, 68.
13   A.W. Gouldner, The Dialectic of Ideology and Technology, Seabury Press, 1976, 160.
14   D. Kellner, op. cit. 51.
15   J.G. Blumler, 'Journalism Research for Democracy: Launching a Tradition?', paper for World Association for Public Opinion Research Conference, 1982, 1.
16   For example, during the 1984-85 coal strike a zealous social scientist countered the finding that the news gave more time to pro-strike miners than to the Coal Board with the suggestion that, 'The greater time given to NUM representatives may simply confirm the definition of the issue [as] 'the miners' strike' rather than 'the coal dispute' or some other variant' (J. Clarke, letter, The Guardian, 17 September 1984). Maybe – but such reasoning puts the broadcasters squarely in a no-win position.
17   A. Fountain, quoted in D. Jones et al, Media Hits the Pits: The Media and the Coal Dispute, Campaign for Press and Broadcasting Freedom, 1985, 20. An eight-week sample of coverage had shown pro-strike miners and their families receiving 89 minutes, anti-strike miners and their families 12.5 minutes, and NCB spokesmen 36.5 minutes. See A. Hetherington, 'Is TV News Impartial?', The Listener, 17 January 1985.
       The Campaign for Press and Broadcasting Freedom includes among its aims, 'To challenge the myths of 'impartiality' and 'balance' in broadcasting, and 'objectivity' in newspapers by campaigning for the genuine presentation of the diversity and plurality of society' (Jones et al, Ibid. 44). The Campaign also wants a reconstituted Press Council to 'promote basic standards of fairness', and considers the right of reply 'fundamental to redressing the imbalance in press bias'. Difficult to

define and frequently derided though they may be, terms like 'fairness' and 'balance' really do seem indispensible to the debate.

18   The 1984-85 coal strike provided further illustrations of the tendency to reach over-hasty conclusions of 'bias'. When miners supporting the strike received more coverage in the early stages than the Coal Board and anti-strike miners there were complaints that the broadcasters were favouring the NUM. But this could not be counted as 'bias' without ascertaining a lot more about the character of the resulting coverage. Although there were some complaints that Arthur Scargill was not interviewed firmly enough, other accounts maintained that he was more often treated as an adversary than Ian MacGregor. But here again, findings called for further investigation rather than immediate conclusions. Among other considerations, one would have to consider whether those two very contrasting individuals, with their different attitudes to the media, could reasonably have been interviewed in identical terms.

There were also complaints that the cameras more frequently operated from behind police lines than from amongst the pickets. But again further questions would have to be asked before concluding that there was culpable bias.

19   On the nature of 'bias' and the investigation of bias see C.R. Hofstetter Bias in the News, Ohio State U.P., 1976, and C.R. Hofstetter and T.F. Buss, 'Bias in Television News Coverage of Political Events: A Methodological Analysis of Broadcasting', Journal of Broadcasting, 22(4), 1978, 517-530.

CONCLUSION

9

The need for scholarly standards is by no means the only conclusion to be drawn from this sad affair. It offers further cause for reflection to academics, broadcasters and all who have based intellectual or political castles on the sand of the Glasgow study. That includes some students of the media. The initial reception of the two major volumes was generally to the credit of the profession. Critics who were disposed to welcome their findings nevertheless identified the weaknesses, drawing attention to several of the points developed in the course of the preceding chapters.[1] Many of the defects of the Bad News series have been recognised in the appropriate academic circles for years, to the point where the present study might even be seen as embellishing at length what 'the trade' has long known. Yet even a decade after the event, 'the trade' still also contains irreducible defenders of the Glasgow theses, their attitude reminiscent of Thurber's lady: 'Mere proof will not convince me.' And there are still media studies courses which leave student unaware that Bad News is anything less than definitive, while introductory texts and specialised monographs in media studies continue to incorporate central elements of the Glasgow case quite uncritically.[2] As earlier remarks have suggested, nowhere is the need for rethinking greater than among those 'critical theorists' who so gratefully grasped Bad News as empirical support for their analysis of the media's role in society. In the words of Hall, hailing the 'profound theoretical revolution' his new model had already accomplished, 'Extensive empirical work is required to demonstrate the adequacy of its explanatory terms, and to refine, elaborate and develop its infant insights.'[3] Quite so.

Others who might usefully think again include those who have produced schemes for media reform predicated to some degree on the Glasgow critique. The Group's own attitude to reform is by no means clear. The two major volumes contain no obvious prescriptions for change, but Really Bad News, written by four members of the Group, includes a list of 'minimum demands' relating broadly to redefinition of the aims of broadcasting, matters of control, access and recruitment (159). There and elsewhere a variety of schemes are canvassed, ranging from proposals to introduce a right of reply or a Freedom of Information Act to demands for 'democratisation' of management, recruitment or access. Setting aside the merits or otherwise of these proposals, it is by no means clear they would in fact resolve the particular problems Bad News identifies, either because they seem of marginal relevance (a Freedom of Information Act), or because they might create as many difficulties as they resolve (notably schemes for 'democratising' television). If, in essence, the social role of the media is to 'reflect and reinforce the power structure of the society in which they operate', to legitimate the consensus and the status quo, we need both a better picture of how the prescriptions relate to the disease, complete with a consideration of the side effects, together with clearer indications of how so radical a transformation of a key sustaining element in 'the power structure' is to be achieved.

These issues are most immediately important to the unions. There has long been a tendency within trade unionism, which has drawn sustenance from the Glasgow volumes, to see the media as implacably hostile. As the press officer of the National Union of Mineworkers put it:

> '[Those] who own, control and manage the means of mass communication were, and remain, monolithically marshalled in total opposition to our fight to protect and strengthen Britain's nationalised coal industry, the jobs within it and the communities that depend on it.
>
> The industrial correspondents, along with broadcasting technicians, are basically our enemies' front-line troops...[We] discovered a long time ago that no amount of 'access' for industrial correspondents from trade union officials stands a chance against similar briefings between respective employers.'{4}

The Glasgow studies use nothing like that language, but where they have kinship with it is in the general argument of the chapter on 'Trade Unions and the Media', that even those unions that made an effort to strengthen their public relations reaped little, if any, benefit in terms of more favourable coverage. In their different styles they convey a common pessimism which has important implications for the scale of union communication activity, and the degree to which it looks inward to the membership, or attempts to reach a wider public.

Sadly, it seems inevitable that this study's criticism of the Glasgow analysis will be seen as an act of hostility to the unions, illogical and inaccurate though such a conclusion would be. On the contrary, it is the pessimists who do the unions a disservice, with their disposition to treat 'the meejer' as a uniformly hostile bloc, and their implication there is little point in making the effort to put their case across. Some sections of Fleet Street are, of course, only too happy to present the unions in a bad light, although McQuail's careful analysis suggests that even there the picture is less black and white than is often alleged. But it really does the unions no service to encourage the belief that The Sun and the Nine O'Clock News are really sisters under the skin, or that they might just as well not make the effort to improve their under-funded, low-status public relations departments. The unions operate in a climate where, whatever the value of cultivating members' loyalties through improved internal communications, they neglect the attempt to speak to the public and their own members through the general media at their peril.{4} It is no kindness to the unions to encourage them in the belief that when they are unpopular the fault lies more in their stars than in themselves.

Another area where the Glasgow volumes have had a lasting influence is on relations between researchers and broadcasters. Journalists have an almost unlimited capacity for positively savage mutual criticism, but they are by no means immune from a corporatist closing of the ranks against criticism from outside the 'trade'. An initial reaction to the challenge of radical media sociology, was to 'put up the shutters' and then 'retreat into the bunker', as a senior television journalist put it. Even the far more measured critiques of scholars like Schlesinger and Tracey — whose work, ironically, was contemptuously brushed aside by the Glasgow Group — were invoked as reasons for refusing cooperation to would-be researchers.{5} Media studies were seen as, in the main, politically partisan and unscholarly. As the chairman of the Media Studies Association sadly acknowledged:

> 'It is now axiomatic among many media professionals that communications courses and research mean an attack on what they

daily do.'{6}

At no time would such an impression have been well-founded. There is no reason to believe that most teaching of media studies was anything but professional. But there is a grain of truth in it, and relations were scarcely helped by incidents such as the proposal at a highly respected English provincial university to run a series of public lectures under the title 'Lies, Damn Lies and the Media'.{7}

While such episodes are best seen as isolated pinpricks, it was not entirely surprising that there was an equal and opposite reaction from the broadcasters, with the director-general of the BBC reportedly being moved to suggest that the Corporation might 'examine the aims and politics of sociology' (More Bad News 418). Few broadcasters were aware of the cool professional reception the Glasgow volumes received, or realised that they were no more typical of media studies than 'Red Robbo' of Longbridge was of trade unionism, and that for every Bad News there were several examples of properly scholarly work, reflecting a healthy range of methodological approaches. Just occasionally one suspected that the deficiencies of the Glasgow study served as an convenient excuse for avoiding more scholarly based critical analyses. Be that as it may, and it is no more than anecdotal suspicion, the outcome was a legacy of hostility that television studies has still not entirely escaped.

The Glasgow Group professed surprise and sadness at the reaction to their work, quoting Paul Lazarsfeld's comment that:

'If there is any one institutional disease to which the media of mass communications seem particularly subject, it is a nervous reaction to criticism. As a student of mass media I have been continually struck and occasionally puzzled by this reaction, for it is the media themselves which so vigorously defend principles guaranteeing the right to criticise.'{8}

While over-reaction by a few broadcasters did them no credit, the Glasgow comment also shows a lack of understanding. The broadcasters' reaction mingled anger, alarm and incomprehension. Anger because it was widely suspected that underneath the academic trappings there lay a more overtly political enterprise. Whatever the truth of this might be, the suspicions were scarcely allayed by a later claim by members of the Group that their work 'provided the necessary weaponry for the cultural struggle over broadcasting' (Trade Unions and the Media 134). Alarm because under the apparently powerful and confident exterior of the broadcasting institutions one rapidly reaches insecurity and vulnerability, especially when their future is under scrutiny, as it was during the Annan enquiry and has been in a variety of ways over the ensuing years. And incomprehension because the broadcasters were in many ways at a loss to know how to respond to a critique which effectively swept away the customary terms of the debate about balance and fairness, dismissing them as unattainable and ideologically undesirable. In their place was a claim to have revealed the hidden essence of the agenda the news was unwittingly constructing, through a decoding process of which the Glasgow Group appeared to be both the inventors and privileged guardians.{9}

Nevertheless, the director-general of the BBC was surely mistaken in arguing that 'there would be no sense' in attacking Bad News in detail.{10} Either the Glasgow Group had a case or it had not. If it had, then a positive response was clearly called for; if it had not, then detailed rebuttal was preferable to the generalised dismissals and abuse with which some senior broadcasters greeted Bad News. If they thought the attack could be disposed of so summarily they were mistaken. As it was, writing in 1982 Anthony Smith could still comment:

'One problem with the current stage in the evolution of journalism research in Britain is that the profession and institutions have so far sniped without responding to what has been said...'{11}

Not that such a circumstantial response would necessarily have resolved the matter. After Peter Sissons and Paul McKee of ITN produced a detailed response to a critique of ITN coverage of the 1980 Labour Conference by three members of the Group, the original criticisms were reproduced virtually unmodified in Really Bad News the following year.{12} And members of the Group continued to maintain that broadcasters had traduced them without refuting their evidence.{13} (A sad sidelight on the debate about bias' is that Sissons' and McKee's offer to provide free transcripts of the material attracted only five takers.)

Despite the difficulties of dialogue, the Sissons and McKee reaction was the wiser one. For with their own needs for access, disclosure and openness the news organisations have a special responsibility for (and interest in) going the extra mile in tolerating criticism and accepting that the hand that feeds may well be soundly bitten. As Sir Michael Swann commented while chairman of the BBC:

'And such is life; it is the failures and the gaps that are held against us, while the successes are taken for granted. But media men, of all people, can't complain about that. It is they, after all, who decree that 1,000 upright men leading good and constructive lives are not news, while one ne'er-do-well fills the columns of the press for days on end.'{14}

It is remarkable, even shameful, that there is still no comprehensive publicly available permanent record of television news and news scripts in Britain, despite the valiant efforts of the British Film Institute, and latterly the support of independent television. It is easier to conduct research on the Jerusalem Post, nineteenth century issues of The Darlington & Stockton Times or the most abstruse doctoral dissertation than to study the past output of the principal news medium of our day. In recent years it has become easier and cheaper to record material for research purposes, and attitudes towards copyright, if not yet the law itself, have fortunately become more relaxed. But there is still a long way to go. Even after the Annan Committee had added its voice to those calling for a comprehensive national television archive the view persisted that it could not properly be supported from the licence fee. Yet one of the basic principles of British broadcasting is accountability. Although there are many dimensions to accountability, time is of absolutely central importance. There are many questions which either may only become apparent over time, or can only be answered with reference to output over some substantial period. Throughout its existence the BBC has shown a keen awareness of its responsibility to history in the preservation of paper records. The result has been a magnificent quarry for a whole range of works on the history of broadcasting which take a much-valued place in fleshing out accountability. It seems unthinkable that there should be less concern for the preservation and availability of its creative output. If the costs and possible inconveniences of the proposals spring to mind, a more supportive approach might also produce benefits. There could be no greater incentive to scholarship than the knowledge that access to the original material was readily available. One reason Bad News held the field so long, to the broadcasters' chagrin, is that it was so difficult for others to retrace the Glasgow

Group's footsteps.

But despite Sissons' and McKee's experience the broadcasters should also contribute more effectively to the debate, making what contribution they can to raising its level. Latterly there have been signs of greater readiness to join issue with the critics.{15} This is welcome, not simply for all the best liberal reasons about the role of debate in a free society, but because the issues are important and the stakes are high.

This study has had the limited aim of assessing the Bad News critique rather than of promoting some alternative analysis of industrial reporting. Accordingly these concluding reflections have no pretention to be anything other than impressionistic and suggestive. As a matter of personal judgment rather than 'science', ITN coverage seemed in general to be competent, fair and more diverse in its 'frames of explanation' than could ever be guessed from the Bad News account. As we have seen, it was by no means without blemish; mistakes were made, opportunities missed. Explanation and context were at times overlooked and at times insufficient. There were items to which the unions could legitimately take exception − though by no means every failing told against them. On occasion ITN omitted material which may have been favourable to them, but potentially prejudicial material was at times passed over or received littler emphasis, while at other times facts or views favourable to management were not reported. Often there was really no means of saying that errors or omissions told against one side rather than the other.

Some weaknesses were directly attributable to the haste with which the news is produced. But many of the problems that have been identified in industrial reporting seem to relate more to notions of what is 'news' in our society than to how they were reported once they had been recognised as such. It is a commonplace that news is more readily concerned with negative than positive occurrences, with events more than non-events, processes or situations. It is difficult, for instance, to see how any conventional interpretation of 'news' could have led to the managerial deficiencies of British Leyland Motor Corporation or of the company's problems of underinvestment being reported as frequently as the tuners' strike. But such routines of news behaviour do not work against the unions alone. If management failings received relatively little attention during the survey period, so did overmanning, demarcation problems and the deficiencies of union organisation. Nor were the unions invariably shown in a negative context. There was coverage of their participation in the National Economic Development Council, their role in the social contract and in routine wage bargaining. There were even occasional 'good news' stories like the London dockers' agreement to let an Antarctic supply ship sail and the Solsgirth miners' production record. Nevertheless, 'trouble at t' mill' was unquestionably more frequently found newsworthy than harmony. And it must be admitted that in a sense the very nature of trade unionism makes it more vulnerable than management. By and large the unions have an honourable tradition of debate, of conducting many of their arguments in public, of being readily accessible to news personnel.{16} For both better and worse much of what they do is more open to scrutiny than the workings of management, whose arguments can usually be conducted more discreetly.

The reality of industrial life is that on any given day the vast majority of workplaces are operating normally, most workers rarely or never strike, and shop stewards' energies are directed far more towards avoiding industrial action than to precipitating it.{17} Yet strikes and the hotheads or mischief-makers that conflict tends to attract are also realities; the media did not invent Jamie Morris, the Shrewsbury pickets or that ambulance drivers' spokesman who was prepared to let patients die if need be during the 1978-79 'winter of discontent'. Neither did they invent George Ward of Grunwick, Eddie Shah of the Messenger group or the feudal owner of the Globtik Venus – though the more neanderthal *patrons de choc* seem more skilful at avoiding the cameras than their union counterparts. Industrial action is emphatically not the norm; nor is demagogy or intimidation when it does occur. While it is not suggested that television news asserts anything different, the recurring focus on the atypical which is at the heart of 'news', may well lead some people to assume strikes and abuses of union power to be more frequent than they actually are – especially if they possess little independent information about industrial relations. Paul Hartmann's findings along these lines provide grounds for serious reflection.{18}

The potentially damaging consequences of any confusion between the exceptional and the commonplace are obvious. This is a major element in the unhappiness about the media's handling of their affairs that is apparent among even 'moderate' trade union leaders. It is by no means clear that management escaped unscathed either from the news' predilection for negative situations. It is even less clear that the outcome of ITN's output during the survey period was in any sense to legitimise management, industry or capitalism. It is not easy to imagine the mythical habitual viewer emerging thinking any better of any of them. At a guess, and it can be no more than a guess, one would have been tempted to emerge feeling less well about almost everyone involved.{19} The broadcasters can quite easily reply that this was, after all, a period during which British manufacturing industry was in decline, that in many respects reality itself was grim. Not a few of the 'sunrise' projects the media have singled out for upbeat reporting over the years proved to offer false dawns; there have been failures of uncritical reporting too. And the broadcasters would also point to programmes like 'Union World' or 'The Money Programme', which often adopt a more 'positive' approach, and to the frequent appearances of spokesmen from both sides of industry in current affairs sequences such as 'Today' and 'The World at One'.{20} But if critics are too prone to overlook this wider, more constructive context, the fact that the news has so much greater a reach than current affairs and feature programmes means that the problem still remains. But to the extent that it is a problem, it is one of how television reports industry as a whole, rather than one of simple bias against the unions.

The preoccupation of the news with negative situations is of course not confined to industry. During the 1970s there appear to have been widespread popular misapprehensions about the extent of student unrest or denials of freedom of speech in British universities — some of it among trade unionists.{21} Who can gauge what the implications of these misconceptions may have been for public policy? In recent years an exaggerated impression of the risks of burglary or assault seems to have led to many elderly people living more restricted (if safer) lives. The introduction of sound broadcasting of Parliament affected many people's perceptions of the incidence or rows and boorish behaviour at Westminster.{22} Further research in hand by the present writer suggests that at certain periods the reporting of British local government and the European Community concentrated heavily on situations which are unlikely to raise them in public esteem. Even the broadcasters are not immune: a rash of really quite trivial stories about star salaries, foreign junkets and waste in early 1985 encouraged an embarrassing image of a financially profligate BBC just when it was submitting an unpopular application for a higher licence fee.

Obviously all these examples call for further evidence and argument. But they suggest that if there is a problem it is by no means confined to industrial relations, with the concomitant conclusion that the trade unions were singled out for odium in some unique way. The tendency for negative coverage to be preponderant either in straight terms of time or in vividness apparently affects a much wider range of groups and institutions, by no means all of which could be considered potentially threatening to social order, some of them actually being part of the 'power structure'. (It could, incidentally, be argued from both a right- and left-wing standpoint that at the time of the Glasgow survey, when 'tripartism', 'neo-corporatism' and 'incorporationism' were at their height, that the unions were very much part of the 'dominant social order'.) It may be that prevailing conceptions of 'news' mean that since few individuals or institutions are capable of making 'positive' news with any frequency, even the fairest and most balanced coverage can be damaging. Michael Robinson has in fact argued — albeit controversially and in an American context — that routine network news has been a 'delegitimising agency' for a number of public institutions.{23} As we argued in the last chapter, there can be no question of substituting one simplistic view of the implications of media behaviour for another; it is entirely within the bounds of possibility that television tends at one moment to legitimate and at another to destabilise. At present we really do not know, but any further research that does not leave room for both possibilities would at the very least be assuming what has yet to be established.

The other problematic area is the highly compressed nature of television reporting at the time. The average duration of dispute items during the survey period was a mere 70 seconds — roughly 210 words of text at conventional newsreading speeds. As table 9 shows, there was considerable variation around the mean. Coverage of most major disputes included some brief updating items which made no pretence to do more than mark the most recent development, and a number of longer reports allowing more space for explanation and interviews with participants. Several of these stories included items which were quite lengthy in terms of the prevailing conventions of television news — though many went out at lunchtime when audiences were relatively small. The most serious questions arise over stories which were minimally reported — the industrial civil servants, the Liverpool dustcart drivers and the British Rail workshop supervisors. Coverage was never more than bald and basic, with no direct input from participants and only the most summary of explanations.

Such coverage was uninteresting and uninformative rather than anti-union — the kind of reporting John Birt and Peter Jay had in mind in

Table 9: Duration of News Items

Dispute	Total coverage	Shortest item	Longest item	Average duration
		seconds		
Car industry	2,265	10	240	57
NHS consultants	2,360	18	412	103
Fleet Street/NGA	1,553	19	276	78
Glasgow dustcart drivers	3,276	11	216	74
Scots ambulance controllers	742	16	178	82
Daily Mirror/NATSOPA	397	13	139	44
Railway signalmen	1,749	8	357	73
Morriston Hospital	264	20	97	33
British Airways	897	23	350	69
London docks	3,587	15	240	85
Industrial civil servants	229	16	67	46
Westminister Hospital	903	18	207	82
Liverpool dustcart drivers	177	12	44	22
Daily Mirror/SOGAT	763	14	273	85
BR Workshop supervisors	470	14	65	29
Imperial Typewriters	430	22	215	86

their celebrated criticism of television news' 'bias against understanding.'{24} The danger was less of a 'dominant frame' than of an absence of frame. It is commonplace to argue that television provides a headline news service, and that those wishing to know more can turn to a current affairs programme or their morning paper. But many strikes are not picked up by 'Newsnight' or 'TV Eye', while readers of the tabloid press will often find it adds little to their knowledge. Television has yet to think through satisfactorily how best it can discharge its responsibility to them.

It has often been said that the coal strike of 1984-85 provided television with the greatest reporting challenge it has had to face. In one sense that is obviously the case: this was the biggest single story the news has ever covered, and one of the most controversial. Television inescapably became an actor as well as an observer. But whatever the ultimate verdicts on the way it responded to the challenge, the event was so far 'off-scale' that there may be only limited lessons for the handling of more routine events. With good fortune, the news will never again be called on to cover such an industrial Passchendaele. But the task of handling the day-to-day stoppages is never-ending. In that sense the routine is the greater challenge than the great occasion.

We began with Arthur Scargill's complaint that 'The Nine o'Clock News' and 'News at Ten' amounted to 'pure bias' in covering the coal strike. But he went on to acknowledge fairer coverage by 'Panorama', 'TV Eye' and 'Channel Four News'. The reference to Channel Four News is interesting. For it is produced by ITN, using many of the same journalists following essentially the same professional routines as the apparently irredeemable 'News at Ten'. Whether bias is said to derive from institutional or management factors, or from the system of recruiting and socialising journalists, it seems hard to explain how there could be significant qualitative differences between Channel Four and 'News at Ten'. Indeed, there seems no way of reconciling judgments like Scargill's, which are heard from both sides of industry, with the kind of view that treats television as an essentially undifferentiated vehicle for instilling the dominant ideology.

It is doubtful whether Channel Four News displays any significant ideological differences from other news programmes. Where it does differ is in giving rather greater attention to industry and commerce, possibly in carrying more 'positive' industrial news, and in a readiness to run a number of stories at greater length than is customary elsewhere. It is no more dedicated to fairness, balance and impartiality than its competitors, but its longer items not only allow a rather wider range of views to be expressed but tend to leave participants and their supporters feeling they have had a reasonable hearing. Most people do not expect television to swallow their case whole; they do look for it to be stated comprehensibly, even if briefly. Much of the dissatisfaction with industrial coverage, though the problem is by no means confined to industry, springs from frustrations at the tendency of television first to concentrate on atypically negative situations (and for the average worker a strike is a rare and painful experience), and then report these in such brief compass that those involved feel, however balanced the report, that they have in some way been diminished. Or, as Blumler has put it, they 'claim not to recognise themselves in stereotypical and constricted portrayals of their activities in the news media'.{25} Broadcasters are not always as sensitive to these frustrations as they might be. To them, thirty seconds may seem a substantial slice of airtime; to participants, the resulting tightly-edited clip, however fairly balanced, may well appear a travesty of a complex situation.

The way through this minefield is far from easy. But first, let it be noted that if Channel Four News is seen as a welcome innovation, the possibilities of progress 'within the system' are being recognised in a way for which the more pessimistic theories of media in society leave little scope. The implication of the advent of Channel Four is not that it should be replicated elsewhere, but that the increase in channels has made possible both a greater diversity of news styles and a wider representation of views than a decade ago. It is not so long since some senior television newsmen gave a patronising reception to lay suggestions that a 50-minute television news was feasible; it now has a permanent niche. In their differing ways, 'News at One' and 'News at Ten' on ITV and the lunchtime and 'Six O'Clock News' on BBC1 have all responded to the need for more background, explanation, and better pacing of items. Indeed, television news has changed perceptibly in the decade since the Glasgow survey, whether in the greater variety of programme formats (mingling 'news' and 'current affairs' in ways which had previously been thought heretical), or in the development of new presentational techniques, especially with the advent of computer graphics displays.

Yet some of the old problems remain, whether the continuing overcompressed verbal shorthand in some bulletins, the use of over-emphatic or unclear language in others, or the enduring tendency to clutter the screen with distracting visuals. The failing of the initial coverage of the Glasgow dustcart drivers' strike, which we discussed in an earlier chapter, was not the imposition of a 'health hazard' dominant frame, but the intrusive use of library film which drew attention away from a verbal report which, within its very limited confines, was a model of succinct clarity. And one still does not have to watch the news for very long to find instances where it cuts away to film that adds little to the words and may even cut across them. The intention to improve communication is evident in a wide variety of caption cards and graphic displays, yet it seems that the thought and ingenuity going into them is still not matched in terms of investigation of their efficacy in conveying information to the audience. Far too much of the debate about television has turned on issues of bias; important though these are they are surely secondary to issues of how successfully television communicates what, and to whom. One cannot watch television news for long without recognising both its immense professionalism and the capacity for improvement. And there are many within broadcasting who are even more aware of the challenge to do better.{26} Therein lies the hope of dialogue, and the need for dialogue.

For too long the Bad News episode has soured the dialogue between broadcasters and academic researchers. It is time that it was put behind us. Broadcasters have to come to terms with the fact that media studies are here to stay, and that most of its practitioners are thoroughly scholarly and professional, although what they say may at times be remote from the realities of the news room or over-fond of jargon. A handful of academics still need to realise that media studies is not a continuation of revolution by other means, and that what counts is their scholarship rather than their ideological stance. The necessary dialogue between broadcasters and students of media will never be easy — any more than the relationship between broadcasters and government can be, and for some of the same reasons. The best to be hoped for, in the well-worn phrase, is a state of creative tension. But since the tension has been more evident than the creativity for much of the past decade, that at least would be progress.

1 See notably, D.C. Anderson and W.W. Sharrock, 'Biasing the News: Technical Issues in 'Media Studies'', Sociology, 1979, 367-385; S. Cohen, review of Bad News, New Society, 9 September 1976; I. Connell, review of More Bad News, Marxism Today, August 1980, 30-31. P. Edwards, review of More Bad News, Industrial Relations Journal, 12(1), January-February 1981, 72-3; P. Elliott, review of More Bad News, Sociological Review, 29(1), 1981, 169-171; D. McQuail, review of Bad News, Sociology, 11(2), 1977, 393-4; P.V. Miller, review of Bad News, American Journal of Sociology, 53(2), 1978, 989-990; G. Skirrow, 'More Bad News – A Review of the Reviews', Screen, 21(2), Summer 1980, 95-99; A. Smith, review of More Bad News, Media, Culture and Society, 4(2), 1982.
2 See notably, D. McQuail, Analysis of Newspaper Content, Cmnd. 6810-4, HMSO, 1977; O. Boyd-Barrett, C. Seymour-Ure and J. Tunstall, Studies on the Press, Royal Commission on the Press Working Paper 3, HMSO, 1977, and J. Tunstall, Journalists at Work, Constable, 1971.
3 S. Hall, 'The Rediscovery of 'Ideology': Return of the Repressed in Media Studies', in M. Gurevitch et al., Culture, Society and the Media, Methuen, 1982, 88.
4 See P. Wintour, 'The Lamp the Miners Failed to Light', The Guardian, 20 May 1985; N. Myers, 'Mines of Misinformation', The Guardian, 3 June 1985; J. Torode, 'Don't Blame the Organ Grinder – Try the Monkey', The Guardian, 11 June 1985.
5 P. Schlesinger, Putting 'Reality' Together, Constable, 1978; M. Tracey, The Production of Political Television, Routledge and Kegan Paul, 1977. For the Glasgow Group's comment on these see More Bad News 479.
6 T. Robinson, Times Higher Education Supplement, 6 November 1981.
7 Private communication inviting the writer to participate, 4 August 1982.
8 Quoted More Bad News 418.
9 Annan noted that the Group's submission was among those raising 'resentment, not to say bewilderment, among the journalists in broadcasting with whom we discussed this outlook' (Report 276). Discussing the Glasgow case on 'The Man Alive Debate', David Holmes of the BBC said, 'Where we're not helped is by your lack of any certainty as to whether you're scientists or polemicists....You put forward 'scientific' findings in a sort of polemical wrapping...which makes it very difficult indeed to accept your book....We look for assistance in all sorts of places, but we don't find them in your book' (BBC2, 28 July 1982).
10 Quoted More Bad News 418 from The Leveller, January 1978.
11 A. Smith, review, Media, Culture and Society, 4(2), 1982.
12 G. Philo, J. Hewitt and P. Beharrell, 'The Bias in the Television Image', New Statesman, 23 January 1981; P. Sissons and P. McKee, 'Legal, Decent and Honest', New Statesman, 20 March 1981.
13 G. Philo, letter, The Guardian, 1 June 1982.
14 BBC Record, January 1974.
15 See, for example, correspondence, The Guardian, 20 August 1982, 13 February 1985, 2 March 1985.

16 Additionally, some styles of traditional trade union discourse, while appropriate for a mass meeting, may come across badly on television.

17 Smith et al quote the Donovan Commission in 1968 to the effect that unofficial strikes 'have such serious economic implications that measures to deal with them are urgently necessary', adding that since then strikes and days lost had increased. 'The judgment must therefore be that the economic implications are no less serious now than they were in 1968.'

However, in an average year 'only 2 per cent of United Kingdom manufacturing plants which employ only 20 per cent of manufacturing workers experience strikes large enough to be recorded by the Department'. Strike activity tended to be concentrated in a few industries and areas. Depending on the method of calculation, Britain ranked sixth or seventh among the 15 countries with which valid comparison was feasible (op.cit. 12).

18 P. Hartmann, 'News and Public Perceptions of Industrial Relations', Media, Culture and Society, (1), 1979, 155-270; D. Morley, 'Industrial Conflict and the Mass Media', Sociological Review, 24(2), 1976, 245-268.

19 Smith et al suggest that foreign correspondents derived from the media the impression that our industry was riddled with strikes, and that this may have affected Britain's standing as a trading nation. However, the judgment is impressionistic and does not specifically discuss television (op. cit. 12 and 85-86).

20 See, for example, 'Business and Industrial Items on 'Today': 1 January – 22nd February 1985', BBC, duplicated, 1985.

21 Cf. 'Seldom a look at what universities are about, but at the slightest hint of a conflict, instant programmes with a rare capacity for getting hold of the least responsible bystanders.' Such was Sir Michael Swann's epitome of vice chancellors' perceptions of television coverage (BBC Record, January 1974). He added, 'I have also heard the same word from industrialists, from councillors, planners, all sorts of people, including of course MPs.'

22 For a contrary assessment see J.M. Cross, 'The Sound Broadcasting of Parliament', Independent Broadcasting, June 1982.

23 M.J. Robinson, 'Public Affairs Television and the Growth of Political Malaise: The Case of 'The Selling of the Pentagon'', American Political Science Review, 70(2), 1976, 409-432; M.J. Robinson, 'Television and American Politics: 1956-1976', The Public Interest, (48), Summer 1977, 3-39; also D. Cater and R. Adler, Television as a Social Force: New Approaches to TV Criticism, Praeger, 1975. For further discussion of the 'dysfunctional' view of television's role see D. Kellner, 'Network Television and American Society', Theory and Society, 10, 1981, 31-62.

24 P. Jay and J. Birt, The Times, 28 September, 30 September, 1 October 1975; 2 and 3 September 1976.

25 J. Blumler, 'Journalism Research for Democracy: Launching a Tradition?', 1982, 1.

26 A. Protheroe, 'The BBC's Journalism and the 1984-85 Miners' Strike', BBC, May 1985.

PART 2: NEWS SCRIPTS

This study has had two main aims. The first has been to examine the validity of key elements in the Glasgow critique of television's handling of industrial disputes, to the extent that they refer to coverage by Independent Television News and can be analysed through the verbal component of the output. One of the recurrent grounds of criticism of the Bad News volumes has been the extent to which the authors either proceed by pure assertion or deploy a limited and untypical range of quotation. Consequently, wherever this has been appropriate this study has made frequent and extensive use of the ITN scripts. But however much the citations are multiplied, sceptics may quite understandably wonder whether one exercise in selective quotation is simply being rebutted by another, falling back on their initial predispositions or calling 'a plague on both your houses'. There is really only one way of dispelling such suspicions − by reference to the original sources. The Glasgow studies did not present a single fully-documented example. The primary materials are to all practical intents and purposes quite inaccessible to the private individual. Consequently, this study bridges that gap by presenting the text of the ITN reports on industrial disputes beginning in the first four months of 1975, which have been under review in the preceding chapters.

If the primary aim is to present the evidence by which the competing cases can be assessed, a second intention is to permit alternative and independent judgments. The present study has repeatedly emphasised the diversity of interpretations that could be attached to ITN's output. Its challenge to the Glasgow critique was not simply aimed at one particular line of analysis which the evidence in the event did not sustain, but to the whole enterprise of imposing a single narrow, restrictive analytical frame on a highly complex set of verbal messages. This is not to say that news output can be interpreted in whatever way our fancy may lead. Those who perceive alternative readings may reasonably be asked to state their criteria and produce their evidence — in short, to bend themselves to the discipline of reasoned exposition that has been attempted in the preceding pages. But at least that possibility for other critical insights exists, as it did not before.

Finally, although this was not a primary purpose, the presentation of the full text of ITN's output makes this the first generally available casebook of British television news output. The following pages reproduce the verbatim text of ITN's reporting of industrial disputes during the survey period under discussion. The lay-out is doubly chronological. That is, disputes are arranged in order of the first occasion on which they were reported, and then the material on each dispute is printed in date order. The exception is the coverage of the car industry, where the character of the case study discussion earlier made it desirable to keep all reports on the industry together in one sequence. Editorial changes have been limited to avoiding confusion and uncertainty in the mind of the reader, rather than achieving a high standard of consistency in spelling and layout. Irregularities are almost inevitable in material prepared under considerable time pressure by a varied group of individuals. The great majority of these untidinesses were in fact not apparent on air.

The form of presentation may be sufficiently unfamiliar that some explanation of layout and terms may be helpful. This is perhaps best based on a brief example:

12. 10 March 1975 22.00 Item 12   Platt
(Previous item: London dock strike)
REGGIE/GLASGOW/VTR ULAY

> Glasgow City Council are to ask the Government to send troops to clear 50,000 tons of rat-infested rubbish from the city's streets.

TAKE ULAY   This follows warnings that parts of Glasgow may soon become
45″ AVAIL   uninhabitable.

> The refuse has been accumulating over eight weeks because of the strike by 350 dustcart drivers, who want pay parity with private haulage drivers.

RT: 22″
(Next item: Whitehall industrial workers' strike)

The first line tells us that this is the twelfth time ITN reported the Glasgow dustcart drivers' strike, and that the item went out in News at

Ten on 10 March 1975. It is marked in the script as item 12 in the running order, and thus ran well down the bulletin. (The numbering of items is usually identical to that stated in ITN's running orders, excluding headlines and the commercial break, but occasional items are renumbered to allow for scheduled items being dropped or late news being added as an extra item.) Also from the ITN script we learn that the sub-editor responsible for the item was called Platt. The 'sub' is usually identified by surname, sometimes by initials ('MDW'), and occasionally by first name ('Sarah'). And at times it is not stated at all. When provided it is one element that helps to indicate the degree of continuity in the handling of the story in the news room – though sub-editors are of course not entirely autonomous agents in preparing the item for transmission.

The information that coverage of the Glasgow stoppage was preceded by an item on the London dock strike comes from the programme running order rather than the script. In most cases this is the short title (or 'catchline') listed in the running order. However, where ITN's catchline did not make the item's content sufficiently clear, or where the meaning would now be lost because of the lapse of time, an expanded and more informative version has been substituted. A few catchlines were so cryptic they could not be traced, and so they have had to be left in their original form.

This brief indication of the previous story provides a pointer to the setting of the item. In this instance, as well as being well down the bulletin, it was clearly part of an industrial disputes sequence which continued with coverage of the strike by industrial civil servants. The need for coherent composition of news programmes meant that dispute stories were frequently grouped. In fact, a quarter of such items were preceded by reporting of another dispute, and nearly as many were followed by coverage of one. It has at times been suggested that the juxtaposition of strike stories and pay stories may have set up patterns of implied connection in viewers' minds. In fact, however, only just under one in ten dispute items were led by an item on pay and slightly fewer were followed by one. Other financial, economic or industrial stories preceded in one in six items and followed in one in five. This left just under half which either led the programme or were preceded by a piece of domestic or foreign news with which any relationship would appear much less apparent. Half the following items likewise 'changed the subject'.

The text follows ITN's microfilm record of scripts and transcripts faithfully, including minor inconsistencies of spelling and style. However, the punctuation and, occasionally, spelling has been edited to improve intelligibility, since this was attributable to ITN's audio typists rather than to the contributors themselves, whether journalists or interviewees.

All but a few ITN scripts are given a 'slug' before the text that is to be read. In the example given 'REGGIE' identifies the newsreader, Reginald Bosanquet. This is essential in News at Ten scripts because there are two newsreaders and it is necessary to identify responsibilities. There are similar identifiers elsewhere for 'LEONARD' (Parkin), 'GORDON' (Honeycombe), 'ANDREW' (Gardner) and 'SANDY' (Gall). Scripts for single-handed programmes do not identify the reader. Following the identifier, if any, comes the catchline by which the item is identified in the running order, in this case, 'GLASGOW'. Then may come one or more references to special technical inputs to the item. In the example above 'VTR ULAY' warns that the newscaster will at some point be 'voice over' videotape, whether recorded on the day or drawn from the ITN library. Similar terms – not always the same owing to last minute changes – may appear as technical cues at the side of the script. In the example above the VTR operator would come in with videotape of accumulating rubbish from roughly the end of the first sentence through to the end of the item. The mention of '45″ AVAIL' indicates that there is sufficient material to see the item through to the end. Examples include:

OB	Outside Broadcast.
LIVE INJ(ECT)	A live report from either a reporter in the studio or down the line from some remote point.
PHONO	A voice-only report, usually late news phoned in by a journalist over a caption picture.
FILM ULAY	Newscaster reading over film. Film was still in fairly extensive use at this time, particularly for library material.
SISSONS FILM	Film report by the journalist named.
STUDIO INTVW	Studio interview.
SLIDE	Newscaster seen reading to camera but with a picture, map or diagram superimposed over his shoulder.

STILL   Newscaster reading over a full-screen picture.

CAP   Newscaster reading over a caption card, possibly setting out figures or otherwise graphically presenting information.

SUPER   Caption superimposed on film or videotape at the moment of transmission to identify participants or locations.

Other cues include FLUP for film reports, or VTR UP for videotape inserts. T/C is used occasionally to cue telecine, and camera changes are signalled as N/C. 'SOF UP' cues in film sound. The marginal annotation sometimes indicates the text of the supercaption in full or abbreviated.

Though the proliferation of marginal annotations does not make for easy reading, for anyone accustomed to watching television news, the technical direction and cues provide at least a partial guide to the missing visual element.

'RT: 22‴' in our example means that the item ran for 22 seconds. Many items contained several segments, and usually the segments are timed separately. Most timings are taken from the ITN scripts, but where this is not provided the approximate timing is given, based on conventional newsreading speeds of 180 words per minute.

Finally, the identification of the following item, derived on the same basis as the 'Previous item', helps further to situate this item in the structure of the programme.

1: HOSPITAL CONSULTANTS' WORK TO CONTRACT

1. 1 January 1975 22.00 Item 9   Purvis
(Previous item: Pakistan earthquake)
AG/CONSULTANTS/LAMBERT FILM/SUPERS
Hospital consultants begin a 'work-to-rule' tomorrow throughout the country to try to put pressure on the Government in the dispute about pay and private patients.
The effects will vary from hospital to hospital. To try to find out why people who normally earn more than seven thousand pounds a year are taking this action, Angela Lambert spent a day with a consultant surgeon at a Kent hospital.

FILM   **Lambert:** It's nine o'clock and the surgeon prepares for this morning's seventh operation − 4 of them quite minor, 3 including one on this small boy, major and possibly complicated. This theatre handles some 3,000 operations a year and Mr Rex Hunter performs about half of them working 10-12 hours a day, never less than 6 days a week. Finally the unconscious child gets his panda back. I asked Mr Hunter why he thought the consultants would reject Mrs Castle's terms.

SUPER   **Hunter:** The first thing is a man should be allowed to do what he
HUNTER   wants to do in his spare time and not be penalised for it. It's very simple. I don't think any workman in the country would sacrifice his income just to do casual work in his evenings or weekends, would he? The other thing is that by the nature of our profession we have to serve our patients to the best of our ability, and we tend to work longer hours than we are being paid for. This is throughout the country. I wouldn't think it's really unreasonable to expect to be paid something for overtime.

Lambert: Now it's the ward round with a colleague. A chance to reassure the patients by discussing their problems. He has 10 minutes for his lunch before driving off [to] visit patients at home. 12 and a half thousand hospital consultants like Mr Hunter have until Thursday to make up their minds whether to accept Mrs Castle's package. They claim that in the past the National Health Service has relied far too much on the goodwill of doctors. They have always been overworked and, certainly by comparison with Europe and America, underpaid. Now they're rebelling. Operations have to be backed by paper work − notes on the case, letters to the patient's GP. It's 4 o'clock and Mr Hunter has at least another 2 hours of operations ahead of him. After that, with luck, and barring emergencies, he can go home. Angela Lambert, NAT, Ashford hospital.

RT: 18″ + 2'38″

(Next item: Dr Christian Barnard)

2. 2 January 1975 13.00 Item 2   JO
(Previous item: IRA extends ceasefire)
DOCTORS/STUDIO INTVW
> 11,000 hospital consultants throughout Britain began their work-to-
> rule or work-to-contract today to protest about the new contract
> offered to them by the Government.
> It's the first work-to-rule ever by consultants in the NHS and the
> British Medical Association says there's every evidence of massive
> support this morning.
> The consultants say the contract they've been offered will put an end
> to the independence of the medical profession, and they're meeting
> this afternoon to decide what to do next. One sanction they're
> threatening is wholesale resignation from the NHS, which according
> to Mr. Clifford Astley, Chairman of the Central Committee for the
> Hospital Medical Services — that's the group that represents the
> consultants — could come in a matter of a few weeks.
> The junior hospital doctors — that's all those below consultant level —
> have pledged their support for the consultants, and are threatening to
> take action of their own unless their demands for a 40 hour week are
> met.
> They've written to the Secretary of State for Social Services, Mrs.
> Barbara Castle, asking for a meeting next week.
> The effect of the present work-to-rule is expected to be cumulative.
> Emergencies will be covered but waiting lists for non-urgent
> treatment will grow, and out-patients clinics will be cut back.
> But if the junior doctors also take action, then the NHS could be
> reduced to an 'emergency only' service.
> With me is the Secretary of State for Health Services, Mrs. Barbara
> Castle.

STUDIO   **Kee:** Mrs. Castle, on the face of it, it seems a terrible indictment of
INTVW   you as an employer that the very top people in the medical
          profession should be forced for the first time in history to take this
          action.

          Castle: Well, I think the position is, as with the nurses earlier, that I
          have inherited the pent up frustration of years by the consultants.
          This is something I inherited throughout the whole of the health
          service, and I'm hopeful that just as we did give the nurses a fair deal,
          then in the same way we shall be able to agree with the consultants a
          fair deal for them, because you see, the interesting thing is that in this
          new contract I am offering them I am giving them something they
          have asked my Conservative predecessors for in vain — namely a

contract which is a closed contract. That is to say they get paid for a defined number of hours, and if they do extra sessions, or if they do emergency calls at weekends and at nights, they will get paid extra. It's a more workload sensitive contract — it meets their major point that they have been working long hours for which they haven't been paid.

Kee: Yes, but their answer to this of course is that certainly you have given them payment for overtime, which they've always wanted to have, but you've given it to them on terms which totally undermine the independence of their profession — on terms which make it impossible for them to do what they want to do with their own spare time, because they are now penalised if they take on private medecine.

Castle: I have given it to them on the terms which have obtained under the existing contract ever since Nye Bevan introduced the National Health Service in 1948. It is not I who am trying to take away the independence of the profession. I..., it is they who are trying to put back the clock, because you see at present, under their existing contract, there has always been a differential in pay between the man who does the private practice and the chap who says, 'No, I will have no outside commitments, I will make myself totally available to my National Health Service patients.' Now I should think that's a commonsense principle. If a man is totally available, with no outside distractions, he should continue to be recognised. Now this is what I want to do, and it is not a new principle, and when they say I'm undermining the independence of the profession, do they think it's been undermined all these years while the differential has obtained? No, I think this is a bogey that they are introducing as a distraction, and I think it would be quite wrong to do what they want me to do, which is penalise the man who makes himself whole time available to the Health Service.

Kee: I don't think you can fairly refer back to the principles that have obtained, because you are changing all those principles, as you rightly claim, with this new offer. Surely now by giving a differential of 18% to people who work full time in the National Health Service, and don't have any private medecine, you are really trying to implement a political dogma. You are not remedying grievances, you are offering an inducement to comply with political dogma.

Castle: No, I am trying to continue what has always been part of the compromise Aneurin Bevan entered into with the profession. Now I'm offering a compromise to them. I am not saying they must not do private practice, I am...

Kee: But you are penalising them for doing private practice...

Castle: No, I'm sorry, it is they who want to penalise the man who says, 'I won't do private practice'. That man at present gets a differential of 18%, and I say to the profession, 'Look, I'm not attempting to impose a whole time service on you, not even imposing this contract, if you don't want it. You're free to reject it and go on as you are now, but the compromise that I'm offering you...'

Kee: But they...

Castle: But I'm offering them a compromise they can continue to have, the freedom to do private practice, but where the man says, 'No, I won't, I won't have outside distractions', I think it would be wrong to take from him the differential he's got now.

Kee: But now, whether this is as reasonable as you make it out or not, they don't think so, and the fact remains that you've reached a major crisis in the National Health Service. In the last 10 years we've seen 4,000 doctors born and educated in this country leave because they don't like the conditions – mustn't you do something better than you've done so far to stop this happening?

Castle: Well, I'll tell you what we've got to do. We've got to sit down and have a look at this contract together, because I think this mood is due to an entire misunderstanding of the contract. You see, what shocks me is this. First the profession threatened me with a strike unless the Government produced a firm statement of what it was prepared to accept, and produced it the Friday before Christmas. So I did that. Then they said, 'Oh, you've brought it on a take it or leave it basis.' I said, 'Look, take this contract away, discuss it with your members. The details are negotiable – the principles aren't, but the details are. Then let us meet after Christmas. Suspend your action, let us meet after Christmas, and then, you will be able to see more clearly how it affects all your members.' Oh, no. They were all geared up for a strike. They've had a strike in their system, I think, for sometime because of the years of frustration when consultants' pay has been held down under the pay policy of the Tories.

Kee: But you see, you say you'll negotiate in any new meeting over details, but not the principle. It's the principle they're objecting to.

Castle: Yes, but I don't think they understand, you see, just the nature of the principles. It is true that some of them, not all – we don't know exactly how many do respond favourably to the contract, and how many feel outraged by it. But it is true that people like Dr. Brian Lewis want to go very much further. They want a complete items-of-service contract, which means they get paid piece work. For an operation they get so much. For a visit they get paid so much — a kind of American system which would destroy our health service. Now I had to tell them that the principle was not negotiable, because the Government is already going a long way by being prepared to put extra money into their pockets for work that at present they don't get paid for, and in our present economic situation, the Government has really gone a very long way to try and meet what I feel, and the Government feels, is some of their legitimate grievances.

Kee: But you will meet them once again?

Castle: Oh, but I'm ready to meet them at any time, and I have already told the junior hospital doctors I will gladly meet them next week.

Kee: Thank you very much Mrs. Castle.

RT: 6'52"

(Next item: Share prices tumble)

3. 2 January 1975 17.50 Item 4   Purvis
(Previous item: Burmah Oil's difficulties hit share prices)
CONSULTANTS/DOCTOR FILM/CASTLE FILM

Hospital consultants throughout the country have started their first ever 'work to rule' in protest at the new contract being offered to them by the Government.

One of the terms of the new contract is that the doctors would be compensated with extra pay if they agree to work solely for the National Health Service. The effects are expected to build up in hospitals, as consultants work only the hours laid down in their contracts. A consultant in West London spoke to Derek Taylor.

VTR UP   **Doctor:** Within that time we shall give priority to the emergency
SUPER: BOLT   admissions coming into hospital of course, and we shall organise our affairs such that the patients admitted for routine work will be those who have conditions which might [imperil] their lives and we shall organise our outpatients work in such a way that we see instead of at the moment 15 to 20 patients in a clinic, I shall probably see about 6. But of those the greatest majority will be patients who have conditions which their doctors regard as being a danger to their lives.

Taylor: So something like 10 to 12 new patients would not be seen each day while you're working to contract.

Doctor: That is absolutely correct.

Taylor: And what about hospital operations?

Doctor: Well we shall try in future to keep our operating sessions within the hours which are designated for in our contract, and during that time the number of patients that we have in conditions such as a disease requiring lifesaving surgery I usually... completely to occupy that operating time.

Taylor: Would you be prepared to resign over this issue?

Doctor: I would personally, yes.

Taylor: And how many of your colleagues?

Doctor: Well, this is something that we don't exactly know, and we're conscious of the fact that many young men with mortgages and expenses, with families, feel that the risk involved is too great. But I would have thought that at the present time probably about 40 to 50% of the consultant body would actually be prepared to go as far as resignation.

[programme continues]

The Social Services Secretary, Mrs. Castle, has accused the consultants' leaders of issuing a 'call for anarchy'.

She said it was a tragedy that blackmail of the Government was being tried through industrial action. She wanted all consultants to study the new contract. And to discuss it with the Government.

RT: Approx. 2'09″

(Next item: Junior hospital doctors' pay)

4. 2 January 1975 22.00 Item 7   Purvis
(Previous item: Junior hospital doctors' pay)
ANDREW/CONSULTANTS/DOCTOR/CASTLE FILM/SUPERS

The report also seems to have hardened feeling among the top hospital doctors – the consultants – who today started a worktorule in their separate dispute with the Government over new contracts.

One called it 'another deliberate slap in the face of the medical profession'.

The effect of the consultants' action is expected to build up gradually as they work only the hours laid down on their present contracts. A consultant in West London explained to Derek Taylor how the action was affecting his working week:

FLUP   [interview with Bolt as at 17.50, then continuing]

SUPER: **Castle:** This contract is a compromise. In it we have made a large number of concessions to the views the consultants have put forward during the months of negotiation in the joint working party. Just before Xmas the consultants' negotiators were threatening me with industrial action [if] the Government did not produce a ·full statement of what it was prepared to do. Now we've produced that statement, and what I said to the negotiators then was, 'Take away this new contract, and look at it. Discuss it with your members, then come back, and we'll talk after Xmas. In the meantime for heaven's sake suspend industrial action which can damage patients.' Now in the end we'll have to get together again. I'm willing to do that any time and I have already made it clear for instance that I'm prepared to meet the junior hospital doctors as they have asked me to do. I stand ready to talk any time, but I think it is tragic if industrial action should go on in the meantime.

RT: 26 2'10
(Next item: Watergate)

5. 8 January 1975 13.00 Item 5
(Previous item: Vietnam fighting)
DOCTORS/STUDIO INTVW STEVENSON
          The dire troubles of the National Health Service, which is already having to cope with a worktocontract by 11,000 consultants – comes under an even bigger threat today, when representatives of the two other major groups of doctors in the service see the Secretary of State for Social Services, Mrs. Barbara Castle...
          [remainder of the item was about the junior hospital doctors]

RT: Approx. 18″
(Next item: Football)

6. 10 January 1975 17.50 Item 7   Black
(Previous item: Ginger Marks)
DOCTORS
          Scottish hospital consultants, meeting in Edinburgh have unanimously rejected the Government's proposed National Health Service contract.
          They've given the Government one month in which to reopen what they call 'meaningful negotiations' on their pay and conditions.
          Failing this, the Scottish consultants will join their English counterparts in working to contract.

RT: 18″

(Next item: Dentists' pay demand)

7. 13 January 1975 17.50 Item 3   O'Connell
(Previous item: Shore Commons statement on aircraft hijacking)
CASTLE/SLIDE

    Also in the Commons the Secretary for the Social Services Mrs. Castle said that industrial action by National Health Service consultants is damaging the interests of patients in some parts of the country.

SLIDE: Mrs. Castle denied that she had used the talks over pay as a means of imposing a full-time salaried service.

    She said the Government's proposals formed 'a reasonable offer' which met the consultants' wish to have a contract which took into account the number of hours they actually worked.

RT: 27″

(Next item: Foot Commons speech on Social Contract)

8. 13 January 1975 22.00 Item 9   O'Connell
(Previous item: Glasgow dustcart drivers' strike)
LEONARD/MRS. CASTLE/SLIDE

    There's been the hint of a peace move in the consultants' dispute.

    The Social Services Secretary, Mrs Castle, told the Commons that the Government had no wish to delay any pay award due to the doctors in April. If the profession desired, Mrs Castle said, the Government were willing to take the 'exceptional step' of asking the Review Body to price the terms of their new contracts before the consultants actually agreed to accept them.

    Later, the Hospital Consultants & Specialists Association said that Mrs. Castle's contract was totally 'unacceptable'. They said they'd be unwilling to sell their independence 'at any price'.

RT: 35″

(Next item: Foot Commons speech on Social Contract)

9. 16 January 1975 22.00 Item 4A   Sheppard
(Previous item: NGA strike)
REGGIE/CONSULTANTS/SLIDE

    Britain's 11,000 consultants have agreed to resume talks with the
SLIDE: Social Services Secretary, Mrs Barbara Castle.

    The move follows a conciliatory letter from Mrs Castle, in which she offered to spell out how much more money the doctors would get under a new contract before they agree to accept it.

    But the consultants have stressed that the talks are only

'exploratory' and they're to continue their worktocontract, which began a fortnight ago.

RT: 26"

(Next item: Cowley tuners' strike)

10. 23 January 1975 13.00 Item 7   JO
(Previous item: London busmen's strike)
WELLINGTON HOSPITAL/LAMBERT FILM

Hospital consultants who've been working to contract for the past three weeks are going to the Department of Health today — or their representatives are — to try and find a way of getting talks on their future going again.

Meanwhile, waiting lists for hospital beds continue to grow in most National Health hospitals and many patients are having to wait longer and longer for routine consultations. But one hospital where there are no problems at all is Wellington hospital in London...

Angela Lambert explains:

[remainder of the item was about the opening of this new luxury private hospital]

RT: Approx. 26"

(Next item: Edrich)

11. 5 February 1975 13.00 Item 4   Stevens
(Previous item: Northern Ireland gun battle)
DOCTORS/THIRKETTLE FILM

It's almost exactly a month since hospital consultants throughout Britain began their work-to-rule over pay grievances. Caused quite a fuss at the time, but doesn't seem to have made much difference since — that is provided you enjoy good health, or aren't waiting for an operation or can afford private treatment anyway. If you don't come into any of these categories, it's a very different story. The consultants' work-to-rule (or 'work-to-contract' they like to call it) IS hurting patients all right. (Odd for doctors to be doing that really.) But those lists of non-urgent operations waiting to be done are certainly getting longer and the out-patients' clinics more crowded. From the doctors' point of view, more and more of them are getting so fed up with pay and working conditions in our National Health Services that they're deciding to emigrate.

Joan Thirkettle's been to some who've already taken that step:

[Interviews with a senior registrar, a GP and a junior hospital doctor, all complaining about pay and conditions but not referring directly to the consultants' dispute.]

RT: 52″ + 3'36″

(Next item: Ethiopia fighting)

12. 17 February 1975 22.00 Item 8   Tristram
(Previous item: Geoffrey Rippon refuses to serve in Shadow Cabinet)
REGGIE/CONSULTANTS/SLIDE

SLIDE   The Social Services Secretary, Mrs. Castle, has appealed to hospital
consultants to resume talks on a bigger pay offer on Thursday — and
call off their work-to-rule.

But negotiators for the consultants say this isn't likely. They
claim Mrs. Castle's views on several issues are still unknown.

Consultants have been on a work-to-rule in England and Wales
for the past six weeks.

Mrs Castle claimed in the Commons that one of the consultants'
professional bodies — the Hospital Consultants' & Specialists'
Association — have demanded rises of 119 per cent.

RT: 33″

(Next item: Bank workers' pay claim)

13. 20 February 1975 22.00 Item 7   Black
(Previous item: Morriston Hospital strike)
REGGIE/CONSULTANTS/TAYLOR FILM/CAPS/SLIDES

Britain's 11,000 hospital consultants are to continue their seven week
work-to-rule, and their leaders are to seek an 'urgent interview' with
the Prime Minister to discuss their grievances.

SLIDE   Dr. Derek Stevenson, Secretary of the British Medical
Association, stressed that his members did not believe they were
taking any kind of industrial action — but were simply honouring
their contracts to the letter.

SLIDE   But the Social Services Secretary, Mrs. Castle, said the
consultants WERE breaking their Health Service contracts.

The Review Body's recommendations on the consultants' pay
will be announced in six weeks' time. Derek Taylor asked Mrs.
Castle if the Government were hoping that when the doctors saw the
size of their proposed increase they'd withdraw their support for the
negotiators:

FLUP SUPER: **Castle:** I think it's true to say that many consultants feel frustrated
CASTLE   and a bit desperate because they have had to wait 12 months since
their last increase. Now I understand they are due to be brought into
line — I'm not opposing them on that. And as far as repricing the
existing contract is concerned I do believe it will make a difference

when the review body has given them a normal pay increase. But if they wish me to negotiate a new contract — a complicated matter — they can't expect me to do that while queues are lengthening at hospitals and while they are breaking their existing contract. That I think no Government would do.

RT: 41″ + 38″

(Next item: Mrs Thatcher formally declared Conservative leader)

14. 7 March 1975 17.50 Item 11   Mawer
(Previous item: Two rescued in tunnel collapse)
DOCTORS
        The Prime Minister has refused to discuss the hospital consultants' dispute with them until they call off their work-to-rule. He told the British Medical Association, in a letter he was sure there was enough common ground to get a settlement.

RT: 22″
(Next item: Bank rate)

15. 14 March 1975 13.00 Item 7   Stevens
(Previous item: IRA ceasefire uncertain after shootings)
PRIVATE BEDS/ARCHER FILM/STUDIO INTVW
        A new hospital wing was opened in Blackpool this morning by Mrs. Castle, the Social Services Secretary — an event one might think which should call for mutual congratulations among *everybody* concerned with our overstretched health services.
        But in this case it served only to point up the *divisions* among those people — because senior consultants at that Blackpool hospital pointedly stayed away from the ceremony.
        The cause of this snub to Mrs. Castle is the continuing dispute over a new pay contract for the hospital consultants.
        And linked with that dispute, of course, is the growing row over private patients within the National Health Service.

[Item continued with a report on private practice in an eye hospital, followed by an interview between Leonard Parkin and Bernard Dix of NUPE on the campaign about private beds. The interview included these passages:]

Dix: Let's be clear first of all. It's not just my members. This Government is committed to phasing out private patient facilities from the health service.

Parkin: But your members are trying to accelerate this by political industrial action.

Dix: Our members are in fact trying to offset the consequences of the consultants' work-to-contract — their dispute which is depriving National Health Service patients of facilities, and our members are saying that in a situation like this, then if there is any diminution of service, it should be the private patients who experience that, not the national health patients.

[Later] **Dix:** ...our members are saying that if as a result of the consultants' taking action, that some patients suffer, as they do, then the people who must suffer the most must be the private patients because their need is not a social need or a medical need, they are there because they can pay to go there...

RT: Not available

(Next item: Portuguese political situation)

16. 14 March 1975 22.00 Item 8   MDW
(Pevious item: Prices)
REGGIE/CONSULTANTS/VTR

The Hospital Consultants and Specialists Asociation, which represents 5,000 of Britain's 12,000 medical consultants, is to step up action in their fight with the Government over Health Service contracts. Apart from not working overtime, members will refuse to work in areas they consider to be understaffed or illequipped, and may ask authorities to close wards, or even whole hospitals.

John Doyle asked the President of the Association, Mr Terence Beatson, if this action would increase the threats to patients.

TAKE VTR
(NO PRESOF)
SUPER:
BEATSON

Beatson: We have never disguised the fact that the action we are taking, which is, I might say, distasteful to us in the extreme, will result in patients having to wait longer times for their treatment.

Doyle: Now you do say in fact, that you complain of a negative attitude on the part of the Prime Minister, but Mr Wilson has said that he will meet you if only you'll first call off your sanctions. Now why don't you do that?

Beatson: Well, you call this sanctions. We call it working the hours for which we're paid. What Mr. Wilson and Mrs. Castle are inviting us to do is go back to working long hours of unpaid overtime, with nothing in return but vague promises. This is not good enough, and you must reflect on why members of a profession such as ours after 26 years of working in the National Health Service, have regretfully decided to make this stand.

Doyle: How can you then claim not to be penalising patients when in fact waiting lists have in many places trebled over the last two or three months?

Beatson: We do not claim not to be penalising patients. Unfortunately, this is happening. I sincerely hope that the patients who are being penalised by having to wait to come into hospital will complain to their Members of Parliament and to their hospital authorities.

Doyle: Aren't you then using patients in your campaign?

Beatson: In any public service which is a monopoly, if the staff in that service wish to protest against their conditions of service, they have inevitably to use the people to whom they give the service.

RT: 28″ + 1'33″

(Next item: Trade figures)

17. 18 March 1975 13.00 Item 2
(Previous item: Westminster Hospital dispute)
CONSULTANTS REACTION/STUDIO INTVW

Meanwhile there's little sign of the consultants' work-to-contract dispute being solved. With me in the studio is a consultant surgeon, Mr. Keith Able, an executive member, in fact, of the Hospital Consultants & Specialists Association.

STUDIO   **Kee:** Mr. Able, between the militancy of the unions, we've just seen
INTVW   at work in the Westminster hospital, and your militancy, what's to
UP   become of the poor patients in the National Health Service?

Able: Well, I rather agree that they're the people who are most likely to suffer. Although there are two different forms of discontent emerging in the health service, I think they're very different in principle. The action by the NUPE members at the Westminster Hospital is in our opinion the application of industrial action for the furtherance of political ends.

Kee: Isn't that exactly what you're doing for your ends as consultants?

Able: No, I don't think our ends are political at all. Our argument with the Government is over our contracts. It is not over the application of a political principle that private patients should or should not be allowed to be treated in any particular kind of hospital.

Kee: However, it's not unconnected is it, because the reorganisation of the contracts is tied in with the Government's plans for phasing out private beds, and certain of what you might describe as bribes were involved for you in the rearrangements, and you don't like the rearrangements generally.

Able: Well, the move to change the consultants' contract was

initiated by the profession some time ago, and during the course of
last year, the Owen Working Party discussed with the Government
all aspects of the consultants' contract, and at the Government's
request, on the agenda for discussion was the question of private
practice. In fact, that question of private practice had virtually no
more than ten minutes discussion throughout the whole of those
negotiations, so that the profession, who agreed to work the health
service when it was instituted 25 years ago, and at that time the
Government agreed that private practice should continue, has had no
means of discussing with the Government how private practice
should be phased out, and our view is that it isn't up to a militant
minority within the health service — because this is what these people
are at the Westminster — to determine the policy in regard to private
beds throughout the country.

Kee: On the other hand, it could be said that the phasing out of
private beds was in the Labour Party's election manifesto, the
Labour Party won the election, and therefore, they're not in a
minority — they're representing the majority opinion.

Able: Well, I don't agree with you at all. I think that far less than
half the population — in fact I think it was only 30% of the
population, or 33%, voted for the Labour Party. So if you're talking
about majority, I would say that the majority of the people in the
country who bothered to vote in the last election didn't want the
Labour Party manifesto. Even within the health service, there are
still, even amongst the Labour Party people, there are still plenty of
people who don't want to see this sort of behaviour going on in our
hospitals.

Kee: What's this further militancy we hear threatened this morning?
What might you do to sharpen the position up?

Able: In regard to the consultants' action?

Kee: Yes.

Able: Well, I think one of the things that we're intending to do is to
recommend that our members should no longer take part in any
medical committees other than staff committees, and that we should
discontinue the scheme or the catchment whereby overseas doctors
are assessed as to their professional capabilities before they're given
registration in this country.

Kee: This could only lead to further damage to the health service in
the end, though?

Able: No, I don't think it will, actually. I think it might improve the standards.

Kee: Thank you very much, Mr. Able.

RT: 3'18"

(Next item: Cabinet discusses British membership of EEC)

18. 17 April 1975 13.00 Item 5   Sarah

(Previous item: Saigon)

CONSULTANTS/STUDIO INTVW/SUPER

At home — the chance of an end to the 15-week work-to-contract by hospital consultants hangs in the balance after an all-night meeting between representatives of the British Medical Association and the Social Services Secretary Barbara Castle.

After the meeting, which lasted nearly 15 hours, the BMA negotiators said they'd recommend a return to work by their members at a meeting tomorrow — a decision they took after seeing the text of 2 letters which Mrs Castle will send to tomorrow's meeting. The BMA says the letters are 'comprehensive' and provide a basis for reopening negotiations.

However, another, more militant organisation, the Hospital Consultants & Specialists Association, which claims to represent about half Britain's 11,000 consultants, have said they'll order their members to carry on the work-to-contract. They're angry because they weren't invited to last night's meeting. Up till then they'd co-operated closely with the BMA.

It was the breakdown of negotiations over a new contract last December that triggered the work-to-contract. Since then waiting lists for operations have doubled and tripled in some areas. And some patients have been told they'll have to wait over a year for an appointment. With me in the studio is David Bolt, who was one of the BMA's negotiators at last night's meeting.

STUDIO **Kee:** What in fact is the basis for negotiation that's emerged from
INTVW this?
SUPER:

DAVID BOLT **Bolt:** Well, we have for some time put aside the idea of a completely
BMA NEGOTI- new contract for consultants at the present time. And what we've
ATOR been concerned with is modifying our present contract in such a way as to particularly help those consultants who have an excessive workload.

Kee: In what way?

Bolt: Well, in that context, two particularly valuable things came out of last night's meeting: the fact that the Secretary of State has agreed in principle to people being recalled to their hospitals out of hours for emergency purposes; and that it should be possible for them with their employing authorities to negotiate for extra sessions of work in areas where there is too much work to be done within their existing contracts. So those are two very helpful things. A number of other, perhaps rather lesser, things were included. We're arranging a shortening of the incremental scale for newly appointed consultants, so that they get to the top of their salary scales in half the time that they do at the moment. There will be payments for the evermounting administrative work, payments for introducing a family planning service into the hospitals, and in fact the extension of London weighting to the consultant body.

Kee: One gets the impression from what you're saying that this has really been a dispute all about money, but one got an impression at the time that perhaps it was a dispute about something deeper than that — the very status of consultants in the National Health Service, and their rights to practise elsewhere.

Bolt: That is absolutely right. There are two letters, which you've heard, coming to the Association from the Secretary of State. One covers the items I've already listed. The other represents the conclusions we have reached with the Secretary of State on the subject of the option of a consultant on appointment, or subsequently, to elect either to work whole time in the National Health Service, or to work on the basis we call maximum part-time, allowing him the option of private practice, and as the agreement on which this was previously based was a very ill-defined one, a great deal of time has been spent in defining reasonably precisely on the one hand his rights, and on the other hand what the Secretary of State can reasonably expect from a part-time consultant.

Kee: Of course, all you're really saying this morning is that a basis for negotiations now exists. How optimistic are you that these negotiations will now be successful?

Bolt: I think that there are very good grounds for supposing that on the terms that I've already mentioned, we shall succeed in thrashing out the details to a point where we shall all have something to offer our colleagues. On the one or two other items that we would very much like to help on, the situation is rather less forthcoming. We've had some improvements in our superannuation scheme proposed, but nothing as substantial as we would have liked. We would have liked something firm on the subject of direct reimbursement for the use of cars and telephones — that is not a very promising situation. Nor is there any great promise on the subject of payment for providing on-call service.

Kee: These sound peripheral matters from your point of view, but of course I must point out that a large number of consultants, as represented by the Hospital Consultants & Specialists' Association, seem to think that there aren't really good grounds for negotiation even yet, at all.

Bolt: Well, obviously this is a point of view, but as far as the representation of the profession is concerned, it must be remembered that although it may well be that the HCSA has a membership equivalent to half the consultant body, a very large proportion of those are in fact members of both the organisations, so that in fact, shall we say, we can claim to represent them as much as the HCSA can. Apart from that, I think that we have been very anxious to end this dispute and to continue to give the kind of service to the public that we're accustomed to doing, and having seen what appears to us at least to be the basis on which fruitful talks can take place, it would seem to us to be quite wrong not to seize it.

Kee: Thank you very much Mr. Bolt. And the patients who've been waiting so long will be glad to hear that news, I'm sure.

RT: 1'14" + 3'30"

(Next item: Scottish alcoholics)

19. 17 April 1975 17.50 Item 11   Maimane
(Previous item: Murder)
DOCTORS/SLIDE

Hospital consultants seem to be split over a decision to end their 14week work-to-rule. The British Medical Association's decision to end the action has been rejected by the Hospital Consultants & Specialists' Association, who represent nearly half the 11,000 consultants.

SLIDE   They're angry because they were not told about the allnight talks between the BMA and the Social Services Secretary, Mrs. Castle. All negotiations with the health service are done by the BMA, and up to now the two associations have been united in the dispute over a new contract.

RT: 31"

(Next item: Former Clay Cross councillors face £5,000 surcharge)

20. 17 April 1975 22.00 Item 8   Maimane
(Previous item: Israelis)
LEONARD/DOCTORS/SLIDE

There's a row among hospital consultants over the British Medical Association's decision to call off their 14-week work-to-rule.

SLIDE:

The decision has been rejected by the Hospital Consultants & Specialists' Association, which represents 5,000 of the 11,000 consultants. They're angry because they weren't told about last night's talks between the BMA — which negotiates for ALL doctors — and Mrs. Castle, the Social Services Secretary.

The BMA is to advise consultants to end their work-to-rule while negotiations are re-opened about a new contract with the health service. Tonight representatives of over 1,000 consultants from the south east voted overwhelmingly to call off the work-to-rule and restart talks.

RT: 38"

(Next item: Murders)

21. 18 April 1975 17.50 Item 3(i)
(Previous item: Continuation of item on doctors' pay award)
DOCTORS/CASTLE VTR and SUPER

Apart from the pay award, another dispute has been solved today. The 11,000 National Health Service hospital consultants have decided to call off their work-to-contract and are to start fresh talks with the Government. And they've also been awarded increases ranging from 27 to 31 per cent.

Anthony Carthew asked the Social Services minister Mrs Castle if the salary increases were justified:

VTR UP
PRESOF

Castle: But these top professional people, we've got to keep them within the Health Service by rewarding them fairly, and I'm totally against trying to run a pay policy always at the expense of people in the public service, because I happen to believe in our National Health Service, and I think the people who work in it have got as much right as anybody in outside industry to get a proper reward for their work.

Carthew: You don't think you've given in any way?

Castle: I'm not giving in — it's not been I who have recommended these rates, it's an independent review body, but if you are talking about the discussions that I have had this week with the consultants, the clarification discussions which led their representatives to recommend the withdrawal of sanctions, no, I think all we have been doing is clarifying the situation. We've been clarifying what is [the] present contractual commitment of a consultant, and we have agreed that the long-established practice still remains under which even the maximum part-time consultant in the Health Service has got an overall commitment to give substantially the whole of his time to the National Health Service.

RT: 49″ + 1'20″

(Next item: Cowley strike)

22. 18 April 1975 22.00 Item 2   Jamieson
(Previous item: Railway pay negotiations)
LEONARD/DOCTORS/CAP/CARTHEW VTR/SUPER

[The start of the story dealt with the doctors' and dentists' pay award.]

N/C   Apart from being awarded a pay rise the consultants today decided to call off their work-to-contract, and start fresh talks with the Government.

Anthony Carthew asked Mrs Castle, the Social Services Secretary, if she thought the salary increases were really justified.

VTR UP
SUPER

[text of interview as at 17.50 but continuing:]

Carthew: Do you think this is going to permanently damage relationships between doctors and Government?

Castle: I want to get my relationships with the people who work in the National Health Service right. I met a pentup frustration. Nurses, as you'll remember, radiographers, everybody. Gradually we've got everybody's pay reviewed, and making them feel that they haven't been left to fall behind. This report and the Government's acceptance of it finishes that round of discussions, and I think we can really expect a new atmosphere in the Health Service now.

RT: 53″ + 1'52″

(Next item: Cowley strike)

23. 20 April 1975 18.07 Lead item   Jill
CONSULTANTS/VTR/SUPER

TITLE:
FILM ULAY
22″ AVAIL

The leaders of 5,000 hospital consultants have decided that their work-to-contract campaign should go ON – and that they shouldn't yet follow the line of the British Medical Association, who called it off last week.

The Council of the Hospital Consultants and Specialists Association say they're not satisfied that there has been enough progress in the consultants' contracts dispute to merit reopening negotiations.

I asked the Association's vice-president, Mr Stanley Simmons, if

VTR UP

they were making their point by force:

SUPER
STANLEY
SIMMONS

Simmons: No, I think that's an unfair assessment of the situation. What we are going to do in the meantime is to first of all write to the

Secretary of State and express our dismay at being excluded — we do represent approximately half the consultants in this country — that's 5,000 doctors. We will express our dismay. We will then do what we think is the proper and responsible action, and that is to ballot our members on whether or not they see within the documents a significant change in stance and if they see within them grounds for lifting sanctions. Indeed, if they do, we will abide by that. But in the meantime it would clearly be wrong, without having all the facts available to us, and indeed without being able to present them to our membership, to make a decision. But I must say Council were fairly unanimous, indeed, I think, unanimous but for one member of Council, that these documents do not contain the assurances which would guarantee professional independence in the future.

RT: 33″ + 1'03″

(Next item: Foot speech on withdrawal from EEC)

24. 20 April 1975 22.00 Lead item   Jill
DOCTORS/VTR/SUPER

TITLE: The leaders of 5,000 hospital consultants — almost half of the total
ULAY 22″   number — have decided that their work-to-contract campaign should go ON, and that they shouldn't yet follow the British Medical Association's decision to call it off.

The Council of the Hospital Consultants & Specialists Association say they can't be bound by the BMA decision because they were excluded from the talks which led to it. But the BMA claimed tonight that they were absent from their own choice.

The Association also say that they're not satisfied that there's been enough progress in the dispute over consultants' contracts, to merit re-opening negotiations.

I asked the Association's vice-president, Mr Stanley Simmons, if they weren't now making their point by force.

VTR SUPER   [interview text identical to 17.50]

RT: 47″ + 1'03″

(Next item: Junior hospital doctors pay)

2: THE PROBLEMS OF THE CAR INDUSTRY

1. 3 January 1975 13.00 Item 10
(Previous item: Cricket)

> Mr Wilson is to make a major speech on the economy in his Huyton constituency tonight. It's likely that he'll comment on the Government intervention to help companies in difficulties and deal with the threat of unemployment that faces British workers, as major companies struggle for survival.

RT: Approx. 16″

2.   [programme continues]

> Item on prospects of saving Aston Martin, which had gone into receivership, not available.

RT: 50″

(Next item: Stock exchange prices)

3. 3 January 1975 17.50 Item 5
(Previous item: Fodens receive Government aid)

> Item on prospects of saving Aston Martin, which had gone into receivership, not available.

RT: 16″ + 1′13″

(Next item: U.K. gold reserves)

4. 3 January 1975 22.00 Item 5   Jill
(Previous item: Government aid for Fodens)
ANDREW/WILSON/VTR/SUPER

> The Prime Minister tonight defended the Government policy of stepping in to help companies where jobs were threatened.
> But he also gave workers a blunt warning: He said: The Government couldn't intervene just to turn a private loss into a public loss.
> It was up to workers to cut what he called manifestly avoidable stoppages, and to curb 'unrealistic' demands.
> Mr Wilson — who was speaking in his Huyton constituency — singled out the car industry, and British Leyland in particular, to illustrate his point.
> He said the Government's rescue of Leyland was 'the most important, spectacular' decision in the fight against unemployment.
> It was their aim to put production, exports and jobs on a secure and profitable basis — as they could be, with the necessary investment.

PRE SOF: But, he said, this didn't depend on the Government alone.

VTR UP **Wilson:** 'In a very real sense, the success of public intervention – Government intervention – to fight the threat of unemployment means a full contribution – and that means a fair day's work for a fair day's pay by everyone for whose job security we are fighting. Parts of the British Leyland undertaking are profitable. Others are not. But public investment and participation cannot be justified on the basis of continued avoidable loss making. Our intervention cannot be based on a policy of turning a private liability into a public liability. This means, against the acknowledged background of established collective bargaining and safeguards, efficient working methods and steady week in, week out production...'

SUPER GLYN MATHIAS **Mathias:** In November over 35% of the cars sold in Britain were imported from abroad and an important contribution to unacceptable failure to compete by our home factories was the loss of production due to strikes. He referred especially to the Austin factory of British Leyland which he said was responsible for about 20% of the man days lost in the car industry last year. And the car industry as a whole was making a disproportionate contribution to loss of output through disputes.

Wilson: '...and an appropriate degree of public ownership and control involved, the Government could not justify to Parliament or to the taxpayer the subsidising of large factories involving thousands of jobs. Factories which could pay their way, but are failing to do so because of manifestly avoidable stoppages [of] production.

Industrial relations and the settlement [or] avoidance of disagreements within the established arrangements – these are a continuing [process] and public financing will not call for any interference with them.

But what is at stake in Britain in 1975 and the years after that is the future of the employment of our people. I repeat that that from now depends not only on Government finance and participation, wherever that occurs, but on the wider and wholehearted participation of all whose future, and whose families' future, depend [on] the success of the decisions the Government have taken and which we will take and which we intend to see through. Thank you for listening.'

Mathias: This was a stern message to come from a Labour Prime Minister. But it was received politely enough by an audience here in a Labour club in his constituency. But the speech was clearly prompted by a growing number of companies going to the Government for help and the large sums of public money involved. Mr Wilson clearly expects a greater degree of restraint from the work force and firms where the Government have stepped in to help and his appeal [was] directly to working people not to rock an already leaky boat. Glyn Mathias, NAT, in the Huyton constituency.

[Next item continues]   Jill

SANDY/REACTION/SLIDES

Mr. Wilson's comment on British Leyland got a cool reception from one Labour MP − Mr Leslie Huckfield of Nuneaton.

He said the Prime Minister clearly knew very little about the car industry. The real cause of the trouble was the chronic failure of management to invest, he said.

SLIDE   But the Opposition's employment spokesman, Mr. James Prior, − and the British Leyland spokesman − supported Mr. Wilson's remarks.

Mr. Prior said Mr. Wilson was 'at last stating some home truths which others have been expressing for a long while'.

RT: 28"

[programme continues]   Jill

ANDREW/COWLEY/FILM ULAY

As if to underline Mr Wilson's remarks British Leyland's

ULAY UP: 16" Austin-Morris plant in Cowley announced that 12-thousand men are being laid off because of a strike by 250 workers.

The striking workers are engine tuners who want to be graded as skilled workers.

They rejected a plea to call off the strike which could cut production by a thousand cars a day.

RT: 22"

6. [programme continues]
Item on hopes of saving Aston Martin not available.

RT: 11" + 1'13"

(Next item: UK gold reserves)

7. 4 January 1975 13.13 Lead item   Purvis

TITLE ULAY The British Leyland plant at Cowley in Oxford − specially picked out by Mr Wilson in his warning last night about strikes − is at a standstill for a second day because of industrial trouble.

Twelve thousand workers at the plant are being laid off because 250 engine tuners who want to be higher graded are stopping work on Monday.

In his speech last night, Mr Wilson warned workers in general, but car workers in particular, that the Government could not justify subsidising large factories which were losing money because of 'manifestly avoidable strikes'. The speech has been welcomed by some Conservative MPs but condemned by some Left-Wing Labour members.

RT: 37″

(Item continued with a CBS report on unemployment in the USA)

8. 4 January 1975 17.14 Lead item   Purvis
TITLE ULAY   The British Leyland plant at Cowley — specially picked out by Mr. Wilson in his warning about strikes last night — has shut down for the weekend because of industrial trouble.

Twelve thousand workers are being laid off because 250 engine tuners, who want to be graded higher, are stopping work on Monday.

In his speech last night, Mr. Wilson warned workers in general and car workers in particular, that the Government couldn't justify subsidising factories which were losing money because of 'manifestly avoidable strikes'.

The speech has been supported by some Conservative MPs, Mrs.
STILL: Jill Knight called it 'rather late, but extremely welcome'.
STILL: The Labour MP, Mr. John Lee, said 'point taken, but it is not the whole story'.
STILL: Another Labour MP, Mr. Denis Skinner, said Mr. Wilson should 'look around him and see precisely who were the real wreckers'.
RT: 58″

(Next item: Callaghan meets Vorster)

9. 4 January 1975 22.30 Item 3   Purvis
(Previous item: Callaghan meets Vorster)
COWLEY/HATFIELD FILM/SUPERS
Mr Wilson has got a mixed reception from his speech last night, warning about the effects of strikes on the Government's policy of helping out companies in trouble.

In the speech, Mr. Wilson warned workers in general, and car workers in particular, that the Government couldn't justify subsidising factories which were losing money because of 'manifestly avoidable strikes'.

The Prime Minister's speech has been supported by some
STILL: Conservative MPs: Mrs Jill Knight called it 'rather late, but

STILL:
STILL:

extremely welcome'.
A Labour MP, Mr John Lee, said 'Point taken, but it is not the whole story', and another Labour MP, Mr Dennis Skinner, said Mr Wilson should 'look around and see precisely who were the real wreckers'.

One factory referred to by Mr Wilson, British Leyland's Austin Morris plant at Cowley in Oxford, has shut down for the weekend because of industrial trouble. Keith Hatfield reports:

FLUP:

The Austin and Morris car plant at Cowley is not totally shut down. 12,000 men have been laid off because 250 engine tuners want their jobs regraded. It's the kind of strike that has contributed significantly to the dire economic difficulties of British Leyland. The engine tuners want to be upgraded to the top skilled rate which they hope would eventually mean higher pay, but there's no promise of this at the moment. The management insist on a single production workers' rate. It was this Cowley sector of British Leyland that was singled out by the Prime Minister for particular criticism. He said it was responsible for 20% of the days lost in the entire car industry last year.

SUPER
BRADLEY

Bradley: I would say that with the car industry in the state that it is now, if you abolish the strikes, all you would be [heading] for is an automatic three days a week anyway, because you could be overproducing in the same way as you did before the war, so the whole of the industry's got to be looked at from top to bottom, and I don't mean vice versa, from the top first of all, to the bottom.

Hatfield: Many of the British Leyland workers now laid off by the strike were in the Cowley workers' social club for their Saturday pint, but they are not paid while the cars are not made.

Bradley: (unintelligible)

Hatfield: Why are there so many unnecessary strikes?

Bradley: Well, I think it's because there are so many different grades up there, I mean, you've got about 13 grades of workers up there, it's stupid. I think there should be about five grades and that's it.

Worker: The Assembly plant, that's where they want to take it up, in there. But I think it's well, it seems to me to be a put-up job all the time. It's just the same blokes in it all the time.

Hatfield: The Cowley plant manager has said that to call off the strike would be a 'statesmanlike' decision [to] the benefit of British Leyland. Meetings are fixed for the beginning of the week, but meanwhile British Leyland's losses mount at the rate of 1,000 cars a day. KH, ITN, in Cowley.

RT: 56″ + 2′01″

(Next item: Sport)

10. 5 January 1975 18.07 Item 3   Purvis
(Previous item: Freighter crashes into Tasman Bridge)
JACK JONES/FILM/SUPER/RW
  Mr Jack Jones, head of Britain's biggest union, has asked the Prime Minister to meet union leaders to talk about the speech on 'avoidable strikes' which Mr Wilson made on Friday.
  Mr Jones, leader of the Transport Workers Union, said they should discuss wage structures, worker participation and to what extent management and the old Industrial Relations Act were responsible for present problems. Michael Oliver spoke to him.

Oliver: Now you've said that you don't want to fall out with the Prime Minister publicly — isn't it possible to look at his speech...

Jones: Well, I believe he's a logical and able man, and I simply want the chance, along with other trade union colleagues to talk with him about what we can do positively, involving management too, because management has a great responsibility in British industry, and we've got to find ways and means of improving cooperation, including the conveying of maximum information about the financial circumstances of the company, to the work people. This in the past has been very absent I'm afraid.

RT: 33″ + 39″

(Next item: Callaghan to call constitutional conference on Rhodesia)

11. 5 January 1975 22.15 Item 3   Purvis
(Previous item: Freighter crashes into Tasman bridge)
  [identical to 18.07]

RT: 33″ + 39″

(Next item: Roy Jenkins orders ex-detainee returned to N. Ireland)

12. 6 January 1975 13.00 Lead item   Morrison
CAR INDUSTRY/STUDIO INTV/SUPER
  But first British Leyland.
  This morning the Industry Secretary, Mr Benn, has been meeting British Leyland union leaders to brief them on the Government's plan to give massive financial aid to the company.

And one of the union leaders at that meeting has called for a 12-month 'strikes truce' at the firm. Mr Roy Sanderson, a member of the executive council of the Electrical Trades Union, said that the truce would be one way Leyland workers could recognise the 'dire straits that the corporation is in'. On the other hand Mr Bob Wright of the AUEW has said that there could be no question of trade unionists giving up their rights to strike.

His call follows the Prime Minister's statement at the weekend criticising British Leyland for its poor strike record, and giving a blunt warning that firms with a history of what Mr Wilson called 'manifestly avoidable stoppages' could not expect to be bailed out with public funds.

At the moment Leyland's Cowley plant is closed down, with 12,000 men laid off, because of a strike by 250 engine tuners. Though as a result of talks this morning the plant will be open tomorrow and union leaders are urging the men to report back at the works tomorrow.

So how do British Leyland see the future?

Here in the studio with me is British Leyland's industrial relations director, Mr Pat Lowry.

STUDIO
INTV

Kee: First of all, your reaction to this one year strikes truce — is it likely to be representative, that, do you think, of the attitude of most of the workers at British Leyland?

Lowry: I can't speak for the workers at British Leyland, but I can say this, that at British Leyland, we would be delighted if it was possible for such a truce to operate, and for such a truce to hold.

Kee: Now yesterday we heard Mr Jack Jones saying that Mr Wilson's diagnosis wasn't in itself enough, and that management was very largely to blame, or was at any rate partly to blame for these apparently stoppable stoppages of work — how do you take that criticism?

SUPER PAT
LOWRY IND.
RELS.
DIRECTOR
BRITISH
LEYLAND

Lowry: Well, obviouly there isn't time here to diagnose every stoppage that British Leyland has had and apportion blame one way or the other. I will say this though, that some of the reforms which British Leyland has been trying to introduce into its industrial relations in the last two or three years, reforms which we thought and still think are absolutely essential for the survival of the company, were almost bound to generate some friction, and so if the criticism was that we had been responsible for causing strikes but the results of these strikes were going to lead to better long-term industrial relations, well then I'm not ashamed to admit the charge, but I would deny strongly that our actions in the short term are deliberately designed to promote stoppages, and I would also deny strongly that the vast majority of stoppages we get are caused by some defect or default on the part of management.

Kee: Well, shortly, what would you say they are caused by?

Lowry: Well, this is a very difficult thing to deal with shortly. I talked about the reforms that we've been trying to introduce, which themselves have generated friction, and we still have in the company what I regard as a highly unsatisfactory basis of collective bargaining. We have something like 400 different bargaining units for our 160,000 employees, and we're bargaining every day of the year — literally every day of the year.

Kee: Doesn't this amount then to a criticism of the unions themselves — it seems so odd that the unions have so little control apparently over their own men — is that because of what you were now mentioning?

Lowry: Yes, I think partly this is the reason — I don't blame the unions exclusively for this — we're all victims of inheritance, and we have jointly inherited an awful hotch-potch of bargaining arrangements, and jointly we have now got to try and introduce a better basis of bargaining in future. I believe with a better basis and more comprehensive basis of bargaining we can avoid some of the disputes and some of the friction which we experience at the present time.

Kee: Are there any other causes? For instance, to put it bluntly, do you think there are people at work in British Leyland who simply want to disrupt the thing?

Lowry: There are obviously some. I mean, if [I] was to refer briefly to Cowley, which I thought got a certain amount of rather unjustified criticism over the weekend, because Cowley's record in the long term has been bad — there have been political extremists at work in Cowley, in the recent past, but as a result of actions which the union itself took earlier this year, changes were made, and as a result, since then the atmosphere in Cowley has been very much better, so clearly there are elements that are at work in the motor industry, but I never exaggerate this, I think one's got to keep it in the right perspective.

Kee: What's the reality of the danger to jobs in British Leyland if these sort of strikes go on?

Lowry: Clearly there must be a danger to jobs. Our problem at the moment in a very substantially contracting market is to hold what share of the market we have and, if possible, to increase it. The customer is going to be ever more insistent that he's able to buy a car immediately and is no longer prepared to wait whilst management and employees are in dispute over some problem, so unless we can avoid strikes and find a better way of doing our business, clearly we shan't be able to hold our share of the market, and clearly that has a severe impact on the jobs of the people that we employ.

Kee: On the other hand, isn't it true that with the Government coming to the aid of British Leyland, in spite of Mr Wilson's words of warning, workers are likely to think, well, anyway our jobs are safe, because that's why the Government's come in?

Lowry: There is obviously this risk, and I would just say this. That within the company, and indeed, on Friday of this week, we are holding a conference of our shop stewards, senior shop stewards, white collar representatives, at which we are going to spell out the facts about the company, and at which we shall be emphasising as strongly as we can that it doesn't matter who owns the company, who puts money into the company, that these problems are still going to have to be dealt with and we are still going to have to live in a very very competitive situation, both nationally and internationally. Government money will give no guarantee that customers will buy cars.

Kee: Thank you very much Mr Lowry.

RT: Approx. 4'00"

13. [programme continues]
CHRYSLER

More bad news for the car industry. Chrysler have announced that 4,000 workers at their Ryton plant in Coventry are to go on a three-day week from next week.

This follows a similar move just before Christmas for 5,000 workers at Chrysler's Linwood plant in Scotland.

RT: 16"

(Next item: Illegal immigrants)

14. 6 January 1975 17.50 Lead item   Jill
CARS/GREEN LIVE/WRIGHT FILM/SUPERS

TITLE FILM   British Leyland are re-opening their Cowley works, after only one
ULAY 20"   day of a shutdown in which 12,000 men were laid off.
AVAIL
               But there was bad news today for Chrysler workers. The

company are putting their Ryton Plant in Coventry on a 3-day week, from next week until the end of the month. Chrysler — who blame a 'depressed' market — had already announced a 3-day week for their Linwood Plant in Scotland. About 9,000 men will be affected at the two plants.

The decision to re-open Cowley was taken after talks between Leyland management and union officials. The unions agreed to recommend that the 250 engine tuners, whose strike led to the shutdown, should return to work pending talks on Wednesday.

Here's our industrial correspondent, Michael Green:

GREEN LIVE: SUPERS: MICHAEL GREEN INDUST. CORR.

British Leyland management are pretty optimistic that the tuners' strike will now be called off and that Cowley can get back to normal. These hopes are underlined by the news that the strikers' shop stewards are recommending a return. If the strike is called off there's no doubt that the political pressure generated by Mr Wilson's attack on 'unnecessary strikes' — and he singled out Cowley in particular — will have accelerated the settlement.

Apart from the current dispute, the industrial climate at Cowley has shown a marked improvement in recent months and the feeling in the industry is that the Prime Minister's remarks have blown a much needed breath of realism into negotiations.

The growing switch to short-time working in the industry as a whole, coupled with natural redundancy fears in some plants, have also made workers more reluctant to take precipitate action.

The future of British Leyland — which is still far from clear — was discussed this morning by Mr Benn the secretary for industry, and leaders of all the motor unions. Next Monday the unions will meet Sir Don Ryder, the Government's industrial adviser who's in charge of the Leyland investigation.

One of the union leaders at today's meeting — Mr Roy Sanderson of the electricians' union — suggested beforehand that a one year moratorium on strikes at Leyland would help.

But apparently he didn't press this idea during the meeting.

After the talks I asked Mr Bob Wright, an executive member of the engineering union, if Mr Benn had asked the unions to help in any particular ways:

FLUP SUPER BOB WRIGHT ENGIN- EERING UNION

Wright: Yes, he wants full participation in examining all the problems that exist, including the financial and company policy on investment and many other things and of course to secure the best possible industrial relations and worker participation.

Green: Its been suggested that industrial action be abandoned altogether for a period. Would you favour that?

Wright: No, we didn't fight the Industrial Relations Act to voluntarily ban strikes and we wouldn't do it in Leyland — and I don't think that [other] unions would sensibly try to do that. They'd only create a backlash from their own members.

RT: 44″ + 1'18″ 49″

15. [programme continues]   Mawer
SHORT TIME/LEWIS VTR/SUPER/REWRITE
One of the areas where workers knew some weeks ago they'd be on a three-day week is the west of Scotland. Chrysler's 7,000 employees at Linwood in Renfrewshire were told of the decision before Christmas. Martyn Lewis reports:

VTR UP   **Lewis:** It was an announcement in Scottish papers on New Year's
SUPER   Eve which broke the news to workers at Chrysler's Linwood Plant
MARTYN
LEWIS   — so while 2,000 men clocked in for work today 5,000 more were at
REPORTING   home — learning to live with a 4-day week.
FROM
SCOTLAND   **Workman:** I think it's ridiculous...

Lewis: But if there isn't work for them to do?

Workman: There must be work somewhere for them...It's no great shock to us. It's bad but it's no shock.

Lewis: How do you think things are going to develop here?

Workman: Badly.

Lewis: Do you think so?

Lewis: 9,000 reasons for the four-day week can be found in yards outside the factory and on the Glasgow dockside. For that's the number of unsold cars which Chrysler in Scotland alone have put into mothballs. Deliveries are at a fraction of the level a year ago — Chrysler see little point in churning out more products at a high price just to see them stand in the rain. Martyn Lewis, ITN, Glasgow.

RT: 13″ + 1'08″

(Next item: Share prices)

16. 6 January 1975 22.00 Lead item   Jill
LEONARD/COWLEY/SMITHFILM/SUPERS
Good evening.
    British Leyland are to re-open their Cowley works tomorrow, after only 1 day of a shutdown in which 12,000 men were laid off.
    The decision follows talks between Leyland management and union officials. Afterwards the union agreed to recommend the 250

engine tuners, whose strike led to the shutdown, to go back to work and await further talks. Leyland management are optimistic that the strike will be called off.

Neither side would say tonight whether there'd been any political pressure for a quick settlement, after Mr Wilson's warning about 'avoidable' disruption in the car industry. He'd singled out the Cowley plant for its record. Here's our industrial correspondent, Giles Smith.

TAKE GILES LIVE   The shop stewards' decision to recommend a return to work came after a secret three hour meeting tonight with full-time officials inside the Cowley plant. Earlier there'd been talks between British Leyland and engineering union officials which, it appears, were hastily arranged following the comments of the Prime Minister on Friday. I understand that national officials of the engineering union were in touch with Cowley over the weekend to see if a return to work could be negotiated at least until national talks had been held on Wednesday. After tonight's meeting AUEW Convenor, Doug Hobbs, had only a brief comment:

Hobbs: [transcription not available]

FILM SOF   **Smith:** Other officials refused to comment at all. These included district secretary, Mr Malcolm Young, and shop steward Mr Allan Thornett. He was the man at the centre of last summer's strike when Leyland sought to have him removed from union office because, they claimed, he was seeking deliberately to disrupt production.

Tonight, though, it's still far from certain peace has come to Cowley. Despite the Prime Minister's message, the political pressure, and the efforts behind the scenes of national officials, the decision is still up to the 250 tuners at their meeting early tomorrow morning. And even if they vote to return until Wednesday, the threat of further action remains if their claim isn't met at the national talks.

RT: Not available

17. [programme continues]   Jill
SANDY/BENN/WRIGHT FILM/SUPER/SLIDES
British Leyland's future was discussed earlier at a the meeting between the Industry Secretary, Mr Benn and leaders of all the car unions. One of the union leaders at the meeting – Mr Roy Sanderson of the electricians union – suggested that there should be a one-year strike 'truce' at Leyland. But he didn't press this idea during the talks. Our industrial correspondent, Michael Green, asked Mr Bob Wright, an executive member of the engineering

union, if Mr Benn had asked the unions to help in any particular way:

FLUP   [as at 17.50]

RT: 1'12"

18. [programme continues]   Jill
LEONARD/CHRYSLER/STILLFRAME/LEWIS VTR/SUPERS

Workers at Chrysler's Ryton plant in Coventry are to go onto a 3-day week, from next week until the end of the month.

Chrysler — who blame a 'seriously depressed' car market — had already announced a 3-day week for their Linwood Plant in Scotland.

About 9,000 men will be affected at the two plants.

Martyn Lewis reports:

VTR UP:
SUPER
MARTYN
LEWIS
REPORTING
FROM
SCOTLAND

Lewis: An announcement in Scottish papers last week put a date on something that Chrysler's Linwood workers already knew was coming — and today while 2,000 men clocked in to work as usual 5,000 of their colleagues were learning to live with a 3-day week.

Worker: It's ridiculous.

Lewis: How do you think things are going to develop here?

Worker: Badly.

Lewis: Do you think so?

Lewis: More than 9,000 reasons for the short-time working can be found in yards outside the factory and on the Glasgow dockside, for that's the number of unsold cars Chrysler has already put into mothballs in Scotland alone. Delivery's just a fraction [of] last year's level and Chrysler see little point in running the production line just to fill their stockyard. But it's not only cars that are affected. Sewing machines are yet another product for which demands are slack. 4,000 workers at Singer's Glasgow factory go on a 4-day week from this Friday. Most I talked to seemed to feel it was preferable to redundancy. 2 other firms here — Hoover and Honeywell — already had a good response to a plan for more than 2,000 voluntary redundancies at their Scottish factory.

SUPER:
HAMISH
GRANT
SCOTTISH
CBI

Spokesman: ...I think we've got to have an end to unofficial strikes — we've got to knuckle down and do a fair day's work for a fair day's pay. It seems to me that in the last year or two there's been too much pay for too little work and that situation's got to be reversed.

Lewis: But Scottish industry still has its bright side — shipbuilders Scott Lithgow still have bulging order books. John Brown Engineering is in an expansive mood and the coil country around

Aberdeen and Inverness is booming, with unemployment at a minimum. Honeywell even say that 40 firms have telephoned to offer jobs to their redundant workers. But for most of these jobs workers would have to move home — even learn new skills — And that's something which up to now many have been reluctant to do. Martyn Lewis, NAT, Clydeside.

RT: 16" + 2'03"

(Next item: Doctors' pay)

19. 7 January 1975 13.00 Item 3   Morrison
(Previous item: Bomb trial stopped after juror compromised)
COWLEY/HATFIELD FILM/SUPER

British Leyland's Cowley works has been getting back to full production this morning after the decision by 250 engine tuners to return to work pending further talks tomorrow.

A report on this marginally good news from Keith Hatfield.

FILM SUPER: The 12,000 Austin Morris men flooded back to work for this
HATFIELD   morning's shift. They'd been laid off for the day yesterday; whether
COWLEY   they stayed at work depended on a meeting of engine tuners. 250 men want to be regraded as skilled workers, rather than production workers. The management say that if they strike, the plant has to be shut down. The company just hasn't room to stockpile the cars. On the recommendation of their shop stewards, they decided to return to work, pending talks tomorrow between senior management, and national union officers in London. It was a two to one vote in favour.

Official: We are having a meeting 7.15 Thursday morning, if they haven't completed the....by then, we're back on the road, and we'll stay out indefinitely then.

Hatfield: There's no way back after that?

Official: There's no way back. The members are adamant. If the company don't concede on Wednesday, we're out and we stay out until they do.

Hatfield: But with the engine tuners back at work for the time being, the Austin Morris plant, singled out by the Prime Minister for particular criticism, was also back in full production. The cost of just one day's layoff is 1,200 cars worth £1 3/4 million. So it all hangs on tomorrow's meeting. The District Secretary of the Engineering Union has warned that if British Leyland want to continue producing cars, they must come up with what he calls positive proposals tomorrow. If they don't, he says that it's very likely that the 250 engine tuners will walk out again, and the whole Austin and Morris car plant could well be closed down by Thursday. KH, FR, in Cowley.

RT: 14″ + 1'39″

20. [programme continues with item on offers for Aston Martin, in receivership — not available]

RT: 30″ + 3'00″

(Next item: Interview with Neil Marten MP, on EEC)

21. 7 January 1975 17.50 Item 3   Maimane
(Previous item: CBI seeks meeting with Wilson on economic situation)
COWLEY/HATFIELD VTR/SUPER

The 250 car tuners at British Leyland's Cowley plant have called off their strike after only one day. But their engineering union District Secretary has warned that all 12,000 Cowley workers could be laid off again in a new strike, from Thursday, if British Leyland don't make 'positive proposals' at tomorrow's meeting with national officers.

The car tuners are demanding a higher staff grading which would in time mean better pay.

Keith Hatfield reports:

VTR SUPER: [the remainder of the report followed 13.00 down to '…£1 3/4 million pounds']

RT: 30″ + 1'09″

(Next item: Building)

22. 7 January 1975 22.00 Item 9   Maimane
(Previous item: CBI seeks meeting with Wilson on economic situation)
LEONARD/COWLEY/FILM/SUPER

The 250 engine tuners at British Leyland's Cowley plant returned to work after their one-day strike which caused 12,000 other car workers to be laid off. But the local union leaders warned that they could be out again on Thursday unless British Leyland made 'positive proposals' about their claim to be up-graded as skilled workers.

Keith Hatfield reports:

FILM SUPER: [remainder of item as at 17.50]

RT: 21″ + 1'10″

(Next item: Enoch Powell optimistic about future of Northern Ireland)

23. 8 January 1975 17.50 Item 13   Jamieson
Previous item: Fleet Street dispute)
COWLEY
        We've just heard that British Leyland have failed to reach an
agreement with union leaders on the claim by 250 engine tuners at
the Cowley factory to be reclassed as 'skilled' rather than
'production' workers.
        Earlier, union leaders said they'd go on strike tomorrow if their
demand wasn't met.

RT: 18″

(Last item)

24. 8 January 1975 22.00 Item 7   Purvis
(Previous item: NGA strike)
ANDREW/LEYLANDS/STILL
        It looks as though the strike which shut down British Leyland's
Cowley Plant on Monday could be back on again tomorrow.
        The management today refused to accept the claim by 250 engine
tuners that they should be graded as skilled workers and the men will
decide their next step tomorrow morning. If they do strike, twelve
thousand other Cowley workers could be laid off.

RT: 21″

(Next item: Fleet Street dispute)

25. 9 January 1975 13.00 Lead item   Sarah
COWLEY/SMITH FILM/SUPER/VTR INTVW/SUPER
        Now British Leyland, and this morning the 250 engine tuners at
British Leyland's Cowley plant voted by a narrow majority of 14 to
resume their strike over their claim to be reclassified as skilled
workers. They'd gone back to work for two days while new talks
with the management went on − but those talks, [the] engine-tuners
say, got them nowhere and now they're out again − within a week
of the Prime Minister's warning that what he called unnecessary
strikes were putting jobs in the car industry at risk. And indeed as a
result 12,000 other British Leyland car workers may have to be laid
off immediately. Our industrial correspondent, Giles Smith reports:

FLUP   The decision to continue the strike came after a 2-hour meeting of
the 250 tuners. The vote was close. 123 to 107, but the minority have
agreed to abide by the decision. One of the tuners explained:

Smith: How do you feel about the 12,000 other people who are now

SUPER GILES
SMITH
REPORTING

liable to be laid off?

Tuner: I feel sorry for them. I don't like [them losing] money, but we have a very just case. We are not engine tuners, we are motor mechanics.

Smith: And you don't fear more political intervention by people like Mr Wilson?

Tuner: I'd like Mr Wilson to intervene, and get the full facts of the case.

Smith: The men have decided not to meet again for another week, so the prospect of Cowley's 12,000 other workers being laid off immediately is now strong. This is something many of them appear to resent.

Smith: How do you feel about the decision of the men to continue?

Worker: We think it's disgusting.

Smith: So what do you think the attitude of the other 12,000 workers will be?

Worker: Well, I think they all feel the same as us. Because nobody can afford to lose money — in any case with the country in the state that it's in, the thing is, we're all going to be on short time anyway, aren't we? We've got our wage review coming up within the next month or so — well, of course, the thing is now it is jeopardising the whole thing. The offer now will be accepted because the men won't be able to afford, nobody will be able to afford, to be out of work.

Smith: So less than a week after the Prime Minister's intervention, this dispute is right back to square one. Mr Wilson calls this sort of stoppage 'manifestly avoidable'. After the events of the past few days, this particular strike is looking manifestly unavoidable. GS, FR, Cowley.

N/C

[Kee] Well, earlier this morning I spoke to Maurice Edelman, who's MP for Coventry North West — in the heart of the motor industry country...

VTR

Kee: After Mr Wilson's very sharp warning a few days ago, how do you account for this incredible hardness on the part of the men in the car industry, as exemplified here?

Edelman: Well, unhappily, it's a mood of confrontation, and that's been going on for a long time. Until and as long as the workers in the industry don't feel that they are participating fully, and as long as you don't have a discipline imposed by the trade unions themselves — so long are you going to have the sort of trouble which we're facing now.

Kee: But Mr Wilson's made it quite clear, that in British Leyland's case, which is going to have Government help, there was a limit to the amount of help that would be available in cases where you get stoppages of this sort. Now why is it that the men concerned don't seem to listen to this, or be affected by it?

Edelman: Well, I think the message hasn't been brought home in the first place.

Kee: He spoke very clearly, didn't he?

Edelman: He spoke clearly, and I think it's a proper beginning, but the essence of the message is that there is a world crisis in the motor industry. It derives, of course, in the first instance, from the rise in the price of oil and petrol, and the result has been that production has been reduced by 25%. In Europe alone there are 300,000 cars in stock, and I think that until the workers in the industry − and management too, for that matter, because they have at least as much blame as the workers. But until they realise that the crisis which threatens their companies, and threatens the name of very famous companies − until that time, you'll have this running sore inside the industry.

Kee: Do you think Mr Wilson might implement his threat to discontinue Government aid, for instance over the Cowley works?

Edelman: Well, I think there comes a moment when the taxpayers themselves will say 'Enough is enough', and we won't go on. After all, we've seen famous names like Rolls Royce, or in another sphere Burmah Oil, which overnight have become threatened, and have threatened to disappear. Now there does come a moment when the Government cannot pledge more public money, and unless it's going to be sure that eventually there's going to be an adequate return to the nation for the money that's put in.

Kee: But it seems as if in this case the men concerned think that as the Government is involving itself with the company, their jobs are safe, so they can afford to do this sort of thing. Now what can be said to them − or should Mr Wilson take action and make clear that their jobs would go by the board if they continue?

Edelman: Well, I think that Mr Wilson must come back to the argument, and he must give a proper shake-up to the management, and to workers in the industry, and explain to them the terrible danger which is threatening companies like Chryslers, Leyland and so on. But the danger isn't only local to Britain. It's a danger to the whole of the western motor industry, and what we are on the eve of now is really cut-throat competition between the motor companies of western Europe, which is going to be a direct threat, not only to the jobs of the few workers but indeed to the companies themselves in this country.

Kee: But then, will the danger ever seem to be there so long as the Government continues to bail out people like this?

Edelman: Well, I've always urged that any investment of public money should be accompanied by full public accountability, and again that goes not only for management but for workers as well. I believe that as far as the British motor industry is concerned, the ultimate logic is that there must be public ownership where you've got public money invested.

Kee: Public ownership didn't stop the miners' strike.

Edelman: No indeed. I don't believe that public ownership is going to be some sort of magic formula to end disputes inside the motor industry, but if you have public ownership with proper worker participation, and proper trade union involvement, then I think you can have a kind of internal discipline imposed by the trade unionists and the workers themselves, which you can't have in terms of the present confrontation between management and workers.

Kee: Mr Edelman, thank you.

RT: 36″ + 1'30″ + 9' + 3'55″

(Next item: Actors)

26. 9 January 1975 17.50 Lead item   Purvis
LEYLAND/TITLE ULAY/SMITH FILM

TITLE ULAY The car tuners at British Leyland's Cowley plant are back on strike, but this time the management are trying to keep car production going for as long as possible.

N/C While the 250 tuners were on strike on Monday, the whole Cowley labour force of 12,000 was laid off. This evening, the plant, at Oxford, is still open.

Our industrial correspondent, Giles Smith reports:

FILM The tuners' vote was close enough − 123 to 107 − to raise hopes that it might be reversed at a meeting in a week's time. For the time being, though, the minority have agreed to abide by the majority view. How do the tuners feel about other workers who may be laid off?
[follows 13.00 report down to ....'We're all going to be on short time anyway, aren't we?']

Smith: Although Leyland are clearly going to get tacit support from other unions for their decision to try and run the production lines without the tuners, there must be a limit to this, and the lay-offs could start by Monday. So, less than a week after the Prime Minister's intervention, this dispute is right back to square one. Disruption of the huge Cowley complex by this strike which Mr Wilson called manifestly avoidable, now seems manifestly unavoidable. GS, ITN, Cowley.

RT: 22″ + 1'32″

27. [programme continues]   PURVIS
LEYLAND LEADOUT
Overall car production in Britain last year was down twelve per cent on the previous year — according to figures from the Department of Industry.
        The decline was worst in the last five weeks of the year, when production was down fourteen per cent on the same period in 1973.

RT: 17″

(Next item: Doctors' pay)

28. 9 January 1975 22.00 Lead item   Purvis
ANDREW/LEYLAND/SMITH VTR
        Good evening.
        The British Leyland plant at Cowley in Oxford is open and making cars tonight, although the engine tuners there are back on strike.
        While the 250 tuners were on strike on Monday, the Cowley labour force of twelve thousand was laid off. But when the tuners walked out again this morning, British Leyland decided to keep production going as long as possible — which will probably be until the start of next week.
        From Cowley, our Industrial Correspondent, Giles Smith reports.

VTR UP The tuners' vote was close enough — 123 to 107 — to raise hopes it might be reversed at a meeting in a week's time. For the time being, though, the men who voted to return have agreed to bow to the majority view. But how do the tuners feel about the other workers who may be laid off?

FILM   [Tuner as at 13.00 and 17.50]

        [Smith] Leyland are clearly aware of the lack of support for the tuners among the rest of the Cowley workforce. Hence their decision not to start laying off 12,000 at once. They're relying on pressure on the strikers from other workers.

FILM: [Worker as at 13.00 and 17.50]
WOMEN

[Smith] Although Leyland are clearly going to get tacit support from other unions for their decision to try and run the production
VTR lines without the tuners, there must be a limit to this. If the tuners are solid in their strike the mass layoffs could start by Monday. And
VTR that would affect production of Leyland's brand-new car, code-named the ADO 71 which could be seen around Cowley today undergoing rigorous tests.

FILM: TO So less than a week after the Prime Minister's intervention, this
CAMERA dispute is right back to square one. Disruption of the huge Cowley complex by this strike which Mr Wilson called 'manifestly avoidable' now seems manifestly unavoidable. Not the most hopeful of scenarios for Lord Stokes' teach-in tomorrow with all his shop stewards at Longbridge. GS, NAT, Cowley.

RT: 29″ + 1′53″

29. [programme continues]   Purvis
REGGIE/CARS/VTR ULAY
VTR ULAY Overall car production in Britain last year was down twelve per cent on the previous year, according to figures from the Department of Industry. The worst period was the last five weeks of the year. There was an even bigger slump in sales of both British and foreign cars in this country — twenty five per cent down — which helps to explain the backlog at factories like Ford's Halewood Plant.

RT: 23″

(Next item: Doctors' pay)

30. 10 January 1975 13.00 Lead item   Mann/LP
CARS/THIRKETTLE FILM/SUPERS/SLIDE
In spite of the new strike by 250 engine tuners at British Leyland's Cowley plant, cars are still coming off the assembly line and output last night was down only twenty per cent.

When the tuners struck last Monday the other 12,000 workers were laid off. They went back to work on that occasion, but went back on strike again yesterday in support of a claim to be upgraded to skilled status.

This time no-one's been laid off. Production's going on without them and the other assembly line workers have been praised for their efforts by the British Leyland management.

The firm intends to keep up production if they can and the main workforce has been told to turn up for work as usual on Monday. So far, the tuners are not planning to meet again until next Thursday.

SLIDE

Meanwhile in Birmingham today 400 delegates from all the British Leyland factories are being given a state of the company report by the chairman, Lord Stokes. He'll also be outlining plans to improve relations between the shop floor and the office upstairs.

Strikes — avoidable or otherwise — are not the only problems facing the British car industry at the moment. Sales last year were down by nearly a quarter.

Joan Thirkettle reports.

SUPER:
THIRK

Last year the British motor industry sold a quarter of a million cars less than in 1973. The home market for new cars is falling fast, and some forecasters say it will be down from its peak of 1 ¾ million to about 1 million by the end of the year. The problems started in 1973. The price of steel rose dramatically, petrol and insurance went up, hire purchase payments were tightened, and strikes within the industry lost sales. The car makers are really worried by the forecasts for 1975. They can't afford to have cash tied up in large stocks of cars which they can't sell, so they're cutting down on production. Men are being laid off, others have been put on short time working. Some say the worst is yet to come, and there's been talk of car plants going to the wall.

SUPER:
BOYD

Boyd: I don't believe that you'll see any major factories closing down. There's always a tendency for the smaller people to have less chance of survival, so it's very much a question of the strong surviving in this particular market — there could be further short-time working and that depends very much on the level of industry. We at the present moment are finding it extremely difficult to forecast what the industry will be, and we are looking at it almost from a day to day, and certainly a week to week basis.

Thirkettle: Ironically, some foreign manufacturers, particularly the Japanese, did quite well in Britain last year. They were able to snap up the orders that British plants failed to meet, but the Japanese don't think this is quite fair. They say they produce cars which people want.

SUPER:
ELLISON

Ellison: I think this is possibly because we've had the cars which people want to buy. Now if you look round the British market for a small car to run about town in, you've got two options — you've got a Mini, which is basically about 15 years old, or you've got a

Hillman Imp, which is basically about 10 years old. If you want to buy a more modern conception of a small car, you've got to go to an importer. You've either got to go to Renault, or to Fiat, or perhaps to us. I think we've sold a lot of Cherries and Sunnies, which alone have accounted, those two series have accounted for about 67% of our sales last year. We have cars there which people want to buy.

Thirkettle: A backlog of unsold British cars is already building up. If sales are to improve, and present output to be maintained, the car industry has got to boost exports, cut back on foreign imports, and get the government to ease hire purchase terms. If not, cut backs in production, and massive layoffs are inevitable.

RT: 1'15" + 2'38"

(Next item: CBI visit to Prime Minister)

31. 10 January 1975 17.50 Lead item   Mawer
LEYLAND/TITLE SLIDES/STILLS/SISSONS VTR/LOWRY VTR/SUPERS
SLIDE: British Leyland's chairman, Lord Stokes has called for a fundamental change in the way the company's management and unions work together.

He was speaking in Birmingham to top management and 400 shop stewards from Leyland's 59 factories about the company's present position and prospects.

Lord Stokes echoed the Prime Minister's words last week about unnecessary strikes when he said that no Government would be willing to invest taxpayers' money in an undertaking that is clearly unprofitable.

POSS   And Leyland's finance director, Mr Alex Park, was even tougher.
STILL   He said: 'If we have no credibility the fundamental question we cannot avoid is 'Do we have any future at all?'

From Longbridge, here's our industrial editor, Peter Sissons.

VTR UP   This was only the second meeting of its kind ever held by British
PETER   Leyland. The first was last May, but since then much has changed,
SISSONS   and the whole tone of the approach today reflected a new urgency.
INDUSTR-   The entire board of British Leyland had their say, then answered
IAL EDITOR   questions, and by all accounts leant over backwards to impress on their shop stewards the gravity of the company's position, and the urgency of eliminating those manifestly avoidable interruptions to production. The theme of the conference, said Lord Stokes, was the need for fundamental changes in attitudes if British Leyland was to survive. The corporation's finance director, Mr Park, said the key to profitability was the number of units made and sold. Last year, he said, if production had been uninterrupted, an extra 200,000 units

could have been made, and figures for 1975, he added ominously, were a most worrying continuation of the 1974 performance. John Barber, the managing director, warned that only by stepping up performance could the company get through the economic recession without major redundancies. And British Leyland's industrial relations director, Mr Pat Lowry, said that 'As a corporation we are sick and tired of handling our industrial relations on a constant basis of potential confrontation'. Mr Lowry went on to make what he called a significant declaration of management philosophy, with the authority of the full board. He promised an open and participative style of management, if possible, more information for, and greater communication with employees, and what he called the highest possible level of managerial honesty. And he proposed a new British Leyland constituent assembly, which would be the basis of consultation between both sides on any appropriate matters.

RT: 39" + 1'48"

(Next item: CBI visit Prime Minister)

32. 10 January 1975 22.00 Lead item   Tristram
ANDREW/KEITH JOSEPH/SLIDES/ROLLER CAPTION/JULIAN
LIVE/ROLLERCAP
        Good evening.
SLIDE   The Conservative Shadow Home Secretary, Sir Keith Joseph, has called for a reversal of the Government's economic policies to prevent what he called an 'avalanche of bankruptcies and massive unemployment'.
        Speaking in Edinburgh tonight Sir Keith said the Government should cut their spending; raise taxes on drink and tobacco — but reduce taxes on companies; end price controls for private firms; and increase prices for nationalised industries.
        Our political editor says the speech may renew efforts to persuade Sir Keith to stand for the Conservative leadership.
        Sir Keith also criticised government borrowing at high rates of interest.
        Much of the money, he said, goes to subsidise wasteful use of labour.
ROLLER CAP   'to keep more men at Cowley than are needed to make cars, while Oxford buses are short of men; to keep the railways overmanned while London Transport is short of men; to give away public money to form Benn's people's communes'.
END CAP   Sir Keith said the tragic thing about this 'Santa Claus' policy was that healthy sectors of the economy were being 'bled white and

killed off to subsidise the unviable, the overmanned and undermanaged'.

Here's our political editor, Julian Haviland...

JULIAN LIVE   This is a blockbuster of a speech — packing a lot of dynamite against a number of beliefs which most people in this country have held for several years and would perhaps like to go on holding, if they can — including some beliefs by which the last Conservative Government lived.

(When Sir Keith laments that 'by trying to spend our way out of unemployment, we spend ourselves deeper into it', it isn't only Labour he's criticising. And when he sympathises with firms which invested because Governments urged them to invest, and which are now as a result burdened with debt, then it sounds like an apology for his own and his colleagues' past actions.)

But mostly he attacks. He attacks government for bailing out 'a few ailing giants' — he presumably has British Leyland in mind — and says there can be no substitute for restoring profitability.

SLIDE
ROLLER CAP   'Massive unselective bail-outs may on their own make matters worse', he says, 'because they spread the belief among unions that, however unrealistic the wage claims and restrictive the practicies, the

END CAP   firm cannot be bankrupted — the government safety net is spread below them'. They are wrong, he says, whatever the Government may believe, for if too many fail, the safety net will break and down we will all fall.

Sir Keith is going to be criticised — for example, for insisting that government spending should be cut but, like all politicians in opposition, not saying how. But he's not likely to be misrepresented or misunderstood, which he's complained of before: his message could hardly be plainer.

If this speech appeals to people beyond the Conservative party — as seems very likely — it may prove of major importance. And then

SLIDE   something else could happen. Sir Keith has ruled himself out of the coming contest for the Tory leadership. But his party are still looking desperately for someone who has something new to say and can say it clearly.

Sometimes the reluctant candidate is wanted most, and they may start asking themselves again whether they cannot persuade him.

RT: 1'02" + 2'09"

(Next item: Oil profits)

33. 10 January 1975 22.00 Item 6   Mawer
(Previous item: CBI visit Prime Minister)

REGGIE/LEYLAND/SISSONS VTR/SUPERS/SLIDE/STILL

The British Leyland chairman, Lord Stokes, has called for a fundamental change in the way the company's management and unions work together.

He was speaking in Birmingham to top management and 400 shop stewards from Leyland's 59 factories at a conference on the company's present position and its future.

Lord Stokes recalled the Prime Minister's comments about 'unnecessary strikes' when he said that no Government would be willing to invest taxpayers' money in an undertaking that's clearly unprofitable.

From Leyland's headquarters at Longbridge in Birmingham, our industrial editor, Peter Sissons, reports:

VTR UP   This was only the second meeting of its kind ever held by British Leyland. The first was last May, but since then, much has changed, and the whole tone of the approach today reflected a new urgency. The entire Board of British Leyland had their say, and then answered questions, and by all accounts leant over backwards to impress on their shop stewards the potential gravity of the company's position. The corporation's finance director, Mr Park, said the key to profitability was the number of cars made and sold. Last year, he said, if production had been uninterrupted, an extra 200,000 could have been made – and figures to date for 1975 showed, he added ominously, the most worrying continuation of the 1974 performance. And British Leyland's industrial relations director, Mr Pat Lowry, said that as a corporation 'We're sick and tired of handling our industrial relations on a constant basis of potential confrontation'. Mr Lowry went on to make what he called a significant declaration of management philosophy. He promised more information for, and greater communication with, workers, and what he called the highest possible level of managerial honesty, and he proposed a new joint assembly, which would be the basis of future consultation. I asked Mr Lowry about a warning from another director that only by stepping up performance could the company get through the economic recession without major redundancies. Was this a threat to the unions?

SUPER: PAT LOWRY INDUSTR-IAL RELATIONS DIRECTOR   **Lowry:** There were no threats made at today's meeting. We tried to be as factual about the present market situation as we can. We emphasised the fact that there is an intense competitive situation world-wide in the auto industry, that we in British Leyland have to recover our share of the market as quickly as we can, and that our ability to employ people in the numbers we employ them today depends on that. We can't forecast what way the market is going to go, and so, it was right and proper I think, that we warned people that we couldn't give guarantees, that there would not be redundancy, although we have assured people that so far as it's possible to do so, we would accommodate any problems initially with short time working.

Sissons: What sort of response are you looking for?

Lowry: We're looking for a collaborative response to these proposals. I've invited the shop stewards and staff representatives today to look at them as a serious, sincere attempt to avoid confrontation and to introduce a better degree of understanding at all levels within the company.

Sissons: Reaction from the 400 shop stewards was subdued, but not sceptical. There are clearly political differences with the management. Many want the company completely nationalised, with workers themselves on the main board, but there seems to have been a general welcome for the Board's frankness, and the proposals for closer consultation.

SUPER:
EDDIE
MCGARRY
JOINT
CHAIRMAN
BLMC SHOP
STEWARDS

McGarry: Oh I think it was a most useful conference — a far greater improvement on the last one, and it was a cool appraisal of [the] shrinking market, and indeed, there was no dramatics at all, as I said, a cool, calm appraisal of the present situation, and I think it's done quite a bit of good, because our people in British Leyland are thirsting for the truth of the situation.

RT: 30" + 3'26"

(Next item: Concorde sales prospects)

34. 11 January 1975 17.12 Item 5   Maimane
(Previous item: Clive Jenkins criticises Healey)
COWLEY

The 250 engine tuners at British Leyland's Cowley plant have asked the engineering union to make their strike official. The request will be considered on Tuesday. The men went on strike last Thursday in support of a claim for a higher staff grading.

RT: 14"

(Next item: Glasgow dustcart drivers' strike)

35. 11 January 1975 22.30 Item 5   Maimane
(Previous item: Clive Jenkins criticises Healey)
COWLEY
        [as at 17.12]
RT: 14"

(Next item: Glasgow dustcart drivers' strike)

36. 13 January 1975 17.50 Item 10   O'Connell
(Previous item: Glasgow dustcart drivers' strike)
CAR TROUBLES/SLIDE/STILL
            Now the troubles in the car industry.
SLIDE: Sir Don Ryder — the Prime Minister's industrial adviser — met
            leading trade unionists from British Leyland to discuss ways of
            improving industrial relations, and solving the company's money
            problems.
            The company say they are maintaining 80 per cent production
            despite the strike by 250 engine tuners, because of the continuing co-
            operation of other workers at the plant.
            At the Vauxhall plant at Ellesmere Port, in Cheshire, there was a
            strike in the body building section.
            The dispute is over a management scheme for transferring men to
            other work to prevent more than 400 workers being made
            redundant.
            Chrysler factories in Scotland and the Midlands have gone on a
            three-day week from today because of a cut-back in production.
RT: 42″
(Next item: Trial date set for IRA bombers)

37. 13 January 1975 22.00 Item 12   O'Connell
(Previous item: Prices)
ANDREW/CAR TROUBLES/SLIDES
            British Leyland have won an order worth £2 million to supply
            machine tools and other equipment to a car firm in South Korea.
            The equipment will be made at British Leyland's Cowley plant
            where production has been cut by 20% because of a strike by 250
            engine tuners.
SLIDE   During the day, Sir Don Ryder — who is heading the
            Government enquiry into the company's cash problems — had talks
            with trade union representatives from the firm. He said afterwards
            that they had reached total agreement on carrying out a 'speedy
            enquiry'. The Chrysler car company say their plants in the Midlands
            and Scotland are likely to remain on a three-day week until at least
            the end of the month because of falling sales.
RT: 40″
(Next item: EEC)

38. 16 January 1975 17.50 Item 6(i)   O'Connell
(Previous item: Daily Mirror dispute)

LEYLAND/TAYLOR FILM/SUPERS/PAGE TWO

The two hundred and fifty engine tuners at British Leyland's Cowley plant have voted to continue their week-old unofficial strike – at least until Monday.

FLUP

UP NATSOF
AT 14"
SUPER
MALCOLM
YOUNG

At a meeting this morning the men decided to wait for the outcome of talks between the union and the management tomorrow on their claim for an upgrading. Afterwards Derek Taylor spoke to union officials.

Young: There was a vote...

Taylor: Was it overwhelmingly in favour of staying out?

Young: Nearly overwhelming, there was only 7 votes against.

Young: That's all I have to say.

SUPER BOB
CLARK

Clark: It was spelt out by Malcolm Young conclusively that they should leave the decision to the membership, to the Executive Council, to do all the negotiating for them, which they've done.

Taylor: Do you expect that they will decide tomorrow to make the strike official?

Clark: No, I don't.

Taylor: Will you go back if they don't?

Clark: I think that something will transpire from those talks tomorrow.

Taylor: Do you think there'll be some sort of offer tomorrow?

Clark: Yes, I do, quite honestly. Let's be honest, I don't think they're going to call a meeting in London just for a waste of time, are they?

RT: 28" + 56"

(Next item: Search for kidnapped girl)

39. 16 January 1975 22.00 Item 5   O'Connell
(Previous item: NHS consultants' work-to-contract)
ANDREW/LEYLAND/FILM ULAY

The week-old strike by 250 engine tuners at British Leyland's Cowley plant is going to continue for the time being.

FLUP

The men have voted to wait for the outcome of talks tomorrow with the management, before deciding whether to go back to work.

The strikers – who are mainly members of the Engineers Union – want to be up-graded.

RT: 18"

40. [Programme continues with item on short-time working by Jaguar: not available]

RT: 37″

41. 17 January 1975 17.50 Item 6   Chamberlain
(Previous item: Prices)
CAR WORKERS/SLIDES
          More short-time working in the car industry.
SLIDE   Up to 6,000 car workers at Vauxhall's plant at Ellesmere Port in
VAUXHALL   Cheshire are to go on a three-day week from the end of January.
ELL. PORT
          Vauxhall said it was because of the general down-trend in car
          markets, but they said there would be no cut-backs at their factories
          at Luton and Dunstable.
SLIDE   In London, British Leyland are having informal talks with union
BR. LEYL. representatives of the 250 engine tuners who are on strike at Cowley.
MOTIF   They're asking to be upgraded.

RT: 30″

(Next item: Jack Jones on Social Contract)

42. 17 January 1975 22.00 Item 12   Martin
(Previous item: Healey)
SANDY/LEYLAND/SLIDE
SLIDE: BRIT. Talks between British Leyland and the engineering union to end the
LEY. MOTIF   engine tuners' strike at Cowley have broken up with no agreement
          after 11 hours.
          It's understood British Leyland is still refusing to agree to the
          tuners' demand for upgrading to skilled status.
          Union representatives will report to a mass meeting on Monday.

RT: 14″

43. [programme continues]
          [Item on Vauxhall short time working not available]

RT: 16″

(Next item: Closure of Imperial Typewriter factory)

44. 20 January 1975 13.00 Lead item   Mike
COWLEY/GREEN PHONO
          Now the decision by the 250 engine tuners at British Leyland's
          Cowley factory to stay on strike.
          A report from our industrial correspondent, Michael Green.

PHONO   …an hour and a quarter, and there was obviously a lot of opposition to the strike continuing. In the end the slim majority to stay out which we saw last week was maintained, but this time it was narrower — 91 to return to work, against 104 wanting to continue the strike — that's a majority of only 13. The question now is how soon British Leyland starts laying off thousands of other assembly workers. For a week now the company has been keeping production down to 80% of normal, and stockpiling cars for the tuners to attend to when the dispute is settled, but now they're running out of room to store these cars, and so it's expected production will have to stop shortly — probably by next Wednesday; when that happens, up to 12,000 workers will be made idle. Talks on Friday in London failed totally to solve the tuners' claim to be made skilled rather than production workers, and the men's leaders are obviously hoping that there'll be a change of heart by British Leyland. MG, FR, Cowley.

RT: 10″ + 59″

(Next item: Shooting and hijacking at Orly)

45. 20 January 1975 17.50 Item 4 Chamberlain
(Previous item: TUC-Labour Party meeting)
COWLEY/FILM U'LAY

UP FILM
ULAY
The strike of more than 200 engine tuners at British Leyland's plant at Cowley is to go on.

END ULAY
ON WORDS
20″ AVAIL
N/C
A meeting decided by only 13 votes to carry on the stoppage over a claim for up-grading. The men will meet again next Monday.
A British Leyland spokesman said later that tomorrow's day shift had been called in, in an attempt to keep production going. But our Industrial Correspondent says it's feared production will be halted by the end of the this week — which will mean laying off up to 12,000 workers.

RT: Approx. 31″

(Next item: Fleet Street dispute)

46. 20 January 1975 22.00 Item 4 Chamberlain
(Previous item: Shooting and hijacking at Orly)
LEONARD/COWLEY/GREEN FILM/SUPERS

SLIDE BL
FACTORY
The strike by more than 200 engine tuners at the British Leyland plant at Cowley is to go on.
The men voted by only 13 votes to carry on the stoppage over their claim to be up-graded. They won't meet again until next Monday.

RT: 15″

Next item: Banks reduce base rates)

47. 20 January 1975 22.00 Item 11
(Previous item: Frazer)
[Item about the Morgan Car Company. Headline was:

'A report on the car firm that hasn't changed its image and ISN'T going bust.'

Full text not available]

RT: 2'55"

(Next item: Herring)

48. 21 January 1975 17.50 Item 5   Chamberlain
(Previous item: Building workers' pay)
COWLEY/SLIDES

SLIDE: The two-week strike by more than 200 engine tuners at British
COWLEY   Leyland's plant at Cowley has been made official by the executive of
            the Engineering Union.

RT: 10"

(Next item: EEC referendum arrangements to be announced)

49. 21 January 1975 22.00 Item 4   Martin
(Previous item: Building workers' pay)
RB/COWLEY/SLIDES

SLIDE BRIT.   The strike by 250 engine tuners at British Leyland's Cowley plant,
LEY. MOTIF   has been made official by the executive of the Engineering Union.
SLIDE
SCANLON   The union's president, Mr Scanlon, said all the executive had
              supported the men's claim to be graded as skilled workers. The
              strikers will now be able to claim strike pay, backdated for 2 weeks.
                  British Leyland are still maintaining 80 per cent of normal
              production at Cowley, but are reviewing the situation daily.
SLIDE PRIOR   In the Commons, the Shadow Employment Secretary, Mr Prior,
              called the move by the Engineers' Union 'a total nonsense'. He said
              the nation is fed up with those who caused avoidable
              unemployment, and no-one was more angry than the other workers
              at Cowley who only wanted to get on with the job.

RT: 44"

(Next item: EEC referendum arrangements to be announced)

50. 22 January 1975 13.00 Item 5   Mike
(Previous item: Comprehensive schools)
ENGINE TUNERS/SLIDE

The two sides in the engine tuners' dispute at British Leyland's Cowley factory have been invited to talks at the Advisory, Conciliation and Arbitration Service to try and settle that hitherto intractable affair.

This morning's invitation is to the British Leyland management and the Amalgamated Union of Engineering Workers who yesterday made the tuners' strike official.

SLIDE: It was Mr Jack Jones, who as leader of the Transport and General Workers represents not only some of the engine tuners but — more important — thousands in British Leyland who stand to lose their jobs through the strike — who appealed to the Arbitration Service, as well as to the TUC General Secretary Mr Len Murray to do all in his power to end the dispute.

RT: 37″

(Next item: Cyprus takes refugee issue to UN)

51. 22 January 1975 17.50 Lead item   Mawer
COWLEY/SLIDE/STILLS

British Leyland and the engineering union have agreed to talks tomorrow at the Conciliation and Arbitration Service to try to solve
SLIDE   the Cowley engine-tuners' dispute. The transport workers' leader, Mr Jack Jones asked the service and the TUC general secretary Mr Len Murray to intervene.
SLIDE   The plant director, Mr John Symonds, said tonight in a letter to all employees that a further deterioration at Cowley 'would be calamitous, with the strongest likelihood of at best a major reduction in manufacturing and employment'.

RT: 29″

(Next item: Petrol)

52. 22 January 1975 22.00 Lead item   Mawer
ANDREW/CAR INDUSTRY/CAPTION/SMITH VTR

Good evening.

On the day it's been announced by the Government that new car sales were down by 25% on 1973, the director of British Leyland's Cowley plant has warned of a 'calamity' if the strike situation there gets worse.
CAPTION   Figures out today show that private car and van registrations dropped from 1,688,000 in 1973 to 1,273,000 last year. And all vehicle registrations were down nearly as much — by 20%. The warning to Leyland employees came in a letter from the plant director, Mr John Symonds, as the company and the engineering

union agreed to talks tomorrow at the Conciliation and Arbitration Service to try to solve the strike of engine tuners at Cowley.

Mr Symonds, said that the strike had meant that Cowley was failing to meet, what he called, its 'survival budget'.

He also gave a warning that a further deterioration would be 'calamitous, with the strongest likelihood of a major reduction in manufacturing and employment at Cowley'.

Here's our Industrial Correspondent, Giles Smith:

VTR UP   Mr Symonds' warning to Cowley's 12,000 workforce is easily the strongest since this dispute started a month ago. In using words like 'calamity' and 'major reduction in manufacturing and employment', he's got the full authority of Lord Stokes. The message is simple: if the dispute isn't sorted out very quickly indeed, the Government may well choose not to help the company in this difficult time. Meanwhile, the problems of the industry as a whole have been highlighted by today's figures showing tens of thousands of the industry's half a million workforce going on to short time, and unsold cars piling up in the car parks. All this in a year when Aston Martin went broke, British Leyland went to the Government for help, and the three Americans, Ford, Vauxhall and Chrysler warned that they might have to transfer operations to the continent.

MAP
(RYTON)
ULAY   Chrysler is probably the worst hit — with their Ryton plant nearby being the worst hit. Between Ryton and their Scottish plant at Linwood Chrysler have 10,000 men on a two day week. [sentence illegible] A thousand have lost their jobs altogether: there's short time working at the Stoke engine plant, and they've got 28,000 unsold cars waiting to go to the dealers. Vauxhall, the General

MAP   Motors subsidiary which should be getting 15 per cent of the market — but isn't — is not much better off. At their plants at Luton,
ULAY   Dunstable and Ellesmere Port, 6,000 of their workers will be going on a three-day week by the end of this week.

MAP (HALE
WOOD)   Of the Americans, Ford is the least affected. At Halewood and
ULAY   their other big plant at Dagenham, the company's sales of Capris and Cortinas continue to go well. There's no short time working yet —
TC4   though not much overtime either. Even they, however, have laid off
SUPER 6   1200 white collar workers. The company's main bright spot is the launch tomorrow of their brand new version of the Escort, a car they hope will help them weather the energy crisis| [pause]

MAP
(COWLEY) The problems of our biggest and only British owned company,
ULAY   Leyland, are well known — particularly at Cowley. Here the jobs of 12,000 are tonight in the balance — and Leyland are not just talking
VTR 5   about temporary lay-offs — until the tuners go back to work.
SUPER 5   Elsewhere, the company's 20,000 employees at Longbridge haven't

worked any overtime for months; and Jaguar, the export leader, have put 7,000 workers on a four-day week. All this is the most depressing scenario for an industry whose exports last year totalled nearly £2,000m — nearly a fifth of the country's overseas sales. If Britain is to make any sort of attempt at clearing the present staggering balance of payments problem, it can certainly not do without a healthy motor industry, with the investment, the manpower and the will to defy the energy crisis and step up sales.

RT: 2'01"

(Next item: Petrol)

53. 23 January 1975 17.50 Item 8   Mawer
(Previous item: Burmah oil sells stake in BP to Bank of England)
CAR TROUBLES/CAPTIONS/SLIDES

SLIDE   British Leyland's Chairman, Lord Stokes, has hinted at large-scale lay-offs and redundancies throughout the group.
            He says in the company's annual report that so far they've avoided this by not hiring more workers and reducing their
SLIDE/AP   worldwide labour force by 10,000 mainly through natural wastage. But, he warns: 'It is increasingly doubtful whether we can hold this position as the economic recession and an accelerating rate of inflation continue, but we have stepped up our cash conservation and profit improvement programmes in order to safeguard employment as far as is humanly possible.'
CAPTION   The report reveals that British Leyland's fortunes changed disastrously last year, mainly because of inflation. The Corporation made a loss after tax of £8.2 million, compared with a profit in 1973 of £26.7 million. But Lord Stokes said they hadn't yet needed to draw on the Government's £50 million loan.
            There's still no sign of a settlement of the Cowley dispute. The engineering union, representing most of the 250 engine tuners who're on strike, had talks with the Advisory, Conciliation and Arbitration Service. The Transport Workers' union and British Leyland management also met officials of the service. The ACAS are now trying to arrange another meeting with the engineering union tomorrow.

RT: 1'13"

54. [programme continues]
            [Item on Aston Martin's financial problems unavailable]
RT: 15"

(Next item: Weather)

55. 23 January 1975 22.00 Item 4   Mawer
(Previous item: Heath on Conservative leadership)
SANDY/CAR TROUBLES/TUNERS' TALKS/SLIDES/CAPTION

There's still no sign of a settlement in the strike of engine tuners at British Leyland's Cowley plant. The engineering union, which represents most of them, had talks with the Advisory Conciliation & Arbitration Service today and its officials are trying to arrange another meeting tomorrow.

SLIDE   British Leyland's Chairman, Lord Stokes, has hinted at possible large-scale lay-offs and redundancies throughout the company. In his annual report he says that so far these have been avoided by reducing the labour force by 10,000, mainly through natural wastage.

But he warned it was increasingly doubtful whether they could hold this position as the economic recession and inflation continued.

CAPTION   The report reveals that British Leyland's fortunes altered disastrously in 1974, primarily because of inflation. In 1973 the Corporation made a £26.7 million profit after tax, but last year the company made a loss of £8.2 million.

RT: 51″

56. [programme continues]   Mawer
ANDREW/CAR TROUBLES/ASTON MARTIN/VTR ULAY

There's been a reprieve for Aston Martin which shut down in December with debts of more than a million pounds.

ULAY UP   At a meeting at the company's headquarters called originally to put Aston Martin into liquidation, about 300 creditors decided to give the firm six months' grace. They were told that two groups — one British and the other foreign — were interested in putting money into the company.

Despite debts, it was estimated that if Aston Martin started trading again, it could make an annual profit of about £370,000 by selling five or six cars a week.

RT: 35″

(Next item: Tate and Lyle profits)

57. 24 January 1975 17.50 Item 2   O'Connell
(Previous item: Share prices boom)
CARS/SLIDE/STILL

The strike by 250 engine tuners at British Leyland's Cowley works will NOT be called off when the men meet on Monday.

STILL   Mr Reg Birch of the Engineering Union, said this after talks in

London today. He said now the strike is official, it's up to the union to make a decision. But he is prepared to attend further peace talks.

In Glasgow, Chrysler's have assured Scottish trade union leaders that the company do not intend to close their Linwood plant — which has been on short time working since Christmas.

RT: 28"

(Next item: Train crash at Watford)

58. 24 January 1975 22.00 Item 5   O'Connell
(Previous item: New York bomb)
SANDY/LEYLAND/STILL B&W/COVENTRY TAYLOR FILM/SUPERS

The strike by 250 engine tuners at British Leyland's Cowley works
STILL   will NOT be called off when the men meet on Monday according to Mr Reg Birch, of the Engineering Union. Mr Birch — who attended arbitration talks in London today — said any return to work would have to be a union decision. But he said he was prepared to attend further peace talks next week.

The Chrysler factories — which have been on short time since Christmas — are to go on to twoday working from the weekend because of a further cutback in production.

Workers at the Linwood factory in Scotland were assured today that their jobs are safe.

RT: 24"

(Next item: Soames opens EEC campaign)

59. 27 January 1975 13.00 Item 5   Morrison
(Previous item: Democracy in Portugal)
COWLEY

That now three-weeks old engine tuners' strike at British Leyland's Cowley plant. This morning they've voted to continue it for another week and meet again next Monday.

But their shop stewards and local union officials will be meeting British Leyland management this afternoon and the shop stewards say they'll call those on strike to an earlier meeting than next Monday if any peace moves emerge.

RT: 22"

(Next item: Government announces enquiry into school government)

60. 27 January 1975 17.50 Item 6   Tristram
(Previous item: Share prices boom)
COWLEY/ULAY

ULAY   Two hundred and fifty engine tuners at British Leyland's Cowley factory have voted overwhelmingly to continue their strike for another week.

After the meeting, union officials began talks at the offices of the Conciliation & Arbitration Service — and they say they'll call an earlier meeting of the strikers if there's a peace move.

The tuners want to be re-graded as skilled workers.

They've already been on strike for three weeks, and their stoppage could eventually threaten the jobs of 12,000 other workers.

But British Leyland say they have no plans for any lay-offs — as yet.

RT: 33″

(Next item: Vietnam fighting)

61. 27 January 1975 22.00 Item 14   Tristram
(Previous item: Tribune Group advocates more planning in industry)
SANDY/COWLEY/FILM ULAY/REWRITE

In the Cowley engine-tuners strike, the unions and British Leyland agreed tonight there should be an independent enquiry into the dispute.

The agreement came during talks at the offices of the Conciliation & Arbitration Service.

But there was NO agreement on the terms of reference for the enquiry — and a union spokesman couldn't indicate whether the 250 tuners would decide to go back to work. Earlier today, the tuners voted overwhelmingly to continue their 3-week-old strike for another week.

FILM ULAY
RT: 20″

They want to be re-graded as skilled workers, and their stoppage could eventually threaten the jobs of 12,000 other workers.

But British Leyland say they've NO plans yet for any lay-offs.

RT: 40″

(Next item: Pre-commercial trailer)

62. 30 January 1975 13.00 Item 3   Mike
(Previous item: Share prices boom)
COWLEY

The engine tuners at British Leyland's Cowley factory have been meeting this morning, but they did not decide to end their three-week old strike — as had been expected by some.

Instead they'll be meeting again next Monday after they've heard the result of further deliberations by the Advisory, Conciliation & Arbitration Service, who yesterday helped set up an independent enquiry into the tuners' demands for skilled status.

RT: 23"

(Next item: Report on Long Kesh prison)

63. 30 January 1975 17.50 Item 9   Chamberlain
(Previous item: Building societies criticise Government scheme for house
building and buying)

FILM ULAY   The 250 engine tuners at British Leyland's plant at Cowley have
UP   decided to continue their three-week strike.
              The men – who want to be upgraded – adjourned their meeting
              until Monday. Today's meeting had been brought forward to
              discuss the outcome of talks at the Advisory, Conciliation &
ULAY OUT   Arbitration Service.

RT: 17"

(Next item: Test match result)

64. 3 February 1975 13.00 Item 3   Mann
(Previous item: Conservative leadership contest)
MOTOR INDUSTRY/SMITH LIVESPOT/SLIDES
              Car tuners at British Leyland's Cowley plant will be back at work
              tomorrow morning after a strike lasting four weeks. They voted to
              return to work an hour ago after hearing a report on talks which
              have been going on between their union and British Leyland
              management under the auspices of the Advisory, Conciliation &
              Arbitration Service. Their claim to be upgraded to skilled status
              hasn't been granted yet but obviously they're hopeful.
              The return to work will enable British Leyland to return to full
              production at Cowley. Since the strike began British Leyland
              production had been cut by 20%.
              Meanwhile, there's more than a little confusion today about that
              trip to Japan planned by top executives of British Leyland.
              Yesterday, they said they were off to Tokyo to negotiate with the
              Jananese car firm Toyota about the possibility of selling British
              Leyland cars over there. But this morning there was a statement
              from Toyota which said negotiations had ended last November and
              had in fact been unsuccessful. Here's our Industrial Correspondent,
              Giles Smith:

SMITH   There's a certain amount of confusion at British Leyland this
LIVESPOT   morning – understandably – and part of it seems to concern the
              translation of the Japanese statement from Toyota. The first
              statement said Toyota would 'find it extremely difficult to re-open
              negotiations' which they said had broken down last year. But a

second translation which reached Leyland an hour ago said only that Toyota denied any deal had been reached, but didn't rule out further talks. At the moment Leyland officials are still trying to work out which translation is the right one — and Japanese being a difficult language, I understand that's quite a job. Well, in the face of all this Leyland are going ahead with their plan to send two of their top executives to Tokyo this week.

SLIDE
SLIDE
      Geoffrey Robinson, boss of Jaguar, will be leaving London in the next day or two, and Jack Reardon, Leyland's director of overseas operations, is already half way there on another overseas selling mission.

The company insist they've firm appointments to see Toyota executives before the end of the week. And as far as they're concerned a deal is still on the cards.

RT: 1'00" + 1'03"

(Next item: British Airways clerical workers' strike)

65. 3 February 1975 17.50 Lead item   Jill
COWLEY/FILM ULAY
TITLE U/LAY The Cowley engine-tuners have called off their 4-week-old strike —
15"   on union instructions.

The 250 men, who want to be upgraded, accepted the instruction, without a vote, at a mass meeting this morning.

They'll go back to work tomorrow, pending the outcome of the enquiry initiated by the Advisory, Conciliation & Arbitration Service.

British Leyland management say that production at Cowley has been maintained at about 80 per cent despite the strike.

RT: 30"

66. [programme continues with item on BLMC: not available]

RT: 38"

67. [programme continues with item on cars: not available]

RT: 31"

(Next item: Conservative leadership contest)

68. 3 February 1975 22.00 Item 3   Jill
(Previous item: Conservative leadership contest)

The Cowley engine-tuners have called off their 4-week-old strike — on instructions from their union. The 250 men — who want to be upgraded to skilled status — will be returning to work tomorrow. Meanwhile British Leyland executives are to go ahead with a visit to Japan, to discuss a major deal with Toyota despite reports that the Japanese car company broke off the talks at the end of last year.

And in another development at British Leyland today, shop stewards from more than 60 of their plants decided to press for TOTAL nationalisation of the company. They've formed a special committee to co-ordinate the nationalisation campaign.

Here's our industrial correspondent, Giles Smith:

SMITH
VTR:

It's been an extraordinary day for British Leyland. First their much heralded Japanese mission appeared to crumble about them; then out of the blue the Cowley tuners ended their strike; and finally they heard their unions were going for nothing less than outright nationalisation to get out of their present crisis. The 250 Cowley tuners' decision was probably the most remarkable. After eight mass meetings in which they've voted to stay out, today suddenly, without a vote and apparently without any discussion, they decided to go back pending the outcome of the independent enquiry into their claim for re-grading. Now Leyland can start getting the un-tuned cars they've had to store at a disused airfield back to the factory for tuning. Perhaps even more perplexing for Leyland, though, was the report that Toyota didn't want anything to do with their plan to step up sales in Japan, a plan widely publicised over the weekend. The company though said they thought Toyota's statement had been misunderstood in translation; and the plan to send overseas sales director, Jack Reardon and Jaguar boss, Geoffrey Robinson, to Tokyo, goes ahead regardless. Despite Toyota's discouraging noises, they insist they've an appointment with the Japanese car giant on Thursday. Finally, the new committee of Leyland shop stewards' decision to ask the Industry Minister, Mr Benn, to nationalise the company whatever Sir Don Ryder and his team recommend. Why did they think outright state ownership would help?

FILM ULAY
24"

ULAY OUT

SLIDE

SLIDE

PRES OF VTR
MCGARRY
RT: 17"

McGarry: Well, it'll do a power of good in so far as one of the main reasons for the intervention of the Government is in effect if the undertaking that it is intervening in is of importance to the economy, and if it is to provide and maintain full employment — that's reason enough for intervention.

Smith: Certainly a confusing day for our biggest and only British-owned motor group. Ironically it was the day in which it was announced that the industry's overall balance of exports over imports last year earned the country more than £1,000m. An

indication of just how important to the country the industry is going
to be.

RT: 38″ + 1'57″

(Next item: Guildford bombings hearing)

69. 14 February 1975 22.00 Item 19   Maimane
(Previous item: Enoch Powell comments on Thatcher's victory)
RB/LEYLAND BUSES FILM/SUPER
British Leyland have ridiculed a claim that the American Central
Intelligence Agency sabotaged a shipload of their buses being
exported to Cuba in 1964. An American newspaper columnist, Jack
Anderson, claims the ship carrying 42 buses was sunk in the Thames
in a collision arranged by the CIA because of America's trade
boycott of Cuba. The claim's also been denied by the Port of
London Authority, who held an enquiry into the collision.
Ray Moloney reports.

FILM SUPER: It's a great STORY...but the only HARD facts are that two ships
MOLONEY   did collide and that one of them — THIS one... the East German
REPORTS   Magdeburg — WAS carrying a cargo of forty-two buses for
Cuba...at a time when the United States was opposed to ANYONE
— but particularly its allies — trading with Cuba.

But...both the Magdeburg and the Japanese ship with which it
was in collision had pilots from Trinity House on board...and —
although it MIGHT be possible to find out in advance which pilots
would be on duty on a particular day — there is no way anyone could
discover which pilot would be on which ship...which means you'd
have to bribe dozens of pilots to be sure of getting a
collision...something which — to say the least — seems a little
unlikely.

Furthermore...the forty-two buses which went down were
replaced by another shipment within a few months without any
problem...and a further five hundred were subsequently shipped to
Cuba.

So...if the CIA didn't like buses for Cuba they were very selective
and their dislike seems to have died away very quickly.

After talking to Leylands...the Port of London Authority and the
Cuban Embassy this — if you'll forgive me — is one you could drive
a bus through.

RT: 27″ + 1'04″

(Next item: Report on children's reading skills)

70. 17 February 1975 22.00 Item 5   Jill
(Previous item: Minister announces increases in food prices)
GORDON/LEYLAND/FILM/SUPER

Six thousand workers at British Leyland's Jaguar plant, in Coventry, have been laid off indefinitely because of a strike at one of the company's factories.

The strike's held up the supply of car bodies to Coventry and production is almost at a standstill.

Meanwhile in London, Leyland's chairman, Lord Stokes, told shareholders at their annual meeting that some sort of partnership with the State was inevitable for large companies like theirs – and that the high rate of inflation meant finance was required on a 'massive scale, undreamed of in the past'.

Lord Stokes also said that he'd taken a voluntary cut of £17,000 in his salary – which last year was almost £48,000.

FLUP:
SUPER:
GILES SMITH
REPORT-
ING

Lord Stokes and his fellow directors faced a barrage of hostile questions from shareholders, many of whom have seen their shares falling in value more than 50p to just 7. Many were critical of the chairman himself, but the well publicised attempt by Mr Veal to have the board removed was ruled out of order because it hadn't been submitted as a motion at the right time, and when it came to a motion for re-electing three board members who, under the rules of the company, have to resubmit themselves to the shareholders, the disgruntled shareholders forced a vote. In the end, the three directors, who included Mr Pat Lowry, Leyland's labour relations director, were re-elected, but only after votes of about 3 to 1 among the 1,000 shareholders present. The meeting ended after two hours with a grim warning from Lord Stokes that this year was likely to be equally worrying as the last.

RT: 39" + 50"

(Next item: Scottish Daily News)

71. 18 February 1975 22.00 Item 8   Maimane
(Previous item: Report on children's reading skills)
REGGIE/FORDS/SUPERCAP

The Ford Motor Company has announced plans for short-time working at four of its plants. Over 11,000 employees – about 20% of their work force – will be affected – and tonight the unions threatened 'disruptive action' against the plan.

SUPER/CAP   Under it eight thousand workers at Dagenham in London will alternate between three and four day weeks. Workers at three other plants will go on a four-day week. But they'll all get 80% of their basic pay for the days they're not working.

RT: 28"

(Next item: London rates may rise 80%)

72. 24 February 1975 17.50 Item 8   Martin
(Previous item: Railway signalmen's strike)
CARS

The engineering union have told 600 toolmakers at British Leyland's West Bromwich plant to call off their strike, which has now put SLIDES SPLIT 12,000 people out of work. After discussions between union leader Mr Scanlon and British Leyland's Industrial relations manager, Mr Lowry, the union said there will be talks on the differential dispute when the men return to work.

The stoppage, now in its third week, has affected Jaguar and Mini production.

RT: 25"

(Next item: Miners' pay ballot)

73. 24 February 1975 22.00 Item 8   Smith
(Previous item: Labour Party and TUC Liaison Committee meet)
REGGIE/CARS

Vauxhall, the smallest of Britain's big four motor groups, has told its 26,000 workforce that 2,300 of them will have to be made redundant. Otherwise, the workers were told, short time working will have to continue indefinitely.

The redundancy warning mainly affects the company's plant at Ellesmere Port, in Cheshire, where they want 2,000 of the 10,000 workforce to volunteer for redundancy.

The Ellesmere Port factory, which makes Vivas and Magnums, is at present on a three-day week.

Our industrial correspondent points out that although all the country's major motor groups are working some sort of short time at the moment, Vauxhall is the first to say it wants to get rid of workers altogether.

But there's better news for Chrysler workers. 7,000 men on a three-day week at Linwood were told they could be back on a five-day week by April if the car market doesn't get any worse.

RT: 54"

(Next item: Cont.)

74. 25 February 1975 17.50 Item 9   Green
(Previous item: York)
CHRYSLER
        Now, the future of Chrysler's operations in Britain. A letter to the
Government from Chrysler in America says that the company's
subsidiary in this country has too much production capacity for the
size of the market.
        The letter, from the president of Chrysler in America, Mr
Riccardo, was published in a written Commons reply by the
Secretary for Industry, Mr Benn.
        Chrysler say they need the support of the British Government
and their employees here, if they're to remain a strong competitor in
the British market. The letter also asks for a cut in vehicle taxes and
relaxation of hire purchase restrictions.

RT: 34″

(Next item: President Ford and nomination of chief trade negotiator)

75. 26 February 1975 22.00 Item 7   MDW
(Previous item: BR signalmen's strike)
LEONARD/BAC/CARS
        [first part of item dealt with BAC strike]
        At the British Leyland car assembly plant at Longbridge,
Birmingham, another 1,000 men have been laid off because of a pay
strike by 600 toolmakers. British Leyland have now laid off 13,000
men, because of the three-week old dispute.

RT: Approx. 14″

(Next item: Lord Chalfont attacks extremist subversive elements)

76. 27 February 1975 17.50 Item 7   MDW
(Previous item: BR signalmen's strike)
LEYLAND/FORDS
        The strike of toolroom workers at the British Leyland plant at Castle
Bromwich in Birmingham is to continue for at least another
fortnight.
        The men voted to stay out in defiance of their union leaders, who
told them to return to work so that negotiations could be resumed.
        Already the 3-week old strike has led to more than 13,000 other
British Leyland workers being laid off, and another 1,200 will now
be made idle.
        And Fords announced this afternoon that short-time working at
their Dagenham plant will continue through April. This means
8,000 workers will now lose eleven working days in April, as well as

the six they will lose in March.

RT: 38″

(Next item: Motorways)

77. 6 March 1975 13.00 Item 9   Sarah
(Previous item: BR signalmen's strike)
VAUXHALL/LEWIS VTR/SUPER

Thousands of Midlands car workers converge on the House of Commons this afternoon to lobby MPs about the parlous state of the car industry. At the moment, 46,000 men in the industry are on short-time working.

One of the plants affected is Vauxhall at Ellesmere Port. The management there has taken the unusual step of actually asking 2,000 workers to volunteer for redundancy — with of course the appropriate redundancy payment — and they've had a somewhat surprising response, as Martyn Lewis reports.

VTR UP
SUPERS: M.L.
REPORTING

For six weeks now the production lines here at Vauxhall's Ellesmere Port factory have been shut down every Thursday and Friday, as the makers of the Viva range find themselves with a smaller and smaller share of a shrinking car market. And just 10 days ago, the management decided to go even further. They decided the time had come to get rid of 2,000 of their 9,000 hourly paid workers. As a first step they appealed for voluntary redundancies. But they certainly never anticipated the staggering reaction they would get. By midnight last night more than 2,500 men had joined the queue to quit, unable to resist the offer of golden handshakes ranging from a few hundred to £3,000 — much of it tax-free. The response prompted the local employment exchange to set up a special job shop for Vauxhall workers alone in one of the factory canteens. All day men taking time off from what work there is file through in the hunt for new jobs. And the jobs they now want could hardly be further removed from the production lines of the motor industry. (SOF)

SUPER: ALAN
DAVIES MGR
ELLESMERE
PORT
EMPLOY-
MENT
EXCHANGE

Davies: We have been very surprised at the sort of jobs these men are interested in. We originally thought they'd be most interested in the engineering industry, but in practice we found that they were looking for jobs... insurance salesmen, supermarket managers, firemen, so really we've had to get a load more jobs in. In these sort of occupations.

Lewis: Most seem undeterred that only 600 jobs are available locally for the two and a half thousand men who are leaving. Some plan to take a Government grant of up to £1,000 to help them move to another area where jobs are more plentiful. Others have settled for the retraining schemes, or are thoroughly disillusioned with the motor industry. Take Martin Hewings, 28, quality control inspector, 8 years with Vauxhalls:

Hewings: I feel as though I want to get out of the industry, start a new career.

Lewis: Isn't it quite difficult to make a break like this?

Hewings: No, not at all. It's such an individual area, isn't it?

Lewis: James Anderson, 42, production operator. 7 years with Vauxhalls. Have you found another job?

Anderson: No.

Lewis: Are you worried about that?

Anderson: Well, I hope to get a Government training course, as a heavygoods vehicle licence driver, you know.

Lewis: Steve Parsons, 19 years old, production operator. Just 9 months with Vauxhalls.

Parsons: No, I'm thinking of going back into office work, you know.

Lewis: Is the money as good?

Parsons: No, it's not very good at all.

Lewis: But you feel it's something you've got to do?

Parsons: Yes. I'm looking for a career now instead of money. I've been chasing the money, and so now it's career.

Voxpop: I'm prepared to take the money and take a chance. Otherwise, you're not going to get a job if you leave it till last, so the best thing to do is take the money while it's going and get out and look elsewhere. You don't want to be at the back of the cart when there's nothing else left.

Lewis: This redundancy scheme is costing Vauxhall more than £2 million. The only bright spot on the horizon is a strong hint that as a result the 7,000 men who remain may soon be able to return to a full 5-day week, but the unions fear that it's the thin end of the wedge — that could set the pattern for many more redundancies in the British car industry in the months to come. ML, FR, Ellesmere Port.

RT: 31″ + 3′38″

(Next item: Callaghan calls for revision of ECSC Treaty)

78. 6 March 1975 22.00 Lead item   Thompson
ANDREW/CARS/SISSONS LIVE/LEWIS VTR/SUPERS
Good evening.
British Leyland have warned the Government that up to 30,000 jobs could be permanently lost unless car sales are given a substantial boost in the Budget next month.
British Leyland currently employs 165 thousand workers, of whom 25 thousand are on short time.
Senior executives of the company have now told the Government's chief industrial adviser, Sir Don Ryder, who's investigating Leyland's affairs, that if the market for cars continues to decline, the company will be forced to shed between 20 and 30 thousand workers over the next 18 months.
Here's our industrial editor, Peter Sissons:

TAKE
SISSONS LIVE
British Leyland's blunt warning has been given privately to the Government by Leyland executives in the last few weeks. At the moment, there's no question of compulsory redundancies — last year Leyland shed 10,000 workers by voluntary means, and they're currently discussing with the unions further voluntary redundancies — 1,000 at Jaguars and 400 at their Coventry engine works.
But the feeling among the Company's top managers is that this may only be the beginning. Indeed, many of those I've talked to are becoming daily more despondent. They're waiting now for Mr Healey to make things different, for, on unchanged policies, and on present market trends, the Company's internal estimate is that they have between 20 and 30,000 employees too many. Ironically, figures out soon will show British Leyland with its highest market share for years — more than 40%. But it's a market which has shrunk by a quarter inside a year, and no recovery is in prospect.

VTR ULAY
Take the Morris Marina, manufactured at Cowley. The production lines are turning out 3,500 cars a week. Only 3,000 a week are being sold. On present demand, the company recognises that the present workforce can't be maintained indefinitely.
In Britain at the moment there are 400,000 new unsold cars, and massive competition among dealers to shift them, but still the stockpile grows. Accordingly British Leyland want the Chancellor in next month's Budget to relax hire purchase and make it easier and cheaper to buy cars. There's also a strong feeling that there should be import controls, particularly against the Japanese.
But amid this dismal scene, there was some brighter news tonight. 4,000 workers at Chrysler's Coventry plant, currently on a 3-day week, are to go back to 5-day working to meet an order for Iran. It could keep them busy until the end of the year, but there's no

similar relief for Chrysler's employees on short time in Scotland.

Chrysler continues, however, to have chronic problems, and last month their market share in Britain took a further fall. There now isn't a volume car manufacturer in Britain who isn't trying to shed labour, and there's growing evidence that the uncertain future for the industry is communicating itself to the men on the shop floor.

From Vauxhall's factory at Ellesmere Port in Cheshire, a report by Martyn Lewis:

SUPER:
MARTYN
LEWIS
REPORTING

[follows 13.00 item down to '…disillusioned with the motor industry', then jumping to the Vox Pop comment and Lewis' wind-up, concluding 'ML, NAT, Ellesmere Port'.]

RT: 45″ + 2'19″ + 2'15″

(Next item: Attack on Tel Aviv hotel)

79. 10 March 1975 22.00 Item 16   Sissons
(Previous item: Balance of payments figures)
REGGIE/LEYLAND/SLIDE

British Leyland will be given a big boost tomorrow by the latest figures for car registrations. They'll show that the Company captured nearly 45% of Britain's car market last month. They've only done that once before, four years ago.

For the first time ever, British Leyland models occupy the top three places among the best sellers. Top is the Mini, which, with more than 13 ½%, has achieved its biggest market share since records began 12 years ago.

RT: 27″

(Next item: Sport)

80. 12 March 1975 22.00 Item 10   Thompson
(Previous item: GIRO to offer loans and overdrafts)
REGGIE/LEYLAND/SLIDE

British Leyland is planning to cut back 1,200 jobs at its Austin-Morris assembly factory at Longbridge, Birmingham, over the next two months, mainly, it's hoped by voluntary redundancies.

A company spokesman said tonight the cuts would be chiefly among engine and gearbox workers. Talks are being held between management and the unions involved.

RT   19″

(Next item: Trudeau visits London)

81. 19 March 1975 17.50 Item 3   Jill

(Previous item: Glasgow dustcart drivers' strike)
LEYLAND
>British Leyland have cut back production at two of their component plants in Birmingham. This will mean short-time working for nearly 5,000 more men.
>Most of the men affected will be on a three-day week from Monday.
>This brings to 25,000 the number of Leyland workers soon to be on short-time — nearly a sixth of the company's entire labour force.

RT: 21″

(Next item: Labour MPs oppose British membership of EEC)

82. 19 March 1975 22.00 Item 2   Jill
(Previous item: Healey blames wage increases for inflation)
LEONARD/LEYLAND/AIRWAYS
>British Leyland are putting 5,000 of their workers at two component plants in Birmingham on short time. Most of the men will go on a three-day week from Monday.
>This will bring to 25,000 the number of Leyland workers on short time — [nearly] a sixth of the entire labour force.
>British Airways are to cut their staff by 13-hundred. 400 pilots are among the 'surplus' workers who'll be phased out by retirement or retraining for other jobs.

RT: 27″

(Next item: Glasgow dustcart drivers' strike)

83. 20 March 1975 17.50 Item 7   Jamieson
(Previous item: Unemployment figures)
LEYLAND
>820 more British Leyland car workers at Castle Bromwich, in Birmingham, are to begin a three-day week from next Monday. This brings the number of British Leyland men on a reduced working week to 30,000.

RT: 13″

(Next item: Report on Self-Employed)

84. 25 March 1975 22.00 Item 14   Lloyd Roberts
(Previous item: Agreement on Concorde services)
REGGIE/LEYLAND/GREEN FILM/SUPERS
>British Leyland have launched a new luxury model — the Austin Morris 18-22 range. The car could make a vital contribution to the company's survival at a time when [its] future is being carefully

examined.

British Leyland have already secured 50 million pounds worth of credit facilities from the Government and an official report on the company's future will probably be in Government hands by the end of the week.

Our industrial correspondent, Michael Green reports:

FLUP M.G. REPORTING

Employment prospects for thousands of workers, as well as millions of pounds of taxpayers' money, now backing British Leyland, are riding on this new model range. More than four years of development have gone into the wedge-shaped European-styled vehicle. Aerodynamic shape — a total departure for Leyland's volume cars — helps cut petrol consumption by a claimed 10% on the old 1800 model. Prices are around £2,100 for the basic model, up to more than £2,800 for the luxury Wolseley version. With all the major car makers except Chrysler recently pinning their faith on the new models in the fight to stay in business and preserve jobs, Leyland can't afford this car to fail. There are now 8,000 of these cars in the showrooms, and production initially will be around 1,600 a week. All sales this year will be for the home market in Britain, but from the end of the year, Leyland's plan a big European sales drive. Leyland's Austin Morris division is at last showing signs of shrugging off its troubled past, and much of the credit for this must go to the division's managing director, Mr Keith Hopkins. But does he think it's a good time to bring out a new luxury model?

KEITH HOPKINS MAN. DIR AUSTIN MORRIS

[Hopkins] The motor industry as a whole is in a depressed state, British Leyland and indeed Austin Morris are getting a larger share of the UK car market at the moment, and although there's a trend to buy smaller cars, more economical cars, this doesn't mean that everyone's going to buy smaller cars, and although you say it's a luxury car, a lot of people are prepared to buy luxury. It's at a very aggressive price level.

Green: Production is one thing, but sales another. Might there not be a danger to employment if sales don't go really well?

Hopkins: Well, that's always the danger of course. One can't forecast the market, but all the signs are that we have from the trade — the distributors and dealers, and indeed from the various members of the media who've seen it — is that it looks a winner.

RT:

26" + 2'02"

(Next item: National Front march held peacefully)

85. 27 March 1975 17.50 Item 8   Mawer

(Previous item: Liverpool, Glasgow dustcart drivers' strikes)
LEYLAND/SLIDE

> British Leyland have called for another 1,900 voluntary redundancies at their Longbridge plant. The company have already asked 1,200 workers there to accept redundancy.
>
> They say the latest redundancies are needed to prevent the plant going on a three-day week.
>
> The announcement came as the report of a secret three-month investigation into British Leyland was handed over to the Industry Secretary, Mr Benn, by the Government's chief industrial adviser, Sir Don Ryder.

SLIDE:

> The report's so confidential the Company hasn't seen a copy and the chairman, Lord Stokes, won't be getting one.
>
> It's believed to recommend an investment in British Leyland of up to 1,000 million pounds in the next ten years — most of which would have to come from the Government.

RT: 43″

(Next item: Stonehouse case)

86. 27 March 1975 22.13 Item 5   Mawer
(Previous item: Hue fighting)
LEONARD/LEYLAND/SISSONS VTR/SUPER

> British Leyland have called for another 5,900 voluntary redundancies at their largest plant — Longbridge, in Birmingham.
>
> They've already asked 1,200 workers there to accept redundancy terms.
>
> The company say the latest redundancies called for would save the assembly plant having to go on a three-day week.
>
> Earlier today, the report of a secret three-month investigation into British Leyland by Sir Don Ryder, the Government's chief industrial adviser, was handed over to the Industry Secretary, Mr. Benn.
>
> Here's Peter Sissons:

VTR UP:
SUPER:
PETER
SISSONS
INDUSTR-
IAL EDITOR

> Sir Don's report is one of Whitehall's most closely guarded secrets. The Board of British Leyland, including the Chairman, Lord Stokes, is totally in the dark about what it contains. They've opened every door and every book to Sir Don's team — the price they've had to pay for going to the Government for massive financial help last December. But they don't know what's going to happen to them.
>
> Nor, it seems, does Sir Don. He is after all the Government's chief industrial adviser, not hatchet man. He's presented Mr Tony Benn, the industry minister, with the most detailed appraisal of

Britain's biggest exporter ever undertaken. He's scrutinised its problems and suggested ways in which they may be overcome — some of them extremely radical. But the final decision what to do now rests with the Government. They've set no date for the publication of the report, nor promised that the whole of it will ever be made public at all.

What then, are the most important things Sir Don has done?

CAP Firstly, he's had to decide how much public money is needed. This depends of course on what size firm is envisaged. He's seen all the firm's future plans, the plans for new cars. If they're to go ahead at least £500 million pounds will be needed in the next 7 years. If not all of them are thought sound or necessary, then plant closures may be inevitable. So, on the money side, the Government has almost certainly been presented with a set of options.

CAP Secondly, he's had to look at the size and efficiency of the corporation. He will have noted the widespread overmanning which was part of the price Leyland had to pay for buying out the old piecework system.

CAP Thirdly, Sir Don will have examined the prospects for selling cars over the next few years. He's been told by Leyland Executives that on present trends the market will shrink so much that the corporation will not need up to 30,000 of its present workforce — that's getting on for 20% — within 18 months. [illegible] Mr Healey will help car sales in his budget next month.

Fourthly, the presence of a former managing director of Ford UK in Sir Don's team has led many Leyland executives to expect some radical proposals for the corporation's structure. The most widely tipped possibility is that Leyland will be divided into four new divisions. A single car division — incorporating the present Rover/Triumph, Jaguar, and Austin Morris concerns. A truck and bus division. An international division — embracing Leyland's overseas interests, and a fourth company to mop up special products such as construction equipment.

ULAY And then there's the overriding question of ownership — will Leyland be completely nationalised? Sir Don will almost certainly leave this to Mr Benn, while pointing out that the cheapest way to achieve public control would be to put in the money Leyland needs and create new shares which the Government would hold — rather than go to the additional expense of compensating existing shareholders.

One thing is beyond dispute, the entire future of this important company, and of the people who work for it, is now totally in the melting pot.

RT: 19″ + 2′47″

87. [Programme continues]   Mawer
ANDREW/VAUXHALL
        Two other car manufacturers have announced price increases
because of rising costs.
        Vauxhall models will go up immediately by 6.8%. This will
mean the Viva two-door will cost another £97 at £1,450.
        And some Volkswagen and Audi models will go up by 6.2 per
cent from the first of April.

RT: 20″

(Next item: US oil)

88. 29 March 13.10 Item 5   Mawer
(Previous item: London docks containerisation strike)
CHRYSLER/SLIDES/SUPERS
        The price of Chrysler cars is to go up by an average 6.8 per cent from
Tuesday. Commercial vehicles will cost 8.6 per cent more.
        In the past week, Ford, British Leyland, Vauxhall and
Volkswagen have all announced price increases of between five and
seven per cent.
SLIDE/SUPER   Chrysler's decision means a Hillman Imp will now cost an extra
SLIDE/SUPER   £85 at £1,179. And an Avenger De Luxe 1300 two-door, £98 more at
£1,443.

RT: 32″

(Next item: Liberal leader criticises Labour Party)

89. 4 April 1975 17.50 Item 9   Kallenbach
(Previous item: London containerisation strike)
VAUXHALL/VTR/ULAY
        At the Vauxhall car plant at Ellesmere Port in Merseyside over 200
VTR UP   shop stewards from the Amalgamated Union of Engineering
Workers took over the reception area and administrative offices in
protest against the company's plan to re-introduce short-time
working.
        A meeting with the management has been arranged for next
week. Before Easter when 2½ thousand men took voluntary
redundancy, the management had said short-time working would
come to an end.

RT: Approx. 25″

(Next item: Not available)

90. 4 April 1975 22.00 Item 10   Kallenbach
(Previous item: BR workshop supervisors work-to-rule)

REGGIE/VAUXHALL/LEWIS VTR/SUPERS

Workers at the Vauxhall plant at Ellesmere Port in Cheshire took over in a 'token' demonstration which lasted for more than eight hours. They were protesting against the company's plan to re-introduce short-time working.

Martyn Lewis reports:

VTR UP: It was a takeover designed with publicity rather than disruption in mind. At eight o'clock this morning, after a mass march among the production lines, 200 shop stewards moved in to commandeer all main gates, telephone and tannoy systems, and the administration offices with their reception area. The men were shocked and annoyed at Vauxhall's announcement that short-time working was to return to the Ellesmere plant. 8,000 workers here were only able to go back to a full five day week a fortnight ago, after two and a half thousand of their colleagues had responded to a management appeal for voluntary redundancies. Now it seems with sales folding and a stockpile of unsold Vauxhalls growing, those redundancies have not made as much difference to the situation as the men were led to believe they might.

SUPER JOHN   **Worker:** We was at a meeting for the JNC on wage negotiations
TURNBULL   yesterday, when this dropped like a bombshell. Works did not give
AUEW   the membership in the plant any warning whatsoever after coming
CONVENOR   off the short working week back onto a five day system.

Lewis: The shop stewards were careful not to let their takeover interfere with the running of the plant. Supplies flowed in as usual, and full production was maintained throughout the day. In the face of the token takeover, the management hastily promised that no final decision would be taken until after further talks with the unions next week. The plant manager, who called the news extremely regrettable, said tonight he found the men's reaction understandable. And there are indications that the decision to make the Viva production line bear the brunt of Vauxhall's cut-back programme was taken over his head. ML, NAT, Ellesmere Port in Cheshire.

RT: 14″ + 1′42″

(Next item: Annan Committee)

91. 9 April 1975 17.50 Sp   Maimane
(Previous item: Not available)
CHRYSLER/SPARE

The British division of Chrysler motors lost nearly £18 million last year. The company blames wage controls. The American-owned company say they intend to remain in business in Britain, and will NOT be asking the Government for any financial help.

RT: Approx. 17″

(Next item: Not available)

92. 9 April 1975 22.00 Item 8   Maimane
(Previous item: Petroleum & Submarine Pipelines Bill & North Sea oil)
ANDREW/CHRYSLER/LADBROKES

The British division of Chrysler motors lost nearly £18 million in six months last year. The company blamed inflation, wages and the decline in car sales. But it says it intends to remain in business in Britain, and will NOT be asking the Government for any financial help.

And the Pools firm Vernon's said tonight it had called off its £17 million bid to take over the betting firm of Ladbrokes.

RT: Not available

(Next item: Bomb injures 15 at Newry)

93. 11 April 1975 22.00 Item 11
(Previous item: Electricians' strike)
[item on Aston Martin not available]

RT: 27″

(Next item: Giles)

94. 18 April 1975 17.50 Item 4   Simons
(Previous item: Consultants' work-to-contract)
COWLEY/FILM ULAY

ULAY   A strike at British Leyland's car factory at Cowley has stopped production and put 6½ thousand men out of work.

The strike's by 2,700 back-up men who provide spare parts for the production line; they walked out when the firm said they would have to go on short-time working.

RT: 18″

(Next item: Retail prices)

95. 18 April 1975 22.00 Item 3   Simons
(Previous item: Consultants' work-to-contract)
REGGIE/COWLEY/ULAY/SLIDE

A strike at British Leylands car factory at Cowley has stopped production and put 6½ thousand men out of work.

ULAY UP: The strike is by 2,700 men who feed parts to the production line.
RT: 23" They walked out when the firm said some of them would have to go
on short time.
But there's better news from Vauxhall's at Ellesmere Port on
Merseyside. There 5,000 engineering workers have accepted the
latest pay offer of between £7 and £8 pounds a week.

RT: 28"

(Next item: Minimum Lending Rate)

96. 22 April 1975 22.00 Lead item   Sissons
ANDREW/LEYLAND/SISSIONS LIVE
Good evening.
British Leyland, Britain's biggest car firm, is now in such deep
financial trouble that it's unable to pay a £20 million tax bill which
fell due this month.
Customs and Excise have agreed to postpone payment of the
money indefinitely until the Government's plans for the company
are known. The rapid worsening of British Leyland's position was
discussed today by the Cabinet, and the report of Sir Don Ryder, the
Government's chief industrial adviser, is being rushed out and is
likely to be published on Thursday afternoon.
Here's our industrial editor, Peter Sissons:

LIVESPOT It's now clear that Sir Don Ryder and his team and the Government,
feel that urgent action is needed to keep British Leyland solvent. The
tax the company can't pay is the first really concrete sign of the scale
of its cash shortage. The £20 million is Leyland's second quarter
instalment of value added tax and the special 10% extra tax on new
cars. It's not unknown for the Customs and Excise to agree to
postpone payment if a company has pressing cash difficulties – but
there's been nothing on this scale before. If a company has the
money, the authorities generally do collect it. But the Excise seem to
have taken the view in this case that Leyland could only pay its tax
by defaulting on payments to its suppliers – something the
Government are not prepared to see happen. Tonight the company
would not comment on these matters, except to repeat they still had
cash available – £40 million of the £50 million guaranteed by the
Government last December. But it's the flow of cash which enables a
company to function, and Leyland have already approached the
Government for £50 million more, so it can continue to trade
normally.
What the company are desperately anxious to see is Sir Don
Ryder's report. From Lord Stokes downwards, they're totally
demoralised at the vacuum the company is now in, but they should

be put out of their misery soon. Sir Don's team will meet Mr Tony Benn tomorrow, and publish most of their findings, probably on Thursday afternoon. An expurgated version of the report is now at the printers. But not much has been left out — only those details which would give secrets to Leyland's competitors.

So what's in the report? Well, I gather it's dynamite. It sets out not a set of options, but a radical survival plan for British Leyland to go on. It says to the Government, if you want British Leyland to go on, the money must be found to make it as efficient as its international competitors. How much money? Something like £700 million over the next 3 or 4 years, is the likely estimate. The report will turn out to be scathingly critical of British Leyland as it stands, accusing the company of having more out-of-date equipment than any car firm in the world, of needless and wasteful duplication of components, and of actually competing with itself by having too many models.

The new organisation envisaged by Ryder will, it's likely, concentrate immediately on rationalising components, and cutting down the number of models. All this will not necessarily mean fewer jobs. Ryder wants Leyland to have the capacity to expand output when world trade picks up and to start hitting back at foreign manufacturers.

There's also a detailed critique of Leyland's present management structure, and proposals for a new one. These will, it's expected, leave a number of Leyland's top people no alternative but to resign.

At the moment, amazingly, they have no knowledge whatever of the changes proposed, but the agony should soon be over.

RT: 32″ + 2′45″

(Next item: Communists reject peace talks in Vietnam)

97. 23 April 1975 13.00 Item 5   Stevens
(Previous item: Northern Ireland bomb injures boy)
FORD SITUATION/HTV VTR

More trouble in the car industry — Fords this time, or should I say again?

Workers at the firm's plant in Swansea are staging a sit-in as a protest against the management and its methods — and this morning they locked out the members of that management.

Stuart Leyshon of HTV reports:

VTR UP   The sit-in began early this morning after the suspension of two men.
SUPER   Their workmates on the night shift decided to lock out the
STUART
LEYSHON   management and staff. Then hundreds of men on the morning shift
REPORTING   arrived, and blocked the main gates with lorries and other vehicles.

The sit-in could be a long one. The men are demanding the reinstatement of the suspended workers. As one of the leaders said this morning: 'We'll sit in until we get what we want', but he emphasised that it would be a peaceful occupation. As the works management held an emergency meeting in a hotel in Swansea city centre two miles away, preparations were being made for a long occupation of the plant, which manufactures axle and transmission units, and employs 2,200 men. Shop stewards were making arrangements with canteen staff for plentiful supplies of sandwiches and tea. Earlier today there'd been talk of an all-out strike at the plant, but the men decided against it because, as a shop steward said, it would put them in a bad light. The men's spokesman promised, 'We will try to conduct ourselves as responsible people.' Stewart Leyshon, for First Report, Cardiff.

RT: 17″ + 56″

(Next item: Authors demonstrate for Public Lending Right Bill)

98. 23 April 1975 17.50 Lead item   O'Connell
BRITISH LEYLAND/TITLE FILM/SLIDES/CAPTION
Dealings in British Leyland shares on the Stock Exchange have been suspended at the request of the directors. There's been mounting speculation that the Government are preparing [to] nationalise the company. The Industry Secretary, Mr Benn, is to make a statement in the Commons tomorrow about Government plans for British Leyland.

CAPTION   The directors did not consult the Government about suspending share dealings and the move came as share prices fell to 6¼ pence — one penny above their lowest recorded level. Five years ago they were at 91 pence.

SLIDE: The British Leyland chairman, Lord Stokes, went to a meeting with Mr Benn today and was shown for the first time a copy of the confidential Ryder report on the company.

SLIDE   The report is believed to be highly critical of British Leyland's top management and it's thought it will recommend a £1,000 million pound investment programme spread over the next five years.

RT: 55″

(Next item: Problems of steel industry)

99. 23 April 1975 22.00 Item 3   O'Connell
(Previous item: Labour Party NEC and TUC)
ANDREW/LEYLAND/SISSONS VTR/CAPTION/SLIDES/SUPERS
Now the problems of British Leyland.
Dealings in the Company's shares on the Stock Exchange have

been suspended, at British Leyland's request, as speculation mounts that the Government are preparing to nationalise the firm.

SLIDE: The Industry Secretary, Mr Benn, is to make a statement in the Commons tomorrow about plans for the company's future. And it's been widely predicted he will announce a massive injection of State aid.

CAPTION: British Leyland share prices have now fallen to 6¼ pence — one penny above their lowest recorded level. Five years ago they hit a peak of 91 pence.

Here's our industrial editor, Peter Sissons:

SISSONS VTR The suspension of Leyland's shares wasn't the only significant happening today. The company's chairman, Lord Stokes, and the managing director John Barber saw Sir Don Ryder's report for the first time when they called on the Industry Secretary Mr Benn. But they still weren't allowed to take a copy away with them. Lord Stokes went back to Leyland's London headquarters, cool, but very angry. One of his aides told me he was disgusted at the way the Government was treating the company and its 165,000 employees. Lord Stokes, however, was said to be in a fighting, rather than a resigning mood, wanting very much to be associated with British Leyland in the future. The future shape of the company will now almost certainly be known tomorrow, and the Government will become the majority shareholder, although part of the 700 million pounds needed for modernisation over the next 3 or 4 years will come from other sources, probably channelled through the organisation Finance for Industry. But there's the more immediate problem of the company's rapidly deteriorating cash position, and there's likely to be a quick Government injection of another £50 million. The company confirmed today that they were unable this month to pay £20 million pounds worth of taxes they owe the Customs and Excise, but they said they had agreed to make payment in full next month. In the meantime they stressed they were still able to pay their suppliers. There are 6,000 firms who supply British Leyland with parts, and probably a million workers who depend directly or indirectly on them for a livelihood. And that, in a nutshell, is the reason why any Government would have to keep the company solvent.

FLUP News of the latest developments was a hot topic for discussion at a meeting in Birmingham of shop stewards from all Britain's factories. They'd got together to voice concern at the growing recession in the industry. Ray Moloney asked the joint leader of British Leyland's shop stewards how he reacted to the suspension of dealings in the company's shares.

McGarry: Oh, it doesn't come as any surprise at the moment. Possibly in the present climate, probably they have more information than we have, possibly this is why Lord Stokes has been called to see Tony Benn, but I would imagine in this situation where we're in the twilight of changing over, I hope, from private enterprise to public ownership, that that would be the normal thing to do.

Moloney: What are you expecting from the Ryder report? It sounds pretty grim from what we hear.

McGarry: Well, it's grim, but not as grim as we knew it was going to be, and it would appear from what we have heard, whether it's true or not we shall have to wait and see what Ryder does say in his report, and I hope by the way that the men in...will be consulted on that, and that is the people who work in British Leyland. But it looks like he has hallmarked the representation that we made to him, on the, for example, the antiquated machinery that we've got — because nowhere, nowhere in this country are people required to work with such antiquated machinery as we are, and maintain the sort of high levels of production that we do with the machinery that we've got. Yes, we're in a bad position, but it's no worse than we expected when Ryder started investigating.

RT: 34″ + 3′05″

(Next item: Problems of the steel industry)

100. 24 April 1975 13.00 Item 3   Morrison
(Previous item: Unemployment figures)
LEYLAND

SLIDE   British Leyland. And it's going to be the Prime Minister himself who'll give details to the House of Commons this afternoon of the Government's rescue plans. This will coincide with the publication

SLIDE   of at least part of the report by Sir Don Ryder which the Government commissioned. Mr Tony Benn, Secretary for Industry, who will become virtual boss of the thing if forecasts of a massive state holding to come prove right, Mr Benn might have been expected to make the statement to the House, but it's thought he might have been subjected to some ribald questioning about possible contravention of the Common Market competition policy. Inappropriate in this solemn moment of truth for the British motor industry.

RT: 44″

(Previous item: Vietnam fighting

101. 24 April 1975 17.50 Lead item   Mawer
LEYLAND/SLIDE/SISSONS LIVE OB/VTR INTERVIEW/SUPERS
 The Government have accepted a report on British Leyland which
calls for a massive injection of public money and a major shakeup of
the car company's structure and top management.
 Announcing this to the Commons today, the Prime Minister said
the Government would take a majority shareholding in British
Leyland. Talks, he said, were already under way with the company
on implementing the report — compiled by a team of investigators

SLIDE under Sir Don Ryder, the Government's chief industrial adviser.
 An abridged version of the report just published recommends an
investment of £1,500 million over the next seven years. And
allowing for inflation that figure could become £2,800 million.
 And the report's believed to be highly critical of top
management, although these criticisms haven't been published.
SLIDE But a reshuffle's already under way. Lord Stokes, the present
chairman, is to become honorary president, and the managing
SLIDE director, Mr John Barber, is being sacked. He'll be replaced by Mr
SLIDE Alex Park, the present finance director.
SLIDE In his Commons statement, Mr Wilson said the vast amounts of
public money involved represented one of the greatest single
investments in manufacturing industry which any British
Government has contemplated. The Government, he said, hadn't
come lightly to their decision. But there was no doubt about the
importance of the company to the economy: as many as a million
jobs were at stake; and if the Government hadn't helped, British
Leyland would have had to go into liquidation or appoint a receiver.
 Our industrial editor, Peter Sissons, reports from the Department
of Trade.

TAKE   It's pretty clear there's never been anything like this report
SISSONS OB before. The sheer scale of the rescue operation, the vast sums
LIVE   involved, and the number of jobs at stake. Although itself British
Leyland employs 170,000 people, perhaps a million others, in 6,000
firms, depend directly or indirectly on the firm's survival, and the
fact is, as the Prime Minister said in the House of Commons, that
British Leyland, as it stands, faces within a matter of days going into
liquidation or appointing a Receiver. So what is in this long-awaited
report? Firstly, the Ryder team concluded that British Leyland
should be saved, but urgent action must be taken to remedy its
weaknesses and make it competitive in world markets. It must stop
making cars that compete directly with other British Leyland cars,
and reduce the number of different body shells, engines and
transmissions.

On finance, the report concludes that since British Leyland was formed in 1968, profits were wholly inadequate, and insufficient to maintain the business on a viable basis. Hence the enormous and quite unexpected sums to be raised. Half the 2,800 million pounds could be generated from within the company, but most of the rest would have to be found or underwritten by the Government, and £900 million of this within the next three years. An important condition of the injection of such money by the Government will be proven stagebystage progress towards reducing industrial disputes and improving productivity. A new joint structure of management and unions, meeting on councils and committees will be required to seek agreement on the action required, and make periodic reports to the Government, but there'll be no day to day Government intervention. The existing organisation of British Leyland comes in for heavy criticism and will be radically changed. And slimmed down. Instead of the existing structure with each individual company having its own management structure, British Leyland will become four new companies – Cars, Truck and Bus, Special Products and British Leyland International. Each a profit centre in its own right. Changes in top management, naming names as well as functions, are recommended in the full report, but details have been left out of the expurgated version published. I gather they're substantial and involve the promotion of some of the company's most promising second-line management. The report really does indict the way British Leyland has been managed. On industrial relations, the Ryder team says it does not subscribe to the view that the ills of British Leyland can be laid at the door of a strike-prone, work-shy labour force. In proposing progress towards the new system of industrial democracy, the report says 'Means must be found to take advantage of the ideas, enthusiasm and energy of British Leyland's workers in planning the future of the business on which their livelihood depends'. Well, with me right now is the man who presided over the team which wrote that report, Sir Don Ryder:

Sissons: Sir, Don, what would have happened if Leyland had been given no help?

Ryder: Well, there would have had to have been a vast slimming down, via possibly a receivership, with all the implications to the company, to the workforce, to the country, to our exports and our position overseas.

Sissons: And that would have happened soon?

Ryder: Well, there is of course, as everyone knows, a cash crisis.

Sissons: There are enormous sums involved, quite staggeringly enormous sums, difficult to comprehend, but we don't seem to have any guarantee that they will give us a viable car company.

Ryder: You don't have a guarantee, but the team, my colleagues and myself, are convinced that we have in British Leyland, potentially a great national asset, and if this vast investment programme is started right away, well then we have very great hopes that by 1982, we shall be in a leading world competitive position, and let us not forget that already British Leyland is our biggest exporter. I think last year it exported £500 million worth as well as all the employment, the companies depending on it, and of course if this disappeared, it would not only be a loss of £500 million of exports, but there would be a vast import bill because people would still want to go on motoring.

RT: 1'45" + 4'25"

102. [programme continues]   Mawer
COWLEY

At British Leyland's Austin Morris assembly plant at Cowley about 3,000 back-up workers ignored their shop stewards' recommendations and accepted the company's pay offer. The Cowley stewards wanted across-the-board increases instead of British Leyland's proposed graduated pay scales. Today's acceptance means all five groups of workers at Cowley have accepted graduated pay offers.

RT: 23"

103. [programme continues]
DAGENHAM/FILM U/LAY

At Ford's Dagenham plant about 1,200 workers have been laid off because of an industrial dispute.

MUTE ULAY   The men work in the body plant and were sent home after a walk-out by 18 door-hangers. Hundreds of unsold cars are already piling up at the plant because of a fall-off in sales. The workers are already on a three-day week and they have been told not to return to work until May 6th unless an early settlement is reached.

RT: 24"

(Next item: Unemployment figures)

104. 24 April 1975 22.00 Lead item   Mawer
REGGIE/LEYLAND INTRO/STILLS
        Good evening.

The Government are to take a controlling interest in British Leyland as part of a plan to inject a vast amount of public money into the car company, drastically reorganise its structure, and reshuffle the top management.

REPORT
STILL

The Prime Minister said in the Commons talks had already started with the company on implementing the proposals – which are in the report made by a team of investigators under Sir Don Ryder, the Government's chief industrial adviser. A censored version recommends an investment totalling £2,800 million over the next seven years. It suggested the Government should offer the 20,000 shareholders 10p a share to get a majority holding in the company, and that British Leyland should be reorganised into four separate divisions with better worker consultation.

Top management are believed to have been strongly criticised in parts of the report not published, and a reshuffle's under way.

SLIDE

Lord Stokes, the present chairman, who joined the Leyland Motor Company 45 years ago as an apprentice, is expected to be offered the presidency of the new company.

Mr Wilson paid tribute to his past achievements and said he hoped Lord Stokes would stay on as ambassador for the company overseas.

SLIDE:

Mr John Barber, the managing director for two years, who joined Leyland in 1967 as finance director was replaced today during a two and a half hour board meeting.

SLIDE:

The present finance director, Mr Alex Park, was appointed acting managing director. He's been with the company just over a year.

Here's our industrial editor, Peter Sissons:

SISSONS LIVE

Today it came out into the open: British Leyland would have been bankrupt within a few days unless the Government acted. But this is no rescue operation: it's an unprecedented, almost a revolutionary, root and branch restructuring of one of Britain's more important companies. The employer, indirectly, [of] a million workers in 6,000 other firms, who supply it.

CAP

To enable it to pay its bills, there'll be £50 million immediately, but over the next seven years, a staggering £2,800 million is required. This is the money Ryder estimates Leyland needs to make it strong and competitive. Half, hopefully, can be raised by the company itself, but most of the rest will come from the taxpayer.

I asked Sir Don Ryder, was there any guarantee that at the end of it all, Britain would have a viable car company.

TAKE RYDER
VTR

[Interview as at 17.50 from 'You don't have a guarantee.']

[Sissons] Sir Don makes a number of specific and far reaching proposals in his report.

CAP   That the company should produce new and fewer models; stop competing against itself, and cut down on the duplication of components.

CAP   That there should be a massive programme to modernise the factories. A large proportion of the machinery is old, outdated and inefficient.

CAP   And there's to be a completely new system of worker consultation – seen by the Government, certainly, as one of the most important recommendations. Ryder says his team does not subscribe to the view that all the ills of British Leyland can be laid at the door of a strike-prone and work-shy labour force. And the Prime Minister emphasised in the Commons that unless there were fewer stoppages and productivity, the Government would not feel obliged to keep putting money in. Accordingly, a new system of industrial participation has been recommended, with joint management/union councils and committees. I asked the Secretary of State for Industry, Mr Benn, if this meant the workers would have a management role in the company.

TAKE VTR   **Benn:** They put a proposal for a two-tier board, which goes a bit ahead of Government thinking, and so what is proposed at the moment [is] these joint councils. But the TUC of course have the object of joint control in the end, and the Government on its side will be making a major statement about industrial democracy. But it is part of our belief that people who invest their lives in industry are entitled to as much account as those who've invested their money, and that will be reflected, I hope, in the new arrangements.

Sissons: So you would hope that we move from the new arrangements to something which gives even greater control to the workers?

Benn: Well, I think the people who build the cars are the people in whom really we are investing. The old plant and equipment, much of it'll go out of the window. So we've got to build on our belief in them, and try to draw from new arrangements the best from them and for them. And that, applied throughout British industry on a similar ten-year strategy, and this country would be back on its feet again. This is the real problem of Britain we've been talking about today, and I think they've come out with a solution that is really going to make a big difference.

[Sissons] Then there are Ryder's proposals for the structure of the corporation itself.

CAP   Here's the organisational set-up as it is today, with a large central staff, as well as numerous divisions.

CAP

And here's the proposed Ryder setup. As expected, a smaller central staff, and four companies each a profit centre in its own right. Cars, Trucks and Bus, Special Products and International. The number of Managing Directors has been halved. Ryder's proposals for top management appointments haven't been published, and so

STILL

STILL

far only one has been made. John Barber, the present managing director of the entire corporation has resigned, and Alex Park, the former finance director, has been appointed acting managing director.

He will be Leyland's chief executive, responsible for implementing the Ryder plan. He's 49, a qualified engineer and accountant, but has only been in the motor industry since January 1974. He's highly regarded by his staff, who describe him as firm but fair. He said recently: 'I've always been regarded as a bloody rebel.' He enjoys, I gather, playing the electric organ at home.

STILL

Also still there are Lord Stokes — said to be on top of the world that so much money has been pumped in, and pleased with his new

STILL:

ambassadorial role. And I gather that Pat Lowry, the corporation's talented and patient director of personnel, is also firmly part of the new set-up.

But there are still big jobs to be filled, and there's likely to be no hurry about it. The managing director of the new Car division, for one — already being tipped here is the young managing director of Jaguar cars, Geoffrey Robinson. And the post of the non-executive chairman of the corporation? It's possible that Sir Don Ryder himself will take this on.

But at Leyland's London headquarters tonight there was a feeling of relief. Although Leyland's top managers have reservations about the report, there seems a determination to get on with the job and justify the hopes being pinned on them.

[Newsreader] British Leyland shop stewards on the whole welcomed the Government plans: some criticised the lack of detail about worker participation, and others were disappointed that it wasn't to be full nationalisation.

The joint chairman of the shop stewards, Mr Eddie McGarry was asked by Trevor MacDonald whether there will now be an improvement in industrial relations.

VTR UP

SUPER:

EDDIE

MCGARRY

BLMC SHOP

STEWARDS

McGarry: Well, our record of industrial relations if you investigate it, is not as bad as it's painted. For every strike we've had...

MacDonald: But it could be better?

McGarry: Of course it could be better, and I think it's going to be better, by the way, given the proper opportunity, given the right tools and equipment and machinery to do the job, in short— give us more elbow grease and we shall compete with the best in the world in the products that we produce.

MacDonald: Is that how you see the potential for British Leyland?

McGarry: Well, of course that's how we do, that's how we've always seen the potential for British Leyland, by the way. We have been hampered by antiquated machinery and insufficient supplies for longer than we care to remember, and no chance at all to compete with competitors abroad, foreign competitors. But if we're given the right sort of tools, the right sort of equipment, as this very welcome money by the public will give us the opportunity to justify their confidence in us, the Government's confidence in us, and our confidence in the future.

[Newsreader] In his statement to the Commons, the Prime Minister said the vast amounts of public money involved represented one of the greatest single investments in manufacturing industry that any British Government had ever contemplated.

The Government, he said, hadn't come lightly to their decision. Our political correspondent, David Rose, was in the House.

TAKE VTR   This may well have been one of the gravest statements ever made in the Commons, as Mr Edward Heath claimed. The trouble was that the Shadow Cabinet couldn't quite convince themselves, let alone anyone else, that they'd have done things differently. While some Conservative backbenchers were appalled at this lame goose getting over two and a half billion pounds, no member of the Shadow Cabinet seemed prepared to say they'd have let British Leyland go to the wall...and lose perhaps a million jobs in the process.

So criticism of Mr Wilson and this decision was not harsh. Only Mr Heath gave a stern lecture on the need for a reappraisal of management and union attitudes. The former leader of the Conservative Party warned bleakly: 'More public ownership will not solve anything'.

The Prime Minister answered Mr Heath pleasantly, agreeing with much of what he said, which is more than could be said of his answer to Mr Michael Heseltine, the Shadow spokesman for Industry. Mr Heseltine had seen some ulterior motive in Mr Wilson's making the statement rather than Mr Benn.

Mr Wilson was at his most crushing. 'You trivialise everything', he told Mr Heseltine, and rather unkindly, Mr Wilson suggested that Mr Whitelaw, in charge in the absence of Mrs Thatcher, should have recognised that answering for the opposition today was not a job for a lad.

Labour MPs laughed, Tories jeered, and members of the public in the Gallery who might have thought they were witnessing a historic occasion, looked disappointed.

RT: 1'10" + 6'13" + 1'13" + 1'37"

(Next item: Unemployment figures)

105. 25 April 1975 13.00 Item 5
(Previous item: EEC referendum arrangements)
BRITISH LEYLAND/SMITH FILM

After yesterday's major Government programme to save British Leyland, our biggest motor group, Leyland shares were quoted again on the Stock Exchange this morning, after being suspended since Wednesday. The shares have advanced to 9¼p −¾p below the Government offer of 10p.

FLUP   The company's new acting managing director, Mr Alex Park, was at Leyland headquarters in London bright and early, and later in the morning emerged briefly to talk to reporters including our industrial correspondent Giles Smith, who asked him if he had any plans to meet union leaders.

SOF UP   **Park:** Not today. We're...Life is a bit hectic for me today, and I'm going to need the weekend to sort myself out.

Smith: How do you feel about the proposal that workers' representatives could be on the board of the various companies?

Park: What's wrong with that?

Smith: You'd like that?

Park: Yes.

Smith: Do you think that workers should have a say in the models you produce? The way finances are organised?

Park: It's far more than that. They also have to accept the responsibility and share the responsibilities that go with it.

Smith: They've often been accused in the past of not doing so.

Park: Well, to me, performing is now a dual role. It's as much theirs as ours.

Smith: How do you feel about...Mr Barber?

Park: Very sad. Mr Barber was the man who introduced me to the company.

Smith: How do you feel about the new position of Lord Stokes?

Park: Well, I've been trying to find out about it this morning myself. So until I can understand it, I really couldn't speak too much about it because I really don't know a lot about it yet.

Smith: And what do you feel about [the chairmanship being] non-executive?

Park: Well, I don't know that that is so. Or anybody else. One has to have a chairman. Some companies have executive chairmen. Some people have non-executive chairmen.

Smith: Do you feel you're in charge of British Leyland as of this moment?

Park: I'm gradually beginning to feel that, if one can allow me the time to just find my feet.

Smith: Do you feel now that there is a real chance that this company will go forward...

Park: Well, let me answer this, that I came to this company 15 months ago, and if I didn't think there was a future for British Leyland, I would never have come.

Smith: Is that future brighter after the Ryder report?

Park: Yes.

Smith: So things were really wrong?

Park: Well, some things were wrong, yes.

Smith: And can they be put right to make the whole thing viable?

Park: I think so, yes. I believe so. But cooperation is a very important thing, and cooperation means you share responsibility and duties.

Smith: You'll get that cooperation?

Park: I think we will. If we play fair.

RT: 22″ + 2'04″

(Next item: Report on Portuguese elections)

106. 25 April 1975 17.50 Item 2   Mawer
(Previous item: Mr Benn carpets head of British Steel)
LEYLAND/PARK FILM/SUPER

British Leyland shares were quoted again on the Stock Exchange following their suspension on Wednesday at 6¼ pence.

At the close they stood at 9 pence.

FLUP   The company's new acting managing director, Mr Alex Park, was at British Leyland headquarters in London early today. Later he emerged to talk to reporters and our industrial correspondent, Giles Smith, asked him if he had any plans to meet British Leyland union leaders.

SOF UP
SUPER ALEX PARK
ACTING MANAGING DIRECTOR B.L.

[edited version of 13.00 runs down to '...it's as much theirs as ours', and then resumes at Smith's question 'Do you feel you're in charge of British Leyland at the moment?' and runs to 'Some things were wrong, yes'.]

RT: 13″ + 1′12″

(Next item: Problems of the steel industry)

107. 25 April 1975 22.00 Item 5   Mawer
(Previous item: Pensions)
REGGIE/LEYLAND/SMITH FILM/SUPER

After the Government's decision to rescue British Leyland the company's shares, which have been suspended since Wednesday, were quoted again on the Stock Exchange.

They rose 2¼ pence to close at nine pence − a penny less than the price per share the Government propose to offer shareholders.

The new managing director, Mr Alex Park − said he was staggered at his appointment after only 15 months with the firm.

FLUP

He was at British Leyland's London headquarters early today, studying the Ryder Report on the company. He talked − briefly with reporters and our industrial correspondent, Giles Smith, asked him if he had any immediate plans to talk to the unions:

SOF UP
SUPER

[edited text of interview as at 17.50]

RT: 23 + 1′12″

(Next item: Stock exchange)

108. 30 April 1975 22.14 Item 7
(Previous item: EEC)
AG/LEYLAND

[Item on strike by clerical workers at Dunlops, with knock-on effects for BLMC factories, not available.]

RT: 1′19″

(Next item: Seaman)

3: THE NATIONAL GRAPHICAL ASSOCIATION – NEWSPAPER PUBLISHERS' ASSOCIATION DISPUTE; DAILY MIRROR/NATSOPA DISPUTE

1. 8 January 1975 17.50 Item 9   Purvis
(Previous item: TUC statement in advance of NEDC meeting)
NEWSPAPERS
> One of the printing unions, the National Graphical Association, are to resume industrial action against the national and evening papers printed in London.
> The timing of the action is to be left to the union's negotiators, whose pay talks with the Newspaper Publishers broke down yesterday. Before Christmas, action by the union forced the papers on some days to print only one London edition.

RT: 22"
(Last item)

2. 8 January 1975 22.00 Item 5   Purvis
(Previous item: Cowley tuners' strike)
REGGIE/NEWSPAPERS/SLIDE
> There's more industrial trouble ahead in Fleet Street. One of the printing unions, the National Graphical Association, is to resume the industrial action which forced national and London evening papers to print only one edition on some nights last month.
> The union's negotiators, whose pay talks with the publishers broke down yesterday, will decide when it starts.

RT: 21"
(Next item: TUC statement in advance of NEDC meeting)

3. 14 January 1975 22.00 Item 13   Tristram
(Previous item: Parliament)
LEONARD/NEWSPAPERS/SLIDE
> The Newspaper Publishers' Association say they'll resist industrial action threatened by 7,000 workers in the National Graphical Association.
> The dispute could affect most national papers printed in London and Manchester – except those in the Daily Mirror Group.
> After talks broke down today, the union said they'd NO choice but to resume action to restore their pay margins.

RT: 19"
(Next item: Wash)

4. 15 January 1975 13.00 Item 7B   Mann
(Previous item: Scottish ambulance controllers' strike)
INDUSTRIAL WRAP
> And trouble still simmering in the newspaper industry in London:

The Daily Telegraph lost 300,000 copies this morning because members of the National Graphical Association – the men who work in the newspaper machine rooms, at a crucial moment stopped work in order to hold a meeting about claims for more money. They say that after the breakdown of talks with the Newspaper Publishers' Association last night, they now have no alternative but to take what is quaintly called industrial action of this sort.

RT: Approx. 28″

(Next item: Holiday)

5. 15 January 1975 22.00 Lead item   Black
ANDREW/NEWSPAPERS/GREEN INTERVIEW FILM/SUPERCAPS
Good Evening.
      There's a risk tonight of a new shut down in Fleet Street from Saturday morning – and perhaps for some time to come.
SLIDE
(GOODMAN)   Lord Goodman, chairman of the Newspaper Publishers' Association, has warned that if the National Graphical Association, the compositors' union, has not given an undertaking that industrial disruption will cease by nine o'clock on Friday, then the publishers will sack all 7,000 members of the union.
      Disruption today cost the Daily Telegraph and the Sun 360,000 and 170,000 copies respectively.
      The dispute is over the erosion of a traditional wage differential between the NGA and the other five print unions. But the Daily Mirror and other IPC newspapers are NOT affected by tonight's moves, because the group is no longer a member of the Publishers' Association. Our industrial correspondent, Michael Green, asked Lord Goodman if he thought that tonight's threat was really necessary:

FLUP CAP   **Goodman:** The decision we've made is unavoidable. The action
GOODMAN   taken by the [NGA], if it's allowed to continue, will bleed the industry white, because they are systematically progressively disrupting individual newspapers each night in a most damaging fashion so as to cause appalling losses, and if this continues the industry will be totally ruined, there's no argument about it. Hence we must take protective action to save the industry.

Green: Isn't there a danger though that if the newspapers shut down some that are in a precarious financial situation might not be able to reopen?

Goodman: There's very certainly such a danger, yes. But it's not a danger we can do anything to avert except with the step [which] with the greatest reluctance and the utmost concern and anxiety we've been compelled to take.

Green: In a nutshell, why has such a dispute over such a small amount [as] 1%, escalated into such a situation?

Goodman: Well, to put it in a nutshell, I think one would require to occupy most of your evening programme to explain it, but trying to put it in a nutshell it's this: it is not a dispute about one third of 1% in the sense that we are reluctant to pay that amount of money which is something less than 40p per man for 200 or 300 men. It's not that at all. It is that we are not able to offer the NGA a better contract than what's been offered to the other 5 unions for reasons which are entirely beyond our control, for which we had no responsibility. Since the NGA were not members of the TUC the other unions would not negotiate with them simultaneously, and the five of them did among themselves. In the result, when we arrived at an agreement with the other 5 unions, that agreement was the one that we had to offer to the NGA, and that they find unacceptable because it erodes a differential by 40p or something less, or by this famous one third of 1%, and that is the situation in a nutshell.

RT: 52″ + 2′40″
(Next item: IRA truce)

6. 16 January 1975 17.50 Item 4
(Previous item: Mrs Barbara Stonehouse arrives back from Australia)
NEWSPAPERS/SLIDE/BONFIELD FILM

National newspapers have agreed to extend their deadline to dismiss 7,000 printers tomorrow morning.

The agreement was made in the High Court where the printers' union, the National Graphical Association, had asked for an injunction against the Newspaper Publishers' Association. They had threatened to sack the men if they didn't call off action disrupting production.

The union had already rejected the ultimatum to end the dispute by nine tomorrow morning. The deadline is to be extended until after another sitting of the High Court tomorrow.

SLIDES: Both the Employment Secretary, Mr Foot, and his opposition counterpart, Mr Prior, have appealed to the union to call off their action. Mr Foot said newspapers faced a desperate situation.

The proprietors issued their ultimatum after the Daily Telegraph and Sun had together lost 500,000 copies yesterday through the dispute. The Telegraph lost another 350,000 copies today.

The union are demanding up to 40p a week to maintain pay differentials with five other Fleet Street unions. The proprietors say if they agreed it would mean new pay negotiations with the other unions. Angela Lambert asked the union's general secretary if he accepted this argument:

Bonfield: Well, it doesn't necessarily follow. We've asked for an adjustment of this differential, because we had a specific undertaking from the NPA last year that this differential would be preserved.

FILM SUPER:
JOHN
BONFIELD
NGA
GENERAL
SECRETARY

Lambert: The NPA have threatened what amounts to a lockout. Do you think they'll carry out this threat?

Bonfield: I wouldn't like to commit myself as to whether they'll carry it out initially. I know there's a good deal of confusion and division on their side about this, so it is a question of whether they will, but I wouldn't look further than that. But certainly they won't carry it out for very long, as we experienced three years ago when the same issue came up. Unfortunately, you can only make sense, or get sense out of some of these people when there is a dispute. This is the tragedy of this thing.

RT: 1'06" + 57"

(Next item: Daily Mirror dispute)

7. [programme continues]   Maimane
MIRROR LEADOUT

The Daily Mirror, who do not belong to the NPA, lost over a million copies of today's issue because of a different dispute, this time with NATSOPA, another of the Fleet Street unions. The management have warned that there'll be 'widespread compulsory redundancy' if the union continue to demand that staff who leave are automatically replaced.

The management say the newspaper industry is grossly overstaffed.

RT: 24"

(Next item: Cowley tuners' strike)

8. 16 January 1975 22.00 Item 4   Maimane
(Previous item: Reaction to ending of IRA truce)
ANDREW/NEWSPAPERS/SLIDES/FILM/SUPER

SLIDE   Fleet Street newspapers have agreed to wait until after a High Court hearing tomorrow morning before acting on their ultimatum to dismiss 7,000 printers if they continue industrial action. This already has lost two newspapers 850,000 copies in the last two days.

The High Court is hearing an application by the printers' union, the National Graphical Association — the NGA — for an injunction to stop the threatened dismissals.

SLIDE   The Secretary for Employment, Mr Foot, has invited ALL six

Fleet Street unions and their employers, the National Publishers'
Association — NPA — to a meeting tomorrow afternoon, when the
court hearing should have ended.

Mr Foot has asked the employers to suspend any action until after
this meeting. The union has turned down appeals by both Mr Foot
and the High Court NOT to disrupt newspaper production tonight.

Earlier in the Commons both Mr Foot and his opposition
SLIDE   shadow, Mr Prior, appealed to the union to call off their action. Mr
Foot said newspapers faced a desperate situation for their survival.

The dispute is over a union demand for up to 40p to maintain pay
differentials with the other five unions. The employers say if they
agreed the other unions would then demand another pay rise.

Angela Lambert asked the NGA's general secretary if he accepted
this argument.

FILM   [Interview as at 17.50]

RT: 1'13" + 1'27"

(Next item: NHS consultants' work-to-contract)

9. 17 January 1975 13.00 Item 4   Mann
(Previous item: Ronald Biggs)
NEWSPAPERS/SLIDES/FILM UNDERLAY/POSS SMITH LS/STUD INT

A crucial day today for Fleet Street.

With the Financial Times and the Guardian both losing thousands
of copies last night because of industrial action by members of the
National Graphical Association and the Daily Mirror and Sporting
Life not printed at all in London due to a separate dispute with
NATSOPA, national newspapers are facing their most serious crisis
FILM UP   in years. Leaders of the National Graphical Association went to the
High Court this morning to apply for an injunction against
Beaverbrook Newspapers, the Times, the Evening Standard and the
Evening News, to stop 7,000 of their Fleet Street members being
sacked. The Newspaper Publishers' Association — the NPA — had
said they'd dismiss all NGA men this morning if industrial action
FILM OUT   didn't stop. The sackings were postponed pending the High Court
SLIDE   hearing. Mr Justice Megarry is hearing the application. He
MEGARRY   adjourned the court for lunch a few minutes ago.

The NGA have been taking industrial action in support of their
claim for more pay.

SLIDE (FOOT)   The Employment Secretary Mr Foot has called the publishers,
the NGA, and other printing unions to a peace conference this
afternoon in an attempt to solve the crisis.

One printing union, NATSOPA, has refused to go to the talks.
They say they're not in dispute with the Newspaper Publishers, only

with the Mirror, which is NOT a member of the NPA.

The trouble at the Mirror came to a head on Wednesday when 1,300,000 copies were lost because of extended NATSOPA chapel meetings about a pay claim. Last night NATSOPA chapel refused to give assurances of normal working so the Mirror promptly sacked them all and shut down the London presses.

So there we are. An extremely serious situation in an industry already facing severe financial problems. With me in the studio is Tom Baistow of the New Statesman, who specialises in press affairs.

STUDIO
INTERVIEW

Parkin: We often hear that newspapers are in severe danger because of industrial action, yet newspapers don't in principle shut down as a result of them. How much danger is there to any of the papers at the moment?

Baistow: Well, I think the danger is very much greater now than it has been because this year the recession's meant very much less advertising revenue, and your daily newspaper is about half the size it would normally be at this time of year, so from that point of view they're strapped for cash, and as you know, various papers, like the Daily Express, had a loss of £1,300,000 last year, even the very rich News of the World/Sun set-up — Rupert Murdoch's organisation — dropped from £3½ million profit in the [first?] six months of this year to £300,000, so everybody is in difficulty.

Parkin: So it looks, to someone on the outside, as if these strikes are suicidal?

Baistow: Yes, they certainly have that appearance from inside as well as outside, because the National Graphical Association is in fact in dispute not really for much more money, but for 40p for about 1,000 — that is about 15% of their strength on the national papers, and they say that they must have this because traditionally they have 12½% more than any other union in the newspaper industry. It's all about craft, skills and recognition.

Parkin: Isn't there a lot of nervousnesss in the newspaper unions about changes which they feel are going to be forced upon them, and which are there for the taking if the newspapers could persuade the Union to accept them?

Baistow: Very much so. This is really at the bottom of this differential row, because the National Graphical [Association], which claims to be and I think is, the most skilled of the unions, does in fact face within the next two or three years, a big switch over to a completely new system, doing away with the old fashioned hot lead type system, [to] photocomposition, which means retraining and means in effect a row between the unions about who will do which job. This [has] set up a deep feeling of insecurity which is now expressing itself in terms of this 40p claim.

Parkin: Are the management doing enough, briefly, to take the unions into their confidence about what they want to do?

Baistow: I think they're doing it very belatedly. They had lots of opportunities in the past, and they were always quite happy as long as they were making money, to do deals with the unions. On the stronger papers, for instance the Daily Express, which is now one of the weakest — the Daily Express used to give rises without the slightest hesitation, because Beaverbrook felt that this might cripple weaker papers — well, this is coming home to roost now.

Parkin: Mr Baistow, thank you very much indeed.

RT: 1'40″ + 3'06″

(Next item: Jack Jones on the Social Contract)

10. 17 January 1975 17.50 Lead item   Maimane
NEWSPAPERS/SLIDES/CAP/LIVE OB

TITLE FILM In the Fleet Street crisis Mr Justice Megarry has reserved until
SLIDE Monday his judgment in the High Court action by six members of the NGA, the National Graphical Association. They want to stop their newspaper employers sacking them for industrial action which
CAPTION has lost four newspapers over a million copies this week.
SLIDE   The Newspaper Publishers' Association (the NPA) have agreed to delay their deadline for dismissals until after Monday's judgment. But the union have NOT agreed to stop disrupting production.
SLIDE   Peace talks with the Secretary for Employment, Mr Foot, began while the court was still in session. Giles Smith reports from the Ministry.

INTO LIVE **Smith:** These talks have now been going on for more than three
OB hours and certainly the signs of some sort of peace in Fleet Street are
SUPER: GILES [not] bright at all. Mr Foot told the unions and employers when they
AND arrived here the problem was a crisis of quite different dimensions to
SEPARATE any previous one in Fleet Street. And the talks didn't get off to the
LIST AS best of starts when Lord Briginshaw, head of NATSOPA, the
REQUIRED second biggest union in the industry, refused to attend at all, saying
he was too busy. Then the 4 other unions refused to sit around the same table as the NGA, and then half an hour ago the other 4 unions walked out altogether. Well, Mr Justice McGarry's decision to give the judgment in the NGA injunction case on Monday seems to have staved off the threat of mass sackings of NGA [men] in Fleet Street at

least for the time being. But for their part the NGA have given no assurance that their action won't continue tonight and over the weekend. Well, as he left the talks I spoke to Mr Bill Keys, leader of SOGAT, the biggest union in the industry, and asked him if this was a walkout.

Keys: No, we're not walking out. We've agreed with the Minister, and indeed with Jim Mortimer of the CAS that there's no purpose of us staying on any more.

Smith: What are the state of the negotiations?

Keys: Well, the state of the negotiations, well we haven't been negotiating. We came here at the invitation of the Minister, and indeed we have listened to the Minister early on this afternoon, and we haven't at any time met the NGA or the [NPA] as a joint force. Because as far as we are concerned we are not in dispute. The four unions that have been here this afternoon came to an agreement last October.

Smith: There's been a suggestion that there could be major chaos in Fleet Street next week. Do you feel that that could be the case?

Keys: I don't think there's any doubt there will be major chaos in Fleet Street this afternoon or from tonight, unless of course the NGA and the [NPA] can come to some resolution.

RT: 44″ + 50″ + N/A

11. [programme continues]   Maimane
MIRROR/FILM ULAY

As result of a separate Fleet Street dispute, the Daily Mirror is unlikely to be printed in London tonight, making it the second day that over three million copies will be lost. The Mirror group have suspended publication of the Daily Mirror and Sporting Life until a union, NATSOPA, stops disrupting production.

FILM ULAY   The two sides haven't met today and there's a possibility that there'll also be no printing in Manchester tonight. Normally over a million copies are printed there.

The dispute is over a demand by the Mirror group that a new pay agreement must include a clause ENDING the practice of automatically replacing staff who leave the company.

N/C   The Mirror Group are not members of the NPA, and so are not involved in the dispute with the NGA.

RT: 45″

(Next item: IRA ceasefire ends)

12. 17 January 1975 22.00 Item 4   Maimane
(Previous item: IRA ceasefire ends)
SANDY/NEWSPAPERS/STILL/SLIDE/FILM

STILL   The threat of a shutdown by Fleet Street newspapers has been
         postponed till Monday when Mr Justice McGarry will make his
         judgment on a High Court action to stop publishers dismissing
         7,000 members of the National Graphical Association.
             The Newspaper Publishers' Association had threatened to
         dismiss the men for disrupting production over their claim for a 40
         pence pay rise.
             The dismissals which would've shut down Fleet Street papers –
         except the Daily Mirror, which is NOT involved – were to take
         place at nine this morning.

FILM   They were delayed by the court action taken by six members of
         the NGA who claimed it would be illegal for their employers – The
         Times, Daily Express, London Evening Standard and Evening
         News – to dismiss them because of union action. Before the court
         adjourned their union said they would NOT undertake to stop
         disrupting production at any newspaper.

CUE AT 19″   This afternoon leaders of the NGA and four other unions
         attended talks called by the Secretary for Employment with
         representatives of the publishers' association. After the talks ended
         without result, Giles Smith spoke to the general secretary of the
         NGA and the chairman of the publishers' association.

NATSOF AT   **Smith:** Mr Bonfield have you made any progress here at all tonight?
37″
         Bonfield: No progress at all. It's been another waste of time.

         Smith: What's the next move?

         Bonfield: There aren't any moves as far as we're concerned. The
         only thing that's come out of this tonight is an appeal by the Minister
         to leave this issue over to negotiate again in October. This
         proposition has been put to us so many times, and we've rejected it,
         and that was never on. The other unions we understand put up a
         proposition to the NPA earlier this evening in an endeavour we
         understand to be helpful. The NPA turned it down, so it was never
         on [our] agenda.

         Smith: Does your union's industrial action continue tonight and
         over the weekend now?

         Bonfield: The policy and the plans that we have will carry on.

         Chairman Pub.Ass.: I can only react by saying that we have
         already in fact reacted. It's given us no satisfaction, but we've
         reacted.

Smith: One of the unions said here tonight as they walked out that Fleet Street had got the death wish. What do you say to that?

Chairman: Well, I think Fleet Street has been believed to have had a death wish for many years. But somehow it's got an astonishing capacity for surviving death wishes and it's my belief if I can make a prediction that it will survive. But it's an immensely critical situation.

SLIDE

Smith: So after a day of intensive activity, things are right back to square one. The NGA seem as intransigent as ever despite their agreement to meet on Sunday to consider Mr Foot's plan to call it all off. The feeling tonight is that there's very little chance of that, and continuing disruption of selected papers seems certain to continue. The employers, too, though holding their hand until after the court judgment, seem determined to go ahead with their mass sackings, assuming the judge rules for them. The other five unions also, and that includes Lord Briginshaw's NATSOPA which refused to attend tonight's talks, seem determined not to allow the NGA to breach the general agreement.

Perhaps the one really meaningful move of the day, though, was the fact that Mr Foot seems to be lining up with the employers and the other unions. I understood that in making an appeal for a return to normal working, he said in effect that the NGA had come to the end of the line. The big question now is whether the NPA is prepared to stand up to the combined strength of the employers, the other unions, and the Government.

RT: 29″ + 2′12″ + 1′01″

13. [programme continues]   Maimane
REGGIE/MIRROR/FILM/SUPER

The Daily Mirror won't be published tomorrow because of a separate dispute with another union: NATSOPA. No copies of the Mirror were printed in London last night; about a million came out in Manchester, but the dispute has now spread there.

The dispute is over a Mirror demand to end the practice of automatically replacing staff who leave. The union rejects this.

Angela Lambert spoke to the Mirror's chief executive.

FILM UP:
SUPER:
PERCY
ROBERTS

Roberts: We're making no plans to print the Mirror tonight. Lord Briginshaw has said he'll also possibly stop us in Manchester, and again in Glasgow, so the prospects are pretty bleak for tonight.

Lambert: It looks very much like deadlock. When is the situation going to ease?

Roberts: The initiative at this point of time has to remain with the union NATSOPA. We think they should now approach us — and we are possibly in for a long struggle in this dispute.

Lambert: How long can the Mirror survive without printing any papers?

Roberts: A considerable period of time — and we think the principles at stake are so important that even if we reach some sort of agreement and get what we wanted out of it then we would just be postponing the day of destruction. So we've got to find a solution however long it takes.

Lambert: This dispute is surely the last twitch of the noose around the suicide's neck; do you agree with that?

Roberts: Yes, I do. We know the financial position of other newspapers. We've never made any secret of our own position. At the end of April last year we lost about 850 thousand pounds. In the current financial year we shall lose in excess of half a million. These figures are determined when the economy was booming. We've had two cover price increases of the Mirror in one year. Both our Sunday papers have increased their price. If the economy were stable we would still have problems. But in the new situation it's quite terrifying and we believe that unless somebody does something about one of our major problems which we can control, which is over-manning — then I think the suicide note is this ... I think we're talking and we shall have to do something about it.

RT: 23″ + 1'56″

(Next item: Jack Jones on the Social Contract)

14. 18 January 1975 13.10 Item 3   Mawer
(Previous item: Ulster)
NEWSPAPERS

7,000 people who work for the newspaper division of the International Publishing Corporation are being sent protective notices this weekend.

They'll be accompanied by details of the state of the company, which hasn't been able to print the Daily Mirror or the Sporting Life in London for the past two days, because of a dispute with one union, NATSOPA.

IPC say it's extremely unlikely that the Sunday Mirror or the Sunday People will be published tomorrow.

In the other Fleet Street dispute, with the National Geographical Association, the Financial Times was the only newspaper affected.

100,000 copies were lost when machine managers belonging to the NGA halted production.

RT: 38″

(Next item: Scottish ambulance controllers' strike)

15. 18 January 1975 17.12 Item 4A   Mawer
(Previous item: Abandonment of Channel Tunnel project)
NEWSPAPERS
The Mirror newspaper group have warned they'll have to stop operations soon if the dispute with one of the print unions, NATSOPA, goes on much longer. They say the dispute has already cost them almost a million pounds. They've sent protective notice to 7,000 of their employees.

And the group have announced that the Sunday Mirror and the Sunday People won't be published tomorrow in London and Manchester because of the dispute.

RT: 25″

(Next item: Wilson meets Israeli Foreign Minister)

16. 18 January 1975 22.30 Item 6   Mawer
(Previous item: Abandonment of Channel Tunnel project)
NEWSPAPERS
The Mirror newspaper group have warned they'll have to stop operations soon if the dispute with one of the print unions, NATSOPA, goes on much longer.

They say the dispute has cost them nearly a million pounds so far. Because of it, the Sunday Mirror and the Sunday People will not be published tomorrow.

The group, who are part of the International Publishing Corporation, have sent protective notices of dismissal to 7,000 of their employees.

In the other newspaper dispute, with the National Graphical Association, only the News of the World has been affected so far tonight, by hold-ups in the production of London editions.

RT: 33″

(Next item: New Chinese constitution)

17. 19 January 1975 22.00 Item 3   MDW
(Previous item: Hopes of new Ulster ceasefire)
NEWSPAPERS/FILM
There's hope of settlements in the two national newspaper disputes,

following meetings in London tonight.

In the Mirror group dispute, the employers and the NATSOPA printers' union have agreed to talks with the Conciliation and Arbitration Service tomorrow. But the industrial action continues for the time being.

In the major dispute, between the Newspaper Publishers' Association and the other printers' union, the National Graphical Association, the union said tonight they're calling off their industrial action which has already cost the publication of more than a million papers. But the NGA added there'd be further disruption if there was no response from the employers on the proposal that all union conditions be renegotiated in April.

RT: 37″

(Previous item: Scottish ambulance controllers' strike)

18. 20 January 1975 13.00 Item 5   Stevens
(Previous item: Chunnel)
NEWSPAPERS/CAP/STILL

One chapter at least in the struggle between the national newspaper proprietors and one of the print unions ended in the High Court this morning — with a defeat for the men.

The National Graphical Association (the NGA) had sought a ruling from the court that the employers were not entitled to dismiss them.

(The employers had given a warning that the men would HAVE to consider themselves sacked if they didn't stop 'disruptive practices'.)

STILL   But Justice Megarry, giving judgment today, backed the employers concerned — the London Evening News and Evening Standard, the Daily Express and the Times.

The judge said the printers hadn't made out an exceptional case for the High Court to depart from its normal practice of NOT stopping employers from sacking employees.

N/C   It was all pretty academic anyway because over the weekend (while waiting for the judgment) the union suspended their so-called disruptive practices. (And certainly these did disrupt newspaper production.)

And counsel for the newspapers said AFTER judgment was given that they, in turn, would suspend further action on their threat of dismissals.

However, the underlying threat to newspapers, of course, remains. And the Newspaper Publishers' Association have been meeting again to consider new peace proposals from the printers' union.

RT: 1'10"

(Next item: TUC/Labour Party Liaison Committee meets)

19. 20 January 1975 17.50 Item 5   Smith
(Previous item: Cowley tuners' strike)
NEWSPAPERS/ULAY/ULAY/SLIDE

There's a breathing space in both the Fleet Street newspaper disputes.

In the major dispute, the newspaper publishers have said they won't be going ahead with their plan to sack the 7,000 Fleet Street members of the National Graphical Association.

This follows the union's decision yesterday to suspend any industrial action for the time being, and Mr Justice Megarry's

ULAY UP   decision this morning not to grant an injunction stopping the NPA
NEWSPAPERS   sacking NGA members. The Newspaper employers had threatened them all if the union didn't give an undertaking not to stop industrial

ULAY OUT   action. The judge said it wasn't right to grant an injunction in a case
SLIDE   where the employees' jobs would be protected while industrial action was threatened on the employers.

ULAY UP   In the other dispute, talks at the Conciliation and Arbitration Service
CAS   between the Mirror Group and NATSOPA, another printing union, have led to new peace talks. The dispute has stopped publication of the Daily and Sunday Mirror since last Wednesday.

RT: Approx. 55"

(Next item: Banks lower base rates)

20. 20 January 1975 22.00 Item 7   Lloyd Roberts
(Previous item: Commercial break)
REGGIE/NEWSPAPERS/SLIDES/SMITH VTR

The industrial troubles that have been affecting Fleet Street papers are temporarily suspended.

In the dispute which has cost the Daily Mirror group more than £1 million since Wednesday, fresh peace talks have been arranged

SLIDE   with NATSOPA – the print union – after talks with Mr Jim Mortimer, chairman of the Advisory and Conciliation Service.

In the other dispute, the Newspaper Publishers Association said they're not going ahead with their threat to sack 7,000 members of the National Graphical Association: the union had already decided to suspend industrial action.

Earlier a judge had ruled that they COULD sack the men.

Here's our industrial correspondent, Giles Smith:

VTR UP CAP:
SMITH

ULAY UP

ULAY UP

SLIDE

SLIDE

RT:

So, after the loss of more than 22m. copies of Mirror group papers, and the throwing of some of the strongest insults between the two parties, Mr Mortimer today somehow managed to get Mr Percy Roberts, the Mirror Group's managing director, and Lord Briginshaw, the NATSOPA leader, to hold peace talks which only yesterday seemed out of the question. Tonight, in anticipation of these talks, the protective notices sent to 7,000 Mirror employees were withdrawn, and the presses were rolling again. Meanwhile the tangled story of the dispute between the £90 a week printers of the NGA and the proprietors of all the other papers simmered quietly. The six printers who'd taken their case to the High Court were told by the judge it was not right to grant an injunction in a case where the employees' jobs would be protected, while industrial action was threatened on the employers.

Though the Judge did say he doubted whether the employers were entitled to act on the dismissal threat without being in breach of contract.

The employers' dropping of the sacking threat does not however, mean this dispute is over.

Mr Bonfield, the NGA leader, says their dropping of the industrial action is dependent on the NPA agreeing to a renegotiation of all Fleet Street pay rates in April. This is something the NPA have turned down once already, and, I'm told, have no intention of changing their minds on.

Officially they're waiting to hear from the NGA; unofficially, armed with the Judge's ruling, they're clearly digging themselves in for a renewed fight with Fleet Street's highest paid union.

7" + 36" " 1'29"

Next item: IRA truce)

21. 22 January 1975 17.50 Item 10   Black
(Previous item: Ontario)
NEWSPAPERS/SLIDES

SLIDE

SLIDE

At home, three Appeal Court judges have unanimously dismissed appeals by six Fleet Street printers.

Lord Denning, Master of the Rolls, said he was 'in entire agreement' with the judgment given on Monday by Mr Justice Megarry in the High Court when he refused to grant the printers a temporary order protecting their jobs.

The printers had asked him for an order preventing employers from regarding them as having ended their contracts of employment.

The Newspaper Publishers' Association made the threat of

dismissal to the men's union because of disruptive practices.

Lord Denning said the printers' complaints about the publishers reminded him of the French proverb: 'This animal is very wicked — when we attacked him he defended himself.'

RT: 40″

(Next: Pools win)

22. 22 January 1975 22.00 Item 14   Black
(Previous item: Ontario)
SANDY/NEWSPAPERS/SLIDES
        [As at 17.50]

RT: 40″

(Next item: Not available)

23. 29 January 1975 17.50 Item 4   Sam
(Previous item: London bus strike)
NEWSPAPERS

A commitee of the National Graphical Association have recommended a ballot in their dispute with the Newspaper Publishers' Association.

The idea of a ballot is expected to be approved by the union's executive commitee tomorrow. But, members will be urged to REJECT an offer by the employers.

The union — who want to maintain 'differentials' for their members — said that if the employers won't negotiate, the prospect of strike action will be 'very much on the cards'.

RT: 25″

(Next item: Sir Don Ryder)

24. 5 March 1975 13.00 Item 6
(Previous item: Cambodia fighting)
NGA

You can never be quite sure whether you're going to get your newspapers regularly or not these days with disputes liable to appear in the industry almost as frequently as misprints. But one such dispute — that which caused the major disruption a few weeks ago — is now over, the issue having been in suspense while 5,000 print craftsmen voted on the 2-stage pay offer which had been made to them. This in spite of the recommendation of their union, the National Graphical Association, that they should reject it.

RT: 32″

(Next item: Market gardeners)

25. 5 March 1975 17.50 Item 7
(Previous item: Dock strike)
NGA

More than 5,000 skilled printers on national daily and London evening newspapers have decided to accept a 7 per cent pay offer — against the advice of the executive of their union, the National Graphical Association.

Their acceptance, by a narrow majority vote, has ended the threat of an all-out strike that would have stopped newspaper production.

RT: 20″

(Next item: Michael Foot on the Social Contract)

26. 5 March 1975 22.00 Item 6   Mawer
(Previous item: Dock strike)
SANDY/NGA

5,000 skilled printers on national daily and London evening newspapers have accepted a seven per cent pay offer — against the advice of the executive of their union, the National Graphical Association. The offer was accepted by a narrow majority — only 2,424 voted in favour and 2,166 against — a difference of 258.

Their acceptance means an end for the time being to the dispute over pay differentials which has cut production. But the agreement only lasts until September and a member of the NGA executive said the restoration of differentials would be the priority in the next round of negotiations.

RT: 37″

(Next item: Michael Foot on the Social Contract)

4: GLASGOW DUSTCART DRIVERS' STRIKE

1. 11 January 1975 17.12 Item 6   Maimane
(Previous item: Cowley tuners' strike)
DUSTMEN/FILM
> Glasgow's 350 dustcart drivers are to go on indefinite strike from
> Monday.
FLUP   The strike means that Glasgow faces another pile-up of rubbish
on the pavements as happened for four weeks last autumn. The
drivers have asked the national executive of the Transport and
General Workers' Union to make the strike official. They want an
extra £3.35 pence to reduce the differential between their pay and
that of heavy-vehicle drivers working for private companies.

RT: 26″

(Next item: Middle East)

2. 11 January 1975 22.30 Item 6   Maimane
(Previous item: Cowley engine tuners' strike)
DUSTMEN/FILM
> Glasgow's 350 dustcart drivers are to go on indefinite strike from
> Monday.
FLUP   The strike means that Glasgow faces another pile-up of rubbish
on the pavements as happened for four weeks last autumn. The
drivers have asked the national executive of the Transport and
General Workers' Union to make the strike official. They want an
extra £3.35 pence to reduce the differential between their pay and
that of heavy-vehicle drivers working for private companies.

RT: 27″

(Next item: Soyuz docks with Salyut)

3. 12 January 1975 22.00 Item 2   Maimane
(Previous item: Scottish ambulance controllers' strike)
AMBULANCE LEADOUT/FILM
> There'll be no rubbish collected, either, in Glasgow from tomorrow
> when 350 dustcart drivers start another pay strike.
FILM   The dustmen's strike follows another last autumn when Glasgow
RT: 30′   pavements were blocked by uncollected refuse. But this time drivers
from the city's road department will join the strike – and from
Monday week, drivers of buses for handicapped school children will
also stop work.

RT: 21″

(Next item: ANC accuses Rhodesian government of violating ceasefire)

4. 13 January 1975 13.00 Item 3   Stevens
(Previous item: Scottish ambulance controllers' strike)
> More effective than the ambulance controllers' strike — it seems — is the stoppage by 350 dustcart drivers in Glasgow.
> Already rubbish is piling up in the city's streets once again — they've only just got them clear from the last strike before Christmas — and it could get worse, because the drivers say they're on indefinite strike. They're seeking pay parity with lorry drivers in the private sector of the haulage industry.
> And 300 Glasgow Corporation drivers in the education department are threatening to join them. That could affect distribution of school meals and force disabled school children to stay at home.

RT: 34"

(Next item: Conservative interview)

5. 13 January 1975 17.50 Item 9   Mawer
(Previous item: Scottish ambulance controllers' strike)
GLASGOW
> Still in Glasgow — 350 Corporation dustcart drivers began a strike today over a pay claim — two months after a similar strike.
> They want another £2.50 a week to bring their pay into line with drivers in the private sector. 30 men who drive road-gritting lorries joined them. And 500 Corporation maintenance electricians today to strike from next Monday for more pay.

RT: 25"

(Next item: Car industry strikes)

6. 13 January 1975 22.00 Item 8   Mawer
(Previous item: Scottish ambulance controllers' strike)
ANDREW/DUSTMEN/SLIDE
> Still in Glasgow... 350 Corporation dustcart drivers have gone on indefinite strike over a pay claim — two months after a similar strike.
> They want an extra £2.50 a week to bring them into line with drivers in the private sector. Another 30 men who drive road-gritting lorries have joined them.

RT: 18"

(Next item: NHS consultants' work-to-contract)

7. 13 February 1975 22.00 Item 4   FM
(Previous item: Morning Star)

GLASGOW/ULAY

A leading medical authority in Glasgow has tonight claimed that the pay strike by Glasgow Corporation's 350 dustcart drivers — now in its seventh week — is creating a serious health hazard and a menace from the growing number of rats.

Professor Gordon Stewart, who holds the chair of medicine at the University of Glasgow, accused the local health authorities of playing down the seriousness of the situation 'for political reasons'.

ULAY   He said more than 50,000 tons of rubbish have piled up in dumping areas in the city and in lanes and back yards of city tenements. Professor Stewart said it would take 3 months to clear the rubbish — even if the strike were settled now.

RT: 37″

(Next item: Rates)

8. 24 February 1975 17.55 Item 10   Hutchence

(Previous item: Miners' pay ballot)

GLASGOW RUBBISH/MOLONEY LIVE INJECT/SUPER/REWRITE

Glasgow's 350 dustcart drivers are now into the seventh week of their strike for more pay. Ray Moloney reports:

SUPER RAY MOLONEY REPORTING   It was a good idea to beautify some of the older parts of Glasgow by painting murals on the walls, but it's been rather spoiled by the garbage strike. More than 40,000 tons of refuse are now piled in increasingly evil-smelling emergency dumps — a total of 7 of them — scattered throughout the city — the direct result of a seven-week strike, the second in less than six months by the lorry drivers who normally remove it. The lorry drivers received a more than 20% pay increase last November after the earlier strike. Now they want another 14% which Glasgow says it can't pay until new national negotiations are complete. In the meanwhile, the city has spent £55,000 so far, providing bags in which people can store and dispose of their garbage, but as the strike continues, and there's no sign of an end to it, the dumps are rapidly filling up. Some of them are already closed. It took seven weeks to clean up after the last strike and that lasted a month. Even if this one ended today, it'll take a minimum of ten weeks, and now is a peak breeding time for the rats which are increasingly being seen at the emergency dumps. The city authorities insist there's no cause for alarm right now, but if the strike continues, things could get dangerous, with plagues of flies joining a possible plague of disease-bearing vermin. RM, ITN, Glasgow.

RT: 6″ + 1'23″

(Next item: Milford Haven polluted by oil spillage)

9. 24 February 1975 22.00 Item 18
(Previous item: Not available)
LEONARD/GLASGOW RUBBISH/MOLONEY VTR/SUPER
       In Glasgow, 350 dustcart drivers are now into the 7th week of their
       strike for more pay.
          It's estimated that there are 40,000 tons of rubbish piled up in the
       streets, and some Scottish MPs are worried about the risk of disease.
       From Glasgow, Ray Moloney reports:

SUPER: RAY   It was a good idea to beautify some of the older parts of Glasgow
MOLONEY   by painting murals on the walls, but it's been rather spoiled by the
REPORTING   garbage strike. More than 40,000 tons of refuse are now piled high in
       a total of seven emergency dumps throughout the city − the direct
       result of a seven-week strike, the second in less than six months by
       the lorry drivers who normally collect it. The dumps are within
       sight, sound and even worse, smell, of houses and apartment blocks
       with an obvious risk to health. Refuse is piled in back gardens, it's in
       bursting bags outside blocks of flats and it's along pavements in the
       city centre. The lorry drivers received a more than 20% pay increase
       last November after the earlier strike. Now they want another 14%
       which Glasgow says it can't pay until new national negotiations are
       complete. In the meanwhile, the city has paid out £50,000 so far
       providing bags in which people can store and dispose of their
       garbage, but as the strike continues, and there's not even a sign of it
       ending, the dumps are rapidly filling up. Some are already closed. It
       took seven weeks to clean up after the last strike, and even if this one
       ended tomorrow, cleaning up would take a minimum of 10, and
       now's the peak breeding time for rats, which are appearing
       increasingly at the dumps. City officials insist there's no real cause
       for alarm right now, but if the weather warms up, the probability of
       a plague of flies will join the threat of diseasebearing vermin which
       Glasgow's already facing, with daily less and less time to head either
       of them off. RM, NAT, Glasgow.
RT: 16″ + 1'50″
(Next item: Not available)

10. 10 March 1975 13.00 Item 5   Morrison
(Previous item: London dock strike)
GLASGOW RUBBISH/VTR ULAY/ST. INTVW/SUPER
       In Glasgow, where the dustmen's strike, or rather strike by dustcart
       drivers, is now in its ninth week, piles of noxious rubbish continue

to accumulate in the streets.

About a thousand tons a day are being added to what now amount to well over 50,000 tons. Some has been collected in special dumps set up by the Corporation, but there are also plenty of unauthorised dumps in alleys and tenement back courts.

One man who is seriously worried about all this as a danger to public health is Gordon Stewart, Professor of Community Medicine in Glasgow University. He's in our Scottish studio.

Kee: Professor Stewart, just what exactly is the health hazard here?

Stewart: The collection of garbage leads to rats and flies — the stuff decomposes, and in many ways it becomes highly objectionable. But of course it also is a source of infection which can be spread by the rats and by the flies, which in this delightful weather will start multiplying — they are doing so already.

Kee: But one wonders why after nine weeks, something more disastrous hasn't yet happened in this sense?

Stewart: Well, it takes a little time for these things to happen, and there's no purpose in being prematurely alarmed, but the point is that accumulation of garbage on this scale now becomes very difficult to handle in lots of ways. There's a danger of fire. If there is a fire, then the fumes that come off from this stuff could in themselves be quite noxious, and that might make it difficult for firemen to deal with any outbreaks that might occur.

Kee: Can't something be done, and presumably one hopes, is now being done, to minimise the risk — other than merely removing the stuff? What can be done to prevent the risk of infection?

Stewart: The only thing that can be done satisfactorily is to dispose of the rubbish. There are intermediate steps that can be done, and which I dare say the Corporation is taking — such as issuing plastic bags, and inspecting sites for evidence of rats and all that kind of thing, but this doesn't get at the basic difficulty. And the basic difficulty can't be overcome until there is some plan which has been worked out for dealing with such an enormous amount of stuff. It's... It will just have to be worked out step by step, where the transport is going to come from, who's going to drive it, who's going to remove the stuff, how it's going to be rendered safe — can any fires be adequately dealt with, contained, how can rats be exterminated? All those things are practical points and must be squared up to, and even if we decided now, it would take some little time. My concern arises not only from the pile-up of garbage — that's bad enough in itself, it's offensive as well as a threat to health

— my concern arises also because there is this constant delay in taking any action, and this is a neglect of the public interest.

Kee: Do you blame the Glasgow council for this?

Stewart: It's hard to blame any one authority, and blame is hardly the word. It seems to be becoming very confused. Decision is delayed because the strikers have to be consulted, and they in turn have to consult people in London, and the Corporation seems to spend about as much time negotiating this in London as in Glasgow — and meanwhile the situation gets worse.

Kee: And meanwhile, how much longer before serious disease might break out?

Stewart: It depends on the weather, it depends on all kinds of other things — not least to the extent to which the general public continue to co-operate. They're co-operating very well at the moment in trying to handle this menace. But if nothing is done by spring, by, say, April, then I would think that there would be a real, very real hazard during the succeeding months. Remember, it will take months to clear it up, even when people start.

RT: 36″ + 3′00″

(Next item: Childminding Charter)

11. 10 March 1975 17.50 Item 6A   Platt
(Previous item: London dock strike)
GLASGOW/VTR ULAY
          Glasgow City Council are to ask the Government to send troops to
TAKE ULAY   clear 50,000 tons of rat-infested rubbish from the city's streets.
45″ AVAIL   This follows warnings that parts of Glasgow may soon become
uninhabitable.
          The refuse has been accumulating over eight weeks because of the
strike by 350 dustcart drivers, who want pay parity with private
haulage drivers.

RT: 21″

(Next item: Whitehall industrial workers' strike)

12. 10 March 1975 22.00 Item 12   Platt
(Previous item: London dock strike)
REGGIE/GLASGOW/VTR ULAY
          Glasgow City Council are to ask the Government to send troops to
clear 50,000 tons of rat-infested rubbish from the city's streets.

TAKE ULAY   This follows warnings that parts of Glasgow may soon become
45″ AVAIL   uninhabitable.
The refuse has been accumulating over eight weeks because of the strike by 350 dustcart drivers, who want pay parity with private haulage drivers.

RT: 20″

(Next item: Whitehall industrial workers' strike)

13. 11 March 1975 13.00 Item 6   Morrison
(Previous item: Whittle kidnapping)
GLASGOW RUBBISH/LIVER INJECT/STV/SUPERS

In Glasgow it's looking increasingly likely that troops will now be called in to clear the 60,000 tons of refuse piled up in the streets because of the strike by drivers of the city's rubbish collection department.

The Minister of State at the Scottish Office, Mr Bruce Millan, is flying to Glasgow later today to meet a deputation from the council. They'll be putting a formal request for Government help in clearing the rubbish, which, as we were told on First Report yesterday, is rapidly becoming a serious danger to health.

Les Wilson of Scottish Television reports:

LIVE INJECT   Today is the 58th day of the strike and the rubbish has been piling
FROM LES   up at an estimated thousand tons a day. The weather is getting
WILSON   warmer, and now we're approaching the peak breeding time for
REPORTING
FROM   rats. The Corporation's been criticised for not acting swiftly enough
GLASGOW   and getting the rotting refuse out of the city sooner. But now, Glasgow councillors feel that it's imperative to clean the city up. This afternoon, the Lord Provost and senior councillors will formally ask Minister of State, Mr Bruce Millan, for help. But is there any alternative to calling in the troops?

SUPER: DICK   **Dynes:** We haven't specifically stated that we want troops in to clear
DYNES   the rubbish away. All we are saying to the Government is that they
LABOUR   are the main health authority throughout Scotland. We are putting
GROUP
LEADER   the problem to them, and I don't think there is any alternative. From
GLASGOW   our view, or from their view, other than using the troops. I don't
COUNCIL   think there's any question of that.

Wilson: OK, it's fine if the Army clear it up, but surely the only long-term solution is to get the men back to work.

Dynes: Oh, we're entirely in the hands of the men, but it's coming through to me, I've gained certain knowledge that the men haven't had a mass meeting for the best part of two months now, if my information is correct. But the men have been isolated by everyone – Government, members of Parliament, the public and the Corporation, and by their own union, and we're really in their hands, and I'm sure that at the end of the day, when that day is, they'll see sense and return to work. I don't think there's any alternative there either for themselves. They've lost a great deal of money from all of this, and I'm sure that they're quite anxious to return. I would hope so anyway.

Wilson: Is there now a health hazard in Glasgow? An extreme one?

Dynes: Oh, I think when you're talking about 60,000 tons of rubbish lying around, it's always a health hazard. As to how critical it is or immediate is another question, but there's one thing for sure – that we cannot allow it to remain there any longer without taking positive action in order to get rid of it.

Wilson: How long will it take to clear away?

Dynes: Well, this is very difficult to determine. If we brought troops in they're not specialised, or even geared up lorry-wise I would imagine, in the same way as the Corporation would be. So I wouldn't like to say how long it would take, but it would certainly take a couple of months anyway.

RT: 33″ + 2′08″

(Next item: Bikes)

14. 14 March 1975 13.00 Item 4   Sarah
(Previous item: Building)
GLASGOW RUBBISH/FILM ULAY

Glasgow Corporation dustcart drivers voted this morning almost unanimously not to return to work – despite an offer including £90 a week for three months to clear the thousands of tons of rubbish from the City.

ULAY (RT: 26″)   They've been on strike for ten weeks and about 60,000 tons of rubbish have built up in the streets. Rats and flies are already a major health hazard. Now that the drivers have decided not to return Glasgow Corporation will have to decide whether to ask the Government to move in troops.

But Mr Alex Kitson, the National Executive Officer of the Transport and General Workers' Union, who addressed this morning's meeting warned the Corporation that this would be 'an act of folly on their part.'

RT: 41″

(Next item: Tories)

15. 14 March 1975 17.50 Lead item   Martin
DUSTMEN/FILM U'LAY/ARCHER VTR/SUPER
TITLE FILM ULAY — RUBBISH

The Government have said they're ready to send troops to clear 60,000 tons of rubbish from the streets of Glasgow if the city council asks for them.

This follows the decision of the city's 350 dustcart drivers to continue their nine-week-old strike.

This morning they rejected a temporary offer that would have run until national negotiations produced a permanent settlement.

From Glasgow, Geoffrey Archer reports:

TAKE
ARCHER VTR
SUPER
GEOFFREY
ARCHER
REPORTING

The strikers were defiant this morning as they left their mass meeting, with only one of them voting against the decision to stay out. They've been offered bonus rates to clear up the mess, which had been agreed by Glasgow Corporation. But the central issue of extra pay for men with heavy goods vehicle licences remains unresolved. And so the men stay out. Glasgow Corporation insist that this is a national, not a local, issue.

Kitson: What's got to happen now is that either Glasgow Corporation, and ourselves as a union, have got to pressurise for this situation to be cleared up at national level, or they go back and fulfil the promise that if it wasn't satisfactorily dealt with at national level, they'll negotiate locally, and I think they've got a responsibility to the citizens of Glasgow, and in the light of the circumstances they should get off this hobby horse and take into consideration the problems that the citizens that are in Glasgow are going through.

Archer: The Lord Provost of Glasgow, Sir William Grey, said he was appalled and distressed by the decision. He has called a special meeting of the full council tomorrow, unprecedented on a Saturday, to discuss the matter. But they may simply decide the dispute is out of their hands, and give the Government the problem of dealing with the potential health risks here. It's most unlikely Glasgow's Labour-controlled Corporation will themselves wish to be seen calling for the use of troops to clear the rubbish and in effect, to break the strike. GA, ITN, Glasgow.

RT: 2'00"

(Next item: Trade figures)

16. 14 March 1975 22.00 Item 5   Platt
(Previous item: Funeral)
REGGIE/RUBBISH/ARCHER VTR/SUPERS

The Government say they'll send in troops to clear 60,000 tons of decaying rubbish from the streets of Glasgow if the city council asks for help.

This follows the decision of the city's 350 dustcart drivers to continue their nine-week old strike. One union leader said calling in the troops would be an act of folly.

TAKE
ARCHER VTR
SUPER:
GEOFFREY
ARCHER
REPORTING

From Glasgow, Geoffrey Archer reports... The strikers were defiant this morning as they left their mass meeting, with only one of them voting against the decision to stay out. They've been offered bonus rates to clear up the mess, which had been agreed by Glasgow Corporation. But the central issue of extra pay for men with heavy goods vehicle licences remains unresolved. And so the men stay out. Glasgow Corporation insist that this is a national, not a local, issue.

SUPER:

Kitson: What's got to happen now is that either Glasgow Corporation, and ourselves as a union, have got to pressurise for this situation to be cleared up at national level, or they go back and fulfil the promise that if it wasn't satisfactorily dealt with at national level, they'll negotiate locally, and I think they've got a responsibility to the citizens of Glasgow, and in the light of the circumstances they should get off this hobby horse and take into consideration the problems that the citizens that are in Glasgow are going through.

Archer: The Lord Provost of Glasgow seemed shaken by the decision. He called a special full meeting of the Council for tomorrow:

Lord Provost, what initiatives do you think are left in this dispute?

SUPER: SIR
WILLIAM
GRAY

Grey: The initiatives I think will finally come from the Government, and action will be required from the Pay Board.

Archer: What do you think will be decided at the full Corporation meeting tomorrow?

Grey: The Corporation can decide theoretically that they're going to take no action at all. And just allow the situation to deteriorate. But although there is no health hazard in existence at this moment, there is in fact a potential health hazard and we must ensure that that potentiality is never realised and the rubbish is cleared before any fatalities or anything arises out of it.

Archer: Do you think the government will bring in troops?

Grey: I think it is highly likely.

Archer: What effect do you think that will have on the dispute?

Grey: Well, I'm not concerned about this in the first instance. My main concern must be the health and safety of the citizens.

Archer: The soonest troops could move in to clear rubbish is next Tuesday, which leaves three days for the parties involved to seek some new compromise if they are to avoid military involvement. GA, NAT, Glasgow.

RT: 21″ + 2'22″

(Next item: Trade figures)

17. 15 March 1975 22.30 Item 3A   Black
(Previous item: Portugal/Spinola)
RUBBISH/ARCHER VTR/SUPERCAP/SLIDE/TITLE + FILM ULAY

One thousand troops are to move in to Glasgow next week to clear 60,000 tons of rubbish which has piled up during the nineweek dustcart drivers' strike. Medical teams will accompany them to monitor health risks.

The city Corporation voted by 84 votes to 10 to ask for Government help in dealing with the rubbish, which is creating a serious health hazard.

SLIDE: ROSS   Tonight Mr Archie Hood, convenor of the drivers' shop stewards committee, threatened to ask for support from every other trade unionist in the country to protest at the move. He said: 'It is a pretty shocking thing when a Labour Government is using troops for strike breaking in this way. I have never known a Labour Government to act like this. I think they are trying to to starve us out.'

Geoffrey Archer reports:

While political militants picketed, Glasgow Corporation decided to ask the Government for help. Convinced of the health risk to citizens of Glasgow, the Secretary of State for Scotland said plans would immediately be made to send in the troops. I spoke to him:

Archer: If they're bringing in troops, which in effect, will use troops to break the strike, isn't there a danger of strong reaction from other trades unionists here?

Ross: This is an unofficial strike, but I think everyone in Glasgow appreciates that you've got to take into account, and the government must take into account, the whole question of the health risk involved.

Archer: Apart from the potential health hazard, fire is another risk, whether started by accident, or by someone who can't stand the sight and smell of the refuse any more. The danger is to the homes nearby. Firemen attend to all the blazes promptly. At the big collection centres, away from the houses, a steady stream of householders drive in their plastic sackfuls of rubbish for disposal. 60,000 tons of it are waiting for the soldiers when they start work next Tuesday or Wednesday. Their first priority will not be dumps [like] these, but the rubbish collected round tenement buildings. Soldiers will probably by-pass confrontation with strikers wherever possible by avoiding established sites and taking the rubbish to [near] tips outside Glasgow. It's the dustcart drivers who are on strike. The binmen themselves are at work manning the dumps. Ironically one of them here was reading in his quiet moments a book called 'The Plastic Nightmare'. GA, ITN, Glasgow.

RT: 46″ + 1′38″

(Next item: Chassis)

18. 17 March 1975 22.00 Item 5   Maimane
(Previous item: Hospital pay beds dispute)
LEONARD/GLASGOW
          The Scottish TUC are meeting leaders of the Glasgow dustcart drivers tonight in an attempt to get talks going again with the city Corporation and avert the arrival of troops to shift the rubbish that's piled up during the unofficial strike. Tomorrow the TUC leaders will meet the Corporation.
          The Scottish TUC warned that if the troops were brought in on Wednesday, industrial relations in the city would be affected for a generation. Already the Glasgow trade[s] council is considering sympathy strikes.
          From Glasgow, Trevor MacDonald reports.

VTR IN   Pressed into the sensitive and rather unpleasant job of clearing
SUPER   70,000 tons of rotting garbage the Royal Highland Fusiliers today
TREVOR
MACDONALD embarked on something [of] a public relations exercise. First they
REPORTING went to City Chambers to discuss the plan of operation for tackling the mountains of rubbish, with the Corporation's health officials. And later even managed to exchange a few words with a small group of good-natured pickets who marched up and down outside the building while the meeting went on, with mildly mocking placards, one of which advised the troops to 'join the Army and see Glasgow.' This afternoon the Fusiliers were back at City Chambers, this time for a press conference at which Brigadier Rendell Webster calmly [f]ended off awkward questions about the involvement of the troops. He said he expected no problems from pickets, agreed that his men had never tackled a job like it before, adding 'But you've got a problem, and we've come to help.' The size of the problem and the Corporation's concern for the health of people living near the rat-

infested mounds of refuse are not lost on the army. They begin work on Wednesday, and by the end of the week troop force working on cleaning up Glasgow will reach 1,000 men and 250 vehicles. The cool detachment with which the military view their assignment is in stark contrast to the growing tension in the city here tonight about the intervention of the troops. Secretly officials are hoping that even now it might be necessary not to actually use them, if, at a mass meeting tomorrow, the men decide to go back to work. But throughout this dispute the dustcart drivers have stuck rigidly to their guns and there's nothing tonight to indicate that they're willing to back down now.

RT: Not available

(Next item: Shelepin visit to Britain)

19. 18 March 1965 17.50 Item 8   Maimane
(Previous item: Westminster Hospital dispute)
RUBBISH/VTR/SUPER REWRITE
        Glasgow dustcart drivers have rejected their union's appeal to end an unofficial ten-week strike. Instead the Glasgow Trades Council will launch a campaign against troops being brought in to clear 70,000 tons of rubbish from city streets from tomorrow morning.
        The troops have already begun arriving from Edinburgh.
        Trevor McDonald reports:

VTR SUPER   The arrival here just after lunch today of a convoy of army trucks
MCDONALD   in an advance party from the Royal Highland Fusiliers, put an abrupt
REPORTING   end to any speculation there might have been this morning that
FROM
GLASGOW   today's peace moves might end the ten week old strike. The Fusiliers
moved in with their heavy transport vehicles, and late this afternoon confirmed that they were now ready to begin clearing up Glasgow's 70,000 tons of rubbish at dawn tomorrow. That the troops are not exactly welcomed by the striking drivers was even more obvious this morning when the men held a mass meeting at Kingston Hall, on the outskirts of the city centre. They weren't even discussing an end to the strike, they said. Only tactics about effective picketing. But still the talking goes on, although while it does, the Army stands poised to begin their massive garbage disposal job. TM, ITN, Glasgow.

RT: 18″ + 51″

(Next item: Viscountess escapes kidnap attempt)

20. 18 March 1975 22.00 Item 11   Maimane
(Previous item: London IRA bombers sentenced)

ANDREW/RUBBISH/VTR/SUPER

Troops have arrived in Glasgow to clear up about 70,000 tons of rubbish which has accumulated during the unofficial strike of dustcart drivers. The strikers rejected their union's appeal to end the tenweek strike, but negotiations are going on to settle their pay dispute.

The Glasgow Trades Council have launched a campaign against the army intervention but the dustBIN men – who're NOT on strike – will co-operate with the troops.

Trevor MacDonald reports:

VTR IN: SUPER TREVOR MACDONALD REPORTING FROM GLASGOW The arrival here just after lunch today of an advance party from the Royal Highland Fusiliers put an abrupt end to any speculation there might have been this morning that today's peace moves might end the 10-week-old strike. The Fusiliers moved in with their heavy transport vehicles in a convoy which made its way from Edinburgh quietly and without fuss. Late this afternoon, the troops confirmed that they were now quite ready to begin at dawn tomorrow the job of clearing up the tons of rotting refuse. [That] the strikers weren't exactly pleased to see the Royal Highland Fusiliers was made quite obvious this morning when the drivers held a mass meeting at Kingston Hall on the outskirts of the city centre. They didn't even discuss an end to the strike, the men said. Only tactics about effective picketing. Tonight talking is still going on, but whatever its outcome, it's now much too late to avoid the controversial use of the troops. TM, NAT, Glasgow.

RT: 26″ + 59″

(Next item: Cambodia)

21. 19 March 1975 13.00 Item 4A   Morrison
(Previous item: Defence White Paper)
GLASGOW RUBBISH/MCDONALD VTR/SUPER

In Glasgow the first contingent of troops moved in early this morning to start the job of clearing up the 70,000 tons of rubbish piled up in the streets because of the long strike by dustcart drivers.

From Glasgow, Trevor McDonald reports.

VTR IN SUPER: TREVOR MACDONALD REPORTING The troops left their billets in Edinburgh just after half past four this morning. And 90 minutes later, a company of 100 men from the Royal Engineers, the Royal Highland Fusiliers, and the Royal Transport Corps, arrived at the Govan incinerator on the outskirts of the city centre. The operation bore all the signs of precise military planning. In the cavernous transport shed where the men gathered to await their final orders, they climbed into overalls which for reasons of hygiene, they'll now change every day. They then moved the heavy tipper trucks into position. An adjoining office, usually used by the Govan cleansing department for routine administrative work, had been been smoothly transformed into the company's headquarters, and by 6.30 Major Robin Falkland was ready to give his final briefing. On the wall map, the three target areas for the morning's assault were quickly identified, and half an hour later, wearing gloves issued by the city's Cleansing Department, the men boarded the truck. The Royal Highland Fusiliers were on the move. The first collections were made in an old tenement block about a mile and a half from the incinerator. The rotting refuse bags, which had been mounting in number in the tenement close for more than nine weeks were brought out to be slung onto army transport vehicles. These were areas where the Glasgow city Corporation feared disease was most likely to spread if the garbage wasn't moved before the warmer weather arrived. This morning it was bitterly cold. Even so, the stench was unbearable. At Fulmadee, another of the incinerators from which the troops were operating, about 30 striking dustcart drivers gathered to picket army vehicles as they swung into the incinerator. There was some shouting, but it was all very good natured. The men's shop steward, Fergus Hilton, told me there were no plans to interfere in any way with the Army's disposal work, and already the Royal Highland Fusiliers are pronouncing day one a success. TM, FR, Glasgow.

RT: 1'14" + 2'16"

(Next item: Westminster Hospital dispute)

22. 19 March 1975 17.50 Item 2   Maimane
(Previous item: Healey warning on wage rises)
RUBBISH/VTR/SUPER/REWRITE

In Glasgow, troops have begun clearing the 75,000 tons of rubbish piled up by the dustcart drivers' unofficial strike. And in London, the Advisory, Conciliation & Arbitration Service have rejected a request by the strikers' union for an inquiry into their ten-week dispute.

The soldiers have been picketed by dustcart drivers as well as council electricians — who're also on strike. The electricians man the incinerators at the depots where rubbish is destroyed.

Trevor McDonald reports.

VTR SUPER   The troops arrived in Glasgow shortly after dawn today and began
MCDONALD   immediate preparations for the start of the massive clean-up
REPORTING   operation. They climbed into overalls, which are to be changed each
FROM   day, and just after 7.30 after a final briefing, the Royal Highland
GLASGOW

Fusiliers were on the move. Their first targets were the rotting refuse bags in and around the tenement blocks. In nine weeks the size of these mounds of rubbish have grown inexorably, and have caused some concern among the health authorities. Excavators tackled the bigger piles of garbage in the more open spaces. At one incinerator, the pickets were out in force. This soldier appeared studiously disinterested, and unlike his 600 colleagues, seeemed anxious to get on with the unpleasant job which could last for weeks. TM, ITN, Glasgow.

RT: 27″ + 1′01″

(Next item: British Leyland short-time working)

23. 19 March 1975 22.00 Item 3   Maimane
(Previous item: British Leyland shorttime working)
ANDREW/RUBBISH/SLIDE/VTR/SUPER/REWRITE

SLIDE: Glasgow Trades Council tonight voted for a mass demonstration on Friday against troops being brought in to clear 75,000 tons of rubbish which has piled up because of the strike by dustcart drivers. More than 100,000 trade unionists are affiliated to the Council which said that bringing in the troops would cause a deterioration in industrial relations.

Earlier in London the Advisory, Conciliation & Arbitration Service rejected a request by the strikers' union for an enquiry into the dispute.

From Glasgow, Trevor McDonald reports:

VTR/SUPER
MCDONALD
REPORTING
FROM
GLASGOW

By half past seven this morning, the Royal Highland Fusiliers had begun to tackle Glasgow's tons of uncollected rotting garbage. Health officials have expressed the fear that if there was a warm spell, this could pose a danger to health. Even in the bitter cold this morning, it was pretty evil-smelling stuff. For the main part, Glaswegians were happy to see the troops. Pickets were not. (SOF) At one of the three incinerators, leaflets and other literature representing the strikers' point of view were passed on to the soldiers. They were generally accepted, and in some cases rapidly read, before the troops returned to the job they had come to do. (SOF) If the troops were under orders to treat aggressive pickets with courteous disdain, no such restraint was applied to the rats. Fearlessly wielding all kinds of sticks and stathes, they beat, clubbed and stamped on the things, with a distinctly surprising, if professional flair. And to think that only a day or so ago, one medical officer was credited with the comforting prognosis that there was no danger of a plague of rats in Glasgow. But today, one soldier felt that apart from the Army, they also needed the Pied

Piper. TM, NAT, Glasgow.

RT: 29″ + 2'00″

(Next item: Labour MPs oppose membership of EEC)

24. 20 March 1975 17.50 Item 7   Kallenbach
(Previous item: Unemployment exceeds 1 million)
GLASGOW/MACDONALD VTR/SUPER

In Glasgow, the Army have been held up on their second day of clearing rubbish accumulated during the unofficial strike by dustcart drivers. A strike by electricians who operate the incinerators means the rubbish can't be burnt. Trevor McDonald reports on what the Army are doing instead:

VTR: SUPER: They call this place the wilderness. Acres of peat scrubland on the
TREVOR   outskirts of the city. Faced with the virtual shut-down of the three
MCDONALD   incinerators, used yesterday to burn rubbish, today, the Army were
REPORTING   forced to take their collections to this sprawling dump. The trucks
                arrived, and the Royal Highland Fusiliers shovel out the rotting
                bags. In addition to overalls and gloves, the men wear face masks, as
                protection against infection and dust. This departure from
                yesterday's operation has slowed down the rate at which the refuse is
                being moved. Army vehicles have further to go, and there is a fear
                that they're merely transporting a serious health problem. There is
                concern too that rats escaping from decaying piles of rubbish in the
                city may find their way to tenement blocks and shops. By tomorrow
                the Army will have 1,000 men and 250 vehicles on the clean-up job,
                but without the use of incinerators they could well be fighting a
                losing battle. TM, ITN, Glasgow.

RT: 16″ + 56″

(Next item: Dan Smith for trial on fraud charges)

25. 20 March 1975 22.00 Item 7   Kallenbach
(Previous item: Unemployment tops 1 million)
LEONARD/GLASGOW RUBBISH/MCDONALD VTR/SUPERCAP

In Glasgow, the Army have been held up on their second day of clearing the rubbish accumulated during the unofficial strike by dustcart drivers.

A strike by electricians who operate the incinerators means that rubbish can't be burnt.

The Ministry of Defence are considering whether troops involved in the clearup should qualify for a special dirt allowance — of THIRTEEN pence a day.

From Glasgow, Trevor McDonald reports on today's operations:

VTR SUPER: TREVOR MCDONALD REPORTING They call this place the wilderness plantation. Several acres of bleak, forbidding scrubland on the outskirts of the city. With the virtual shutdown of the three incinerators used yesterday to burn the rubbish, today, the Army had no alternative but to dump their collections here. It's as filthy a job as ever, and as a precaution against infection and dust, the men wear face masks. This departure from yesterday's operation has slowed down the rate at which the refuse is being moved. Army trucks have further to go, and it's felt that they might merely be transferring a serious health hazard. There is concern too that those rats which do escape the Army's determined assault could find new breeding grounds in the city. One public health expert today warned that Glasgow could become the garbage capital of the west. If that's to be avoided, the use of the incinerators could be crucial. This is Dalton incinerator, one of the three at which rubbish collected by the Army was burnt yesterday. Today it's not operating, and it now seems that the question of the use of these incinerators has become a fundamental issue in the drive to clean up Glasgow. The electricians know that if they don't operate these incinerators, the Army's disposal job will become just that much more difficult, if not impossible. And while the danger remains that fires will continue to break out at huge dumps like these in various parts of the city, then the urgency of the task facing the Army becomes increasingly clear. TM, NAT, Glasgow.

RT: 24″ + 1'38″

(Next item: precommercial trailers)

26. 21 March 1975 13.00 Item 6   Morrison
(Previous item: Liverpool dustcart drivers' strike)

In Glasgow the use of troops to clear rubbish has brought a protest march by trade unionists from Glasgow and the west of Scotland.

About 500 of them marched through the city centre this morning. The march was organised by Glasgow Trades Council and a spokesman said the Army was being used to break the dustcart drivers' strike.

The march passed off peacefully, though it met a certain amount of heckling and abuse from passers-by.

RT: 26″

(Next item: Government proposals for London docks strike)

27. 21 March 1975 17.50 Item 8   Jamieson
(Previous item: London containerisation strike)
RUBBISH/VTR ULAY/SUPER

VTR UP: In Glasgow, shop stewards representing 50,000 Scottish workers
SUPER: marched to the city chambers to protest against troops being used to
VTR clear away refuse built up by the 10 week old dustcart drivers' strike.
RT: 39" Glasgow's 800 firemen have decided on a policy of non-cooperation
with the Army. They'll only tackle fires in rubbish heaps if there's a
danger to life or property and not while the Army are there.

RT: Approx. 25"

(Next item: Liverpool dustcart drivers' strike)

28. 21 March 1975 22.00 Item 11A   Sara
(Previous item: Continued from Liverpool dustcart drivers' strike)
REGGIE/LIVERPOOL RUBBISH/VTR ULAY/GLASGOW FILM/SUPER
Earlier today, shop stewards representing 50,000 Scottish workers
marched to the city centre to protest against the use of troops. But —
as Trevor MacDonald reports — they won little sympathy from the
public:

UP If the purpose of today's march was to rally support for the
FILM: strikers, their demonstration was a disaster. At several points on the
SUPER: three-mile route to the city centre, the marchers were shouted at,
TREVOR
MACDONALD booed jeered at by people whose rat-infested rubbish has been lying
REPORTING in backyards now for ten weeks. (NATSOF) Before the march
FORM
GLASGOW began, shop stewards warned off members of activist groups who've
become increasingly visible on the picket lines since the troops
moved in. The troops are now fighting a battle they may never win.
Every day, new rubbish is added to an already decaying pile, almost
twice as fast as the troops can cope. Two days ago, the Army cleared
this area of refuse. By mid-afternoon, there were new, menacingly-
growing piles. The use of the incinerators remains a crucial factor.
Today, the only one in operation was at Govan. Without a full-time
use of all three plants, it might be impossible to avert the spread of
disease. The dispute which triggered off the unofficial strike has
driven the two sides further apart now than they ever were. And
even with today's announcement of an increase in the size of their
task force, the Army are digging in for a very long stay. TM, NAT,
Glasgow.

RT: 2'44"

(Next item: Bank rate)

29. 22 March 1975 13.10 Item 3A   Jill
(Previous item: Liverpool dustcart drivers' strike)
In Glasgow, shop stewards of the Transport & General Workers'
Union have suggested that the Glasgow Corporation should be

asked to make a similar offer to their dustcart drivers who're on strike.

RT: Approx. 11″

(Next item: Ian Mikardo MP criticises Wilson on EEC)

30. 22 March 1975 17.50 Item 5   Jill
(Previous item: Cambodia)
DUSTMEN/VTR ULAY

ULAY   Liverpool's dustcart drivers have called off their strike and have
UP: already begun clearing the temporary tips built up during the 9-week
         stoppage.
         The drivers voted overwhelmingly to accept an interim pay offer
         which will give them another £2.63.
         Union leaders have suggested that the Glasgow Corporation
         should make a similar award to the dustcart drivers on strike there.

RT: 22″

(Next item: Trawlermen blockade ports)

31. 27 March 1975 17.50 Item 7   Platt
(Previous item: Liverpool dustcart drivers' strike)
DUSTMEN/VTR ULAY

VTR ULAY But in Glasgow the strike goes on. About 100 men picketed the
          Polmadie incinerator depot in protest at the use of troops to clear the
          rubbish. The Army diverted as many dustcarts as possible from the
LOSE ULAY depot. One lorry went in, but no attempt was made to stop it.

RT: Approx. 16″

(Next item: BL redundancies)

32. 27 March 1975 22.13 Item 10   Platt
(Previous item: Liverpool dustcart drivers' strike)
LEONARD/DUSTMEN/VTR ULAY

TAKE ULAY ...In Glasgow, the dustcart drivers strike goes on. And troops who
24″ AVAIL are clearing the rubbish faced a demonstration from angry residents
           at a tip at Coatbridge near Glasgow. They said the Army trucks
LOSE ULAY were a danger to their children, and they didn't want Glasgow's
           refuse dumped so near their home.

RT: Approx. 17″

(Next item: Trawlermen blockade ports)

33. 1 April 1975 22.00 Item 9   Kallenbach

(Previous item: BR workshop supervisors' work to rule)
REGGIE/RUBBISH/LEWIS VTR/SUPERCAPS
In Glasgow, the Army say they've managed to clear a quarter of the 70-thousand tons of rubbish which has accumulated during the 12-week unofficial strike by dustcart workers.
Martyn Lewis reports:

VTR UP:
SUPER:
MARTYN
LEWIS
REPORTING
FROM
GLASGOW

To be honest, the last fortnight was one which the first battallion Royal Fusiliers, would prefer to forget. Their 4.00 a.m. reveille call has woken them up to a 15-hour day spent among the garbage of Glasgow, but their new emblem, the broom rampant, is a sign of their considerable achievements in the past fortnight. They've been at the dirtier end of a 1,400 man Army team, which helped by local dustmen not on strike has now cleared a quarter of the 70,000 tons of refuse lying around the city. Their main targets have been the 90,000 tenement homes where the health risk is considered greatest. Most seem to accept it as just another job, and the Army say that morale is reasonably high. But it's clearly not what they joined the Army for.

Lewis: What do you think of this work?

SUPERCAP
SECOND

Milne: Terrible.

Lewis: You don't like it?

LT. HAMISH
MILNE FIRST
BT. ROYAL
FUSILIERS

Milne: I don't like it at all. I suppose it's got to be done, and that's that. Somebody's got to do it.

Lewis: Tomorrow the Royal Scots move in and the Fusiliers move out. Their next assignment – Northern Ireland, which, for some, after two weeks in Glasgow, appears with a rosier hue.

Milne: Oh, I think they're quite happy about it really, because it means they're going back to what they've been trained for, which is soldiering. They're not soldiering at the moment, and I think they'll be quite glad to get out of here at the end of it.

Lewis: So this evening the Fusiliers hosed the refuse remnants of their lorries for the last time. Gave their boots a final dip in disinfectant, and drove off in one of their specially chartered buses to the cleansing department showers, with spirits high, and their minds clearly not on their work. (SOF) After making every effort to ensure that they didn't take their work home with them to Edinburgh, they queued up for a cup of tea and a sandwich. And a free beer, courtesy to the troops. As one soldier said, the beer was good, but just look at what we had to go through to get it. ML, NAT, Glasgow.

RT: 11″ + 2'07″

(Next item: Daily Mirror strike)

34. 3 April 1975 17.50 Item 10   Simons
(Previous item: London dock strike)
DUSTMEN
> The Glasgow dustcart drivers' strike is to go on.
>
> No solution was reached at a meeting in London today where the National Joint Council for local government manual workers discussed a claim for the review of pay grading.
>
> The drivers wanted an interim pay offer but this was refused.

RT: 21″

(Next item: Daily Mirror strike)

35. 3 April 1975 22.00 Item 13   Simons
(Previous item: Trawlermen blockade ports)
ANDREW/DUSTMEN/SLIDE
> The Glasgow dustcart drivers' strike is to go on.
>
> No agreement was reached at a meeting in London when the National Joint Council for local government manual workers discussed a claim for the review of pay grading.
>
> The drivers wanted an interim pay offer but the employers turned it down because they said it would break the social contract.

RT: 20″

(Next item: Ulster)

36. 5 April 1975 22.30 Item 9   Kallenbach
(Previous item: BR workshop supervisors' work-to-rule)
TIES/FILM ULAY
FILM ULAY   Finally, some of the troops who've been clearing up the rubbish in Glasgow have designed their own tie to mark their spell of dustcart duty.
> The design, chosen by men of the Sword Squadron, shows a half-emptied dustbin with a rat above it.
>
> The men say they got the idea because they wanted to generate some sort of 'common identity' amongst themselves.
>
> They're thinking of giving one to Mr Roy Mason — the secretary for Defence.

RT: 26″

(Last item)

37. 9 April 1975 13.00 Item 3
(Previous item: Vietnam)
GLASGOW RUBBISH/STV LIVE INJECT/SUPER

Back home, the Glasgow dustcart drivers strike is over. The men voted a short time ago to end their 13-week stoppage and go back to work on Monday.

A report now from Les Wilson of Scottish Television.

LIVE INJ
SUPER:
WILSON

For the 500 drivers, the harsh reality is that their 13-week old strike achieved nothing. They haven't added a penny to their pay, and the troops that have been clearing up the backlog of rubbish have robbed the dustcart drivers of hours of overtime. The men are bitter and disillusioned, many of them, not only with Glasgow Corporation, but with their union as well, which never made the strike official. The Corporation are of course delighted. Unlike Liverpool, they haven't had to make an expensive local agreement. The sting in the tail could come from the Ministry of Defence who haven't yet decided whether or not to send the city a bill for Operation Clean-Up. There is one condition to the men's going back. They are not prepared to work alongside the troops. If the men go back on Monday, the troops will have had to have pulled out, and an emergency Corporation meeting this afternoon will decide if that condition can be met. Dan Duffy, one of the strikers' leaders, said that the men had been starved into submission. He said that the Corporation had ratted on an undertaking they gave last October, to hold local negotiations, and Mr Duffy warned that the Corporation's behaviour had done no good to Glasgow's future industrial relations.

RT: 16″ + 1'00″

(Next item: BR workshop supervisors' work-to-rule)

38. 9 April 1975 17.50 Item 2   Simons
(Previous item: Parliament debates EEC)
GLASGOW DUSTMEN/VTR ULAY/LIB VTR

The Glasgow dustcart drivers have ended their strike because of the hardship they were facing. They will return to work on Monday.

VTR ULAY
UP
RT: 16″

The decision to end the 13-week strike came after a meeting this morning when the drivers' shop stewards recommended they go back. One shop stewards' convenor said 'There's no future in banging our heads against a brick wall'.

LIB VTR
ULAY
RT: 34″

Three weeks ago the Government sent 1,300 troops to clear the mounting piles of rubbish. By then there was 75,000 tons of it. The men went out on strike for an extra £5 a week to give them parity with drivers of heavy lorries. But their employers said this would breach the social contract.

One shop steward said the strike had been of no use because they were up against the Government, the Corporation and the troops.

RT: 47″

(Next item: BR workshop supervisors' work-to-rule)

39. 9 April 1975 22.00 Item 10   Simons
(Previous item: Commercial break)
GORDON/DUSTMEN/VTR

The Glasgow dustcart drivers' strike is over. The men said they wouldn't face any more of the hardship the strike was causing them.

A spokesman for the drivers said 'There's no future in banging our heads against a brick wall. The strike was no use because we were up against the Corporation, the Government, and the troops'.

VTR

The bitter 13-week struggle ended this morning when shop stewards recommended at a 2-hour meeting the men should go back.

Les Wilson of Scottish TV asked a shop steward what happened.

VTR
RT: 37″

Shop Steward: After a long discussion with the membership, the shop stewards recommended that in view of the hardship that our members were facing, in view of the fact that the Corporation weren't prepared to honour any agreement, and were continuing to welsh on the agreements they had made with us, we felt that, well, we've got to go back and try and retrieve the situation in other fashions.

RT: 19″ + 31″

(Next item: Hull dock strike)

40. 11 April 1975 17.50 Item 7   Simons
(Previous item: Rail pay)
GLASGOW TROOPS/VTR ULAY/REWRITE

The troops who helped clear Glasgow's rubbish during the dustcart drivers strike finally pulled out this afternoon – ahead of the municipal dustmen who start work again on Monday.

VTR UP:
RT: 21″

The Lord Provost of Glasgow, Sir William Gray, thanked the troops for clearing away – in three weeks – more than half the 75,000 tons of accumulated rubbish.

As a souvenir each of the 2,500 troops is to get a mug and a miniature bottle of whisky inscribed 'a clean drink from a clean city.' Glasgow will also make a substantial donation to the Army Benevolent Fund.

RT: 27″

(Next item: Libyan arms)

41. 11 April 1975 22.00 Item 8   Simons
(Previous item: Rail pay)
REGGIE/DUSTMEN/VTR ULAY

The troops called in to clear away Glasgow's rubbish during the dustcart drivers' strike have left and the dustmen will be back at work on Monday for the first time in [thirteen] weeks. The troops cleared away more than half the 75,000 tons which built up during the dispute.

VTR ULAY
UP
RT: 21″

Before they left Glasgow's Lord President thanked them personally for their dustcart duties. As a souvenir, each of the 2,500 soldiers will receive a mug and a miniature bottle of whisky, inscribed 'a clean drink from a clean city.' Glasgow will also make a substantial donation to the Army Benevolent Fund.

The only casualty the Army suffered was one soldier bitten by a rat.

RT: 39″

(Next item: Electricians' strike)

42. 14 April 1975 13.00 Item 6   Sarah
(Previous item: Enquiry into Moorgate tube disaster)
GLASGOW DUSTMEN/LEWIS VTR/SUPERS

Glasgow's dustcart drivers went back to work this morning after 13 weeks on strike — taking over from the Army who've been very efficiently [doing] the job during for the last few weeks.

From Glasgow, Martyn Lewis reports...

TAKE VTR
SUPER:
MARTYN
LEWIS
REPORTING

Most of the 350 drivers turned up early at the city depots this morning, anxious to start earning money again after their abortive 13-week unofficial strike. The backlog of 45,000 tons of rubbish remaining to be cleared will ensure plenty of overtime working and bonuses with Saturday and Sunday working as well. Glasgow Corporation, anxious to restore good relations after the bitterness of the last three months, say they're making the bonuses as attractive as possible, and are giving the men a reasonable chance to make up something of what they have lost. But the men claim that the minimum target of 50 tons per week for each truck is a high one. Driver Tom Docherty ruefully admits that he won't come anywhere near the £700 – £800 the strike has cost him in lost wages. Mr Docherty would happily go through it all again.

SUPER: TOM
DOCHERTY
DUSTCART
DRIVER

Docherty: I'd strike for the same point again, because I'm a qualified driver, with experience, professional. We're entitled to this money.

Lewis: Your strike doesn't appear to have achieved anything because the army can come in and do your work.

Docherty: (unintelligible)

Lewis: So why go on strike again?

Docherty: ...principle, and we're still entitled to this money. And I think...we won't go on strike — we definitely will if it comes to the point again, and... we must go on strike for it.

Lewis: Another final comment on the return to work came from one of the 2,000 binmen. During the strike they continued working alongside the Army to clear the refuse.

Binman: (unintelligible) should have been back long ago.

RT: 12″ + 1'38″

(Next item: Lebanon)

43. 14 April 1975 17.50 Item 8   Simons
(Previous item: Government cuts forecast of North Sea oil output)
DUSTMEN/LEWIS VTR

The Glasgow dustcart drivers went back to work this morning after their strike, which lasted 13 weeks. Their main job was to carry on where the Army left off, and clear away the backlog of rubbish — 45,000 tons of it.

Martyn Lewis reports:

[Remainder of item identical to 13.00]

RT: 15″ + 1'38″

(Last item)

44. 14 April 1975 22.00 Item 13   Simons
(Previous item: Civil service pay)
ANDREW/DUSTMEN/LEWIS VTR/CAP

The Glasgow dustcart drivers went back to work this morning after 13 weeks on strike.

Their task is to take over where the Army left off and clear the remaining backlog of rubbish. There's 45,000 tons of it and they've got seven weeks to do the job. Martyn Lewis reports:

VTR UP: [remainder of report identical to 17.50]

RT: 18″ + 1'38″

(Next item: Francis Pym resigns from Conservative front bench)

5: SCOTTISH AMBULANCE CONTROLLERS' STRIKE

1. 12 January 1975 18.07 Lead item   Maimane
AMBULANCE/ULAY

FILM TITLE   Scotland's ambulance service will answer only emergency calls from
RT: 20″   tomorrow morning because of a strike by controllers.
              The 90 officers concerned are striking from seven in the morning
in support of a pay claim and an overtime agreement.
              Their strike starts almost exactly a year after 1,100 ambulance
men in Scotland went on strike for a week before accepting a pay
offer of £2.32p. Most of them are not involved in the new strike, but
it will be difficult for them to carry out normal services without
direction from the striking controllers.
              The strike decision was taken at a two-hour meeting in Glasgow.
The controllers say they were left out of an overtime agreement
reached after the last strike, and also out of a pay agreement made
last November.

RT: 50″

(Next item: Rhodesia situation)

2. 12 January 1975 22.00 Lead item   Maimane
AMBULANCE/VTR

              Good evening.
              The Scottish ambulance service will be reduced to emergency
calls only from seven tomorrow morning by a strike of controllers
who direct the ambulance crews.
              The 90 controllers and about 30 administrative officers decided
on the strike at a two-hour meeting in Glasgow. They are
demanding a pay rise, believed to be £10 a week, back-dated to
November, to restore the differential with ambulance crews who
had an increase in November. The strikers also claim that they were
left out of an overtime agreement which was part of the settlement
of the last strike by all 1,100 ambulancemen almost exactly a year
ago.
              Tomorrow's strike — for an indefinite period — will make it
difficult for ambulance crews, who will NOT be on strike, to
provide a normal service except in country areas where the crew
themselves answer calls without going through the controllers.
              From Glasgow, Brian MacLaurin reports.

VTR UP   Today's all-out strike decision by Scotland's 90 controllers will
SUPERS: B.   have dire effects on the smooth running of the mercy service. From
MACLAURIN   tomorrow morning, senior officers will have to man the
REPORTING   switchboards, and this will mean only emergency calls will be
handled. But unlike the ambulance drivers' all-out stoppage last year

when nonunion labour was brought in to help out, I heard unofficially that this won't be tolerated by the controllers. One told me that if blacklegs man the boards, the strike will be extended to include the drivers as well, and the entire service in Scotland will grind to a halt. After today's mass meeting at the ambulance headquarters in Glasgow, I spoke to a full-time official of the major union involved, the Transport and General Workers':

SUPER: JOHN
MACCALL
TGWU
OFFICIAL

MacLaurin: Mr. MacCall, what will be the immediate effect of this all-out strike?

MacCall: Well, after a decision this evening, it means virtually as far as Scotland's concerned, there'll be no ambulances on the road tomorrow.

MacLaurin: You don't think action like this is totally irresponsible, putting lives in danger?

MacCall: Well, you know, somebody in general can say this is an irresponsible action but, you know, they're very responsible people up till now. They've been abused, the service has been abused, we're getting virtually nowhere, boxing with kid gloves. Now they feel that the gloves have got to come off, and we've got to...

MacLaurin: Could this dispute spread to England?

MacCall: Well, let's say this. Before the meeting this evening I had calls from south of the border. I just don't want to tell you what depots they came from in England, but we had notification from some of the offices in England, and I feel this could possibly spread by Tuesday to England.

MacLaurin: Tonight a spokesman from the Scottish Ambulance Association appealed to members of the public to help out in this crisis and not to call an ambulance unless it's a matter of life and death. BM, for ITN.

RT: 51″ + 1'43″

(Next item: Glasgow dustcart drivers' strike)

3. 13 January 1975 13.00 Item 3   Stevens
(Previous item: Bazooka attack at Orly airport)
SCOTTISH AMBULANCE STRIKE/LEWIS INJ. EX STV/MAP/SUPER
     In Scotland the men who control ambulance crews duly began their pay strike this morning. But the effects of it seem less widespread than people thought it was going to be.
     Hospitals have of course been hit. Out-patients, for example, have had to get lifts to hospital from friends, or forego their

appointments.

MAP

But despite the warning that it was to be an all-out strike, ambulance crews ARE answering emergency calls.

SUPER

And over the north and northwest of the country, in fact, the entire ambulance service seemed to be working normally. Some of the crews in rural areas there don't HAVE controllers to supervise them in any case.

N/C

But the picture's been somewhat different in Glasgow and the west, as Martyn Lewis reports:

TAKE STV INJ
SUPER LEWIS
REPORTING

When the men who send out the ambulances walked out of Glasgow's central control room at 7 o'clock this morning, they left behind the city's chief ambulance officer trying to do the work of 9 men. How did they think he'd get on?

Ambulanceman: Well, as far as I can see, he may manage the road accidents, emergencies, and things like that, but as far as the ordinary routine work — that's the out-patient department — there's normally about five or six hundred patients. So I fancy these patients will need to be brought into hospital today.

Lewis: In fact, the Glasgow Controllers normally handle 800 calls a day. Most of these, routine calls taking out-patients to hospital for check-ups, are in advance. Today the booked booking sheets lay abandoned on empty desks. And switchboard operators, like the ambulance crews still working, firmly turned down all but emergency calls.

(SOF) Twenty-six emergency calls came in in the first four hours of the strike, slightly fewer than usual. chief ambulance officer, David Ramsay, personally dealt with them all, including the first one at exactly 27 minutes after the start of the strike. (SOF) An old man had fallen from a first floor window — a typical emergency said the crew men as they swung into action — and it's clear that so far all emergency calls have been dealt with.

(SOF) I asked the chief ambulance Officer if he would be able to stay in the control room all day:

SUPER:
DAVID
RAMSAY
CHIEF AMB
OFFICER

Ramsay: Yes, as I'm the chief ambulance officer I've got to take over elsewhere and deal with business. I'm in charge of the running of the ambulance service in Glasgow.

Lewis: Who's likely to take your place?

Ramsay: Well, at this stage I don't know if there's anybody.

Lewis: And meanwhile, shop stewards representing the men on strike are in conference at the Transport and General Workers' Glasgow headquarters, discussing the mixed response throughout

Scotland to the strike call and tactics for the days ahead. ML, FR, Glasgow.

RT: 43″ + 2'15″

(Next item: Glasgow dustcart drivers' strike)

4. 13 January 1975 17.50 Item 8   Mawer
(Previous item: IMF and Healey plan for recycling petrodollars)
AMBULANCES/LEWIS VTR

Ambulance services in west and central Scotland have been badly hit by a pay strike of officers, including controllers.

And one of their union leaders has warned that industrial action could spread to major cities in England and Northern Ireland.

The strike isn't total. Officers in the north east of Scotland are reported to be working normally and those in Edinburgh are handling emergency calls. But in the west and central areas, senior staff are dealing with the emergencies.

From Glasgow, Martyn Lewis reports.

VTR SUPER
MARTYN
LEWIS
REPORTING

The men who send out the ambulances walked out of Glasgow's control room at 7 this morning and left behind the city's chief ambulance officer trying to do the work of nine men. This call at 20 minutes past 7 was his first emergency; seven hours later he'd dealt with 81, a pattern repeated throughout the west of Scotland, as the 6 senior officers in this huge area found themselves under increasing pressure. Glasgow controllers normally dictate the pattern of 800 ambulances a day, most of them out-patient calls booked in advance. All these were cancelled today, the booking forms piling up in front of empty chairs. Telephonists who are still at work were ordered to firmly turn down all requests for help except emergencies.
SOF: 'It's only emergencies we're doing.'

Lewis: Quite clearly the senior officers can't carry on like [that] for very long, so what happens then?

SUPER:
DEREK
BUCKLEY
DIRECTOR
SCOTTISH
AMBU-
LANCE
SERVICE

Buckley: Well we shall have to look at some other emergency measures, but I think we'll have to consult elsewhere before I can give any information, of course, of what measures might be undertaken.

Lewis: The possibility of the police being called in was one of the subjects discussed by the strikers' shop stewards who were in conference all day in Glasgow, and they seem only too conscious of the need to preserve a good public image.

JOHN
MCCOLL
TCWU

McColl: I would [say] at least we'll get some feeling back, as we're not as [ir] responsible as everyone says we are, and if we allow the police to cooperate and assist the people in Scotland and have some sort of a service, at least we're being reasonable.

RT: 28″ + 1′43″

(Next item: Glasgow dustcart drivers' strike)

5. 13 January 1975 22.00 Item 7   Mawer
(Previous item: Arabs)
ANDREW/AMBULANCEMEN/MAP/SLIDE/LEWIS VTR/SUPERS
MAP/CHROMA Ambulance services in west and central Scotland are dealing with emergencies only tonight because of a strike of officers who man the control rooms. But those in the north of Scotland haven't joined the strike and in the east they're still at work handling only emergency calls.

SLIDE: The Scottish Under Secretary of State, Mr. Robert Hughes, said in the Commons he regretted the officers' action, especially when their grading and salary structure was due to be discussed on Friday. The officers want the pay differential between them and the ambulance crews restored.

From the hardest-hit area, where 70 officers have totally withdrawn their labour, Martyn Lewis reports:

VTR UP   [report identical to 17.50 with this addition:]

Lewis: That gives hope that the emergency service at least will continue, but the chances of restoring a full normal service will have to wait for the next round of talks on Friday. Signoff.

RT: 36″ + 1′52″

(Next item: Glasgow dustcart drivers' strike)

6. 15 January 1975 13.00 Item 7B   Mann
(Previous item: Scottish teachers' pay)
INDUSTRIAL WRAP
The strike of ambulance controllers in Scotland continues and there's a meeting of ambulancemen from the north-west in Manchester today to decide whether to take any action in support of their pay claim. There's to be a meeting in Manchester between union representatives and managements.

RT: 16″

(Next item: Holiday)

7. 15 January 1975 22.00 Item 17   Henderson
(Previous item: Israeli reprisal raid)
ANDREW/AMBULANCEMEN

Here at home ambulance drivers from the north-west of England, who have been meeting in Manchester tonight, voted to strike from midnight tomorrow in support of their pay claim. But they agree to keep an emergency only service going.

This means that they will join the Scottish ambulance controllers who are still out on strike for higher wages.

RT: 19″

(Next item: Soccer results)

8. 18 January 1975 13.10 Item 4   Mawer
(Previous item: Fleet Street dispute)
AMBULANCEMEN

Scottish ambulance controllers are to meet tomorrow to consider a £9 a week interim pay award.

The Scottish controllers have been on strike since Monday in a dispute over wage differentials. A union official said he thought there would be a split tomorrow over whether to call off industrial action and accept the award.

But the director of the Scottish Ambulance Service, Mr. Derek Buckley, said he was confident the controllers would go back.

RT: 27″

(Next item: Prior on wage settlements)

9. 19 January 1975 22.00 Item 4   MDW
(Previous item: Fleet Street dispute)
AMBULANCEMEN

Scotland's week-old ambulance service strike is to end at seven o'clock tomorrow morning. At a meeting in Glasgow the ambulance officers decided to call off their strike and accept an interim pay offer of nine pounds a week.

And in the north-west of England a similar offer was accepted by ambulancemen on strike there.

RT: 19"

(Next item: Greece and Cyprus situation)

6: THE IMPERIAL TYPEWRITER SIT-IN

1. 17 January 1975 22.00 Item 12
(Previous item: Vauxhall short time working)
        [proposed closure of Imperial factory: not available]

RT: 16″

(Next item: Cyprus situation)

2. 21 February 1975 13.00 Item 2
(Previous item: Leslie Whittle kidnapping)
IMPERIAL TYPEWRITERS/VTR/FILM
        As from this morning, 3,000 workers at the Imperial Typewriter works in Hull and Leicester are out of a job. Despite continuing efforts to save their jobs, Litton Industries, which owns the plants, decided to go ahead with the closure as planned.
        But 300 workers at the Hull works have taken over the factory and say they intend to stay — despite the fact that more than 600 of the work force there have already taken their redundancy pay and left.
        The workers who've decided to stay on say they're looking to the Industry Secretary, Mr Benn for help to save their jobs.
        Mr Benn himself was in Leeds this morning, and he's accused Litton Industries of 'behaving irresponsibly'. He said he was still awaiting a report on the firm commissioned by the Government, but he thought things might have been different if there'd been a planning agreement.
        Our industrial correspondent, Michael Green reports:

FILM   Five weeks ago today, the Imperial workers were told the plants would close, and a rearguard battle to save the 3,200 jobs has been

SUPER: raging ever since. Litton Industries, the American conglomerate
GREEN/   which took over the ailing Imperial Company in 1966, has lost £9
HULL   million trying to revive its fortunes, but its been beaten by a rapid rise in costs — particularly wages, and a slump in sales. Here in Hull, many workers have but little chance of another job.

Vox Pop: There's no prospect at all.

Green: Have you been looking?

Vox Pop: Well, yes, we've been to the Employment, and there's nothing in the Employment in town. There isn't anything. Not for the women.

Green: Are you on the assembly line?

Vox Pop: Yes, we're ever so sorry it's happening, aren't we?

Green: Was there nothing you felt could be done?

Vox Pop: Well, we're trying — that's all you can do, isn't it?

Green: The job situation in Hull is already bad, with unemployment over 4% and jobs for unskilled men hard to come by. Independent consultants appointed by the Government to see if it's worth saving have been urged by the unions to recommend a £3 million grant to keep them going. But the company is convinced this wouldn't be feasible. Littons, which bought the German Triumph-Adler company after it took over Imperial, plan instead to sell the German machines in this country under the Imperial brand name. The company deny accusations that it left things too late to mount a rescue operation.

SUPER:
FREDDIE
ST.CLAIR
IMPERIAL AT
1.49 CUT TO
VTR 20″
AVAIL.

St. Clair: The real problem was that as we got deeper and deeper into our discussions in connection with the productive capacity of…within the Litton organisation, a very dramatic change in the market as a result of a fall in the market it became quite clear that Litton itself would be able to meet its obligations from its German factory, and under these conditions, the least cost-effective of the units was virtually bound to be sacrificed because of the market conditions.

AT 1.59 BACK
TO FILM
AFTER
WORDS 'THE
GOVERN-
MENT
HADN'T
TO DO'

Green: But the workers don't accept this verdict. On Tuesday they went to London to lobby MPs, but Mr Benn the Industry Secretary, told them the Government hadn't decided what to do. What makes the Imperial case so important is that it's one of the few instances where an American company has deliberately shut down its operations in the United Kingdom with the intention of supplying the home market here from abroad. It's bound to make the Government more sceptical about foreign takeovers in the future, and will increase its determination to exert closer control over the multinationals here in the future. MG, FR, Hull.

RT: 1′06″ + 2′29″

(Next item: Doubts about future of Harrier)

3. 21 February 1975 17.50 Item 3   O'Connell
(Previous item: Watergate)
TYPEWRITERS/VTR

In Yorkshire, 300 redundant workers have taken over the Imperial Typewriter factory in Hull and have appealed to the Industry Secretary, Mr Benn, to save their jobs.

SLIDE   Mr Benn has accused the American owners — Litton Industries — of 'behaving irresponsibly' in closing both their Hull and Leicester

CUE VTR
plants from today — putting nearly 3,000 people out of work. More than 600 workers at the Hull factory have already accepted redundancy payments and left. But there was some hope this afternoon for the others taking part in the sit-in.

A consultants report — ordered by the Government — does suggest ways in which production could be started again at the two plants. The recommendations will be the subject of further talks between the Government and trade union leaders.

RT: 21" + 20"

(Next item: British Aircraft Corporation Strike)

4. 21 February 1975 22.00 Item 6   O'Connell
(Previous item: Strasbourg Court ruling on British prisoner)
REGGIE/TYPEWRITERS/GREEN VTR/SUPERS/SLIDE

The Imperial Typewriter plant in Hull has been taken over by 300 redundant workers who have refused to accept their dismissal notices and have appealed to the Industry Secretary, Mr Benn, to save their jobs.

SLIDE
(BENN)
Mr Benn has already accused the American owners — Litton Industries — of irresponsible behaviour in closing both their Hull and Leicester factories, putting nearly 3,000 out of work.

[Our] industrial correspondent Michael Green reports:

GREEN VTR
SUPER
MICHAEL
GREEN
To try to avoid trouble the management closed the plant last night — a day early. But the more militant workers climbed the gates in defiance of this decision to begin the threatened sit-in.

And their leaders were obviously angry at what they regarded as a deliberate attempt by their employers to deceive them:

SOUND UP
ON VTR
SUPER
TGWU SHOP
STEWARD
[Tate:] After we had all left, the management sent us all a special delivery letter, at a fee of 44½p, not forgetting this company is telling us all along the line they have no money. After receiving that letter, the stewards gathered round, and we decided what we was going to do. As we have said all along, there's two roads, and we know which road we're on. This factory belongs to us. Littons have disowned us.

VTR

SOF OUT
[Green]It was five weeks ago today that the Imperial workers were told the plants would close. And a rearguard battle to save the 3,200 jobs has been raging ever since.

Litton Industries, the American conglomerate which took over the ailing Imperial company in 1966 has lost £9 million trying to revive its fortunes.

The workers are bound to be encouraged by the Government's promise of further talks with the unions to discuss the possibility —

no more — of keeping production going.

But as far as the present management's concerned: this is the end of the road.

What makes Imperial's case so important, is that it's one of the few instances where an American firm has deliberately shut down its operations in Britain with the intention of supplying the home market here from abroad. It's bound to make the Government more sceptical about foreign takeovers in the future, and is bound to increase its determination to maintain closer control over the multinationals here in future. MG, NAT, Hull.

RT: 24″ + 1'46″

(Next item: Lloyds Bank loses £28 million)

5. 22 February 1975 13.10 Item 5   Purvis
(Previous item: Ulster)
IMPERIAL/STILL FRAME

STILL FRAME   The sacked workers at the Imperial Typewriters factory in Hull are continuing their sit-in in protest at the closure of the plant by the American owners. Some say they will stay inside for several weeks if necessary until the Government say whether they can save any of the fourteen hundred jobs. A union official is expected to report to the workers today on talks he's had with the Industry Secretary, Mr Benn.

RT: 22″

(Next item: Queen's Caribbean tour)

6. 22 February 1975 17.14 Item 6   Purvis
(Previous item: Croydon)
IMPERIAL/STILL FRAME

STILL FRAME   Sacked workers are still occupying the Imperial Typewriters factory in Hull in protest at the closure of Imperial's British operation by the American owners. They say they'll stay there until the Government announce whether they can save any of the fourteen hundred jobs.

N/C   A union official who's seen the Industry Secretary, Mr Benn, says it would be wrong to raise false hopes.

RT: 22″

(Last item)

7. 23 June 1975 13.00 Item 3   Mawer
(Previous item: TUC General Council adopts pay policy principles)
IMPERIAL/THIRKETTLE FILM/SUPERS

Of course there are those who say that the inevitable unemployment

which inflation brings will itself in the end be the only effective
corrective to excessive wage demands. Nearly 870,000 out of work
according to the official figures. Only 423,000 — less than half —
according to Sir Keith Joseph, working away at his Centre of Policy
Studies. Either way losing your job is something that's gradually
happening to more and more people. When it happened to people at
the Imperial Typewriter factory in Hull after the American owners
closed down the plant in February, the people refused to be closed
down and sat in, hoping to persuade the Government or a private
investor to pump enough money in to keep the factory going. The
Department of Industry is considering the matter at the moment and
should be announcing its decision soon. Meanwhile, the sit-in
continues, as Joan Thirkettle reports:

TAKE FILM
SUPER: JOAN
THIRKETTLE
REPORTING

After more than four months, workers at the Imperial
Typewriter factory in Hull are as determined as ever to continue
their sit-in. Out of an original workforce of 1400, 280 of them still
turn up every day. Despite the fact that Tony Benn, one of the
pioneers of worker participation, has left the Department of
Industry, the workers are still hoping for Government help. Clearly
they see themselves [as going] along the same path as the Scottish
Daily News and Triumph Motor Cycle workers. The Department
has already commissioned a feasibility study. They're anxious to
maintain employment levels in the area, and workers resent the
opinions of some experts who say there's no future for them no
matter what the set up. (SOF) It'll take an initial investment of about
£5 million to get Imperial going again, and it could be a risky
proposition. In the past the bulk of Imperial's products was sold to
the States, but demand is falling heavily. Litton Industries, the
American owners of Imperial, lost £8 million on its British plants
before closing them and retreating to West Germany. They blame
inflation and the three-day week, but one person who thinks there's
much more at stake than simply the loss of a company and the jobs
that go with it is John Prescott, MP for Hull.

SUPER: JOHN
PRESCOTT

Prescott: If a multi-national decides that we'll no longer produce
typewriters and business equipment in this country, that's a very
serious consequence for this country, because (a) it means we now
must import those typewriters from Germany because they decide
to produce in Germany, and it also means that we as a country as
Tony Benn has been saying often enough and Government
spokesmen, that we must decide those areas in which we must
produce — is it two things? Is it cars? Is it typewriters? And we have
to concentrate on special skills, and our specialised skills must be in
that field, and if we give that up, we give up a whole range of areas

of production that we might have, and need to export in order to survive, so the question is much more fundamental than the future of us in Hull.

Thirkettle: But Litton say they've no choice. They feel that wage inflation and soaring costs make it impossible for any country to make typewriters here at a profit, but the events at Imperial demonstrate the ease with which international companies can pull out of Britain, taking jobs and investment with them. One of the aims of the Government's new Industry Bill is to exercise close control over multi-nationals. The loss of Imperial £30 million at a time when we can ill afford it. JK, FR, Hull.

RT: Not available

(Next item: Chrysler workers end strike)

8. 4 July 1975 17.50 Item 5   Chamberlain
(Previous item: Pay dispute at Rolls Royce aero)
TYPEWRITER/LIB.FILM U'LAY

LIB U'LAY   The 70 workers who've been staging a sit-in for more than four months at the Imperial Typewriters factory in Hull may soon be facing a High Court writ.

END U'LAY   The American company which announced the closure of the plant last February with the loss of 1,400 jobs has applied for a writ to regain occupation of the factory.
AVAIL: 22"

Their move follows an announcement by the Department of Industry earlier this week that there was NO hope of creating a British typewriter company based on the Hull factory and another Imperial Typewriter plant at Leicester which has also been closed down.

RT: 35"

(Next item: Jackal)

9. 4 July 1975 22.00 Item 7   Chamberlain
(Previous item: Pay dispute at Rolls Royce aero)
REGGIE/ TYPEWRITERS/ LIB FILM U/LAY

U/LAY   The seventy workers who've been staging a sit-in for more than four
20" AVAIL   months at the Imperial Typewriter factory in Hull may soon be facing a High Court writ.

The American company, which closed down the plant last February with the loss of 1,400 jobs, has applied for the writ to
U/L OUT   regain occupation of the building.

RT: 17"
(Next item: Enquiry into death of baby)

10. 5 July 1975 13.10 Item 5   Mawer
(Previous item: Chemical workers)
IMPERIAL/ SLIDE

SLIDE   Writs were delivered today against 70 former employees at the
               Imperial Typewriters factory in Hull and they've been ordered to
               leave.
                   The writs were pushed through the factory gates but were
               apparently ignored by the former workers who've been sitting in for
               four months.
                   The American company closed down the factory in February —
               but they've said they want to regain possession to fulfil outstanding
               legal and commercial obligations.

RT: 23″

(Next item: Jackal)

11. 16 July 1975 22.00 Item N/A   Thompson
(Previous item: 160 Labour MPs back Reg Prentice in constituency row)
LEONARD/ IMPERIAL/ VTR U'LAY

               Workers at the Imperial Typewriter company in Hull admitted
               defeat today, and ended their sit-in which had lasted more than five
               months.
VTR U'LAY   Nearly eighty men and women were led out from the plant by
UP 42″ AVAIL   union officials. The sit-in lasted one hundred and forty six days.
                   They marked the length of their vigil by a coffin draped with the
               union jack.
                   Many were in tears as they passed through the factory gates.

               (PAUSE 4″)

                   They d all been clinging to one last hope. A new enterprise had
               been promised for the factory. But the firm interested finally
VTR U'LAY   dropped out of the deal.
OUT
RT: 40″

(Next item: Birmingham bomb trial)

7: THE LONDON BUS STRIKE

1. 23 January 1975 13.00 Item 7   Mann
(Previous item: Problems of British civilians in Cyprus)
BUSMEN/STUDIO INTERVIEW/SUPER

Back home, shop stewards from various bus depots are meeting [tonight] to discuss the possibility of a one-day national strike in protest against the sort of violence now prevalent on the buses which killed a conductor in London last weekend.

There were a thousand assaults on busmen in London alone last year. Most big cities are having trouble as well. Even in relatively peaceful towns like Bridgend in Glamorgan, bus crews in the past have banned late night services because they're afraid of attack. With me now is Mr Larry Smith, National Secretary for the passenger services group of the Transport & General Workers' Union.

STUDIO
INTERVIEW
SUPER:
LARRY
SMITH

Kee: How widespread in fact are these attacks, or is it mainly that London . . .

Smith: Well, in London of course it's exaggerated because of the total number of buses and bus crews running in a highly densely populated town, but it's happening all over the country.

Kee: And is it happening in all areas of London?

Smith: Oh, in all areas of London, there's no isolated centre of these attacks.

Kee: Do you think the penalties for the people who are caught perpetrating these attacks are in fact stiff enough?

Smith: Well, if you think a slap on the wrist and telling them to go home and behave themselves is sufficient punishment, no. The facts are of course that the courts are quite lenient with people that are making these vicious attacks on public servants.

Kee: What do you think ought to be done to prevent them, or what could be done?

Smith: Well, firstly, we think that the Home Secretary ought to ensure that if necessary a Bill to Parliament to give power to the courts to treat offenders against public servants in the same way as they would for the police − in other words, that it's quite inadequate to say that the quasi-legal position of a bus conductor who's attempting to enforce the law is in the same way as a postman or a miner. It isn't like that. What needs to be done is to be treated as though he is a legal enforcer of the law, and therefore the penalties about attacking him should be the same as those applying to the police.

Kee: What else might be done to help protect bus crews − I've seen it suggested that a policeman might travel on every bus — it might even come to that. Is that reasonable?

Smith: Well, it ought to be a reflection on our society if that was indeed the case. I don't think busmen themselves believe that that's necessary, but they want to be assured that their morale is not going to be again endangered by the fact that people do not take action. We want the public involved. We want them because it's their transport that's affected and will be affected if buses are removed.

Kee: What about certain technical devices that might help, such as perhaps even a radio on a bus, or alarm signal, something like that?

Smith: Two-way radios, Klaxon horns, flashing lights, these have all been suggested, and are indeed being fitted — but we consider at the end of the road, they're palliatives. If indeed you don't educate the public that they ought to be invoved against these assailants on bus crews.

Kee: On the whole the passengers just let these attacks take place and don't do anything?

Smith: Yes, I can understand if it was a brawl in the street, that people want to avoid, but to be inconvenienced by some youths that attack conductors seems to me not the way in which the public ought to behave.

Kee: Thank you very much Mr Smith. I don't see how anyone could disagree with Mr Smith on that.

RT: 37″ + 3'00″

(Next item: Report on new private hospital)

2. 29 January 1975 13.00 Item 2   Stevens
(Previous item: Censorship row; Mary Whitehouse interview)
BUS STRIKE/LYNDALL FILM

Not a single bus has been on the roads in London this morning. The drivers and conductors — all 20 thousand of them — are taking the day off, to join in the funeral of a colleague of theirs — the conductor Ronald Jones, who died after a personal attack on him in his bus last week.

The action is simultaneously a protest against the general increase in such urban violence which is making their working life a real personal hazard.

SLIDE   Mr Jack Jones, general secretary of the Transport & General Workers' Union, who led thousands of busmen on the funeral march said: 'This is a symbol of the problems we've been trying to impress on successive Governments about assaults, attacks and abuse of the men and women carrying out essential public service.' Lyndall Hobbs reports on the funeral — and the effect of the one-day strike on the London public:

FILM UP:
SUPER:
LYNDALL
HOBBS
REPORTING

Empty bus lanes told the story this morning. On any normal day, five and a half thousand buses are on London's roads. But today, none were in sight, and other traffic was reported 20% heavier than usual, since several tube services also had to be cancelled. It was here, at the Merton depot, in south west London a week ago, that 270 drivers and conductors decided unanimously to stage a one-day token strike in sympathy for their dead colleague, and to demand greater security for London transport bus crews. Mr Jones, a Jamaican, was hit on the back of the head in Lavender Hill, after an argument on his bus, and later died in hospital from his injuries. With assaults on bus crews running at about a thousand a year, Transport Union leaders want an urgent meeting with the Home Secretary, to discuss bus crews having the same protection under the law as policemen. They also intend complaining about the leniency meted out to offenders. Drivers and conductors from garages all over London, along with many country busmen, gathered in the rain at Wandworth Common this morning, before marching half a mile to the African Methodist Church, where a memorial service was held. I spoke to some of the men about the risk they run:

Busman: The trouble is over the last five years it's deteriorating, especially the youngsters. They get on, they don't want to pay their fare, that is where the trouble comes in, especially if you work a route where you have a social club, or something like that, or the pubs, when they come out at night.

Busman: As a natural deterrent, well, as you probably well know, there's an experimental bus out with flashing lights and sirens and things like this.

Hobbs: Do most people just sit back and watch if they see something happening on a bus?

Busman: This seems to be the general attitude of the public.

Hobbs: The effects of the bus strike will be felt all day throughout London and some country areas, but the Transport Union has threatened calling out bus members throughout the country — 160,000 in all, for another stoppage, unless the government meet their demands for action against violence [against] busmen. LR, FR, Wandsworth.

RT: 48" + 2'30"

(Next item: Parliamentary controversy over pensioners' earnings)

3. 29 January 1975 17.50 Item 3   Jill
(Previous item: Lotteries)
BUSES/FILM ULAY/OLIVER FILM/SUPERS

ULAY UP   No buses have been running in London today. The city's 20,000
drivers and conductors stopped work to mark the funeral of Ronald
Jones — the conductor who died last week after being attacked on his
bus.
　　　　Some underground workers joined the 24-hour stoppage, and a
quarter of all the scheduled trains didn't run during the morning
ULAY OUT   peak period.
20″ AVAIL   　　But despite the cut-back in public transport, traffic was up only
about 20 per cent and there were few trouble spots.
　　　　4,000 of the dead conductor's colleagues marched to the
memorial service at Wandsworth. Michael Oliver reports:

OLIVER FILM   The busmen congregated on the side of Wandsworth Common.
UP SUPER: They were both showing sympathy with their dead colleague, and
MICHAEL   protesting against the increasing violence they all have to face
OLIVER   nowadays. Some of the men have suggested installing 2-way radios
REPORTING   in all buses, and others have called for increased legal protection. The
quarter mile walk to the church was led by the Transport Workers'
leader, Mr Jack Jones. Hundreds of the marchers crowded into the
African Methodist Church, but many more to follow the service
outside. Ronald Jones' widow had had flown over from Jamaica to
be present in church. She was comforted by relatives during the
service. Several tributes were paid to the dead man's quiet and
unassuming manner. Mr Jack Jones summed up the busman's life.

SUPER: **Jones:** Working in public transport is no man's paradise. But it's a
JACK   service which helps all working people in this metropolis, and assists
JONES   elderly people, and those who wish to travel. A service worthy of
TGWU   respect, and society owes a simple debt to those who undertake such
public service, to permit the responsibilities to be discharged
without hindrance, and without the fear of physical attack and
abuse.

RT: 33″ + 1'25″
(Next item: Fleet Street NGA dispute)

4. 29 January 1975 22.00 Item 14   Jill
(Previous item: Commercial break)
REGGIE/BUS STRIKE/FILM ULAY/OLIVER FILM/SUPERS

ULAY UP   London has been without buses. 20-thousand drivers and conductors
stopped work for the funeral of Ronald Jones — the conductor who
died last week after being attacked on his bus.

RT: 20″
AVAIL

Some underground train workers also joined in a 24-hour stoppage. Four thousand of Mr Jones' colleagues marched to the memorial service in Wandsworth:
Michael Oliver reports:

FILM UP   [film as at 17.50]

RT: 19' + 1'25″

(Next item: Northern Ireland sectarian murders)

8: BRITISH AIRWAYS

1. 30 January 1975 22.00 Item 18A   Sissons
(Previous item: Duke of Edinburgh)
REGGIE/AIRWAYS

A mass meeting of British Airways' workers is to be held at Heathrow tomorrow to decide whether the airline is grounded from Monday week.

Shop stewards will advise 11,000 engineering and maintenance staff to go on strike, because of failure to agree on a new pay deal. The deal, which has already been accepted by nearly 20,000 other British Airways staff, consolidates threshold payments into basic pay, and gives an additional 15% in two stages. The engineers want 23%.

RT: 28″

(Next item: Test match)

2. 31 January 1975 17.50 Item 3   Miles
(Previous item: Duke of Norfolk ill)
AIRWAYS/FILM/SUPER

The strike that could have grounded all British Airways flights has been averted.

The airline's engineering and maintenance staff at London's Heathrow Airport this afternoon voted to reject their union's strike call — and have accepted the employers' pay offer instead.

Our industrial correspondent, Giles Smith, was at the mass meeting at Heathrow.

FILM: SUPER: The decision to reject the union's advice took the men less than
SMITH   half an hour and from the look at the voting it was almost
unanimous. The decision is a major blow to the authority of the
shop stewards.

Shop Steward: It's the men's own decision that they don't agree
with, so let them strike.

Smith: They've overturned their shop stewards' recommendations.
Why do you feel they felt so strongly?

Shop Steward: I suppose they don't want to go on strike. It's as
simple as that, isn't it? The majority of the people came to the
decision because they don't want to [strike] for the simple reason
that it's quite a good offer.

Smith: Did the fact that the airline's in considerable financial trouble
have anything to do with it?

Shop Steward: It's quite possible, but the whole country's in a lot
of trouble.

Smith: Tonight British Airways, who warned a strike could cripple
the airline, warmly welcomed the vote. Now they face only one
major problem: the threatened walk-out by booking staff if the
airline goes ahead with its plan tomorrow for cabin staff to collect
fares on the new Glasgow shuttle service. Giles Smith, ITN, London
Airport.

RT: 18″ + 1'05″

(Next item: British Caledonian)

3. 31 January 1975 22.00 Item 4   Miles
(Previous item: Stock market)
REGGIE/AIRWAYS/SMITH/FILM/SUPER
The threatened strike that could have grounded all British Airways
flights is off.

A mass meeting of the airline's engineering and maintenance staff
at London Airport rejected their union's strike call, and voted instead
to accept the employer's pay offer.

Our industrial correspondent, Giles Smith, was at Heathrow.

FILM UP   [film as at 17.50]

RT: 16″ + 1'04″

(Next item: Wilson on meeting with President Ford)

4. 1 February 1975 13.10 Lead item   Mawer

SHUTTLE/OLIVER FILM/SUPER

TITLE/FILM ULAY
At London's Heathrow Airport long queues of passengers built up this morning because of a strike by British Airways clerical and ticket staff. Flights to Europe were delayed by up to 20 minutes.

The strike was in protest at British Airways' decision to start selling tickets on board aircraft on their new shuttle service to Glasgow.

Michael Oliver reports:

SUPER: MICHAEL OLIVER REPORTING
Although the shuttle service between Heathrow and Glasgow was begun three weeks ago, with no booking, but a guaranteed seat for anyone who turns up, it wasn't until today that British Airways started collecting fares on board. On the first flight to Glasgow most of the 50 passengers paid their £17 direct to the stewardesses. In protest the ground staff, members of APEX, stopped work. The checking in was left to managerial volunteers. On domestic flights the check in was at the departure gate, but on European flights in the main concourse. The members of APEX fear that the pay on board system will spread to more flights and lead to redundancies among their members, while cabin staff increase. Long queues built up but delays to flights were kept to less than half an hour, and by mid morning, despite the milling crowds, the makeshift system for getting passengers away was working. MO, ITN, Heathrow.

RT:
Approx. 20″ + 54″

(Next item: Ulster)

5. 1 February 1975 17.12 Item 2
(Previous item: Sugar)

Mawer

SHUTTLE/OLIVER FILM/SUPER

At Heathrow Airport, British Airways clerical and ticket staff have gone on indefinite strike over the airline's decision to sell tickets on board aircraft on their new shuttle service to Glasgow.

British Airways were forced to cancel a flight to Helsinki and there were delays on other flights to Europe.

Michael Oliver reports:

FLUP
[Film as at 13.10]

RT:
18″ + 54″

(Next item: Ulster)

6. 1 February 1975 22.30 Item 5
(Previous item: Enoch Powell)

Thompson

SHUTTLE/OLIVER FILM/SUPER
> At London's Heathrow Airport, British Airways clerical staff decided, after a 2-hour meeting, to go on indefinite strike over the airline's decision to allow passengers to buy 'instant tickets' on their new shuttle service to Glasgow.
>
> British Airways are considering extending the buy-your-ticket-on-board idea to their other services. Today they were forced to cancel some flights, and delay others because of the dispute.
>
> Michael Oliver reports...

FLUP   [Film as at 13.10 and 17.12]

RT: 23″ + 55″

(Next item: Ulster)

7. 3 February 1975 13.00 Item 7   Mann
(Previous item: Cheap shirts)
AIRPORT STRIKE/STUDIO INTV/SUPER
> British Airways flights to Europe are still being disrupted by that strike of 450 clerical workers at Heathrow and there's no sign at the moment of any end to it. The trouble is over the new shuttle flight from London to Glasgow, which British Airways introduced last month. On this service you don't buy a ticket from a clerk in advance. You're guaranteed a seat if you simply arrive, walk on the plane and pay on board, like on a bus. The clerical workers are saying no-one should be able to sell tickets but them. Well, British Airways say they'll refer the dispute to the Arbitration, Conciliation & Advisory Service. On the other hand, the clerical workers union leader, Mr Tudor Thomas, of the Association of Professional, Executive, Clerical & Computer Staff, warned last night he was considering extending the strike. He's with me in the studio now.

Kee: Mr Thomas, aren't you really saying, as if it were a matter of principle somehow, that the maintenance of these clerical workers' jobs is really more important than the convenience and efficiency of the service to the public?

Thomas: We're not saying that at all.

Kee: It sounds like that, though.

Thomas: Well, it may sound it to you, but perhaps I could explain why I don't think so.

Kee: Please.

Thomas: In the first place, we have not opposed the introduction of shuttle − I think the economics of shuttle are very suspect, but nevertheless we have not opposed the introduction of a system which will help us to retrieve some of the lost traffic on the London-Glasgow route. What we are saying is that we should have been properly consulted right from the time that British Airways decided to go ahead with this, and we certainly shouldn't have had jobs which are traditionally our members' jobs taken away from us without our agreement. This is precisely what we are saying, but if we go one further — and I think that this has to be looked upon against the background of what my union and my members have done in civil air transport — we'd cooperate. This is the first dispute, incidentally, involving my union, in air transport.

Kee: But can we just be quite clear what the dispute is about. The way you put it it sounds as if it's just a question of your dignity — you weren't properly consulted, but you're not against what's actually happening?

Thomas: Well, I think we're entitled to our dignity in this situation...

Kee: Yes, of course.

Thomas: ...especially with our record in the industry...

Kee: ...but are you against what's happening?

Thomas: We're against the collection of fares, and the uplifting of coupons, as we call it, flight coupons in the air, because, let's be quite clear, amongst the group of staff concerned we agreed to a situation last year where 103 jobs were lost. We've got a reservation system which — I've got the figures, I took them this morning — where we'd 409 staff in 1964; last Saturday we had only 442, which is an increase of 8% and yet from '64 to '73 — I can't take you later because BEA amalgamated with British Airways — but until that time the traffic had increased by 73%. In other words, 8% more staff, partly affected by this, for 73% more production. Now the point I want to make is this: that we have cooperated to the hilt on this, but we do feel that where something is traditionally a clerical worker's job, or administrative worker's job, we're entitled to maintain that, when we participate and cooperate in the introduction of new systems.

Kee: But then in spite of your denial at the beginning of the interview, it seems that you really do at all costs want to keep control of the issue of these tickets, and you are against the tickets being issued on the planes, which does in fact very much speed up and make more convenient the flights to Glasgow.

Thomas: Well, we tried for three weeks up to last Friday a system

310 / NEWS SCRIPT 8

of doing this on the ground, and the study team employed by British Airways had kept a very close watch on the situation, and the figures they came out with at the end of two weeks of this period indicated that there were no delays on the ground at all. People were able to walk onto the aircraft, and, incidentally, I did suggest a position about nine weeks ago that could have avoided all this...

Kee: You'd like the tickets issued, as it were, bus tickets, on the ground by your people?

Thomas: Well, if they want to compete with the railway, which they're telling us they are, you buy your railway ticket at the booking office and you hand it in at the barrier.

Kee: But this is what's been going on for years?

Thomas: Oh, no, no. This will in effect cut out the whole of the reservation system as we know it.

Kee: Will you in fact go to arbitration?

Thomas: I have agreed to meet officials of the CAS this afternoon, because I'm a constitutionalist, so are our union constitutionalists, and it'll be wrong for me not to agree to meet them.

Kee: For the moment, then, you're not extending the strike?

Thomas: I could well be extending it. I'm hoping to contain it, quite frankly, and I've done my hardest to contain it.

Kee: Thank you very much, Mr. Thomas.

RT: 50″ + 3'00″

(Next item: Ethiopia fighting)

8. 3 February 1975 17.50 Item 16   . Jill
(Previous item: Angola independence)
INDUSTRIALS/VTR ULAY

The strike of airport workers over the new London-to-Glasgow shuttle service has now spread to Manchester, and four flights have been cancelled.

Clerical workers there are to black all British Airways flights serving Scotland and London, in support of the Heathrow and Glasgow clerks who object to stewardesses taking fares on the shuttle service.

The Manchester workers are also threatening an all-out stoppage from Wednesday if suspensions, imposed since the dispute began, aren't lifted.

RT: 33″

(Next item: Holidays)

9. 3 February 1975 22.00 Item 9   Jill
(Previous item: Pylon)
ANDREW/AIR SHUTTLE/VTR ULAY
    The strike of airport workers over the new London-to-Glasgow
shuttle service has spread to Manchester.
    Clerical workers there are blacking all British Airways flights to
London and Scotland, in support of the Heathrow and Glasgow
clerks who object to proposals for stewardesses to take fares on the
shuttle service.

RT: 28″

(Next item: Miners pay talks)

10. 4 February 1975 13.00 Item 5A   Mann
(Previous item: American economy)
BRITISH AIRWAYS
    More talks today between officials of British Airways and chiefs of
the white collar union, APEX, to try and end the strike by 300
clerical workers at Heathrow, who are protesting against the selling
of tickets by air hostesses on the new shuttle service to Glasgow on
board the plane as if it were [just] a bus. You may remember we
talked to a top official of the union here yesterday. Not much
progress this morning as far as passengers are concerned. The strike,
and the ban by clerks at Manchester Airport, caused the cancellation
of three flights this morning, and British Airways say there'll be
delays on other flights.

RT: 36″

(Next item: Ethiopia fighting)

11. 5 February 1975 17.50 Item 10   Simons
(Previous item: Eritrea fighting)
AIRWAYS/ULAY
    British Airways have cancelled all their flights between London and
ULAY   Belfast because of the strike by clerical officers. International flights
(RT: 17″) have also been delayed as passengers have to carry their bags to the
aircraft and check in there.
    Representatives from both sides in the dispute have been having
talks this afternoon with the Advisory, Conciliation & Arbitration
Service.
    If the talks fail, the clerical workers union say they will call out
their 7,000 British Airways members in support of the 450 who

began the strike at Heathrow, in protest against the selling of tickets on board planes on the new shuttle service between London and Glasgow.

RT: 41″

(Next item: Miners' production record)

12. 5 February 1975 22.00 Item 7   Simons
(Previous item: Eritrea fighting)
ANDREW/SHUTTLE/SLIDE

SLIDE   Here at home talks to end the strike by British Airways clerical officers broke down tonight without agreement, and APEX, the clerical workers' union, have threatened to call out all 7,000 of their British Airways members.

All British Airways flights in and out of Manchester Airport have been cancelled. So have all flights between London and Belfast. Manchester could face a complete shutdown tomorrow if members of the Transport Workers' Union come out in support of the clerical officers. The strike is in protest against tickets being sold ON BOARD planes on the new shuttle route between Glasgow and London.

RT: 33″

(Next item: Devolution referendum)

13. 6 February 1975 17.50 Item 12   Martin
(Previous item: Renaissance masterpieces stolen in Italy)
AIRPORTS

British Airways have cancelled indefinitely all their flights into and out of Manchester Airport because of the booking clerks' strike there. Other airlines which normally use British Airways' booking facilities are using their own staff to keep services going.

Talks between British Airways and the clerical workers' union broke down last night at the London headquarters of the Advisory, Conciliation & Arbitration Service. No staff meetings are planned until tomorrow.

RT: 25″

(Next item: Lady Plowden to chair IBA)

14. 6 February 1975 22.10 Item 12   Platt
(Previous item: Laker Airways keeps Skytrain operating permit)
LEONARD/AIRWAYS

A plan has been worked out to end the strike by British Airways booking clerks.

The union side of the National Joint Council for Civil Transport is to recommend the clerks to accept it. British Airways say the plan will be put to the staff tomorrow.

The clerks are striking because they fear there'll be redundancies over British Airways' decision to sell tickets on board the new London to Glasgow shuttle service.

RT: 23″

(Next item: Commercial break)

15. 7 February 1975 17.50 Lead item   Thompson
AIRPORT/FILM U'LAY

N/C   The strike by 450 British Airways clerks over the new London to Glasgow 'shuttle' service is over.

FILM   At a mass meeting at Heathrow this afternoon, union leaders
ULAY UP   recommended the acceptance of an interim proposal put forward after discussions with British Airways management.

It means the system on the 'shuttle' service that allowed passengers to buy tickets from cabin staff on the plane, will END at
FILM ULAY midnight on Sunday. Instead, passengers will buy their tickets just
OUT   before boarding from ground staff.
N/C
They will still be guaranteed a seat. If one plane's full, another will be operated.

British Airways clerical staff in London will be back at work tomorrow, and in Glasgow they'll be back on Sunday. Manchester, who'd been out in sympathy, went back two hours ago.

The issue is now being referred to the manpower committee of the National Joint Council for Civil Air Transport.

RT: 57″

(Next item: Laker Airways retain Skytrain permit)

16. 7 February 1975 22.00 Item 5   Thompson
(Previous item: Ebbw Vale demonstration against redundancy)
SANDY/AIRPORTS/FILM ULAY/SLIDE

SLIDE   The strike by 450 British Airways clerks over the new London to
HEATHROW   Glasgow shuttle service has ended. At a mass meeting at Heathrow,
FILM
ULAY UP   union leaders recommended acceptance of an interim settlement put forward after talks with British Airways.

The shuttle service hasn't been scrapped. But from Monday passengers will buy their tickets from the clerks just before boarding.

Passengers will be guaranteed a seat. If one plane's full, another

ULAY OUT
30″ AVAIL

will be put on. But the system which allowed passengers to board the plane and buy their ticket afterwards has been withdrawn.

The shuttle operation — which the clerks feared might lead to redundancies — is to be examined by the manpower committee of the National Joint Council for Civil Air Transport.

British Airways said tonight all their domestic flights will be back to normal tomorrow.

RT: 47″

(Next item: Laker Airways keeps Skytrain permit)

9: THE AVON COMPUTER STRIKE

1. 3 February 1975 22.00 Item 19   Simons
(Previous item: Football results)
SANDY/COMPUTER/VTR/CAP

Finally, a computer in Bristol has gone off the rails and has caused hundreds of people to go on strike.

It belongs to Avon County Council and works out wages for council employees. Recently, it's [been] giving some people thousands of pounds too much in their pay packets and others nothing at all.

Ken Rees of Harlech TV reports:

VTR UP:

The 200 strikers who picketted Avon County Hall today weren't asking for more money — they just want the cash they've already earned. Since the new Avon county took over, they say they never know from one week to the next how much they'll have in their pay packet, or even if it'll arrive at all. So today, 5,000 workers, from canteen cooks to caretakers, joined the walkout. Hundreds of schoolchildren were sent home, while thousands more ate sandwich lunches. Council officials blame the teething troubles of a new authority for this chaos at County Hall. One caretaker received a weekly pay cheque for £2,700 — another for £230 a week, but the men who struck it rich weren't among today's unhappy pickets:

Picket: Well, I joined the Avon County Authority in November, and it took them six weeks before I got any pay through at all.

Rees: Any money at all?

Picket: Any money at all. No money for the first six weeks at all.

TIGHT OUT

Picket: You've got to have your money. You go to work so you expect your pay. Nobody wants to work a month and not get any money, do they?

RT: 20″ + 1′00

(Next: Signoff)

10. BRITISH RAIL SIGNALMEN'S STRIKE

1. 7 February 1975 17.50 Item 12   Simons
(Previous item: Aristide Onassis ill)
RAIL/SLIDE

British Rail have offered an extra £3 a week to nearly 3,000 signalmen, in a bid to end the series of unofficial strikes that have brought chaos to the Southern and Eastern regions over the past three months.

Their union, the NUR, will meet on Tuesday to consider the offer, which would be backdated several months.

RT: 20″

(Next item: Prince Charles reveals a nautical sense of humour)

2. 11 February 1975 17.50 Item 8   Black
(Previous item: Miners' pay)
RAIL

A 24-hour rail strike which would disrupt services in the London area and other parts of the country may still go ahead on Thursday, although the executive of the National Union of Railwaymen have accepted a new pay deal for signalmen.

The union say the new offer will give pay rises of up to £5.35 a week to more than 2,000 of Britain's 8,000 signalmen.

But a member of the signalmen's committee, Mr David Theedon, claims that only 500 signalmen will get more than £3 a week from the latest offer.

Mr Theedon says his committee have appealed to the Prime Minister and the Secretary for Employment Mr Foot, that their case should go to arbitration. If an assurance on this is given, he said, the men will stop their threatened strike action.

(Next item: Morriston Hospital Strike)

3. 11 February 1975 22.00 Item 6   Jamieson
(Previous item: Miners' pay)
     A 24-hour rail strike which would disrupt services in London and
other parts of the country may still go ahead on Thursday, even
though the executive of the National Union of Railwaymen have
accepted a new pay deal for signalmen.
     The union say the new offer will give pay rises of up to £5.35 a
week to more than 2,000 of Britain's 8,000 signalmen. But a leading
member of the signalmen's committee, Mr Theedon, claims only
500 men will get more than £3 a week out of the latest offer.

RT: 30″

(Next item: Inflation)

4. 12 February 1975 17.50 Item 4   Maimane
(Previous item: Miners' pay)
RAIL/MAP
     British Rail say they're making 'intense efforts' to stop tomorrow's
unofficial pay strike by signalmen which would seriously disrupt
services in many parts of England.
     It would be the biggest of the strikes signalmen have staged in the
last three months in their demands for a 15% pay rise.
MAP   The worst-hit areas are expected to be Southampton,
Manchester, Liverpool, Stoke, Crewe and Stafford. Trains into
London's Waterloo, Liverpool Street and Fenchurch Street stations
would also be seriously disrupted.

RT: 29″

(Next item: Bread and electricity prices)

5. 13 February 1975 13.00 Item 4
(Previous item: Turkish Cypriots declare federal state)
RAIL STRIKE/VTR ULAY/LYNDALL FILM/SUPER/VTR SOUTH-
ERN/SUPER/STUDIO INTVW/SUPER
     On the railways hundreds of thousands of commuters all over the
country have had a fairly hellish time this morning trying to get to
work and things'll be no better getting home − this is all because of
the latest unofficial one-day strike by signalmen. British Rail say it's
the most widespread industrial action since the signalmen's
campaign began at the end of last year. A complicated affair this.
The National Union of Railwaymen accepted a pay deal on behalf of
all its members on Tuesday. This would give most signalmen,

though not all, rises of between £2.95 and £5.45 a week — depending on the type of signal box they operate. But the signalmen say that all signalmen should get those increases — and they also are not satisfied with the amount. They want more and propose to strike every Thursday until British Rail agree to all their terms.

VTR ULAY Well, most of the country has been hit by this, this Thursday. In Bristol all InterCity services to London were cancelled — and only a few local services are running.

And the story's much the same in Manchester and Birmingham but as usual commuters in London and the south have had the worst of it.

First, from London, here's Lyndall Hobbs:

FLUP: SUPER: LYNDALL HOBBS REPORTING … was devoid of all trains today, and Fenchurch and Liverpool Street stations were equally peaceful. But outside, disruption will hit the biggest area since the stoppages began. The rebel signalmen [who] have been unhappy since last year's pay review are now challenging NUR figures, saying only 500 men will benefit from the deal. A meeting on February 28th will decide if the case can go to arbitration. Naturally, the strike meant many people switched to cars, and quite early traffic was 20% higher than normal, but … escape the traffic wardens, as no free or extra parking was available. Commuters who struggled in face a grim journey home. The situation depends on whether the evening shift of signalmen join in the strike, but since so many depend on trains getting to work, it's likely to be chaotic.

MONTGOM- ERY VTR SUPER: JAMES MONTGOM- ERY RE- PORTING In the south thousands of commuters who live outside London suburbs, [had] to stay at home today. InterCity services were worst hit in the central south. No trains running to London on the Portsmouth, Southampton, Bournemouth, Basingstoke or Weymouth lines, and there were no services between Portsmouth, Southampton and Salisbury. However, there were half hourly shuttle services between Woking and Alton and from Reading and Basingstoke to Wokingham. There were no trains from the channel ports, and passengers arriving from the continent travelled to London by special buses. Local passengers who caught one train from Folkstone to London were told they might not get back today. Although a few trains had been been running in mid-Kent, British Rail warned that there'll be hardly any services there after three o'clock. However, services on the Brighton/Victoria and Hastings /Charing Cross lines are normal. JM for FR, in Southampton.

(Kee) Well, with me in the studio is Sidney Weighell, general secretary of the NUR, who has just appealed to signalmen to get back to work and [6 words illegible].

STUDIO
INTVW:
SUPER:
SIDNEY
WEIGHELL
NUR

Kee: Mr Weighell, can you seriously expect a response from the signalmen on this, because after all, they've defied the union by going out on strike and saying that the terms you negotiated last week weren't adequate?

Weighell: I would hope so, and out of the 9,000 signalmen, we represent 99.9% of them. And my message to signalmen is this. I understand the problem, not only theirs, but other grades of railwaymen. Last year, April of last year, we got an increase for all grades of railwaymen, improvement in conditions of service. Signalmen benefited from that. We had an 'arbitration award in October, which again gave signalmen increases, and improvements in conditions of service backdated to February. This week we concluded another agreement, that gave substantial increases to a substantial number of signalmen. Tomorrow I'll be presenting another claim on behalf of all railwaymen including signalmen, for a substantial increase in pay. Within 12 months we will have succeeded, and I anticipate concluding the agreement regarding tomorrow's claim by the end of February, that's the deadline, we will have had four increases, including signalmen in these categories, and all grades of railwaymen in that period of time, on no test that can be applied can railwaymen or signalmen say that this union has let them down or failed.

Kee: Except that obviously this is what they're saying.

Weighell: I understand that they have a problem. The tribunal decision left us with certain anomalies about relativities between certain grades, but it charges us with the responsibility of looking again more closely at the scale and responsibility of various grades of railwaymen in order to precisely evaluate their relativity. We're engaged in that task, and at this moment the thing that annoys me is signalmen, rank and file signalmen have been represented at every stage of the process of negotiation. They know everything that we have been doing. They are one of the most powerful voices in our union, and they have been a party to all that we've done in the course of recent years. They have their own annual conference, they can appeal to a parliament of our union, the annual conference in which they have substantial representation. What I'm saying is that if we want to raise the standards of all railwaymen, including signalmen, and solve their problems, and I know about them, I [spend] my life dealing with railwaymen's problems, my father was a signalmen for

40 years, we can only do it in an intelligent and united way with the National Union of Railwaymen – that's the only way, and I'm saying to them, if they look at this intelligently, they will get back to work normally, and let us sort this out within the process – it's the most democratic union in Britain I'm talking about – the NUR.

Kee: When you go to the Rail Board tomorrow, will you be asking for as much as the signalmen on strike today are asking for?

Weighell: Tomorrow I'll be asking for, in accordance with the instructions of my annual conference, for a substantial increase for all railwaymen, in which includes signalmen. And in addition to that I'll be asking them to take up at an early date the responsibilities that the tribunal laid at our door to look at the relative skills of various grades of signalmen, and other grades, to see what further improvements we can make, and I am saying all I want is time to put this right, and what I'm asking for is for a period for them to use their democratic process within this union to argue their case, if they think the decisions that have been made up to now are wrong.

Kee: How much will you be thinking about the social contract when you go there tomorrow?

Weighell: Tomorrow? When I start tomorrow I'll be attempting to honour the obligation that this union entered into when it supported the Congress decision last year. Having said that, I'll be watching other negotiations to see to what extent they also keep within the guidelines. And I'm going to say this quite frankly; I'll be faced with a problem if miners come out with 40, 41, 44,[%] whatever it is – I'll be faced with a problem, I don't deny that.

Kee: Thank you very much, Mr Weighell.

RT: 1'12" + 52" + 48" + 5" + 3'00"

(Next item: Campbell Adamson gives CBI view of Industry Bill)

6. 13 February 1975 17.50 Item 5   Jill
(Previous item: Miners' pay)
RAIL/FILM ULAY

There's been widespread disruption of train services because of the unofficial strike of signalmen – the latest in a series of stoppages that began last October.

ULAY UP   Southern and Eastern regions seem to have been worst hit by the 24-hour strike. In London there were no main line services out of Waterloo and Fenchurch Street station closed down completely.

(PAUSE 2")

The result on the roads has been heavy traffic build-ups and jams.
SLIDE   In the Commons, the Secretary for Employment Mr Michael Foot, appealed to the signalmen to stop their unofficial action – which they threatened to repeat every Thursday.

RT: 38″

(Next item: Ulster bombs)

7. 13 February 1975 22.00 Item 2   Jill
(Previous item: Miners' pay)
GORDON/RAIL/FILM ULAY/MACDONALD FILM/SUPER
Train services were disrupted throughout Britain today when 300 signalmen staged another of the unofficial strikes they began last October.

ULAY UP   The walkout was more crippling than earlier ones, with Southern and Eastern regions worst hit. Many InterCity trains were also cancelled, and Southern say there could be further disruptions tomorrow morning.

RT 24″ OUT   As commuters switched to the roads to beat the rail cuts – there
ON WORDS   were heavy traffic build-ups around London. The signalmen want a 15 per cent increase in their wages, and say next week's stoppages will be even worse.

Their general secretary, Mr Charles Holloway, says the lowest-paid signalman is now getting only 30 pence a week more than a porter, and that their differential has been eroded.

FILM UP   He spoke about the stoppages to Trevor MacDonald:
SUPER:
CHARLES   **Holloway:** These men are going to keep on striking every
HOLLOWAY   Thursday, much as they deplore the inconvenience created to the
GEN SEC
UNION OF   general public.
RAILWAY
SIGNALMEN   **MacDonald:** And you, as general secretary, can do nothing about that?

Holloway: I, as general secretary of the Union of Railway Signalmen have got no responsibility about it at all, and I know full well that if I was to ask my members to resume normal working, they wouldn't take any notice any more than if the NUR militants would take any notice of Sidney Weighell from Unity House.

RT: 24″ + 20″ + 33″

(Next item: Wilson)

8. 19 February 1975 22.00 Item 10   Mawer
(Previous item: Morriston Hospital dispute)

GORDON/SIGNALMEN

British Rail have ·· ..ed that another unofficial 24-hour strike by signalmen tomorrow will cause widespread disruption to commuter and InterCity services.

More signalmen than last week are expected to take part. This'll mean bigger cuts in InterCity services and stoppages in areas not previously affected.

Southern and Eastern Region services into and out of London are again likely to be hardest hit. But trains in North-East England should run normally and there's been no hint yet of industrial action on Western Region.

RT: 28″

(Next item: Old people die from virus infection)

9. 20 February 1975 13.00 Item 4   Stevens
(Previous item: Unemployment rises to 3.1%)
RAIL STRIKE/MOLONEY PACKAGE

It's Black Thursday again — with railway signalmen staging yet another in their series of weekly strikes for what they call responsibility pay. Train services all over the country were disrupted this morning.

A report from Ray Moloney:

VTR UP LIVE COMMENT-ARY FROM BOX SUPERS: RAY MOLONEY NORWICH	It was bad enough last week. It's even worse today…and the striking signalmen say they may step up their action even further…if their demands for an enquiry into their pay are not met…and there's no sign yet they will be. This situation at Norwich was duplicated throughout the country.

It's the first time Norwich has been brought to a total halt. Up to now they've at least had SOME trains running on Thursdays.

SUPER: LEEDS	Today…from Scotland down to the South Coast hundreds of thousands of people were hit…with the damage seen clearly here — at Leeds — where travellers — apparently heeding warnings to check stations first — didn't bother to even look for trains that never
MIX TO FILM U/L CONTINUE LIVE COMMENT-ARY 10″	arrived. The weekly strikes are really beginning to bite into the long-distance inter-city services…with trains between London and the North-East and Scotland — the ones out of St. Pancras and Euston — halted completely. There are no trains in the Manchester-…Leeds…Sheffield…Doncaster or York areas.
11″	London was possibly worst hit of all…with hundreds of commuter
11″	trains cut…and some stations closed completely.

British Rail warns that even the few trains that did run this morning may not be available tonight.

As always…thousands sought to beat the strike with their cars…and — as traffic built up around London into mile-long blocks — they faced what motoring organisations called one long agony.

15″   Despite the opening of special parking spaces in London — the Wall was one of them — there was hardly a space to be had anywhere by
28″   nine-thirty this morning…and — as travellers battled — they faced the threat that — before the end of the month — these one-day strikes may be extended to two or even three days a week.

RT: 12″ + 1'45″

[programme continues]   Stevens
RAIL STRIKE/ UNION REACTION/STUDIO INTERVIEW/SUPER
One MP who's really angry about the lack of Government action
SLIDE   over all this is Sir Bernard Braine, the Conservative MP for southeast Essex, one of the areas worst hit by the weekly strikes. He said this morning it was time for Mr Foot to 'stir himself' — and he went on: 'It's the poor bloody commuters who are supposed to own the railways that I'm worried about. My constituents have had just about enough. Yet the situation's been allowed to drag on for far too long.'
Of course the signalmen themselves rather feel this too.
With me in the studio is Mr Charles Holloway, general secretary of the small, unaffiliated to the TUC but evidently effective Union of Railway Signalmen:

STUDIO   **Kee:** Mr Holloway, a great number of people who have been
INTERVIEW   enduring what we heard then being described as 'the long agony'
SUPER: this morning, must be longing to get at you really for the discomfort
CHARLES
HOLLOWAY   that your men are causing this morning. What would you say to
UNION OF   them to placate them?
RAILWAY
SIGNAL-   **Holloway:** Well, in the first place, we're sorry that they are being so
MEN   inconvenienced, but I would like to make it quite clear that it would appear from the press that the Union of Railway Signalmen are the bad people in this that we organised it. We never did no such thing.

Kee: Who did organise it then?

Holloway: This strike was organised by a strike committee composed of militant NUR men assisted by URS members who thought along the same lines as the NUR men, and they are the people who organised these strikes in their protest to the British Railways Board and to the National Union of Railwaymen in particular, that a very bad deal had been awarded.

Kee: Are you then as leader of the Union of Railway Signalmen, against the strike?

Holloway: I wouldn't like to make a comment on that. It doesn't affect me at all in as much as this union never authorised the strike.

Kee: But Mr Holloway, you say it doesn't affect you at all, and therefore you are not particularly interested in whether the strike's right or not − it affects thousands, hundreds of thousands of people today. You must be either for the strike or against it.

Holloway: Well, the attitude of the men I'm in sympathy with, because they've had such a raw deal. In short, I suppose I could say that I condone their actions in making a fight against this award.

Kee: But not perhaps this particular form of fight?

Holloway: No, I would sooner it be done by negotiation round the Board's table.

Kee: But now here we come to the point − negotiations are going on with the Rail Board by the National Union of Railwaymen − they've specifically taken on the signalmen's problems. Why aren't you waiting until these negotiations have come out one way or the other?

Holloway: Well, these negotiations have been going on for quite a long while, and this strike has been going on, or this destructive position has arisen since the Railway Wages Tribunal issued its findings. I think that the National Union of Railwaymen have certainly had quite long enough to have tried to have come to grips with it, and with the British Railways Board found a solution to it rather than keep on ignoring it and saying it's unofficial and all this, and then we get a three pound a week offer made to the men which the men won't accept because it's not enough − they asked for a clear cut 15% across the board, and until such time as somebody climbs down on this from either the British Railways Board, and the NUR, I'm afraid that this position is going to escalate into something much greater.

Kee: As you've made it quite clear that you're in sympathy with your men, as one would expect...

Holloway: Yes, but it must be stated, unofficially.

Kee: Yes, but also that you don't really approve of the actual strike action they've taken, would you make an appeal to them now to go back to work to stop these strikes?

Holloway: No, I would not, because I think that if I was to make an appeal to go back, to the URS to go back on strike, they wouldn't take a bit of notice of me. I have no right whatsoever to appeal to

NUR members to go back to work. Now I understand overtures have been made in this respect but the militant NUR men just won't wear it.

Kee: So what is the country, who are having to wear it, going to do?

Holloway: I just don't know. I just don't know, and all we can hope is that somebody will come right down to grass roots and agitate for a proper independent enquiry into this position regarding the signalmen.

Kee: But one thing obviously one hardly needs to make an enquiry into is that the union's direction of all this is totally in a chaotic condition, and it's really the commuters who are suffering from your union chaos.

Holloway: Yes, the commuters are suffering as a result of the bad bargaining done by the National Union of Railwaymen on behalf of signalmen.

Kee: Thank you Mr Holloway.

RT: 41″ + 3′00″

(Next item: Morriston Hospital strike)

10. 20 February 1975 17.50 Lead item
RAIL/TITLE FILM/MALONEY PACKAGE/SUPER

Hundreds of trains throughout the country were cancelled today as about half the railway signalmen called another unofficial strike. Tonight more than a million commuters face chaos on their journey home.

The stoppage is the latest — and the most serious — in the series of one-day strikes which began in early November.

Ray Moloney reports:

VTR UP FOR 25″ ANGLIA 20″

For hundreds of thousands of travellers — from Scotland to the South Coast — tonight was the end of yet another long Thursday's agony...with the threat that — before the end of the month — the present strikes may be extended to two or even three — days a week.

Today was the worst day yet...with some stations closed down completely in London...and no trains in Manchester...Leeds...Shef-

TC4 CUT TO FILM V/O FROM BOX 18″

field...Doncaster and York areas. Stations all over the country — most of which have — up to now — had at least SOME local trains each Thursday — closed down totally...and the strikes are cutting harder and harder into the long distance — InterCity — services...with trains between London and the North-East and Scotland — the ones out of Euston and St. Pancras — halted completely. British Rail warned early today that even the few local trains that did run today — and it's mainly the local — commuter — services that are being hit — might not be available tonight.

22″   The striking signalmen are warning that — if their demand for an enquiry into their pay rate is not met — they may extend their action…calling not just one… but even two — or possibly three-day — strikes each week. And — all over the country — the traffic chaos

30″   which follows inevitably from railway strikes gets worse and worse…with people only just recovering from the morning's hunt for a parking space…before they have to face the battle — and it is a battle — to get back out of the cities again.

Parking restrictions remain in force — even though extra areas have been opened — but with no other way of travelling there just isn't enough legal space in the cities to handle the extra traffic… and — next week — it may be even worse.

[programme continues]   Sam

Unofficial leaders of the signalmen say they've twice asked to see the Employment Secretary, Mr Foot — and that if he sets up an independent enquiry, they'll call off their action.

The Department of Employment said tonight that Mr Foot is 'considering a reply'.

Last week, Mr Foot told the Commons he opposed an inquiry.

RT: 19″ + 25″ + 1'11″ + 18″

(Next item: Blockade)

11. 20 February 1975 22.00 Item 5   Sam
(Previous item: Aid)
GORDON/RAIL STRIKE/MOLONEY VTR/SUPER/SLIDE

SLIDE/CK   The Employment Secretary, Mr Foot, has rejected a request by signalmen to intervene in their pay dispute with British Rail.

About half of the country's signalmen went on an unofficial strike again today…the latest in a series of oneday strikes which began last November.

Their leaders said they'd twice asked for a meeting with Mr Foot…and that if he agreed to their demand for an independent inquiry into their pay, they'll call off the action. But Mr Foot told them that the dispute was a matter for the signalmen and their union — and that it would be wrong for him to intervene.

Earlier, the signalmen said that if the dispute wasn't settled by the end of the month, they would step up their action. Ray Moloney reports on the effects of today's stoppage.

For hundreds of thousands of travellers — from Scotland to the South Coast — tonight was the end of yet another long Thursday's

UP VTR
SUPER RAY
MOLONEY
NORWICH 25″

agony...with the threat that — before the end of the month — the present strike may be extended to two — or even three — days a week. Today was the worst day yet...with some stations closed down completely in London...and no trains in the Manchester-...Leeds...Sheffield...Doncaster and York areas.

SUPER
WATERLOO
18″

Stations all over the country — most of which have — up to now — had at least SOME local trains each Thursday — closed down totally...and the strikes are cutting harder and harder into the long distance — InterCity — services...with trains between London and the North-East and Scotland halted completely.

22″

The striking signalmen are warning that — if their demand for an enquiry into their pay rate is not met — they may extend their action...calling not just one...but even two — or possibly three day — strikes each week.

And all over the country — the traffic chaos which follows inevitably from railway strikes gets worse and worse ...with people only just recovering from the morning hunt for a parking space...before they have to face the battle — and it is a battle — to get back out of the cities again.

30″

Parking restrictions remain in force — even though extra areas have been opened — but with no other way of travelling there just isn't enough legal space in the cities to handle the extra traffic...and — next week it may be even worse.

RT:

2'04″

(Next item: Morriston Hospital strike)

12. 24 February 1975 17.50 Item 7   Black
(Previous item: Healey on economy at TUCLabour Party meeting)
SIGNALMEN

The Employment Secretary, Mr Foot, has again said that he will NOT agree to an inquiry into the grievances of the railway signalmen who've staged a series of unofficial strikes over recent months.

SLIDE:

Mr Foot condemned the stoppages and said the signalmen had to understand that they could not secure a fresh hearing of their case by unofficial action.

SLIDE:

But an opposition spokesman, Mr Barney Hayhoe, said Mr Foot's statement added nothing to what he said ten days ago. Mr Hayhoe said the House wanted the Minister to take action to protect the travelling public.

RT:

30″

(Next item: BL toolmakers' strike)

13. 24 February 1975 22.00 Item 10   Black
(Previous item: London containerisation strike)
REGGIE/SIGNALMEN
        The Employment Secretary, Mr Foot, has again refused an inquiry
        into the grievances of the railway signalmen who've staged a series
        of unofficial strikes over recent months.
SLIDE: Mr Foot condemned the stoppages, and said the signalmen had to
        understand that they could not secure a fresh hearing of their case by
        unofficial action.
SLIDE: An Opposition spokesman, Mr Barney Hayhoe, said Mr Foot's
        statement added nothing to what he said ten days ago. Mr Hayhoe
        said the House wanted the Minister to take action to protect the
        travelling public.
RT: 30″

(Next item: Miners' pay)

14. 26 February 1975 17.50 Item 7   Maimane
(Previous item: Industry Bill)
RAIL/VTR/SUPER
        There's to be another unofficial strike tomorrow by a group of
        signalmen who claim it'll be the worst so far and will affect the
        whole country.
        But British Rail say many areas will NOT be affected, and
        Southern Region WON'T be as badly hit as last Thursday.
        The strikers have today refused to join with the National Union
        of Railwaymen in pressing for pay claims acrosstheboard. They
        insist on an official inquiry into their OWN claim before calling off
        their weekly strikes.
        The secretary for Employment, Mr Foot, has refused to set up an
        inquiry.
RT: 32″

(Next item: Developments in Stonehouse case)

15. 26 February 1975 22.00 Item 6   Maimane
(Previous item: Industry Bill)
ANDREW/RAIL/SLIDE/VTR/SUPER
        Signalmen go on unofficial strike again tomorrow in support of a
SLIDE   pay claim and they say it will be the worst day of chaos on the
        railways since they started their action five months ago.
        But British Rail have promised near-normal commuter and
        InterCity services for most areas.
        The striking signalmen want an official inquiry into their claim.

This has been rejected by the Secretary for Employment, Mr Foot.
Ray Moloney asked him why, with the strikes getting worse
every week, he won't act.

VTR UP
PRESOF
'GET WORSE
AND WORSE'
SUPER:
FOOT SEC
FOR EMPL.

Foot: Well, I hope it's not going to get worse and worse, and of
course, we greatly deplore the strike and all the trouble and
inconvenience and hardship for so many people which results from
it, but it would be no good us taking action now to stop this, or help
to stop this disruption, if it caused much greater disruption as a
consequence, and that's what we fear would be the result of the kind
of things people are asking me to do. You see, a year or so ago, there
was much bigger disruption on the railways, and that led to an
inquiry — a full-scale independent inquiry, which made
recommendations, accepted by all the unions concerned — now it's
no good coming along now and saying that the whole of that inquiry
is going to be re-opened. All the other parties to it would be
justifiably outraged, and we can't do that.

RT: 29″ + 50″

(Next item: BAC sit-in)

16. 27 February 1975 13.00 Item 7   Morrison
(Previous item: Motorway pile-up)
RAIL STRIKE/MOLONEY FILM/SUPER

This time last week it was Black Thursday on the railways and it
would have been again today if militant signalmen had had their
way. But they haven't altogether and their one-day strike has caused
less confusion to commuters than last week. It's true that many
commuters have been inconvenienced but they can take some
comfort from the fact that today will be the last of the four one-day
strikes called by the signalmen, and falling support for the action
among signalmen suggests that the threatened escalation to two or
three-day strikes will not now take place. A report on the situation
now from Ray Moloney:

FILM UP
SUPER
MALONEY
REPORT-
ING

Much better this week, both as far as train services and traffic are
concerned — that's the verdict on this the fourth, and hopefully the
last of the one-day, once a week strikes. Only about 340 signalmen
failed to report for duty today, about half the figure for last week.
The worst hit area again was the north-west, from Crewe up to the
Scottish border, rail services are halted completely. There are no
trains in or out of Manchester, and the Eastern region, particularly
East Anglia, is almost completely cut off. But unlike last week,
British Rail is maintaining a good proportion of its long-distance
services, albeit on a reduced basis. London commuters are having a

far easier time today, except for those unfortunate enough to be coming in from the East, who've got virtually nothing. Fenchurch Street, Liverpool Street and Kings Cross are completely shut, the first time that's happened to Kings Cross since the strikes began. Motoring organisations say today's traffic, although definitely heavier than normal, kept moving well, except when it was hit by fog — the biggest build-ups occurred south of the Thames where the fog cut ferry services, funnelling heavier than usual traffic into the tunnels. Now we await tomorrow's meeting of the strikers here in London to find out whether, with support apparently falling away, they now decide to call off the strikes altogether.

RT: 36 + 1'20"

(Next item: Hunt for policeman's killer)

17. 27 February 1975 17.50 Item 6   MDW
(Previous item: Scanlon calls for reappraisal of Social Contract)
RAIL/FILM

Railway signalmen were on an unofficial strike again today. But the effect was not as severe as previous stoppages, although services in the north-west of England, East Anglia, and the commuter services to London from the east were hard hit.

The signalmen will meet in London tomorrow to consider their position, and Ray Moloney spoke to Richard Amott, one of their spokesmen, and asked him about future action:

TAKE FILM   **Amott:** Well, today was the last planned day for a one-day strike.
SUPER: The men have a meeting tomorrow at Kings Cross, when any
AMOTT   decision will be taken. I very much doubt if the men will want to step it up to two or three days, because they've all been suffering monetarily. I would imagine that we may well accept the NUR's offer and hold off action until the end of April. If the signalmen get no satisfaction then, the action is bound to continue and be even worse than it has been now.

RT: 22" + 25"

(Next item: BL toolmakers' strike)

18. 27 February 1975 22.00 Item 7
(Previous item: London containerisation strike)
REGGIE/RAIL/FILM

The railway signalmen's dispute.

Some of the men staged another unofficial strike in support of their pay claim but today's disruption wasn't as bad as the previous strikes and this could be the last one.

Ray Moloney reports:

TAKE FILM
SUPER:
MOLONEY

Once again...it was the North-West and East Anglia which took the real brunt of today's strike...the fourth and — at least as far as their public announcements are concerned — last of the once-a-week...one-day strikes called by the signalmen.

Services stopped completely from Crewe to the Scottish Border.

East Anglia was almost completely cut off...and there were no trains into or out of Manchester.

London commuters had a much easier time today... except for those coming in from the East...who found virtually no services at all.

In London...Fenchurch Street...Liverpool Street and Kings Cross closed down completely...the first time that's happened to Kings X since the strike began.

The signalmen are meeting in London tomorrow to decide on their next move...with the knowledge that only about three hundred and forty joined the strike today... about half the figure for last week.

With support apparently falling away...I asked Mr Richard Amott — of the strike committee — what the future for travellers looks like:

[Amott as at 17.50]

RT: 13″ + 1′24″

(Next item: EEC referendum)

19. 28 February 1975 17.50 Item 7   Maimane
(Previous item: Argentine guerillas kidnap judge)
NEWS WRAP/STILLS/

In London the group of railway signalmen who've been staging weekly strikes have voted to continue their action over a pay award.

RT: Approx. 8″

(Item continues with miners' pay)

20. 6 March 1975 13.00 Item 5   Sarah
(Previous item: Hotel)
RAIL STRIKE/ULAY

The railway signalmen's Thursday strike was, on their own admission, less effective even than last week, this morning.

ULAY UP

Commuter trains in most regions were nearly normal and there were few delays. But Eastern Region still had problems, and Fenchurch Street station in London is closed. In the North East too most local services around Tees-side have been cancelled. And there are no InterCity trains from London to Manchester.

RT: 23″

(Next item: Norton-Villiers Triumph cooperative established)

21. 6 March 1975 17.50 Item 14   Tristam
(Previous item: Vauxhall short-time working)
RAIL/FILM U/L

U/L UP 8″   The latest one day unofficial strike by rail signalmen put a stop to all trains in and out of Fenchurch Street station in London, and to many services in the north east of England.
            And there were no InterCity trains between London and Manchester.
            Elsewhere, most trains ran as usual — and today's strike was the least effective since the signalmen began taking their weekly action — for a responsibility payment.

RT: 24″

(Next item: Michelangelo)

22. 8 March 1975 13.10 Item 3   Barlow
(Previous item: Wilson and Heath on pay)
SIGNALMEN

            Railway signalmen in the Eastern region have decided to abandon their weekly strikes in support of a pay claim. Other regions are expected to follow suit.
            The unofficial stoppages which began last October have been steadily losing support and a spokesman for the strikers said they didn't feel justified in making the public suffer any longer.

RT: 19″

(Next item: Mob violence at meetings in Portugal)

23. 8 March 17.12 Item 3   Kallenbach/Barlow
(Previous item: Wilson and Heseltine on pay)
SIGNALMEN/SLIDE

[text identical to 13.10]

RT: 19″

(Next item: Mob violence at meetings in Portugal)

24. 8 March 1975 22.30 Item 4
Kallenbach/Barlow(Previous item: Wilson and Heseltine on pay)

SIGNALMEN/SLIDE
>Railway signalmen in the Eastern region have decided to abandon their weekly strikes. Other regions are expected to follow suit.
>The unofficial stoppages, which started last October in support of a pay claim, have been steadily losing support and the strikers say they don't feel justified in making the public suffer any longer.

RT: 19"

(Next item: NUJ statement on press freedom)

11: THE EBBW VALE DEMONSTRATION

1. 7 February 1975 13.00 Item 5A
(Previous item: Bomb damages pylon)
EBBW VALE/SLIDE
>Steelworks at Ebbw Vale in South Wales are at a virtual standstill today because of a 24-hour stoppage by workers, who are protesting against the Steel Board's wishes to run the plant down, and the Government's decision to let it.
>This afternoon the workers are staging a march through the town, and they're timing it to arrive at the civic centre at the same time as their MP, Mr Michael Foot, and the Secretary of State for Wales, Mr John Morris. Mr Morris is expected to announce a twelve million pound scheme to offset the unemployment caused by the steel plant's rundown.

RT: 35"

(Next item: Tension in Peru)

2. 7 February 1957 17.45 Item 4   Chamberlain
(Previous item: Wilson)
STEELWORKERS/LIVE INJECT/FILM U'LAY
TAKE INJECT Several thousand steelworkers marched to the civic centre at Ebbw
LIVE   Vale in South Wales this afternoon to protest against the phasing out, and eventual closedown, of steel production in the town.
>About four-and-a-half thousand workers will lose their jobs by 1978 and up to two thousand workers could go this year.
>The Employment Secretary, Mr Foot, who's also the local MP, was shouted down with cries of 'resign' and 'betrayal' when he tried to address the crowd.
>The first one thousand men will be laid off in July. A twelve-and-

TAKE NAT
SOF & HOLD
TO CUE 25″
RT:

a-half-million pound plan has been approved by the Government to help promote jobs in the area.

43″

(Next item: Good day for shares on Stock Exchange)

3. 7 February 1975 22.00 Item 4   Chamberlain
(Previous item: Government promises action on abortion abuses)
REGGIE/STEELWORKERS/MCDONALD VTR/SUPER

At Ebbw Vale in South Wales, several thousand steelworkers marched to the civic centre to protest against the phasing out, and eventual closedown, of steel production in the town. They gave their MP, Mr Foot, who's the Employment Secretary, a hard time.

About four-and-a-half thousand workers will lose their jobs by the time the cuts are completed in 1978. Trevor McDonald reports.

TAKE VTR
SUPER:
TREVOR
MCDONALD
REPORTING
FROM EBBW
VALE

It was, in the words of one speaker, a sad and sombre day for Ebbw Vale. Although as they left the British Steel offices, the demonstrators appeared decidely good natured. Just before the march began, word got round that Mr Foot had arrived in town. At other times such news would have brought general acclaim, as until now Michael Foot has been the hero of Ebbw Vale, Nye Bevan's heir, and the area's Member of Parliament for 15 years. But with the Beswick report on steel closures, and the projected loss of four and a half thousand jobs here, today Michael Foot was deemed the fallen idol. (SOF) At the Civic Centre, where the demonstrators heard about the £12½ million to be spent in Ebbw Vale for new industry, their anger was plainly directed at Mr Foot. (SOF) When the Minister did manage to make himself heard above the shouting of detractors, he offered no easy answers, and very little hope.

Foot: I'm not going to stand here and say something that might be popular in Ebbw Vale...What we've got to do is save the future of Ebbw Vale and the valley towns. That's what I'm seeking to do.

McDonald: Mr Foot plans to talk to the steelworkers again tomorrow night, but he's also likely to hear a lot more from them as well, because in this part of Wales, the future of the steelworks and that of the people are inextricably linked. TM, NAT, Ebbw Vale.

RT: 22″ + 1'48″

(Next item: British Airways clerical staff strike)

12: MORRISTON HOSPITAL STRIKE

1. 11 February 1975 17.50 Item 8   Henderson
(Previous item: BR Signalmen's Strike)
NURSES/STILL
> Five hundred nurses and staff at Morriston Hospital in Swansea have gone on strike because a private patient admitted there, the first since the National Union of Public Employees put a ban on private patients at that hospital nearly a year ago.
>
> A union spokesman said a formal request had been made for the patient to be transferred to a private nursing home, but no action was taken.

RT: 24″

(Next item: 11 old people die from virus infection)

2. 16 February 1975 22.00 Item 9   Tristram
(Previous item: Coach crash)
HOSPITALS/MAP
> There's been a warning that a strike over pay beds at a Swansea hospital could spread throughout South Wales.
>
> Nurses and others workers at the Morriston Hospital in Swansea went on strike five days ago.
>
> Today union representatives of workers in other South Wales hospitals drew up plans to support the strike if the dispute wasn't settled by Tuesday.

RT: 20″

(Next item: Foreign news roundup)

3. 19 February 1975 13.00 Item 5   Mike
(Previous item: 11 old people die of virus infection)
WELSH HOSPITAL/VTR/SUPER
> Now that strike by hospital ancillary workers in South Wales, over the continuing problem of pay beds. An appeal has been made for them to go back this morning by junior doctors from the Swansea hospital where the row began. The strike then spread to three more hospitals in the area. In their plea, the doctors said every hospital employee has a moral obligation to care for all hospital patients.
>
> The ancillary workers' union, the National Union of Public Employees, is meeting tonight.
>
> A report now from Stuart Leyshon of HTV.

SUPER:
STUART
LEYSHON
> The trouble began at Morriston hospital in Swansea just over a week ago, and it could soon involve every hospital in the country. Tonight officials of the National Union of Public Employees in South Wales, meet at Swansea, and the whole of the area is likely to

be hit tomorrow. An official forecast today that it could lead to the most serious trouble in the National Health Service since the hospital workers' strike in 1973. Today 400 staff at Neath General Hospital are on a one-day strike, and at [name not transcribed] in the Rhondda 18 nurses are out. They're supporting the 400 staff at Morriston who claim they've been locked out for refusing to attend the only private patient in the 500-bed hospital. Among the 400 staff are 25 nurses. Most of the union's anger is directed at the consultants. The union claims that because of their powerful position, the health authority cannot make a move. The consultants have called NUPE's action outrageous and inhuman. Yesterday a 7½ hour meeting chaired by an official of the Advisory and Conciliation Service ended in deadlock, and it now looks as if there could be chaos in the hospitals in south west Wales tomorrow. Stuart Leyshon for First Report, Cardiff.

RT: 31″ + 1′ 06″·

(Next item: Interview on use of offenders in community service)

4. 19 February 1975 17.50 Item 5   Mawer
(Previous item: Wages increased by 29% in 1974)
INDUSTRY/SLIDES

In the hospital pay beds dispute in South Wales, ancillary staff at three more hospitals went on 24-hour strike today. Nurses at two others are already on a 48-hour strike.

SLIDE: 400 staff are still out at Morriston Hospital in Swansea, where the dispute began over the admission of a private patient to the maternity ward.

(Item continued with protest at FORD short-time working...)

RT: Approx. 22″

(Next: Continuation of item)

5. 19 February 1975 22.00 Item 9   Mawer
(Previous item: Statement by Egyptian Premier)
LEONARD/HOSPITALS/SLIDE

The woman who started the hospital pay beds dispute in South Wales when she was admitted as a private patient to the maternity
SLIDE: ward of Morriston Hospital in Swansea, left the hospital tonight.
The 400 staff at the hospital have been urged by the West Glamorgan Health Authority to return to work. But the dispute spread today. Ancillary staff at three hospitals in the area went on strike for 24 hours, joining nurses at two more hospitals who're on a 48-hour strike until tomorrow.

RT: 27″

(Next item: BR signalmen's strike)

6. 20 February 1975 13.00 Item 5   Morrison

(Previous item: BR Signalmen's strike)

HOSPITAL STRIKE

> That strike of some nurses and ancillary workers at six hospitals in Wales seems to be over for the time being.
>
> At Morriston Hospital in Swansea where the dispute, over the admission of a private patient, began, the strikers are meeting this afternoon but since the private patient in question has now left, it's expected they'll vote for a return to work.
>
> Staff at five other hospitals in the area who'd come out in sympathy have already gone back.

RT: 26″

(Next item: Conservatives ratify Thatcher as leader)

7. 20 February 1975 17.50 Item 6

(Previous item: Unemployment rises to 3.1%)

HOSPITALS/STILL

> The staff at Morriston hospital in Swansea have called off their strike. The woman who'd been admitted as a private patient to the maternity ward — the cause of the strike — has now gone home. The 500 nurses and ancillary workers at five hospitals in Glamorgan who had walked out in support of the Swansea strike have also gone back to work.

RT: 21″

(Next item: Conservatives ratify Mrs Thatcher as leader)

8. 20 February 1975 22.00 Item 6   Black

(Previous item: not available)

REGGIE/PAY BEDS/STILL

STILL
> The strike by ancillary hospital staff at the Morriston hospital in Swansea has been called off. The workers have agreed to go back on duty at six o'clock tomorrow morning.
>
> The strike was originally called when a private patient was admitted to the Morriston maternity unit — but last night the woman concerned went home.
>
> Earlier today, 500 nurses and ancillary workers at five other hospitals in Glamorgan who walked out in support of the Morriston strike were back on duty.

RT: 27″

(Next item: Consultants' work to contract)

9. 14 April 1975 13.00 Item 4   Morrison
(Previous item: Attempt to assassinate Northern Ireland Secretary)
HOSPITAL BEDS

       The dispute over pay beds in National Health hospitals is back in the
news with the National Union of Public Employees threatening to
withdraw all services to private patients now in Hampshire,
Oxfordshire, Berkshire and the Isle of Wight.

       Hospitals in Portsmouth and Basingstoke look like getting the
first impact. Why now again suddenly: The union say they're taking
the action because one of their members − a NUPE convenor in a
Portsmouth hospital − was struck off his GP's list after attacking the
idea of pay beds at a meeting.

       The GP in question says it was nothing to do with pay beds. He
was reducing his list of patients anyway, and others had been cut off
too. 'This gentleman,' said [the GP], 'is making political capital out
of it.'

RT: 44″

(Next item: Enquiry into Moorgate Tube disaster)

10. 14 April 1975 22.00 Item 12   Hutchence
(Previous item: Arson)
REGGIE/PATIENTS

       Another hospital dispute.

       The National Union of Public Employees is to take industrial
action to close private wards in hospitals in Hampshire,
Oxfordshire, Buckinghamshire and Berkshire. This means paying
patients would lose portering, laundry and catering services.

       The union say the action is being taken because one of their
members claims he was struck off his doctor's list, after speaking out
against having private patients in Health Service hospitals.

RT: 23″

(Next item: Glasgow dustcart drivers' strike)

13: BRITISH AIRCRAFT CORPORATION SIT-IN

1. 21 February 1975 17.50 Item 4   O'Connell
(Previous item: Imperial Typewriter sit-in)
BAC

At Hurn, in Hampshire, 200 production workers barricaded offices at the British Aircraft Corporation plant and prevented their executives from starting work.

The demonstration — by engineering workers — is part of a campaign in support of a pay claim.

The plant makes parts for Concorde and the BAC 1-11 jets.

RT:.   Approx. 17″

(Next item: Maudling mentioned during corruption trial)

2. 26 February 1975 22.00 Item 7   MDW
(Previous item: BR workshop supervisors' work-to-rule)
LEONARD/BAC

Seven hundred British Aircraft Corporation workers have taken over more of the company's factory at Hurn Airport, Dorset.

They're protesting at a £2 a week pay offer which they called 'ridiculous'. A union spokesman said the men were prepared to extend the occupation, which began a week ago.

[continues with British Leyland strike]

RT: Approx. 17″)

(Next item: British Leyland strike)

14: LONDON DOCKS CONTAINERISATION STRIKE

1. 24 February 1975 22.00 Item 9   Black
(Previous item: BL toolmakers' strike)
LEONARD/CONTAINERS/GREEN FILM/SUPERCAPS/SLIDES

SLIDE (JONES)	The leader of the Transport Workers' Union, Mr Jack Jones, has suceeded in getting an official investigation into the London docks container dispute.
SLIDE (HUNTER)	The investigation will be headed by Professor Lawrence Hunter of Glasgow University.
SUPERCAP: GREEN	Our industrial correspondent, Michael Green, reports:
FLUP GREEN DUBBING SCRIPT SOF 13 sec to 22 sec	The picketing, which began quietly a month ago, has now paralysed Tilbury Docks and another East London container terminal. Hundreds of lorries have been turned away in the complex dispute.

The dockers are trying to force the container depots to employ registered dockers. They argue that these depots do work which traditionally belongs to them.

But the haulage workers have retaliated by picketing some dock gates — to bring the issue to a head.

The fear is that the dispute could erupt into a repeat of the 1972 dock strike which brought riotous scenes in London and resulted in five dockers being jailed for defying the Industrial Relations Court. At that time the inland container depots were urged to employ dockers. But not many followed the advice.

Now the dockers want the Government to legislate that all container handling in a five-mile corridor round the main ports has to be done by dockers. And they'll be hoping to see concrete signs of such an intention in a consultative document Mr Foot, the Employment Secretary, plans to publish next month.

Tonight, after he'd seen Mr Foot, Mr Jones was at pains to play down the potential seriousness of the situation.

SUPER CAP	**Jones:** Basically, there is not a conflict between drivers and dockers, because lorry drivers agree that dockers should do work of cargo handling. The difficulty has arisen because of the unauthorised picketing or blacking as it's called, and we want that blacking action to be called off on both sides so that we can get normal working, a proper examination of the problem by the Conciliation and Arbitration Service, and at the same time to go ahead as quickly as possible with the projected legislation.
RT:	14″ + 1′11″ + 28″

(Next item: Signals)

2. 27 February 1975 22.00 Item 6A   Smith
(Previous item: Government plan for half-pay pensions)

REGGIE/DOCKS

> The port of London was brought to a standstill tonight when 3,000 dockers went on strike in support of 3,000 others at Tilbury who'd been sent home by employers.
>
> It's [the] latest development in a long-running dispute between dockers and lorry drivers over who should load and unload containers. The Advisory, Conciliation and Arbitration Service are looking into it.

RT: 21″

(Next item: BR signalmen's strike)

3. 3 March 1975 13.00 Item 4
(Previous item: Reg Prentice comments on Social Contract)
DOCKERS

> Despite an appeal from their union leader, Mr Jack Jones, a meeting of about 2,000 dockers in London voted this morning to carry on blacking lorries in a dispute over who handles containers at terminals away from the docks. The port of London's been at a total standstill since Friday, and very badly held up for 3 weeks. Other ports, including Liverpool, Hull, Manchester and Southampton are considering whether to join the dispute.

RT: 25″

(Next item: Belfast explosions)

4. 3 March 1975 17.50 Item 5   Tristram
(Previous item: Wilson/Prentice and the Social Contract)
DOCKERS/GREEN FILM/SUPER

> In the Port of London, a mass meeting of dockers voted to continue blacking lorries in a dispute over container handling.
>
> Their action has brought the port to a standstill since Friday.
>
> Here's our industrial correspondent, Michael Green.

FLUP

> 2,000 dockers turned out for the meeting in front of the Connaught pub at the Royal Docks. They were strongly urged to continue their blacking campaign, and the shop steward said the picketing at Dagenham storage, the container depot at the centre of the dispute, would continue. Dockers' leaders said they wanted to meet Mr Jack Jones, General Secretary of the Transport Union, and Mr Foot, the Employment Secretary, to get assurances that the container depot work should be done by registered dockers. In the end, the vote to continue the action was all but unanimous. Only three hands were raised against. The effect has been the total paralysis of the London docks, including Tilbury, since the men

walked out at the end of last week. 20 ships are lying idle in the enclosed docks because of the dockers' refusal to handle some container cargoes. The port employers warned this afternoon that far from winning more jobs for dock workers, the action may well drive more business away from the port and reduce the number of jobs. MG, ITN, at the Port of London.

RT: 11″ + 1′01″

(Next item: Mill demo)

5. 3 March 1975 22.00 Item 6   Tris
(Previous item: Wilson/Prentice in row over Social Contract)
SANDY/DOCKERS/FILM/SUPER
        In the Port of London, a mass meeting of dockers voted to continue blacking lorries in the dispute over container handling.
        Their unofficial strike has brought the port to a standstill for the past four days.
        Dockers in Hull decided to respect the London dockers' blacklist of container depots − but there is no suggestion that they'll call a strike.
        Here's our industrial correspondent, Michael Green:

FLUP SUPER   [report as at 17.50]

RT: 20″ + 1′01″

(Next item: Mill demo)

6. 5 March 1975 17.50 Item 6   Mawer
(Previous item: OPEC meeting)
DOCKS/FILM ULAY
        Dockers at several ports, including Hull, Dover, Harwich and Ipswich, have agreed to black cargoes diverted from London, in support of the 9,000 dockers who've been on strike since Friday over the alleged use of unregistered labour to handle containers.

FILM ULAY   Some London dockers met today and were told that men at other ports would be asked for their support. They decided to put off any further decisions about the strike until Monday.

RT: 23″

(Next item: NGA strike)

7. 5 March 22.00 Item 5   Mawer
(Previous item: Moorgate Tube disaster)
SANDY/DOCKS/FILM ULAY
        Mr Jack Jones, the Transport Workers' leader, tonight failed in an

attempt to persuade representatives of London's dockers to call off their unofficial strike. The strike, which is over the long-standing grievance concerning container work, has brought London's docks to a standstill. Mr Jones addressed a stormy meeting of about 300 dockers, including most of their shop stewards. After two hours, Mr Jones left to cries of 'traitor' and 'Judas'. He had tried unsuccessfully to persuade the meeting to await Government legislation later this year.

Dockers at several ports, including Hull, Dover Harwich and Ipswich, have agreed to 'black' cargoes diverted from London. And tonight it was learned that Felixstowe, the country's largest unregistered port, won't be handling diverted cargo either.

ULAY UP
RT: 37″

Some of the London dockers, who met today, were told of their support and of plans to ask men at remaining ports to take similar action. They agreed to put off any decision about their strike until a meeting on Monday.

RT: 55″

[programme continues]   Mawer

The Employment Secretary, Mr Foot, also appealed to the dockers to return to work. He said the Government is doing all it could to speed up legislation to deal with the container handling problem.

Mr Foot's appeal came in a speech defending the social contract to members of the executive of the Transport & General Workers' Union.

Our industrial correspondent, Michael Green reports:

FLUP
SUPER:
MICHAEL
GREEN
REPORT-
ING

Mr Foot got a warm reception from the leaders of what is the country's largest union. But his message, though carefully phrased, was quite stark. Unless pay deals are kept within the social contract guidelines, workers will simply price themselves out of jobs. But he stressed that under Labour, there would be no return to statutory controls.

TAKE
INSERT
SUPER:
MICHAEL
FOOT
EMPLOYMENT
SECRETARY

Foot: What madness it would be for this country if because we haven't solved the problem, which by the way has baffled pretty well every other country in the world, because we haven't solved it in 8 months by sane methods, they therefore say we must return to the insane methods that they had before. Well, we certainly have no intention of doing so. It certainly is necessary, however, that we should seek to make the guidelines complied with as successfully as possible. That's essential in the interests of the employment of the people of this country, because it is the case that our inflation is running at a high level — higher than in most other countries in the west — that was the case when we came into office some 12 months ago, and it remains the case today.

Green: And emphasising the government's fear that Britain's rate of inflation will continue to surge ahead of its rivals, he returned to the ways this threat could be overcome.

TAKE
SECOND
INSERT

Foot: One of the ways in which that can be done is to ensure that the guidelines of the social contract are successfully observed. If we can achieve that, then we will have made a major contribution to warding off the danger of rising unemployment.

RT:

20" + 1'33"

(Next item: NGA strike)

8. 7 March 1975 22.00 Item 12   Green
(Previous item: Queen)
SANDY/DOCKS LEAD IN/GREEN FILM

The London dock strike may be called off next week. After a two-hour meeting between port employers, union officials and unofficial strike leaders, the employers said they were 'hopeful' of a return to work.

The decision will be taken at a mass meeting at the Royal Docks on Monday. Our industrial correspondent Michael Green:

FILM GREEN
DUBBING
SCRIPT

The dockland meeting was supposed to have been secret. And both sides − clearly angry at the leak − were tight-lipped when they emerged. Apparently, though, the employers think they've got at least a 50-50 chance of the strike being called off. And I understand the unofficial dock leaders have been persuaded to recommend a return to work. Two firms − this one, Dagenham Storage, and nearby Robertsons − have borne the brunt of the dockers' fight for the container and freight handling jobs. That's because they ignored the advice − made by an enquiry just three years ago − to employ dockers on container work.

Dockers picketing the gate haven't forced lorries away from the depot. But haulage firms which do deliver are added to a list − known as the Cherry Blossom list − and blacked in the docks from then on. One firm − Instone's − has already gone out of business. Others could easily follow.

CUE

Depots like Chobham Farm are paralysed by sympathy strike action even though it already employs registered dockers:

SUPER:
JOHN
DOUGAN
CHOBHAM
FARM

Dougan: I think if this action goes on it will send a number of small employers of registered men bankrupt. These firms will then close down, and the cargo that goes through their firms will no longer be handled by them, and probably no longer handled by the Port of London. I think it's almost self-destructive. They stand to lose the jobs they already have and have other men out of work.

Green: The cost of the dispute is already enormous to the container firms — a quarter of a million pounds. Port employers — a million pounds in wages to men made idle by the strike.

And exports worth £60 million are held up or diverted. Everyone's anxious for a change of heart when the dockers meet on Monday. MG NAT in the Port of London.

RT: 2'04"

(Next item: Housing Finance Bill provisions)

9. 10 March 1975 13.00 Item 5A
(Previous item: Phnom Penh evacuation)
DOCKS

Representatives of London's 10,000 dockers — out on unofficial strike but expected to go back this morning — in fact voted overwhelmingly at a mass meeting this morning to stay out on strike for at least another week.

They want principally the right to more jobs in container work, and they want to stop container firms moving out of dockland and setting up inland where they don't have to employ dockers.

They also want the employers to give in on a number of other points including that no man should be disciplined for any blacking or picketing activities.

RT: Approx. 33"

(Next item: Glasgow dustcart drivers' strike)

10. 10 March 1975 17.50 Item 6
(Previous item: Funeral of murdered policeman)
DOCKERS/FILM ULAY

The dockers' strike which has paralysed the Port of London for ten days, is to go on for at least another week.

FLUP   A mass meeting of about 3,000 dockers outside the Royal Docks were urged by their shop stewards to stay out until they were promised two days back pay; the return of ships diverted from London; and a pledge that no dockers would be disciplined for refusing to work 'blacked' cargo.

In the end the vote to continue the strike was overwhelming.

Film runs 19" before vote and 29" to end.

RT: 32"

(Next item: Glasgow dustcart drivers' strike)

11. 10 March 1975 22.00 Item 11   Tristram
(Previous item: Stonehouse case)
REGGIE/DOCKERS/FILM
The dockers' strike which has paralysed the Port of London for 10 days is to go on for at least another week.

FLUP   The dockers want more jobs in the container depots — and today a mass meeting of 3,000 men was urged by union leaders to stay out until at least 3 demands are met...

8″ SOF UP   'One, all men in the port to be paid for Thursday and Friday the
SUPER: 27th and 28th February. Two, all diverted ships and cargoes to be
DOCKERS'   returned to the port of origin. And three, no man to be disciplined
LEADER   for refusing to work or handle diverted ships, freight, cargo or
OUT 43″   vehicles. I move...'

CUE N/C   **[Newsreader]**The dockers responded by voting overwhelmingly for the strike to continue.

RT: 52″
(Next item: Glasgow dustcart drivers' strike)

12. 13 March 1975 17.50 Item 6   Henderson
(Previous item: Death at toxic waste tip at Pitsea)
DOCKS/ULAY
FILM UP: 50 London dockers who've been on strike for 12 days have agreed to
FILM ULAY   unload and re-load a supply ship from the Falkland Islands. The
RT: 32″   ship, which arrived on the first day of the strike, at Gravesend, has been waiting to unload a cargo of wool and to pick up essential supplies for 2,000 Falkland Islanders.

RT: 19″
(Next item: Shell-BP profits)

13. 13 March 1975 22.00 Item 12   Henderson
(Previous item: Airport strikes)
ANDREW/DOCKS/FILM/ULAY
FILM UP   And in London, 50 dockers broke off their strike which has been going on for 12 days, to unload and re-load a supply ship from the Falkland Islands. They agreed to do the job without pay after being told that the ship must return with essential supplies for the 2,000 inhabitants of the Falkland Islands. The ship has been waiting in the docks since the first day of the strike.

RT: 24″
(Next item: Guardian editor becomes Controller BBC Scotland)

14. 17 March 1975 17.50 Item 5   Thompson
(Previous item: Westminster Hospital dispute)
DOCKS/FILM/SUPER

N/C   The unofficial strike by eleven thousand five hundred London dockers is to continue for at least another week. The dispute is over jobs at container depots.

FILM UP   The decision was made at a mass meeting at the Royal Docks, and it'll take the stoppage into its fourth week.

         The loss to exports is now estimated at about one hundred and twenty million pounds.

         The employers HAVE met certain conditions for a return to

SOF AT 18″   work, but they've refused to accept the blacking of cargo.

SUPER:
BILLY   **Powell:** To say whether or not it was the chairman of the Port
POWELL   Employers who…normal work, and when he was challenged on
DOCKERS'   what he meant by normal work, he said remove your pickets and
LEADER   stop blacking. Now he knew we couldn't [concede] that. He knew
         we wouldn't concede it.

RT: 11″ + 38″

(Next: Benn)

15. 21 March 1975 13.00 Item 8   Mike
(Previous item: Glasgow dustcart drivers' strike)
DOCKS/FOOT VTR – REWRITE

         With the London dock strike now into its third week, the Employment Secretary, Mr Foot told the Commons this morning that the Government had proposed that dockers should be given sole rights to handle container traffic within five miles of docksides. It's part of the Government's proposals for an extension of the dock labour scheme which it's hoped will solve the current dispute between dockers and drivers.

         Some importers and other bodies have already said that such an extension of dock labour would be a disaster, and our industrial correspondent, Giles Smith, asked the Employment Secretary, Mr Foot, whether he hadn't, in fact, given in to militant strike action.

VTR UP: **Foot:** Well, a lot of foolish people often make such foolish
SUPER: suggestions – in fact these proposals are following what we
FOOT   announced in the House of Commons way back in July, long before
         this present action ever occurred, but of course we did know about the constant danger of industrial trouble in the docks, but it's not any surrender, unless it's a surrender to common sense – it's that I suppose.

         Smith: You may not get this into legislation perhaps until towards the end of the year. How is this going to help the present situation in the London docks?

Foot: Well, I hope that dock workers, when they see what we've proposed, will see that we're going about it in a way that is sensible and fair to them, and the more they see that and the more they recognise also, because dock workers are intelligent people who know what's going on in the world, the more they know that there are problems involved in making changes of this character. They can see that for themselves down there now. They can see that they've got a government that's understood their problem, that has listened to representations made by their union, and representations by others as well of course, and I hope that we will get a response to that. I think the government deserves a response from the dock workers to this proposal.

Smith: Well, you say you've listened to the unions, but in this case the union has two totally opposed factions fighting each other. Isn't this a great danger?

Foot: No, I've listened to people who are the spokesmen for those different views, and we've taken into account the different views that are to prevail inside the same union. Of course we've taken them into account in devising these proposals.

Smith: But in the very nature of the dispute, you can hardly expect to please both sides?

Foot: Well, you know, in a lot of disputes you can't please both sides all the time, but you can out of such discussions produce a coherent way to try and avoid these troubles in the future, and that's what we're doing. We're not laying down an absolute hard and fast way of dealing with everything in each particular circumstance. We're trying to lay down a procedure which can be adapted to new circumstances as they arise, and instead of people condemning that as surrender and using [this] emotive language – I'm sure you wouldn't use such language, but instead of people condemning it in that way, I think they should look at the problem and see how we've tried to devise a solution.

RT: 38″ + 2′16″

(Next item: Soccer)

16. 21 March 1975 17.50 Item 7   Smith
(Previous item: Westminster Hospital dispute)
DOCKS
SLIDE   The Employment Secretary, Mr Foot, has announced new plans

ULAY which he hopes will persuade the 11,000 London dockers on strike to return to work.

They've been out for three weeks now in a long-running dispute with lorry drivers about which of them should handle container traffic.

The Government propose that all work connected with the loading and unloading of ships within a five-mile radius around the docks should be done by registered dockers. And firms employing non-registered men would have to insist on them joining the

LOSE ULAY registered scheme.

Our industrial correspondent says that the Government's decision will be seen as a victory for the dockers and a reverse for the lorry drivers. And it's bound to be resisted by the container companies and small port operators who don't have registered dockers.

RT: Approx. 45″

(Next item: Glasgow dustcart drivers' strike)

17. 21 March 1975 22.00 Item 8   O'Connell
(Previous item: Westminster Hospital dispute)
REGGIE/DOCKS/SMITH VTR/SLIDE/ULAY/MAP/SUPERS

SLIDE: The Employment Secretary, Mr Foot, has asked London's 11,000 dockers to call off their three-week unofficial strike and go back to work.

Mr Foot has promised that the Government will back new plans which would give dockers sole rights to handle container traffic arriving and leaving the dockside.

Here's our industrial correspondent, Giles Smith:

SMITH VTR ULAY UP SUPERS PROBABLY ON VTR Many people will see today's Government statement as a major victory for the striking London dockers in their fight with the lorry drivers whose job it is to handle containers. From the wording of Mr Foot's document it seems pretty well all jobs connected with loading and unloading of ships are going to registered dockers. There will be exceptions but in general it looks as though workers at the big container depots will have to become registered or be sacked. When the proposals become law, after further consultations, a five-mile

MAP VTR 1 ROLL belt around ports will be drawn − in the case of London right out to the far reaches − in which the National Dock Labour Board can specify firms who must employ dockers. I asked Mr Foot how he answered charges that such a scheme would be a disaster for dockland efficiency.

Foot: Well, I think it is very foolish for them to use language of that character. What we are trying to do is to ensure that the scheme can be extended in an orderly manner, and that we don't have the kind of disturbances in the docks which are going on at the moment – I would have thought that was the disaster that had to be avoided. Of course we've – employers have been able to make any representations they want to and still will be able to do so, but we are determined to carry through this scheme in order to avoid disaster, and to prevent the kind of troubles we've got now.

INTO CAM **[Green]:** Whether the concessions are enough to get the dockers to call off their strike when they meet again on Monday remains to be seen. What does seem certain is that the proposals will be hotly resisted by the lorry drivers, whose views in this dispute seem to have been ignored. It'll also be attacked by many port employers particularly those in the small private ports outside the dock labour scheme.

RT: 21″ + 1′40″

(Next item: Strike at House of Commons)

18. 24 March 1975 13.00 Item 4 Mike
(Previous item: Collapse of Middle East peace initiative)
DOCKERS/MEETING/GREEN PHONO

The London dock strike – now in its fourth week – and holding up exports [estimated] at £200 million – is to continue in spite of the Government's peace moves last Friday.

The dockers voted NOT to go back to work at a mass meeting this morning, and our industrial correspondent Michael Green, was there.

PHONO
SUPER:
MICHAEL
GREEN

The decision confirms the worst fears of the Port employers, and the leaders of the transport union. After last week's Government proposals for a sweeping new definition of dock work, which would give dockers the right to work in container depots up to five miles inland from the ports, it did seem that there was a good chance of this damaging strike being called off. But among the shop stewards the feeling has grown that they want some concrete concession now. And in the first instance that means that they want two freight-handling firms – Dagenham Storage and S.J. Robertson – to take on dockers or close down. So this morning the stewards met before the mass meeting and agreed to recommend that the strike goes on, at least until Wednesday when there's to be another mass meeting. Mr Brian Nicholson, the chairman of the unofficial stewards' committee, claimed afterwards that the vote was four to one to stay out, but this was greeted with hoots of derision from some dockers nearby. The press and TV cameras had been excluded from the meeting, but from a distance it looked as though the vote among about 3,000 dockers, was very close indeed. It's understood the dockers' leaders will be meeting the employers later today, and they're also calling for talks with the Secretary for Employment, Mr Michael Foot. But meanwhile, the cost of transferring ships, paying port employees not involved in the strike, exports held up and so on is mounting by millions of pounds a day. The total cost is said to be well over £100 million, and could be getting on for £200 millions. MG, FR at Tilbury docks.

RT: 18″ + 1'31″

(Next item: Trawlermen blockade ports)

19. 24 March 17.50 Item 2   Jamieson
(Previous item: Trawlermen blockade ports)
DOCKS/GREEN FILM/SUPERS

London's dockers have decided in a controversial vote to continue their three-week strike. The decision to stay out until at least Wednesday was taken at a meeting in Tilbury.

Our industrial correspondent, Michael Green reports:

FLUP SUPER: **Green:** The meeting was the first since the Government's plans
MICHAEL   announced on Friday for a sweeping new definition of dock work
GREEN   giving dockers the right to work some inland container depots. But
REPORTING   the decision dashed any hopes for a quick return to work. The vote
            seemed fairly close. Some observers even thought it might have been
            a vote to return but the shop stewards' chairman, Mr Brian
            Nicholson, claimed otherwise.

SUPER: **Nicholson:** Well you see the vote, 4 to 1 in favour of continuing this
BRIAN   strike.
NICHOLSON

            Green: It didn't look quite that enormous.

            Nicholson: It was that enormous. You must know what the vote
            went, right? OK, and we will be now going to meet the Minister
            because we are (fuming) at the way we are being treated.

            Green: Why, after the White Paper last week...

            Nicholson: The White Paper is not to do with this, you know it and
            I know it. What I'm talking about is the lack of consideration, the
            bloodymindedness of the port employers, and they were part of that
            decision. Now they were part of that decision. We didn't go to an
            inquiry to have people say afterwards...well that was the decision.
            We would have had to have abided by it. Now we want someone to

take action and get them to abide by it and this port of ours will be working.

Green: Are you going to see Mr Foot then?

Nicholson: We hope to.

Green: The disastrous effects of the strike on the port were underlined by the port employers this evening. Losses of imports and exports are incalculable, they say, and they've appealed to the Transport Union, Mr Jack Jones, to try once more to get the strike called off. MG, ITN Tilbury Docks.

RT: 9″ + 1'33″

(Next item: Vietnam fighting)

20. 24 March 1975 22.00 Item 6   Jamieson
(Previous item: Plight of the Kurds)
REGGIE/DOCKERS/GREEN FILM/SUPERS
     The London dock strike is to go on. After a mass meeting in Tilbury, the dockers decided, in a controversial vote, to continue their three week dispute and meet again next Wednesday.
     Our industrial correspondent, Michael Green reports:

FLUP   [text identical to 17.50 to end of Nicholson interview]

Green: Apart from the understandable doubts of the stewards' interpretation of the vote, the employers tonight said they were dismayed at the low attendance at the meetings – no more than 2,000 of the port's 11,000 dockers. There are now rumblings that the Tilbury men may well desert their brothers up river and call it off unilaterally, but meanwhile the employers said losses of imports and exports are incalculable, and they appeal to Mr Jack Jones, the Transport Union leader, to try once more to get the strike called off. MG, NAT, Tilbury.

RT: 13″ + 1'52″

(Next item: Benn)

21. 26 March 1975 13.00 Item 6   Mike
(Previous item: Vietnam fighting)
DOCKERS MEETING
     Back in Great Britain, London's dockers have once again voted to continue their month-old unofficial strike. They voted that way last Monday, but called a mass meeting at Tilbury this morning to hear an appeal to go back from the general secretary of the Transport and General Workers' Union, Mr Jack Jones. However, one of the strike

leaders, Mr Brian Nicholson, said the men had voted this morning by a show of hands to stay out by a majority of 3-1.

RT: 27″

(Next item: Trawlermen blockade ports)

22. 26 March 1975 17.50 Item 8   O'Connell
(Previous item: Mrs Sheila Buckley held on theft charges)
DOCKS/FILM ULAY

The three week strike by London dockers is to continue despite a dispute among the men themselves as to how the vote had gone. The decision to stay out for at least another ten days was made at a mass meeting of 4,000 dockers this morning. It was a noisy meeting and at one point scuffling broke out. The vote was on a show of hands, in two stages – first the vote to stay on strike.

FLUP
SOUND UP
AT 6″
CUE AT 10″
(SOUND
LOW)
SOUND UP
AT 22″
AT 24″
CUE AT 27″
(SOUND
LOW)

Then the vote to go back.

There was confusion afterwards. But the leader of the shop stewards claimed there was a three to one majority in favour of continuing the strike.

RT: 40″

(Next item: Trawler sinks)

23. 26 March 1975 22.00 Item 3   O'Connell
(Previous item: Government takeover rescues Harland and Wolfe)
REGGIE/DOCKERS/GREEN VTR/SUPERS/SLIDE?/2nd REWRITE

London dockers have decided to continue their strike for at least another ten days – it's already gone on for nearly four weeks.

Not all the dockers are said to be happy with the decision. And the port employers claimed tonight that the shop stewards were wrong in the way they interpreted the vote.

Michael Green reports:

GREEN VTR
INTO CAM

The pressure was ON the dockers at today's meeting to call it a day.

They've been on strike for four weeks during which the main dockers' union, the Transport and General Workers', has repeatedly urged them to go back.

VTR 4 UP

The Government has produced its plans for extending dock work to five miles outside the ports – apparently answering the dockers' main grievance. And the employers have warned that they're cutting their own throats by driving even more trade away from what was quite recently Britain's most important port.

But the shop stewards – once again – urged the men to stay out. This was the vote for the platform.

The employers maintain that the platform proposition was itself confused and that this may have baffled some of the dockers.

Then came the vote against. And immediately there was a feeling among some experienced observers that the vote was certainly a close run thing and might well have shown a majority wanting to go back.

But the stewards were adamant: the vote, they said, was three to one to stay on strike.

TC 3 UP: The scene was almost a replica of Monday's mass meeting when there were grave doubts expressed about the stewards' declaration
FILM 11″ that the men had voted FOUR to one to keep the strike going.
INTO CAM At TODAY's meeting out of five experienced correspondents from national newspapers, four felt that the vote was definitely in favour of a return to work, while one said that it could have been a dead heat.

Only the Communist Morning Star said the vote was a clear majority for continuing the strike.

The Press Association news agency declared that it was 'possibly even more clearly in favour of a return to work than Monday'.

RT: Not available
(Next item: Trawlermen blockade ports)

24. 27 March 1975 13.00 Lead Item   Mike
DOCKS STRIKE/SISSONS STUDIO SPOT
But first the situation at London docks. A meeting of about 1,000 dockers at Tilbury this morning voted to reject that controversial, to say the least, decision taken yesterday to continue the month-old strike, and go back to work instead. One shop steward, Mr Norman Buckley, said they'd had the guarantee they were seeking about jobs at container depots from the Employment Secretary, Mr Foot, and from the Transport Union leader, Mr Jack Jones. After the vote it was estimated there was a two-thirds majority in favour of ending the strike.

Other shop stewards who were present refused to take part in the vote and said they would only convey the feeling of the meeting to the leader of the unofficial strike, Mr Brian Nicholson.

Peter Sissons is on his way back from that meeting:

Kee: Peter, what actually happened this morning, apart from the vote itself?

Sissons: It was extremely confusing, and it's even confusing as to what the vote means. But basically, what happened was this: no-one seems to know who called the meeting. Some wag in the crowd suggested to me that the press had called the meeting this morning, but in fact it was held outside the Transport & General Workers' Union offices in Tilbury, and officials of the T&G addressed the men, less than a thousand of them, and put to them the argument used by Mr Jack Jones, and Mr Michael Foot that the Government had everything in train, and there was no point continuing the strike, that Tilbury was losing business, and only harm could come to the men and their jobs if they carried on. Well, after this, which went down very well, and was listened to very sympathetically, the representatives of the London docks stewards had their say.

Kee: These were the people who voted yesterday? Can we just get this clear: were the Tilbury dockers present at the meeting yesterday?

Sissons: Oh yes. Yesterday was a meeting of all the dockers which go to make up the group of docks.

Kee: So this was a breakaway meeting as it were from yesterday's meeting?

Sissons: This was clearly a breakaway meeting designed, or I think, engineered, to try to persuade the Tilbury dockers to go back unilaterally. Now what happened was that the meeting closed as these meetings do close, without any decision having been taken, except that it did seem that the meeting had taken on board what they'd been asked to do by the London shop stewards, and that is not to take unilateral action. If there's going to be a vote to go back, everyone will go back together.

Kee: But did they not take a vote to go back?

Sissons: There was then a vote. But people started to drift away in the confusion, and I should think that when there were only 500 left around the platform, one of the Tilbury stewards jumped up and said, 'Well, we're bloody well going back to work: all those in favour?'. And I should think by a ten to one majority – I know all these ratios are highly disputed these days – but by a very clear majority, I don't think anyone could possible dispute this, the few who were left voted to go back to work. Now, I went in and asked one or two of them, who wouldn't be filmed, or anything like that, what that vote meant, and they were unanimous in saying that the Tilbury dockers would not go back unilaterally, but they intended that vote to be an indication to the London dockers, whom they regard as being the sort of militant pacemakers, [that] they couldn't drag the Tilbury men along much longer. And the combined shop stewards, of course the Tilbury shop stewards are outnumbered two to one by the London shop stewards, are meeting sometime now to discuss just what's happening at Tilbury. But Tilbury I don't think is going back unilaterally – but everyone knows now how strongly they feel.

Kee: Thank you very much Peter Sissons.

RT: Not available

(Next item: Fishermen blockade ports)

25. 27 March 1975 17.50 Lead item   O'Connell
DOCKS/SISSONS LIVESPOT/SUPER/FILM or VTR ULAY
TITLE VTR + FILM
At Tilbury today, there were the first signs of a major split in the unofficial strike by 11,000 London dockers, which is now in its fourth week.

A mass meeting of dockers there voted overwhelmingly in favour of calling off the strike. But they've set no date for a return to work.

The Tilbury men are outnumbered by the Port of London dockers and it's unlikely that the strike will be called off until there's a mass meeting representing both sections.

Here's our industrial editor, Peter Sissons:

LIVESPOT UP   Today's meeting at Tilbury, Britain's biggest container port, was
+ VTR ULAY   clearly a direct response to yesterday's mass meeting further up river. This, too, had been attended by Tilbury men, many of whom were clearly dissatisfied with the way shop stewards had interpreted yesterday's vote.

But the revolt on their home ground today was disorganised and confused. They heard officials of their union urge a return to work on the basis of what the Government was doing to make dock-work secure in the face of containerisation. They heard, and many vociferously expressed, condemnation of the way leaders of the unofficial strike were reading the votes at mass meetings. But shop stewards from London urged solidarity, and said that the only meeting that could call the strike off was one representing all eleven thousand dockers in the port. They promised, however, to take the men's feeling back to the 160-strong shop stewards' committee.

U/LAY   At this, the meeting started to break up, and perhaps a third of the thousand left. It was at this stage that one of the Tilbury stewards leapt onto the platform.

SOF UP STRONG FOR FIVE SECONDS

What he decided to do was call for a vote.

SOF UP STRONG FOR ANOTHER TWENTY SECONDS

So most of those who were left at the meeting – about 600 of

Tilbury's 2,350 dockers — voted overwhelmingly to return to work, but set no date for it. Afterwards, individuals shunned publicity but I spoke privately to a couple of dozen, and all expressed the view that this was not so much a vote for a return, as the strongest possible warning to the strike's unofficial leaders that Tilbury wouldn't go along with them indefinitely.

However, afterwards, Mr Harry Freeman, a Tilbury official of the Transport Workers' Union, said he interpreted the vote as 'a direct call for a return to work'. Unconfirmed reports indicate that there has indeed been a trickle of men going back in certain parts of the port. Something the strike leaders will have to consider at their next meeting.

RT: 2'45"

(Next item: Vietnam fighting)

26. 27 March 1975 22.00 Lead item   O'Connell
ANDREW/DOCKS/SISSONS VTR

Good Evening:

There are signs tonight of a major split in the four-week unofficial strike by London dockers.

The Port Employers claim there has been 'a steady trickle' of men reporting back to work during the day.

And at a mass meeting of dockers at Tilbury there was an overwhelming vote in favour of calling off the strike.

The Tilbury men are outnumbered by the Port of London dockers and it's unlikely that the strike will end until there's a mass meeting representing both sections.

But it seemed to emphasise the growing dissatisfaction among some of the 11,000 dockers at the way previous meetings have been handled by the shop stewards.

Here's our industrial editor, Peter Sissons:

SISSONS VTR [Report identical to 1750 down to closing para.]

However, afterwards, Mr Harry Freeman, a Tilbury official of the Transport Workers' Union, said he interpreted the vote as 'a direct call for a return to work'. Reports tonight indicate that employers have indeed had a trickle of enquiries from men wanting to go back in certain parts of the port. Something the strike leaders will have to consider at their next meeting on Saturday.

RT: Not available

                                                                 O'Connell
[Programme continues]
LEONARD/DOCK LEADER/ARCHER VTR

The man at the centre of the London dock strike is Mr Brian

Nicholson, a controversial figure during two dock meetings where the voting has been disputed.

Geoffrey Archer reports:

ARCHER
VTR
NICHOLSON
ON
PLATFORM
T/C

Brian Nicholson has attracted the attention of the cameras only during the last few weeks, as leader of the latest dock strike. But he has been a major political force in the docks for many years. In 1969 he was largely responsible for the Bristow committee reporting on the docks. At the time their proposals were shelved, and in 1972 when Bernie Steer and Vic Turner were briefly imprisoned for being in contempt of the Industrial Relations Court, Nicholson was thought to be the master mind behind the dispute at the time. He is chairman of the docks group of the Transport and General Workers' Union. The recent disputes over who should run the container depots have been largely in the hands of the shop stewards, led by Vic Turner. But in the last few weeks Nicholson has taken over, in his role as local union chairman, even though the strike is unofficial. This has been his bid for ultimate power in the London Docks.

Brian Nicholson lives in Hackney; he's divorced and he has three children. He's a member of the Labour Party and of the national executive of the Transport Union. For the four months prior to this dispute he has been on sick leave with an injured leg.

Nicholson's main political affiliation is to the Institute for Workers' Control, an organisation based in Nottingham which has the late Bertrand Russell as its honorary president. Nicholson is vice president of the Institute whose members include the Minister of State for Northern Ireland Mr Stan Orme, and whose conference this year will be addressed by the Industry Secretary Tony Benn.

Brian Nicholson has written a number of pamphlets on the docks, urging total workers' control throughout Britain so that dock employees can have complete power to dictate terms and conditions of employment. His involvement in recent days in disputed vote counting may have been a set-back to his ambitions as a dockers' leader.

RT: Not available

(Next item: Vietnam fighting)

27. 28 March 1975 22.00 Item 4   Maimane
(Previous item: Daily Mirror dispute)
LEONARD/DOCKS/ROLLER/SLIDE

11,000 London dockers have been warned that their five-week strike is threatening their own jobs as well as those of thousands of other workers.

The warning's in a letter sent to all dockers by the employers, who say their losses so far this year are nearly £6 million.

The letter goes on:

SLIDE/
ROLLER
'Each day that this dispute continues, the job of every man in the port becomes progressively less secure. In addition, the jobs of thousands who work in the surrounding community and whose livelihood depends on the port must also be in jeopardy.'

RT: 32"

(Next item: Commercial break)

28. 29 March 975 13.10 Item 3   Sam
(Previous item: President Lon Nol of Cambodia to leave)
DOCKERS/FILM ULAY

The London dock strike over the manning of container depots, is to go on.

UP FILM
ULAY 26"
About 100 shop stewards meeting at the Surrey Dockers' Club in Rotherhithe decided NOT to bring forward the date of a mass meeting scheduled for Friday.

Among the stewards was the strike leader Mr Brian Nicholson, whose declaration of a 3-1 vote in favour of staying on strike at a mass meeting last Wednesday has been disputed.

Today, Mr Nicholson said it was hoped to extend the strike nationally.

RT: 27"

(Next item: Chrysler car prices)

29. 29 March 1975 17.12 Item 3   Sam
(Previous item: President Lon Nol of Cambodia to leave)
DOCKERS/FILM

The London dock strike over the manning of container depots is to go on – despite a warning by the employers that the unofficial stoppage is, in their words, 'the most serious in the history of the Port of London'.

They said in a letter to all registered dockers that its 'catastrophic' effects are putting thousands of jobs in jeopardy.

FILM UP
About 70 shop stewards met in south east London for two hours, and it had been thought that the stoppage might be called off because of an apparent lack of support from many of the men. Among the stewards was the strike leader, Mr Brian Nicholson – whose declaration of a 3-to-1 vote to continue the strike at a mass meeting last Wednesday has been disputed. He said it is now hoped to extend the strike nationally.

Derek Taylor asked Mr Nicholson why the date of a mass

meeting scheduled for Friday hadn't been brought forward:

SOF UP
AT 26″
BRIAN
NICHOLSON
STRIKE
LEADER
RT:

Nicholson: We never bring the meeting forward or anything else — we'll bring the meeting forward tomorrow. The policy is men. We'll bring it forward tomorrow and let our men know. I've got something concrete to tell our men, we'll have the meeting.

43″

(Next item: Common Market)

30. 29 March 1975 22.30 Item 5   Sam
(Previous item: Egypt)
DOCKERS/FILM/SUPER

The Port of London employers have warned all registered dockers that their unofficial strike over the manning of container depots is, in their words, having a 'catastrophic effect' — and putting thousands of jobs in jeopardy.

UP FILM

But despite the warning, about 70 shop stewards meeting in south-east London voted NOT to bring forward the date of a mass meeting scheduled for Friday...so the strike will go on until then.

The strike leader, Mr Brian Nicholson, said it is now hoped to extend the strike nationally.

CUE AT 20″

Afterwards Derek Taylor asked Mr Nicholson WHY the shop stewards didn't advance the date of the meeting...

SOF UP
AT 26″
SUPER
BRIAN
NICHOLSON
STRIKE
LEADER

Nicholson: We never bring the meeting forward or anything else — we'll bring the meeting forward tomorrow. The policy is men. We'll bring it forward tomorrow and let our men know. I've got something concrete to tell our men, we'll have the meeting.

RT: 54″

(Next item: Common Market)

31. 1 April 1975 13.00 Item 6   Mike
(Previous item: Kurds)
DOCKS/REES PHONO

A mass meeting of dockers in Hull has rejected an appeal for them to join in the London dock strike, which is now in its fifth week. A deputation of shop stewards from the Royal Group of Docks had travelled up from London to make the appeal, and Norman Rees was there to hear the Hull dockers' decision.

REES PHONO
SUPER: REES

[Rees] This is a major setback for the unofficial London strikers — Hull is traditionally one of the most militant ports, and without support here, it's thought that dock workers in other parts of the country can be persuaded to join them. This morning's meeting was attended by about 1,000 men — that's about half the dock labour force, and despite a recommendation by their own shop stewards that they should come out on strike, the vote to return to work was overwhelming. London shop stewards who had addressed the meeting, refused to comment as they left. But ironically, as the Hull dockers return to work just about now, they'll find their port blocked by striking fishermen — nine fishing boats arrived from Grimsby during their meeting this morning, to block the lock gates leading to the port's two largest docks; 22 ships are now trapped inside. NR, FR, Hull.

RT: 59″

[programme continues]

Meanwhile in London itself, there are signs that the dock strike is weakening. Over 100 dockers met at Purfleet in Essex this morning to decide whether or not to go back to work, and though their decision isn't yet known, our reporter who was at the dock gate says it's expected that they'll return to work.

In the studio with me is our industrial editor, Peter Sissons.

STUDIO INTERVIEW

Parkin: Let's look at Hull first, Peter, if we could. How much of a set-back is this for the militant dockers' leaders, led by Brian Nicholson?

Sissons: Well, I think it is a great set-back. They wouldn't have gone to Hull expecting to be rebuffed. As Norman Rees pointed out, Hull has got a tradition of backing the London dockers on the big issues, and you'll recall that we did have a national docks strike a couple of years ago, over this very issue — over containerisation — which led to the Jones/Aldington report, and the proposals they made. So the docks of this country were at a standstill in the recent past over this issue, and Mr Nicholson and his colleagues have now found out that they are not willing to go along the same road again.

Parkin: Does it look, as it appears to me from hearing Norman Rees there — because, as you remember, he said the Hull dockers went against the advice of their own shop stewards — does it look as though the great silent majority are now beginning to assert themselves?

Sissons: Well, when he said they went against the advice of their own shop stewards, their own stewards could hardly, having given [their London colleagues the courtesy of a hearing], then recommend that their request is turned down. So I wouldn't pin too much to that.

Parkin: Well, nonetheless, 1,000 Hull dockers did decide that they wanted to work and not strike.

Sissons: Oh, absolutely. I think we're getting a bit away from the main point, which is that this growing feeling, not just amongst dockers in Hull, and Liverpool by all accounts, but in places like Tilbury, which are part of the Port of London, but with not the same sort of militant tradition as the Royal Docks for example, that what has been done so far by the Government, by their own Union leaders, by the Conciliation and Arbitration Service, to speed up Government proposals, to provide more jobs for dock workers, in places which are now on the fringe, in container work, what is being done is all that can be done, and there is no further point in being on strike. Now this was the feeling that I got clearly at Tilbury last Thursday, when I was there. Of course it's a running sore; of course there has to be some deep-seated cause why men can be on strike for four or five weeks, but I think one is beginning to see the realisation that perhaps there's not much more that can be done.

Parkin: Yes, there has to be a cause why men can be on strike for five or six weeks beyond the determination of some sort to simply disrupt for disruption's own purposes?

Sissons: I don't go along with that at all. There's no doubt in my mind that the issue of containerisation and the related issue of lack of job security is frighteningly...

Parkin: Real to the dockers themselves?

Sissons: Deep-rooted and real to the dockers. And this is the reason. This is the reason the strike is prolonged, and has been so intractable in the various inquiries and committees that have been set up over the last few years to try to resolve this particular issue, that I think we're now beginning to see, and the next mass meeting is on Friday. We're now beginning to see the beginning of the end of the strike. It's not crumbling — I wouldn't go so far as to say it was crumbling.

Parkin: But it is the beginning of the end?

Sissons: ...

Parkin: There we must leave it, I'm afraid. Thank you very much.

RT: Not available

(Next item: Northern Ireland killings)

32. 1 April 1975 17.50 Item 2　　　　　　　　　　　　Jamieson
(Previous item: Shelepin cuts short visit to Britain)

DOCKS/SMITH FILM/VTR ULAY/MAP/SUPERS

MAP
LONDON
DOCKS

The first signs of a return to work by London dockers came this afternoon when about 100 men at the private Purfleet dock began moving cargo — for the first time since the strike began five weeks ago.

Another blow to the dockers came when their colleagues in Hull rejected a call to come out in support. Our industrial correspondent, Giles Smith reports.

VTR UP
SUPERS:
HULL
GILES SMITH
VTR OUT
FILM UP
SUPER:
TILBURY
PURFLEET

The strike leaders' first set-back came in Hull when 2,000 dockers there refused to go on strike in support of the London men. In doing so they rejected personal appeals from two of the London strike leaders who'd travelled north specially for the meeting. Far more damaging for the strike leaders though was the decision of more than half the 200 dockers at the small dock at Purfleet near Tilbury to ignore their leaders' recommendations and go back.

Although their decisions and the subsequent work was surrounded in secrecy — understandably perhaps — it's understood the 100 men were unanimous in their decision. While the Purfleet dock is tiny, Port of London officials claimed tonight that a number of other groups of dockers had begun drifting back to work.

SUPER:
TILBURY

Some of these were thought to be at Tilbury, where strikers mounted a heavy but uneventful picket. More than 500 men there had earlier picketed their own union office demanding to know why they shouldn't go back to work.

INTO
CAMERA

Clearly the solidarity of the dockers is beginning to crumble. Not only have the men here at Purfleet decided to go back to work, but far more significantly, the strike leaders have been unable, or unwilling, to mount a strike picket to dissuade them otherwise, and that could be the most telling lesson of the day.

RT: 1'35"

(Next item: Trawlermen blockade ports)

33. 1 April 1975 22.00 Item 7   Jamieson
(Previous item: Commercial break)
LEONARD/PURFLEET/SMITH FILM/REES FILM/SUPERS/MAP

The first sign of a return to work by London dockers came this afternoon when about 100 men at the private Purfleet dock began moving cargo — for the first time since the strike began five weeks ago.

The strike had another setback when dockers in Hull rejected their appeal to come out in support.

From the Port of London our industrial correspondent, Giles

Smith reports:

FLUP SUPER:
GILES SMITH
REPORTING

Purfleet deep wharf in Essex was the scene of the first small break in the solidarity of the London dockers. An early morning mass meeting led to the men resuming work at 1.25. Nearly half the 200 dockers there decided to ignore the strike leaders' recommendations and go back. Their decision, and the subsequent resumption of work were shrouded in secrecy. Understandably perhaps, both management and men clearly fear a reaction from the strike leaders in the form of picketing. While the Purfleet dock is tiny, Port of London officials claimed tonight that a number of other groups of dockers had begun drifting back to work. Some of these were thought to be at Tilbury, where strikers mounted a heavy but uneventful picket. More than 500 men there had earlier picketed their own union office, demanding to know why they shouldn't go back to work. Clearly the solidarity of the dockers is beginning to crumble. Not only have the men here at Purfleet decided to go back, but perhaps far more significantly, the strike leaders have been unable or unwilling to mount a strike picket here to persuade them otherwise, and that

WIPE TO
REES FILM

could be the most telling fact of the day. GS, NAT NAT, Purfleet.

SUPER:
NORMAN
REES
REPORTING

And there was further discouragement for the London strikers here at Hull. 2,000 Hull dockers, considered among the most militant in Britain, were asked at a mass meeting this morning, to join the London stoppage. Militant shop stewards from London, among them Mr Vic Turner, appealed to the men to come out on strike, but it was a meeting at which the moderates held sway. (SOF) The Hull dockers ignored the advice of their own shop stewards to join the London strikers, and instead, voted overwhemingly to stay at work. It was a barren morning for Mr Turner and the rest of the London militants who afterwards refused to comment on the Hull workers' decision. (SOF) But ironically, as the dockers at Hull returned to work, they found the report blocked by striking fishermen. Ten trawlers from Grimsby blocked the entrance to two of Hull's largest commercial docks. 22 ships are now trapped inside the dock basin. NR, NAT, Hull.

RT:

6″ + 23″ + 1'12″ + 1'18″

(Next item: Trawlermen blockade ports)

34. 2 April 1975 13.00 Item 6   Mike
(Previous item: Trawlermen blockade ports)
DOCKS/SMITH FILM/SUPER

Now the London dock strike…and after yesterday's setbacks for the strike committee when Hull dockers refused to come out, this morning there has been an appeal from leaders of the 1,500 tally clerks in the Port of London for an immediate return to work. They want shop stewards to recommend ending the 5 week old unofficial strike at a mass meeting on Friday.

The Port of London Authority say that up to 60 men men have gone back to work at Tilbury today; and there are reports of more men going back at smaller wharves along the Thames. Our industrial correspondent Giles Smith, went to Purfleet this morning, where the first cracks in the strike appeared yesterday.

FLUP SUPER: GILES SMITH

There were six rather cold and wet pickets at Purfleet deep wharf this morning, following yesterday's decision by 100 dockers there to ignore the strike leaders' recommendations and go back to work. The six had come from Tilbury and the Royal group. They said they'd attempted to stop and talk to the Purfleet men, but none apparently had wanted to listen. They complained bitterly that the Purfleet men should have waited until Friday's mass meeting in Tilbury to put their views. In fact the pickets, noticeable by their absence yesterday, were today greatly outnumbered by the police, who clearly feared incidents if a large picket had appeared. In the event, there was no trouble as pickets and police watched as loads of newsprint were being driven out of the by now active dock. Purfleet is an important centre for newsprint, and its reopening will help to ease the shortage which has hit Fleet Street since the start of the docks strike. GS, FR, Purfleet.

RT: 40" + 53"

(Next item: Ipswich)

35. 2 April 1975 17.50 Item 6   Tristram
(Previous item: Trawlermen blockade ports)
(DOCKS/FILM ULAY

The London dock strike showed further signs of breaking up today.

FILM ULAY   Leaders of 15-hundred tally clerks appealed to their men to end the five-week-old unofficial strike. And at Purfleet in Essex despite pickets, a hundred men turned up for work − 30 more than yesterday.

At Tilbury, 50 dockers were reported to be at work, with more men going back at smaller wharves along the Thames.

RT: 23"

(Next item: Oil)

36. 2 April 1975 22.00 Item 10   Tristram
(Previous item: Trawlermen blockade ports)

ANDREW/DOCKS/FILM ULAY

In London, there were more signs that the dock strike is breaking up.

Leaders of 15-hundred tally clerks appealed to their men to end the five-week old unofficial strike.

FILM ULAY   And at Purfleet in Essex, pickets were ignored by a hundred men who turned up for work today — 30 more than yesterday.

At Tilbury, 50 dockers were reported to be at work, with other men going back to smaller wharves along the Thames.

RT: 25″

(Next item: Miners' pay)

37. 3 April 1975 17.50 Item 8   Sam
(Previous item: Trawlermen blockade ports)
DOCKERS

Tomorrow morning's mass meeting of London dockers to decide whether to end their five-week old strike has been switched from Tilbury to the West India dock.

Shop stewards said the change would make an accurate count easier should there be a close vote.

RT: 15″

(Next item: British Rail workshop supervisors' dispute)

38. 3 April ₁975 22.00 Item 15   Sam
(Previous item: Glasgow dustcart drivers' dispute)
REGGIE/DOCKERS

London dockers are to hold a mass meeting at the West India Dock tomorrow to decide whether to end their five-week old strike over the menning of container depots.

The meeting — at eleven o'clock — was moved from Tilbury because it was thought that the West India dock would make an accurate count easier if the vote is close.

RT: 20″

(Next item: Provisional IRA Council discusses ceasefire)

39. 4 April 1975 13.00 Item 7   Mike
(Previous item: Cambodian peace call)
DOCKS/VTR/GREEN INJECT/SUPER

The London dock strike — which has lasted for five weeks — is over. After a mass meeting inside the main gate of the West India Dock this morning, the strike leader, Mr Brian Nicholson, said the vote had shown 'an overwhelming desire to return to work' and the men

will be going back on Monday.
Over now to our industrial correspondent, Michael Green, who
is with our outside broadcast unit at the docks.

LIVE INJ &
VTR ULAY

The dockers at the best-attended meeting in this dispute so far —
there were probably four thousand of them here, were told at the
outset that nothing had changed since their previous controversial
vote to stay out. Mr Bill Powell, a member of the Transport and
General Workers' Union executive, said he had faith in the
Government's plans to extend dock work, and he had faith in Mr
Foot, the Employment Secretary, but he said he had faith in previous
attempts to safeguard dockers' jobs, and those had proved to be
worthless pieces of paper. The number one docks group demands on
which the dispute has been fought were again reiterated: payment
for the first two days of the dispute, when the dockers claim they
were locked out; that diverted ships should be returned to their port
of origin, and, most important, that dockers should not be
disciplined and therefore allowed to picket container bases, and to
black certain container cargoes coming into the docks. Mr Brian
Nicholson, chairman of the docks group, cut short the meeting and
said there had been calls for a vote. (SOF) Mr Nicholson and some of
his fellow shop stewards left the meeting here bitterly disappointed
men, but the result will be a relief for Mr Jack Jones, General
Secretary of the Transport Union and for the Government as well.
The Port of London, whom I spoke to just now, say they expect the
docks quickly now to get back to normal. MG, MR, at the West
India Docks.

RT: 25" + 2'00"

(Next item: Electricity supply workers' pay)

40. 4 April 1975 17.50 Lead Item   Sam
DOCKERS/SMITH FILM/SUPER

Home news. The London docks strike is over. The men voted to
end their five-week old dispute over the manning of container
depots at a mass meeting at the West India Dock.
     Afterwards, the Port of London Authority, who said work
would resume on Monday, described the stoppage as 'the most
expensive in their history'. They said the strike had cost the
Authority alone more than seven million pounds.

SUPER: GILES
SMITH
REPORTING

An estimated 4,000 of London's 11,000 dockers turned up at the
meeting at the West India Docks at 11.00 this morning. After the
controversy of previous meetings, and the allegations, strongly
denied, of fiddled votes, the shop stewards' committee had agreed to

allow press and television full access to the entire proceedings. From the start it was clear the strike leaders would face strong pressure to end the dispute. Committee chairman, Brian Nicholson, and other leaders like Bernie Steer and Vic Turner, both imprisoned during the 1972 national dock strike, were clearly uneasy after the trickle back to work of the past few days. When Mr Nicholson called the vote this time there was no doubt in anyone's mind. (SOF) After the vote, Mr Nicholson refused to comment. (SOF) Clearly, though, the vote was a major setback to the dockers' leaders' fight to continue militant action on the container issue. The big question now is, 'Will the blacking of the container depots now cease, and what will be the reaction of the lorry drivers, who've been so strongly opposed to the dockers?' GS, ITN, in the Port of London.

RT: 50″ + 1'43″

(Next item: Plane carrying Vietnamese refugees crashes)

41. 4 April 1975 22.00 Item 8   Sam
(Previous item: Commercial break)
REGGIE/DOCKERS/SMITH FILM/SUPER

London dockers – who've been on strike for nearly five weeks – have voted to go back to work on Monday. They decided to end their dispute – over the manning of container depots – at a mass meeting at the West India Dock.

Afterwards, the Port of London Authority said the stoppage was the most expensive in their history – costing the authority alone more than seven million pounds.

Our industrial correspondent, Giles Smith, reports:

SUPER: GILES
SMITH
REPORTING
An estimated 4,000 of London's 11,000 dockers turned up at the meeting at the West India Docks at 11.00 this morning. After the controversy of previous meetings, and shop stewards' committee had agreed to allow press and television full access to the entire proceedings. From the start it was clear the strike leaders would face strong pressure to end the dispute. Committee chairman Brian Nicholson, and other leaders like Bernie Steer and Vic Turner, both imprisoned during the 1972 national dock strike, were clearly uneasy after the trickle back to work of the past few days. When Mr Nicholson called the vote this time there was no doubt in anyone's mind. (SOF) After the vote, Mr Nicholson refused to comment.

Smith: Are you pleased?

Nicholson: I've got a bad leg...

Smith: The vote, though, was a big setback for the stewards, and

368 / NEWS SCRIPT 14

the bitterness was reflected afterwards.

Smith: ...your reaction to the vote?

Steward: Disgraceful.

Smith: Why?

Steward: Because we've gained exactly nothing, have we? The youngest people...but half of them don't want to fight for it.

Smith: So you think you've gained anything?

Steward: [Of] course they gain. If the workers stick together they have [gained]. This vote was no different to the vote we had last Wednesday, or the previous Monday. It was carried to go back to work, and the reason they didn't go back to work was because they was scared. They was scared of a mob, a little mob.

Smith: At this point both our interviewee and the ITN crew were jostled, as his views on picket breaking were being expressed (SOF) As one docker lunged forward we were prevented from filming, though the interviewee was not hurt. After the bitterness, the big question is: will the blacking of the container depots now cease, and what will be the reaction of the lorry drivers, who've so been so strongly opposed to the dockers? GS, NAT, in the Port of London.

RT: 24″ + 2'41″

(Next item: Railway workshop supervisors' dispute)

42. 10 April 1975 17.50 Item 2A   Maimane
(Previous item: Eric Heffer dismissed for defying P.M. over EEC)
DOCKERS

Mr Wilson has criticised militant dockers who he said had dishonestly gained control of the recent strike at London docks.

He said in the Commons dockers had been naturally anxious about the closure of docks, but it was also true that they'd come under the dishonest and deceptive control of militants who'd given false tallies of the number of dockers voting on the strike.

RT: Approx. 22″

(Next item: Not available)

15: INDUSTRIAL CIVIL SERVANTS' STRIKE

1. 7 March 1975 17.50 Item 14
(Previous item: Ladbroke Group bid for Vernons' Pools)
COMMONS
    The Houses of Parliament and many other Whitehall buildings may
be hit on Monday by an unofficial strike of industrial civil servants.
The men, mainly maintenance and power workers, want an interim
pay settlement.
    The Shadow Chancellor, Sir Geoffrey Howe, told MPs that
entrances to the House of Commons would be picketed and that
other staff had been warned not to cross the lines.
    He asked for assurances that the Commons would be able to
carry on its normal business.
    Mr Neil Carmichael, a junior Minister at the Department of the
Environment, said every endeavour would be made to continue the
business of the House.

RT: 35″

(End of programme)

2. 7 March 1975 22.00 Item 13   Mathias
(Previous item: Bank rate)
REGGIE/COMMONS
    A strike at the House of Commons.
    The Houses of Parliament and many other Whitehall buildings
may be hit on Monday by an unofficial strike of industrial civil
servants. The men, mainly maintenance and power workers, want
an interim pay settlement.
    The Shadow Chancellor, Sir Geoffrey Howe, told MPs that the
water supply, heating, cooking and air conditioning in the
Commons could be affected. Entrances would be picketed and other
staff had been warned not to cross the lines.
    Mr Neil Carmichael, a junior Minister at the Department of the
Environment, said every endeavour would be made to continue the
business of the House.

RT: 35″

(Next item: Gliding)

3. 10 March 1975 17.50 Item 8   O'Connell
(Previous item: Glasgow dustcart drivers' strike)
WHITEHALL STRIKE/SLIDES/FILM ULAY
SLIDE   The Employment Secretary, Mr Foot, has appealed to 400
     Government maintenance workers picketing the Houses of
     Parliament, and other Government buildings, to call off their

	unofficial strike and return to work.
FLUP	The strikers started picketing today in support of a claim for an interim pay award. The main hardship suffered by MP's and peers is a lack of hot meals, but if the strike continues, Parliament will be without heating, hot water or lifts.
RT:	25″

(Next item: Trade figures)

4. 10 March 1975 22.00 Item 13   O'Connell
(Previous item: Glasgow Dustcart Drivers' Strike)
ANDREW/COMMONS DEMO/SLIDES/FILM ULAY

SLIDE (FOOT)	The Employment Secretary, Mr Foot has appealed to 400 Westminster and Whitehall industrial workers to end their unofficial strike and go back to work.
FLUP RT: 19″	The strikers are picketing the Houses of Parliament and other Whitehall buildings in support of a claim for an interim pay award. Mr Foot said he knew their grievances were strongly felt but there had been considerable increases in their pay since their last settlement in July. The main hardship today was the lack of hot meals but the outlook for MP's and peers is chilly – with no heating, hot water, or lifts.
SLIDE	The Liberal Leader, Mr Thorpe, claimed the dispute was getting very near to a 'breach of Parliamentary privilege'. Mr Foot said the pay talks were continuing and that any interim award would be in breach of the social contract.
RT:	1' 07″

(Next item: Charter for Child-Minders)

5. 12 March 1975 22.00 Item 12   Kallenbach
(Previous item: Pierre Trudeau visits Britain)
REGGIE/COMMONS STRIKE/FILM ULAY

| FLUP | Four hundred maintenance men at the House of Commons are to step up their unofficial strike over pay. They say there'll now be a 24-hour picket on the Houses of Parliament and other Whitehall buildings.
The strike's been on for 3 days. MPs have had to go without hot meals and heating...and they can't use the lifts.
The Speaker of the House, Mr Selwyn Lloyd, has rejected a Conservative MP's claim that it is a breach of parliamentary privilege.
In the House, MP's had some complaints about their own pay |

and conditions. A Labour MP complained that the Commons is the only place in Britain operating a wage freeze.

SLIDE   Mr Joe Ashton, MP for Bassetlaw, told a private meeting of the Parliamentary Labour Party that MPs existed 'on lousy money and long, rotten hours'.

And many of the MPs at the meeting complained they'd had no increase in salary for over three years.

RT: 51″

(Next item: Publication of Sex Discrimination Bill)

6. 21 March 1975 22.00 Item 9   Hutchence
(Previous item: Government proposals to end London containerisation strike)
ANDREW/COMMONS STRIKE

The strike by industrial civil servants which hit the Houses of Parliament and Whitehall offices over the past two weeks, has ended.

The 500 strikers wanted an interim pay award but the Government said it would be outside the social contract, and they won't be getting it.

RT: 16″

(Next item: Retail Prices)

16: THE WESTMINSTER HOSPITAL DISPUTE

1. 16 March 1975 18.07 Item 9
(Previous item: Jackie Onassis views husband's body)
HOSPITALS/SLIDE

Talks between the National Union of Public Employees and the management of Westminster Hospital have broken down and the union are to cut off all non-medical services to 42 private patients in the hospital from midnight. The patients, who pay around £20 a day, will have no cleaning, meals or portering services.

RT: 18″

(Next item: Ferry)

2. 16 March 1975 22.00 Item 2   Jamieson
(Previous item: Egypt's response to Kissinger proposals)
HOSPITALS/DOYLE FILM/SUPERS

From midnight tonight the 42 private patients at the Westminster Hospital in London will be without all non-medical services.

Meals, cleaning and portering services are being withdrawn following a breakdown in talks between the hospital management and the National Union of Public Employees.

John Doyle reports:

SUPER: The hospital want to close 38 National Health Service beds, to
JOHN DOYLE   decorate wards and give nurses extra holidays. NUPE said the
REPORTING   closures should include private beds, and when the management refused, they announced their sanctions against private patients. What will happen to these patients who pay £20 a day?

SUPER: **Morris:** Well, if you come back at midnight and ask me the same
JAMIE   questions, I'll answer you, 'What private patients?', because as far as
MORRIS   we're concerned, there will be no private patients after midnight. We
CHMN   just will not recognise that they're there.
LOCAL NUPE
BRANCH   **Doyle:** But in fact they are going to be here in reality, so what's going to happen to them?

Morris: They'll probably be asleep in the night, and when they wake up in the morning they'll find that the ancillary staff will not give them what they expect that they would. That means breakfast, cleansing, portering services, etc.

Doyle: What will you do if the hospital say they'll provide alternative arrangements to supply these services that you're not going to supply from midnight?

Morris: It depends what the alternative arrangements are. If it means using other people to do our jobs, then we will black them. We will consider putting up picket lines. We will not cooperate with them. If we find that voluntary workers are being used on the wards, we will then cease to cooperate with voluntary workers anywhere in the hospital.

Doyle: Could you perhaps go on strike?

Morris: No, never. No National Health Service patient will suffer because of what we're doing. That I can promise you.

Doyle: The hospital say they have contingency plans for looking after private patients after midnight, but they're keeping the details a closely guarded secret.

SUPER:
VICTOR   **Ripley:** I think it would be unwise at this stage to try to spell it out.

RIPLEY
REGIONAL
HOSPITALS
PRESS OFFICER

All I can say is that we will attempt to do it from within the resources we already have, within the hospital.

RT:

17″ + 1′54″

(Next item: Portuguese political situation)

3. 17 March 1975 13.00 Lead item
WESTMINSTER HOSPITAL/HOBBS FILM/SUPERS

First the situation at the Westminster Hospital in London, where members of the National Union of Public Employees are having a meeting about now and could well decide on a complete walkout. Since midnight they've banned all non-medical services to private patients because of a dispute with the Hospital management about its use of private beds. However, they're annoyed that volunteers from other departments have been doing their work — getting the private patients their breakfast, for instance.

Here's a report now from Lyndall Hobbs.

So far, the action by NUPE members has had little effect on Westminster's 32 private patients, but the action of volunteers is bound to step up the NUPE ban. Most of the kitchen staff are NUPE members, and this morning a chef that belonged to no union went ahead and cooked breakfast for the 23 private patients in the main building. NUPE was not amused. The other nine private patients in a wing across the road had to make do with a simple continental breakfast of tea and toast. And the porters' refusal to actually take patients their meals was also thwarted by a rush of volunteers from other departments in the hospital, including nurses, secretaries and clerks. After breakfast the same volunteers washed up and made beds with fresh linen, which is always brought in by private contract. Generally, as the hospital put it, there was business as usual, with patients being moved around for X-rays, operations, or treatment as required. This morning's only real victims of NUPE's actions were flowers for private patients left wilting in reception. But bowls of flowers for the National Health wards were delivered as usual. The whole affair was prompted by the hospital's decision to close 38 National Health beds for three weeks over Easter, because of staff holidays and because of building work in some wards. The union has demanded that 10 of the hospital's 52 private beds should be handed over to the National Health Service during that time. Now they threaten a complete walkout. I asked Jamie Morris what the reaction of NUPE members was to volunteers doing their work.

Morris: Well, the movement on the shop floor is to pull out altogether. The branch officers are going to fight against this; I in particular will argue the point very strongly that we should not pull out of the NHS wards. We are here to serve NHS patients, and I will ensure that my members do service them. I only suggest to the hospital, for God's sake get the volunteers off the wards and give us the ten beds because neither we nor the hospital want this to go on as long as it could go.

Hobbs: Meanwhile, as the meeting continues, private patients are not going hungry. Volunteers were standing by to prepare food, possibly not cooked, for lunch.

RT: 26″ + 2′13″

[Programme continues]
CONSULTANTS REACTION/STUDIO INTVW

Meanwhile, there's little sign of that Consultants' work to contract dispute being solved.

With me in the studio is a consultant surgeon, Mr. Keith Able, an executive member, in fact, of the Hospital Consultants & Specialists Association.

STUDIO **Kee:** Mr. Able, between the militancy of the unions, we've just seen
INTVW UP at work in the Westminster Hospital, and your militancy, what's to become of the poor patients in the National Health Service?

Able: Well, I rather agree that they're the people who are most likely to suffer. Although there are two different forms of discontent emerging in the health service, I think they're very different in principle. The action by the NUPE members at the Westminster Hospital is in our opinion the application of industrial action for the furtherance of political ends.

Kee: Isn't that exactly what you're doing to your ends as consultants?

Able: No, I don't think our ends are political at all. Our argument with the Government is over our contracts. It is not over the application of a political principle that private patients should or should not be allowed to be treated in any particular kind of hospital...

4. 17 March 1975 17.50 Item 4   Martin
(Previous item: Shelepin to visit Britain)
HOSPITALS/TAYLOR FILM/SUPERS

Ancillary workers at the Westminster Hospital in London have voted to start a work-to-rule from tomorrow in their dispute over services for private patients.

Members of the National Union of Public Employees banned services to the hospital's private patients after hearing of management plans to close 38 National Health beds for three weeks over Easter. They want ten private beds to be made available to National Health patients. This morning the management used non-union workers to serve private patients.

TAKE
TAYLOR
FILM DEREK
TAYLOR
REPORTING

So far the effect of the NUPE action has hardly been felt by the 32 private patients at Westminster. Some of them had to put up with a continental breakfast, rather than bacon and eggs this morning, but that's been about all. Nurses, secretaries, and even consultants have been carrying meals, flowers and newspapers and the like into the wards. And it's non-union labour which has annoyed NUPE today. On the face of it, this dispute is merely about making 10 private beds unavailable for three weeks, and since 20 private beds are unoccupied anyway at present, it looks as if the real issue is one of principle. The union's proposed work to rule is now likely to have some effect on Health Service patients.

SUPER:
JAMIE
MORRIS

Morris: They'll probably be affected very slightly, whereby it will make the transportation of patients to clinics from wards, and from clinics to wards, a lot slower.

Taylor: But isn't this a nonsense? This is a dispute about private beds, and yet here you are in fact affecting National Health Service patients?

Morris: It could also be argued that management affected National Health patients the minute they decided to take the steps they did take. We are very sorry about the action that we've been forced into taking. I personally recommended against it. I do not like to see National Health patients affected in any way, but obviously I have to go along with the branch's feelings.

SUPER:
DAVID
EVANS

Evans: Well, I think that NUPE have made it quite clear that this dispute is purely to exert pressure on Mrs. Castle and the Department to phase out or abolish the private beds in National Health Service hospitals.

Taylor: It would surely be very simple just to designate 10 private patient beds for National Health Service use over the next few weeks. Why don't you do that?

Evans: Well, I think if the situation was such that we couldn't meet the demand for NHS beds, then we have made it abundantly clear that if this was the situation we would use the private beds to help out the NHS beds. This is not new — we have always done this. No patient has ever been refused admission as an NHS patient if there was a private bed which they could be put into.

RT: 22″ + 2'20″

(Next item: London dock strike)

5. 17 March 1975 22.00 Item 4   Platt
(Previous item: Parliamentary Labour Party row)
REGGIE/HOSPITALS/TAYLOR FILM/SUPERS

Ancillary workers at the Westminster Hospital in London have voted to work to rule from tomorrow in their dispute over private patients. Their action will affect National Health patients, who may not get extras like tea and newspapers.

The workers — who are members of the National Union of Public Employees — have banned services to the hospital's private patients because the management plan to close 38 National Health beds for three weeks over Easter. They want ten private beds to be made available to National Health patients.

Their decision to work to rule came after the management used non-union workers to give the private patients their breakfast.

Derek Taylor reports:

TAKE FILM
SUPER:
DEREK
TAYLOR
REPORTING

On the face of it the dispute at the Westminster Hospital is about 10 beds; empty ones at that. So far the effect of the union's action has hardly been noticed by the private patients; some of them had to put up with a continental breakfast rather than bacon and eggs this morning, but that's about all. Nurses and other volunteers have done the carrying jobs and it's that that's made NUPE decide to work to rule. The row started over this ward; it's closed for the bathrooms to be improved. Because of this, and the fact that a number of nurses are on holiday, 38 National Health Service beds aren't being used for the the time being. The union want 10 of the 38 to be dropped from the list of private beds available. Now that wouldn't seem to be a problem since there are 20 private beds unoccupied anyway, and add to this that over 100 health service beds are also empty and the argument seems academic. I asked the union's leader if the action was really an attempt to pressure the Government on the issue of pay beds in the health service.

Morris: Obviously we hope it would help, but that is not what the dispute is about; the dispute is simply because the hospital management refuses to close private beds while they're closing NHS beds. We also asked them to transfer the private beds or at least some to the NHS. They point blankly refused. In our view they put people's bank balances before their health.

Taylor: So the action that you're taking is going to make the lives of National Health patients less palatable in order to bring them gains later. It's all a bit pointless, isn't it?

Morris: No, it's not a pointless dispute. The dispute is also about an issue that my members feel very strongly about. But we are not paid skivvies, we are National Health Service workers; we work for the National Health Service and we are fed up of being insulted, pushed around and dictated to by a few people who've got money.

SUPER:
DAVID
EVANS

Evans: Well I think that NUPE have made it quite clear that this dispute is purely to exert pressure on Mrs. Castle and the Department to phase out or abolish private beds in National Health Service hospitals.

Taylor: It would surely be very simple just to designate 10 private patient beds for National Health Service use over the next three weeks; why don't you do that?

Evans: Well I think if the situation was such that we couldn't meet the demands of the NHS beds, then we have made it abundantly clear that if this was the situation we would move the private beds to help out the NHS beds. This is nothing new, really, we've always done this. No patient's ever been refused admission as an NHS patient if there's a private bed which they can be put into.

RT: 37″ + 2′50″

(Next item: Glasgow dustcart drivers' strike)

6. 18 March 1975 13.00 Item 2B
(Previous item: Glasgow dustcart drivers' strike)
WESTMINSTER HOSPITAL/ULAY

At Westminster Hospital, union leaders have decided to call a full-scale work-to-rule in the row over private beds and they say this could shortly be followed up with a series of lightning strikes lasting one or two hours at a time.

ULAY UP   Up till now, the action taken by the 400 ancillary workers at the hospital has affected only private patients. This new action will affect National Health patients too; there are more than 500 of them at the hospital. The union say it won't affect the medical side, but it will make life in the hospital much slower. The strikes, however, they concede, if they happened would bring the hospital to a standstill.

The eight-man action committee which decided on the action say it's in protest against volunteers continuing to serve private patients at the hospital. The committee has sent a letter to the Social Services Secretary, Mrs. Castle, asking her to intervene.

RT: 1'13"

(Next item: IRA escape)

7. 18 March 1975 17.50 Item 6   O'Connell
(Previous item: IRA bombers transferred to Armagh gaol)
HOSPITALS/FILM ULAY/REWRITE
Non-medical staff involved in the dispute over beds for private patients at the Westminster Hospital have now started a work-to-

FLUP   rule. They are threatening to bring the hospital to a standstill by one or two hour strikes unless some agreement is reached. The workers — who include porters, cleaners and kitchen staff — say they are angry at the way the hospital management have brought in volunteers to carry out their work in the private wards.

RT: 26"

(Next item: Glasgow dustcart drivers' strike)

8. 19 March 1975 13.00 Item 6   Morrison
(Previous item: Glasgow dustcart drivers' strike)
HOSPITAL
At Westminster Hospital in London the first lightning one-hour strike of ancillary workers started at eleven o'clock this morning and it meant no cleaning or portering services.

The leader of the union action committee which ordered the strike said there will be more stoppages until, as he put it, 'we bring the management to their senses'. This is in their campaign to get the management to close private patients beds equally with National Health patients beds — as the latter being necessary according to the management owing to staff shortage.

RT: 30"

(Next item: Closing headlines)

9. 19 March 1975 17.50 Item 12   Jill
(Previous item: Fall of Hue imminent)
HOSPITALS/S/F
Ancillary workers at London's Westminster Hospital are ready to 'starve out' the private patients, according to their union spokesman, Jamie Morris.

The workers — who are in dispute with the management over plans to prevent the use of 38 National Health beds for three weeks — have been refusing services to all private patients.

Mr. Morris says there are now only two people left in the hospital's kitchens who are prepared to provide meals for private patients — and that it will be impossible for them to cope. If relatives try to bring in meals, union members will set up picket lines.

They've already stepped up their campaign by starting 'lightning' strikes.

RT: 37"

(Next item: Moorgate tube disaster)

10. 21 March 1975 17.50 Item 5A   Taylor
(Previous item: BR ferry strike threat)
HOSPITALS

The pay beds dispute at Westminster Hospital is over.

The union involved — NUPE — have agreed to go back to normal working in return for a promise by the Area Health Authority that private beds will be made available to Health Service patients in an emergency.

RT: 33"

(Next item: Glasgow dustcart drivers' strike)

11. 21 March 1975 22.00 Item 7   O'Connell
(Previous item: BR ferry strike threat)
REGGIE/PAY BEDS/CHROMOKEY

GK   At the Westminster Hospital in London non-medical staff have called off their work-to-rule in the dispute over private patients. 400 staff — including porters, kitchen staff and ward orderlies — have been refusing to work on private wards since the hospital said that 39 Health Service beds were being closed over Easter.

The National Union of Public Employees have advised a return to normal working, and been given a promise that private beds will be made available to Health Service patients in an emergency.

RT: 27"

(Next item: London dock strike)

17: LIVERPOOL DUSTCART DRIVERS' STRIKE

1. 21 March 1975 13.00 Item 5
(Previous item: Interview on Vietnam with Air Vice Marshal Menaul)
LIVERPOOL RUBBISH VTR ULAY/REWRITE

In Liverpool, where dustcart drivers have been on unofficial strike for nearly eight weeks, the medical officer of health says there's a danger of an epidemic of diseases like dysentery and jaundice.

Liverpool City Council Environment Committee met this morning to review the situation. Some councillors have already called for troops to be brought in as they have in Glasgow.

VTR   Last night barricades of rubbish were built across some roads in Liverpool by residents who resent having accumulated rubbish stored at dumps near their homes. Their protest has now been reinforced by the medical officer of health who says children are particularly at risk because of contaminated refuse in the plastic bags.

Councillors and dustcart drivers are meeting this afternoon to see if they can find a settlement.

RT: 44″

(Next item: Glasgow dustcart drivers' strike)

2. 21 March 1975 17.50 Item 9   Jamieson
(Previous item: Continues from Glasgow dustcart drivers' strike)
RUBBISH ULAY/SUPER: LIVERPOOL (TO FOLLOW GLASGOW VTR)

VTR UP   In Liverpool, where dustcart drivers have been on strike for 8 weeks, rubbish was dumped in the streets by local residents as a protest against the conditions near the Wellington Road tip — one of the worst temporary dumps in the city.

Liverpool's medical officer of health has warned that there's the danger of an epidemic if the rubbish isn't cleared.

RT: Approx. 20″

(Next item: Retail prices)

3. 21 March 1975 22.00 Item 11   Sara
(Previous item: Commercial break)

In Liverpool, union leaders are to recommend a return to work by about 300 dustcart drivers — who've been on strike for eight weeks — at a mass meeting tomorrow. The move follows a new interim pay offer by Liverpool corporation.

UP VTR   Residents dragged bags of rubbish off one of the worst temporary
ULAY 32″   tips, in Wellington Road, and scattered them across the streets — and they say they'll do the same every evening until the tip is moved.

Liverpool's medical officer of health has warned that if the rubbish ISN'T cleared, there could be an epidemic...[item continues with Glasgow dustcart strike]

RT: Approx 31″

(Next item: Continuation with Glasgow dustcart drivers' strike)

4. 22 March 1975 13.10 Item 3   Jill
(Previous item: Cambodia)
DUSTMEN/VTR ULAY

ULAY UP   Liverpool's 200 dustcart drivers have voted to go back to work —
           and they'll begin today to clear the temporary tips built up during
RT 15″   their 9-week strike.
AVAIL   The drivers have agreed to accept an interim pay offer made by
           the Liverpool Corporation — and they say they were influenced by
           the health-hazard warning given yesterday by the city's medical
           officer of health.

RT: Approx. 21″

(Next item: Glasgow dustcart drivers' strike)

5. 22 March 1975 17.50 Item 5   Jill
(Previous item: Cambodia)
DUSTMEN/VTR ULAY

ULAY UP   Liverpool's dustcart drivers have called off their strike and have
           already begun clearing the temporary tips built up during the 9-week
           stoppage.
               The drivers voted overwhelmingly to accept an interim pay offer
           which will give them another £2.63. Union leaders have suggested
           that the Glasgow Corporation should make a similar award to the
           dustcart drivers on strike there.

RT: 22″

(Next item: Trawlermen blockade ports)

6. 22 March 1975 22.30 Item 4   Jill
(Previous item: Kurds)
DUSTMEN/FILM ULAY

ULAY UP   Liverpool's dustcart drivers are back at work and have begun
           clearing the temporary tips built up during their 9-week strike. This
           morning they agreed to accept an interim pay award that will give
           them another £2.63.

RT: Approx 12″

(Next item: Trawlermen blockade ports)

7. 27 March 1975 17.50 Item 7   Platt

(Previous item: British Rail ferry strike)

Liverpool's 900 dustmen are back at work after unexpectedly accepting an interim pay offer — which they rejected on Tuesday.

Together with a special bonus to clear the 35,000 tons of rubbish that have accumulated during the nine-week strike, they'll have the chance of earning up to £73 for a 40-hour week...[continues with Glasgow dustcart drivers' strike]

RT: Approx. 17"

(Next item: Continuation with Glasgow dustcart drivers' strike)

8. 27 March 1975 Item 10 Platt
(Previous item: Home Secretary on Northern Ireland detainees)
LEONARD/DUSTMEN/VTR ULAY

900 Liverpool dustmen have gone back to work after unexpectedly ACCEPTING an interim pay offer which they rejected on Tuesday.

With bonuses they'll have the chance to earn up to £73 for a 40-hour week to clear away the 35,000 tons of rubbish which piled up during the nine-week strike...[item continues with Glasgow dustcart drivers' strike.]

RT: Approx. 18"

(Next item: Continuation with Glasgow dustcart drivers' strike)

18: SEALINK FERRY STRIKE

1. 21 March 1975 17.50 Item 6   O'Connell
(Previous item: Rail pay talks)
SEAMEN/MAP

MAP   A threat to Easter holidaymakers. British Rail ferry services from eight ports may not be running over Easter if members of the National Union of Seamen go on strike.

The union have called for a 48-hour stoppage — from noon next Thursday — is a protest at plans to shut down the car ferry service between Heysham and Belfast.

British Rail hovercraft services would not be affected.

RT: 23″

(Next item: London dock strike)

2. 21 March 1975 22.00 Item 6   O'Connell
(Previous item: Rail unions say pay offer is insufficient)
ANDREW/SEAMEN/MAP

British Rail ferry services to Ireland and the Continent over Easter are being threatened by a possible strike by members of the Seamen's Union.

ANIMATE   9 ports could be affected by a 48-hour stoppage from noon next Thursday — as a protest at plans to shut-down the ferry service between Heysham and Belfast. British Rail hovercraft services will not be affected.

RT: 22″

(Next item: Hospital pay beds controversy)

3. 27 March 1975 17.50 Item 6   Henderson
(Previous item: Trawlermen blockade ports)
FERRY STRIKE/MAP/FILM ULAY

MAP   Seamen on British Rail Sealink ferries have begun a 48-hour strike. All Sealink services to the Continent, the Channel Islands and Ireland have been cancelled until midday on Saturday as a protest against the withdrawal of the Heysham Belfast ferry service next month.

FLUP   But at Dover as elsewhere, Dutch, Belgian and French ferries hovercraft have been running their usual services.

ULAY R/T   Passengers have been warned not to turn up unless they have firm bookings, as all the services over the weekend are already fully booked.
20″

RT: 35″

(Next item: Glasgow dustcart drivers' strike)

19: DAILY MIRROR — SOGAT DISPUTE

1. 25 March 1975 17.50 Item 8   Sam
(Previous item: Farmers demonstrate against egg imports)
MIRROR
> The Mirror group of newspapers have dismissed all 1,750 London-based members of the print union, SOGAT — the Society of Graphic and Allied Trades.
> The dismissals came after the union said they'd continue their unofficial action which last night lost the company one-and-a-half million copies of the Daily Mirror.
> Unless the union change their minds, the group say tomorrow's London edition of the Daily Mirror won't be printed. Neither will the 'Sporting Life'.
> The Sunday Mirror and the Sunday People will also be hit and the company say the dispute — which is over pay, could be the final straw for Reveille.

RT: 36″

(Next item: Textile workers demonstrate over industry's plight)

2. 25 March 1975 22.00 Item 8   Sam
(Previous item: Cost of NHS hospital pay beds increased)
REGGIE/MIRROR/SLIDE
SLIDE/CK   The Mirror group of newspapers have sacked all 1,750 London-based members of the print union SOGAT... the Society of Graphic and Allied Trades.
> They did it after the union confirmed that they would continue their unofficial action, which last night lost the company one-and-a-half million copies of the Daily Mirror. The group say that unless the union change their minds, tomorrow's Daily Mirror won't be printed London. Neither will the Sporting Life.
> The company say the pay dispute could also mean closure for the periodical Reveille. The Sunday Mirror and the Sunday People will also be affected.

RT: 36″

(Next item: Pre-commercial trailers)

3. 26 March 22.00 Item 7   Kallenbach
(Previous item: Post Office)
REGGIE/DAILY MIRROR
> The Mirror group of newspapers have started giving notice to more than seven thousand of their nine thousand London employees in expectation of a shutdown which could last for several weeks.
> This is the result of the three day old pay dispute between the

management and the print union, SOGAT – the Society of Graphical and Allied Trades.

Tomorrow's London edition of the 'Daily Mirror' won't be printed but the Manchester edition should appear. There will be a 'Sporting Life' tomorrow.

RT: 25"

(Next item: Pre-commercial trailers)

4. 28 March 1975 22.00 Item 5   O'Connell
(Previous item: Scottish Daily News launch agreed)
ANDREW/MIRROR/GREEN FILM/SUPER

In London, new talks are to be held next Tuesday to solve the dispute that has stopped publication of Fleet Street editions of the Daily Mirror and of the Sporting Life.

The Mirror group have lost more than six million copies in the last two days after sacking 1,750 warehouse workers for taking unofficial action.

Here's our industrial correspondent, Michael Green:

GREEN FILM: No Daily Mirrors have been printed in London since Monday
SUPER: and – barring the unexpected – it's unlikely that printing will
MICHAEL   resume until at least the middle of next week. The paper is still being
GREEN   printed in Manchester, where the normal run is 1.1 million copies.
REPORTING   The dispute is over the Mirror Group's insistence that, as part of a
new pay deal for members of SOGAT, the Society of Graphical and Allied Trades, the long standing practice that any worker who leaves is automatically replaced should be abolished.

Sogat members began a campaign of unofficial industrial action which reached a climax on Monday when half the newspaper's London print run was lost. Next day 1,750 Sogat warehouse staff were sacked and production in London stopped. Employees have been warned that the company is prepared if necessary for a prolonged shut downin order to overcome what they maintain is a massive overmanning problem.

But there's much more to the present Mirror shutdown than a simple manning dispute. It's a reflection of the crisis which faces Fleet Street as a whole. National newspaper finances have been shaky for years, but never so much as they are today. For example, Times Newspapers has warned printing unions that drastic action must be taken to counter losses of more than £100,000 a week. The Guardian is to slim down on both printing and journalistic staff in the face of a £1 million loss this year. Beaverbrook, which publishes the Express and London Evening Standard, lost more than £650,000 in the last six months of last year. And the Mirror Group looks like losing well over £1 million in the current financial year. It's a crisis compounded by the soaring price of newsprint and falling advertising revenue, and with the total sales of newspapers now falling, what was once a circulation war is now a battle for the survival of the fittest. MG, NAT, Holborn Circus.

RT: 22″ + 1′52″

(Next item: London docks containerisation dispute)

5. 1 April 1975 17.50 Item 8A
(Previous item: Exorcism)
mirror 1

Peace talks aimed at ending the Daily Mirror shutdown ended in deadlock less than an hour ago. No copies of the newspaper have been published in London since Monday last week when 1,750 warehouse staff were dismissed over a manning dispute.

RT: Approx. 14″

(Next item: Soccer)

6. 1 April 1975 22.00 Item 10   Tristram
(Previous item: Glasgow dustcart drivers' strike)
LEONARD/MIRROR

Talks to settle the week-old Daily Mirror dispute in London broke down tonight and there'll be NO London editions of the Mirror or Sporting Life again tomorrow.

The stoppages have been caused by the printing union SOGAT — which is opposing management plans on manning and pay.

RT: 16″

(Next item: Ulster)

7. 2 April 1975 22.00 Item 5
(Previous item: Commercial break)
mirror 1

The news that the Sunday People and the Reveille may close is the gravest threat so far from the Mirror Group in its determined campaign to reduce manning levels.

All 9,000 employees — right up to directors — are already under notice to quit. And these notices are due to take effect next week.

The Daily Mirror hasn't been published in London since Tuesday last week. But still the staff go through the motions of producing a paper that will never go on sale.

The 300 or so copies that have been produced each night are said to cost an astronomical £400 each. The dispute came to a head when 1,750 warehouse staff were sacked just over a week ago after taking industrial action against the manning reduction plans.

The warning the management sent out to leaders of other printing unions tonight is clearly aimed at putting maximum pressure on the SOGAT leaders to come to terms.

The dispute has cost the Mirror group well over £1 million in revenue and I asked the Daily Mirror group chairman, Mr Christiansen, if it was worthwhile sustaining such losses:

Christiansen: Oh, very much so. I think the whole progress of Fleet Street is tied up in this dispute. We've got to modernise, I think we've got to cut staffs as time goes by in order to remain economically afloat. Individually, and certainly collectively, we don't know of anybody who's making a profit in the situation at the moment. There are ways and means by which publishing can become a very prosperous and exciting industry again, but it can't be done while we've got this fearful problem of overmanning. We're not trying to throw people on the streets — we've said that all along. Nor do we want to make people redundant. The idea is, what non-automatic replacement means is that as people die or retire, they will not be replaced, and we would expect that in the SOGAT area it would take seven years of people leaving for one reason or another to get down to an acceptable level of argument, level of manning.

Green: One of the Mirror Group executives has said that you might have to be prepared for a very long shutdown. Can you see any chance of a quick solution?

Christiansen: Journalists are always optimists.

RT: 26″ + 2′38″

(Next item: Trawlermen blockade ports)

8. 3 April 1975 13.00 Item 6
(Previous item: BR workshop supervisors' strike)
DAILY MIRROR/BLACK INTVW VTR

Leaders of SOGAT — the Society of Graphic and Allied Trades — are meeting in London this morning to discuss their industrial action which has stopped publication of the Daily Mirror for nine days now.

Yesterday, the management of the Mirror Group of Newspapers threatened to close down the Sunday People and the magazine, Reveille, making 22 per cent of the Group's staff redundant, if agreement isn't reached with SOGAT by next Wednesday.

The dispute is over attempts by the company to abolish the

traditional practice of automatically replacing all workers who leave or retire. The Mirror group's chairman, Mr Percy Roberts, has said there is vast overmanning.

Earlier this morning, I spoke to Sheila Black who's studied the problems facing the whole of Fleet Street.

Parkin: Miss Black, how serious is this threat to Reveille and The People? Is it a real threat, or is it just bluff by the management?

Black: No, it's a real threat — there's no bluff. I think the Mirror Group newspapers proved they'd had enough when they came out of the NPA, which was the Newspaper Publishers' Association.

Parkin: What's the whisper from Fleet Street this morning, then, about the latest talks going on?

Black: Well, I spoke to somebody at the Mirror Group — he was hopeful, he said of course things change from hour to hour, but he said 'I think they realise that we mean business. It's in their hands, the union's hands'.

Parkin: To accept what the management want or...?

Black: Or those newspapers go, and it won't stop at two. It won't stop at two. The public, if they see two newspapers die, are going to start mistrusting all Fleet Street. As it is, they're fed up with seeing newspapers not appear, or not appear in their area. And once anyone cancels a newspaper, or fails to get a newspaper, they won't take it back again. The Mirror last year, when they had trouble in Manchester, lost 7% of their sales. With a tremendous amount of expenditure on promotion, a tremendous amount of effort, they've managed just about to creep back and get that 7% back in a whole year.

Parkin: Do they expect to get back what they've lost in the past week?

Black: I think it's totally impossible. It'll take them years.

Parkin: What's the real root problem? Is it overmanning simply, or is it bad management?

Black: It's bad management in the past. Management of newspapers have really only just begun to think about the problems, and let me say here and now that as far as management goes I think the Mirror Group and The Times stand out as being the real hawks of the business — the people who want to get it right, who want to make newspapers viable. The others are in varying degrees of dovery, but not really approaching hawkery.

Parkin: What are you suggesting? That The Times and the Mirror

Group are prepared to be firm with the unions, but the others are backhanding under the table?

Black: Backhanding under the table is right, and I'm afraid some of them are backhanding all sorts of increases, bonuses, concessions, which they're not reporting to the Newspaper Publishers' Association as they should be.

Parkin: Now there is this overmanning problem, and problems of late retirement in the printing business — what can we do about them?

Black: Well, the only way, and it's a very kind way because it's going to take years to achieve the right degree of manning this way — the only way is the way the Mirror Group, The Times, and a few others occasionally suggest, which is automatic non-replacement. In other words, every job has got to be evaluated, and if a man's needed for it, or a woman, a man or a woman will be hired, but at the moment, anyone who goes, old or young, even if they're in a job watching string tiers, not tying string, they're replaced.

Parkin: I heard of one man who's 82 still going in to Fleet Street yesterday — is that sort of thing true?

Black: That sort of thing is true, and it's been another trouble because the basic wage of all the production unions, of all the printers, was terribly low — there was overtime and bonuses and all sorts of other things that made their take-home pay while they were working terribly high, and then suddenly, zoom, they dropped onto a terrible pension. So they went on working, and that meant a lot of them were working terribly over age.

Parkin: Can you say very briefly what you think the long-term answer is?

Black: The long-term answer frankly is for the unions to get together and have one press union so that they are strong as management, and make management strong thereby.

Parkin: Miss Black, thank you.

RT: 4'33"

(Next item: Stonehouse remanded in Melbourne)

9. 3 April 1975 22.00 Item 11
(Previous item: Electricity workers' pay)
ANDREW/MIRROR

Hopes are high tonight that the dispute which has stopped production of the Daily Mirror in London for the past eight days may be settled in the next 24 hours.

After talks between the Mirror group and the print union, SOGAT, the management expressed 'cautious optimism' that the Daily Mirror and Sporting Life would resume publication tomorrow evening, following more talks tomorrow morning.

The Mirror Group had threatened to close both the Sunday People and Reveille — as well as dismissing 22 per cent of their staff, if the dispute continued for another week.

Meanwhile, plans to start a 24-hour newspaper in Glasgow on May the 6th have run into trouble with the National Graphical Association.

RT: 45"

(Next item: Trawlerman's blockade)

20: ELECTRICIANS' STRIKES

1. 28 March 1975 17.50 Item 4A
(Previous item: Trawlermen blockade ports)
AIRPORT

But Glasgow Airport — closed by an electricians' strike — is likely to re-open next Thursday.

The electricians have agreed to return to work when the airport passes from Glasgow Corporation's control to the British Airports Authority next week.

RT: 14"

(Next item: Money raised to launch Scottish Daily News)

2. 11 April 1975 22.00 Item 9   Tristram
(Previous item: Glasgow dustcart drivers' strike)
GORDON/HIGH FLATS/LAMBERT FILM/SUPERS

A strike by electricians working for local authorities is spreading to Manchester and Swansea.

In seven other cities electricians are already on strike over pay demands.

The strike is having serious effects on people in high rise flats —

especially in Glasgow — because without electricians to do maintenance work, most of their lifts are out of order.

Angela Lambert reports from Glasgow:

VTR UP:
SUPER:
LAMBERT
REPORTING

These high rise blocks in the St. George's Cross area of Glasgow are typical of the flats hit by the strike. There are over 100 flats in each building, and not one lift in working order. Old age pensioners, and mothers with very young children are the worst affected. Some can ask older children to shop for them. Others, who can't cope with these stairs, have been completely marooned for the last three weeks. I asked Mrs Oliver how long it took her to come down the stairs:

SUPER:
OLIVER

Oliver: Well, I've just got to take my time coming down.

Lambert: How long does it take you?

Oliver: Oh, it takes me a while. But I would say about 20 minutes from the top down.

Lambert: And how long to walk back up?

Oliver: And it takes me longer — I've never timed myself really. The first night, as I said, it took me an hour, and I was very tired. I wasn't very well.

Lambert: How do you manage the stairs?

Oliver: Well, as I say, I come down on the one leg and I hold onto the bannister down, and it's the same going back up. There's no other way — I canna fly. I've just got to do what I can.

Lambert: How do you feel about the electricians whose fault it is?

Oliver: Oh, my, but I would rather go now after all this time, on my hands and knees, rather than give them that extra money. Before, if they'd put on the lifts, I'd have been saying, well, they should get their money, but now, no, I'm disgusted, I'm really disgusted. I've got a cold too, and that's not helped me any.

Lambert: Then I asked the leader of the strike committee why the electricians were imposing this hardship.

SUPER:
KELLY

Kelly: Well, right away, I say we regret any hardship that's caused to anybody that's living in tower blocks. I think that the blame has to be put fairly and squarely with the Councils themselves. The authorities have consistently refused to honour an agreement. We have, although we're under tremendous pressure after 12 weeks, instituted an emergency service. We have made them as streamlined as we possibly can to alleviate any hardship — we have turned up for almost any call that has been made on us, but we feel this is a legitimate arm of a strike, and we are using that particular strength that we have.

Lambert: In the Gorbals, local schoolchildren have been running errands and fetching shopping for many old people. The electricians say they will get the lifts going in an emergency, but if you're old and your chest is bad, and you live on one of the top floors, these children are your lifeline to the outside world. AL, NAT, in Glasgow.

RT: 18″ + 2'37″

(Next item: Aston Martin)

4. 26 April 1975 22.30 Item 15   Black
(Previous item: National Front March)
IVOR/INDUSTRY

The 14-week strike by local authority electricians in Scotland is over – they've voted to go back to work on Monday after the employers agreed to the men's demands in full.

The settlement will cost Scottish local councils an extra half-million pounds a year in wages.

RT: Approx. 15″

(Next item: Sir Ian Gilmour deplores rise of left-wing extremism)

21: BRITISH RAIL WORKSHOP SUPERVISORS' WORK TO RULE

1. 30 March 1975 18.07 Item 8   Hutchence
(Previous item: Young Liberals criticise Thorpe)
BRITISH RAIL

Holidaymakers face train cancellations on British Rail tomorrow because of a pay dispute which is delaying repairs in British Rail workshops.

The services worst affected will be those between London, the Midlands and the North West; and London, Bristol and South Wales.

RT: 14″

(Next item: Wade)

2. 30 March 1975 22.35 Item 8   Hutchence
(Previous item: Trawlermen blockade ports)
BRITISH RAIL

> Holidaymakers on their way home tomorrow face train cancellations because of a pay dispute involving British Rail maintenance men.
>
> The services worst affected will be those between London, the Midlands and the North-West; and London, Bristol and South Wales.

RT: 15″

(Next item: Northern Ireland)

3. 31 March 1973 13.02 Item 3   Jamieson
(Previous item: Sir Edmund Hillary's wife killed in plane crash)
TRAINS/REES FILM/SUPER

> Most excursion services in British Rail's London Midland region have been cancelled as a result of industrial action by maintenance staff. Other regions, so far, aren't affected but the situation could well get worse.
>
> Ken Rees reports.

SUPER: KEN REES REPORTING
> The London Midland region has been badly hit by the dispute. A quarter of today's InterCity services were cancelled, as well as nearly all the region's holiday excursions. Trains between London and the north-west either didn't run or had fewer coaches. A work-to-rule by maintenance supervisors has led to a huge backlog of work. As trains come into the workshops for regular safety and servicing checks they join a long queue. 130 main line locomotives out of service − that's over half the region's fleet, and on the busy Bedford/St. Pancras commuter run, only three rail cars out of 50 are left running. Tomorrow the situation will be even worse, with 50 main-line trains cancelled. Commuters, though, will be hardest hit. Dozens of local services in London, Liverpool and Manchester will be cut, and the prospects for the rest of the week are gloomy unless the dispute is settled soon.

RT: 15″ + 50″

(Next item: Vietnam)

4. 31 March 1975 17.50 Item 3RW   Sue
(Previous item: Sir Edmund Hillary's wife dies in plane crash)
TRAINS/MAP/REES FILM/SUPER

> Many trains in British Rail's London Midlands region were cancelled

today because of industrial action by 5,000 maintenance staff.

And up to a quarter of Western Region's inter city services will be cancelled tomorrow. The dispute — which is over last year's pay restructuring agreement — has stopped essential repairs and safety work.

Ken Rees reports:

FLUP SUPER:
KEN REES
REPORTING

The London Midland region was worst hit today, with a quarter of all InterCity trains cancelled, as well as nearly all holiday excursions. Trains between London and the North West either did not run, or had fewer coaches. A work-to-rule by maintenance supervisors over a pay restructuring claim has led to a huge backlog of work. As trains come in for routine maintenance or safety checks, they join a long queue. 130 main line locomotives are now out of service — over half the region's fleet. On one London commuter route, only three out of 50 diesel rail cars are still in service. As the lines of waiting locomotives grow longer, so does the list of cuts in services. Other regions are starting to run into problems, but it's London Midland commuters who will really face problems tomorrow. 60 InterCity services and dozens of local trains in London, Manchester and Liverpool will not run.

RT: 15" + 50"

(Next item: 14 die in Swedish crash)

5. 1 April 1975 17.50 Item 4   Kallenbach
(Previous item: Trawlermen blockade ports)
RAIL PAGE ONE

The leaders of 3 rail unions tonight agreed to reject British Rail's latest 20% pay offer as 'not good enough'.

The executives of the NUR, ASLEF and TSSA are to meet later this week to decide how to press for an improved pay offer.

Services on two of British Rail's regions, London-Midland, and Western, have again been disrupted because of a pay dispute involving five thousand maintenance workers.

RT: 38"

(Next item: Vietnam)

6. 1 April 1975 22.00 Item 8   Kallenbach
(Previous item: Trawlermen blockade ports)
LEONARD/RAIL/SLIDE

The leaders of the three rail unions have agreed to REJECT British Rail's latest twenty per cent pay offer as 'not good enough'. They'll meet later this week to decide how to go about getting an improved pay offer.

Services on two railway regions, London-Midland, and Western, were disrupted because of a separate pay dispute involving five thousand maintenance workers.

RT: 21″

(Next item: Glasgow dustcart drivers' strike)

7. 3 April 1975 13.00 Item 5
(Previous item: Trawlermen blockade ports)
TRAINS

Rail services have been hit again today by the continuing pay dispute between British Rail and their workshop supervisors.

InterCity services from London to the West Country have been reduced by half and the service between London and the Midlands is also disrupted.

On the Eastern Region — main line trains aren't affected but some suburban services ARE.

And a Southern Region official said they've had no cancellations.

One train that IS cancelled — well in advance — is a Grand National special from the West Country to Liverpool on Saturday. It already had 300 bookings — from racegoers in Weston-super-Mare, Bristol, Gloucester and Cheltenham.

RT: 35″

(Next item: Daily Mirror dispute)

8. 4 April 1975 13.00 Item 8   Mike
(Previous item: Electricity workers' pay)
RAIL

One of the leaders of British Rail's 5,000 workshop supervisors has warned that their overtime ban and work-to-rule, over a pay claim, could soon develop into an all-out strike.

Mr David Mackenzie, the Secretary of the Transport Salaried Staffs Association, which represents nearly half the supervisors, said this morning that his men were 'getting fed up with the time the dispute was taking'. He said he would recommend that they continue their present action at tomorrow's union executive meeting but the final decision was 'out of his hands'.

Meanwhile the dispute has hit train drivers in every area this morning except Southern Region. The worst affected was Western Region, whose services to Bristol and South Wales were cut by half.

RT: 40″

(Next item: Sectarian murders in Northern Ireland)

9. 4 April 1975 17.50 Item 11   Hutchence
(Previous item: Power workers' pay)
RAIL

There has been more disruption on British Rail because of the overtime ban and work-to-rule by the 5000 supervisors in the railway workshops. And British Rail warn the situation will get WORSE over [the] weekend.

InterCity services between London, the Midlands and South Wales will be cut by about half.

RT: Approx. 18″

(Next item: Not available)

10. 4 April 1975 22.00 Item 9   Sam
(Previous item: London containerisation strike)
ANDREW/RAIL/ELECTRICITY

Hopes for a settlement of the railway workshop supervisors' dispute − over pay differentials − rose tonight when British Rail agreed to talks to the unions next Tuesday. Earlier, British Rail said they wanted the dispute to go to arbitration.

Despite agreeing to talks, British Rail have warned that services in some regions will be cut by 40 to 50 per cent over the weekend.

Meanwhile, the Department of Employment have criticised ...(continues with power workers' pay)

RT: Approx. 22″

(Next item: Power workers' pay)

11. 5 April 1975 13.10 Item 3   Maimane
(Previous item: Cambodia)
RAIL

Here at home, some train services have been cut this weekend by the overtime ban and work-to-rule of workshop supervisors who're in dispute with British Rail over pay. One of the worst-hit regions is London Midland, where trains out of Euston will be cut by 40% today and 50% tomorrow.

British Rail have agreed to open talks on Tuesday with the supervisors' unions to settle the dispute.

RT: 24″

(Next item: French criminals seize ten hostages)

12. 5 April 1975 22.30 Item 8   Maimane
(Previous item: French criminals seize ten hostages)
RAIL

Some train services have been cut this weekend because of the overtime ban and work-to-rule of workshop supervisors who're in dispute with British Rail over pay. One of the worst-hit regions is London Midland, where services out of Euston were cut by 40% today, and will be cut by 50% tomorrow.

RT: 18″

(Next item: Glasgow dustcart drivers' strike)

13. 8 April 1975 22.00 Item 13   Keith Thompson
(Previous item: Manchester airport strike)
ANDREW/RAIL

There are hopes tonight that the overtime ban and work-to-rule by five thousand supervisors in railway workshops may be called off tomorrow. It's been in operation for more than a fortnight, disrupting rail services in all parts of Britain.

The supervisors' negotiators have been given an offer from the Railways Board on their claim for improved pay differentials. It will be considered by the executives of the 4 unions involved tomorrow, and one union leader said a settlement now looked 'more optimistic'.

RT: 31″

(Next item: Relations between EEC and the Commonwealth)

14. 9 April 1975 13.00 Item 4A
(Previous item: Glasgow dustcart drivers' strike)
RAILWAYS

And there's good news for Rail travellers too. After an offer from the Railways Board last night one of the unions involved in the overtime ban by railway supervisors says they are ready to end the sanctions 'if other unions agree'.

The Railways Board offer has not been disclosed, but the unions' original demand was for a 15% increase in salaries ranging from £2,000 to £2,700 to restore their differentials.

RT: 26″

(Next item: Hull dock strike)

15. 9 April 1975 17.50 Item 2A   Maimane
(Previous item: Glasgow dustcart drivers' strike)
RAIL

The pay dispute which has disrupted train services for a fortnight has been settled. The three unions have accepted an offer from the British Railways Board, and the workshop supervisors will end their work-to-rule immediately.

But it's believed, it'll take some days for train services to return to normal because there's a backlog of maintenance on rolling stock.

RT: 18″

(Next item: Hull dock strike)

16. 9 April 1975 22.00 Item 12   Hutchence
(Previous item: Hull dock strike)
GORDON/MANCHESTER/RAIL

[first part on Manchester airport strike]

And the pay dispute which has disrupted train services for a fortnight is also over. The three unions involved accepted an offer from British Rail, and the workshop supervisors will end their work-to-rule immediately.

But it'll take some days for train services to return to normal, as there's a backlog of maintanance to be done on rolling stock.

RT: Approx 20″

(Next item: Leslie Whittle murder hunt)

22: THE HULL DOCK STRIKE

1. 9 April 1975 13.00 Item 5
(Previous item: Glasgow dustcart drivers' strike)
HULL DOCKERS

> Just three days after the London dockers' return to work after a five week strike, 2,000 dockers at Hull have decided to strike one day a week and ban all overtime.
>
> The Hull dockers say this will go on until employers honour an agreement to make a pay rise based on the retail price index.
>
> Talks broke down on Monday when the employers offered a 7½% increase. The dockers want between 11 and 12%.

RT: 26"

(Next item: Blizzards)

2. 9 April 1975 17.50 Item 4   Jamieson
(Previous item: BR workshop supervisors' work-to-rule)
HULL DOCKERS/SLIDE ?

> 2,000 dockers at Hull have begun an overtime ban and a series of weekly one-day strikes over a pay dispute.
>
> A dockers' spokesman said they'll continue their action until the employers honour an agreement to offer a pay rise based on the retail price index.
>
> Last Monday the employers offered a 67 and a half per cent increase.

RT: 17"

(Next item: Manchester airport strike)

3. 9 April 1975 22.00 Item 11RW   Jamieson
(Previous item: Glasgow dustcart drivers' strike)
ANDREW/HULL DOCKERS/SLIDE/REWRITE

> 2,000 dockers at Hull have begun an overtime ban and a series of weekly one-day token strikes over a pay dispute.
>
> A docker's spokesman said they'll continue action until the employers honour an agreement to offer a pay rise based on the retail price index.
>
> And tonight 900 Manchester dockers also stopped work over a pay dispute.

RT: 21"

(Next item: Manchester airport strike)

23: THE NEWMARKET STABLE LADS' STRIKE

1. 30 April 1975 13.00 Item 7
(Previous item: Stonehouse case)
STABLE LADS/BROUGH SCOTT FILM

Strikes in themselves are scarcely news any more, but this is a rather unusual one, because it's the one called by the stable lads at Newmarket racecourse, the first time stable lads have ever been on an official strike in this country. It began at midnight last night, but so far it's won mixed support. Here now is a report from Brough Scott.

FLUP   It was lovely at Newmarket this morning, but also very sad, because to the sound of hoofbeats and skylarks added the more raucous cries of the first official picket lines to be established at this headquarters of the turf. The dispute is over an extra £4.70 claimed by the Transport & General Workers' Union which represents over half of the 800 Newmarket stable lads. The trainers have offered three pounds, and I asked picket Ian Ramidge how he reacted to the trainers' claim that there was no more money in the kitty left:

Ramidge: Well, they're still going on holidays for a month at a time, and they're still running about in big cars and, you know, I think there's money there. How can they afford to give their lads backhanders...

Scott: How far will you take the picketing?

Ramidge: Well, just within the law. You can't go outside the law.

Scott: And how long do you want to go on?

Ramidge: We want to get back to work tonight if we can. We want to take it to arbitration, and if the arbitrator says we aren't worth a rise, then we'll all go back to work quite happy. If he says we are worth a rise, then we'll get a rise.

Scott: At John Winter's yard, 11 out of 30 lads were out on strike, and a makeshift staff were exercising the horses, and even Lester Piggott's chauffeur was giving a hand with the mucking out. Winter is leader of the Trainers' Association, and I asked him why he wouldn't go to arbitration.

Winter: Well, there's no more money. I have an expensive car, and I drive 30,000 a year, and I do a lot of work in my car, but in actual fact, I don't even own it. And I mean, that's part of the business. I mean, if you cut down on that there's still not enough money left over. My standard of living is dropping the same as everybody else's. Talking personally, and all we're trying to do is to preserve what we've got at the moment because even without this strike racing in Newmarket is going to contract considerably at the end of this year and next year.

Scott: For the moment, tomorrow's 1,000 Guineas meeting looks like being badly disrupted. With no starting stalls, photo finish, catering or even TV coverage. Brough Scott, for First Report, at Newmarket.

RT: 20″ + 2'16″

(Next item: Closing headlines)

2. 30 April 1975 17.50 Item 11   MDW
(Previous item: Northern Ireland election)
STABLE LADS

FILM UP   Stable lads at Newmarket have started their strike for higher pay — but first indications are that less than half of them are supporting the action.

Despite the strike, the three day Newmarket meeting, which includes the 2000 and 1000 Guineas classic races, will start on schedule tomorrow. But there are likely to be no starting stalls, catering facilities, television coverage, or photo finish.

RT: 21″

(Next item: Closing headlines)

3. 30 April 1975 22.00 Item 18   MDW
(Previous item: Soccer)
ANDREW/STABLE LADS/FILM

The striking Newmarket stable lads have threatened to step up their action for higher pay.

A union official says pickets will attempt to stop all locally-trained horses getting onto the Newmarket course for tomorrow's opening day of the classic meeting. This could affect runners in the One Thousand Guineas.

Already the meeting looks like having to do without starting stalls and photo finish equipment.

The stable lads started their strike at midnight but because less than a third of the Newmarket lads are supporting the action, they've had only mixed success so far.

Our racing correspondent, Brough Scott, reports:

TAKE FILM   It was lovely at Newmarket this morning but also very [sad],
SUPER   because to the sound of hoofbeats and skylarks were now added the
SCOTT   more raucous cries of the first official picket line to be established at this headquarters of the turf. Only 30% of the town's 700 stable lads

were actually out on strike, but the proceedings were pretty efficient. At the moment, lads average £35 for a seven-day week.

The dispute is over an extra £4.70 claimed by the Transport General Workers' Union which represents over half of the lads. The trainers have offered £3, and I asked picket Ian Ramidge for his opinion.

Ramidge: Well, they're still going on holidays a month at a time, and I mean, they're still running about in big cars, and you know, I think there's money in the game.

Scott: John Winter, leader of the Trainers' Federation, would not agree: 11 of his 30 lads are out out on strike, and a makeshift staff were exercising the horses. Even Lester Piggott's chauffeur was giving a hand with the mucking out. I asked him about the apparent difference in lifestyles.

Winter: Well, there's no more money. I have an expensive car, I drive 30,000 a year, and I do a lot of work in my car, but in actual fact I don't even own it and I mean, that's part of the business. I mean, if you cut down on that there's still not enough money left over. I mean, my standard of living is dropping same as everybody else's.

Scott: So, who is right? Lads, who want more than £35 for their seven day week, or trainers who are sure that any increase in charges will lose them owners, and therefore lads their jobs? BS, for NAT, at Newmarket.

RT: 2'06"

(Next item: Payoff)

The remaining coverage of this strike fell outside the survey period.

APPENDIX

HAROLD WILSON'S SPEECH ON GOVERNMENT AID TO INDUSTRY

at Cantrell Labour Club, Huyton, 3 January 1975.

Advance text as circulated by the Labour Party information department. Passages in bold were carried verbatim in ITN's report. Passages in italic were summarised. Harold Wilson occasionally departed from his circulated text, but these differences made no significant difference to his message. Emphasis is his.

'In a New Year broadcast last Sunday I warned that in Britain, as in the western world as a whole, the great danger we face, as great now as that of inflation, is the threat of recession and the consequential unemployment. But every one of us knows that these twin menaces to our economic stability and the living standards of the average family are not so much strangers one to another, as allies.

'For a year now our prices have been gravely affected by the four-fold increase in oil prices, and by the other prices inflated by world pressures. In these circumstances we cannot afford *any* avoidable surge in production costs – which would work through relentlessly to household costs – caused either by thoughtless or by calculated sectional demands for higher living standards which are unrealistic in the year or two ahead. Demands which, even if attained by a show of strength, would be won at the expense of less well off sections of the community – and which even those who sought and secured them would soon find have depreciated into worthlessness. Not only that, they would find that what they have achieved could be a powerful accelerator to the growth of unemployment – a threat to their own jobs.

'From the day we took office, Her Majesty's Government have warned of the dangers of world recession, and have pressed in every international forum where we have a part to play, for joint international action, and for individual action by our trading partners and colleagues.

'The Government's internal policies have been directed to maintaining a high level of employment. These policies have been extended from the purely financial and budgetary to direct intervention where jobs have been threatened. And, not least, because there are many employed in the motor industry here on Merseyside, I want to stress this tonight. *The most important, the most spectacular, Government industrial decision in the fight against unemployment, was our announcement before Christmas, that the Government have come to the rescue in the case of British Leyland.'*

'Several weeks ago it became clear that while British Leyland could survive and indeed prosper as a much smaller unit, a costly investment and modernisation programme would be required if the firm were to be maintained, as they and the Government want it maintained, as a major *producer,* a major *exporter,* and a major *employer of labour.* Investment on the massive scale required would not, it was clear, be forthcoming from private financing: it has to be Government investment, with appropriate Government participation in the equity and in control.

'We were already engaged in an urgent study of the help required, when the firm's even more critical and immediate liquidity problem became clear. Urgent action will be taken, on the basis of the most thorough examination of the circumstances and needs of the firm.

'*Our aim is to put production, exports and jobs on a secure and profitable basis. Because British Leyland can be made profitable, given the necessary investment.*

'**But the achievement of that aim does not depend on the action of Government alone. In a very real sense, the success of public intervention to fight the threat of unemployment means a full contribution, a fair day's work for a fair day's pay by everyone for whose security we are fighting.**

'**Parts of the British Leyland undertaking are profitable. Others are not. But public investment and participation cannot be justified on the basis of continued** *avoidable* **loss-making. Our intervention cannot be based on a policy of turning a private liability into a public liability.**

'**This means, against the acknowledged background of established collective bargaining and safeguards, efficient working methods and steady week-in, week-out production.**

'*In November, the last full month for which figures are available, the total car sales in Britain — themselves heavily down on last year — 35.64 per cent were imported from abroad. An important contribution to this unacceptable failure to compete by our home factories was lack of continuity of production due to strikes.*

'*In the Austin/Morris sector of British Leyland more than 350,000 man/days were lost through disputes in 1974 — getting on for two-thirds of this in one works. This sector was responsible for about 20 per cent of the man/days lost in the car industry last year. This in an industry which itself makes a disproportionate contribution to the loss of output through disputes, for with just over 2 per cent of the total employees in the whole of Britain it accounted for one-eighth of all the man/days lost in 1974 (a year which included the coalmining dispute) and getting on for one-third of the total national loss in 1973.*

'Whether this loss of production was acceptable or not with private capital involved, or whether private capital was unable to deal with such problems, is a matter now for historical argument. What is not a matter for argument, for the future, is this. With public capital, and an appropriate degree of public control involved, **the Government could not justify to Parliament or to the taxpayer the subsidising of large factories, involving thousands of jobs which could pay** their way, but are failing to do so because of manifestly avoidable stoppages of production.

'Industrial relations and the settlement or avoidance of disagreements within the established arrangements, are a continuing process and public financing will not call for any interference with them.

'But what is at stake in Britain in 1975 and the years after that is the future of the employment of our people. I repeat that *that*, from now on, depends not only on Government finance and participation, wherever that occurs, but on the wider and whole-hearted participation of all whose future, and whose families' future, depend on the success of the decisions the Government have taken and will take and which they intend to see through.'

INDEX (to Part I)

Abercombie N., 119
Able, K., 55
Adamson (NUM), 22
Adeney, M., 78
Advisory, Conciliation & Arbitration Service, 52, 96, 107n, 117
Aims of Industry, 5-6, 71
Ambulance controllers, 45n, 49, 51, 54, 57, 60
Annan Committee, 5, 10, 20, 30, 65, 71-72, 74-76, 81, 90, 136-138, 147n
APEX, 116-117
Army, 23, 41, 83, 89-91
Association of British Chambers of Commerce, 71
Avon County Council, 42, 45n, 59, 68

Bachrach, 16
Balance, 19, 25n
Baratz, 16
Baistow, T., 56
Benn, T., 10, 13n, 98, 111-113, 115
Bias, 5, 10-11, l6, 19, 24n, 25n, 48, 67, 119, 128-130, 132n, 137, 144
Birch, R., 96
Birt, J., 14, 30n
Blumler, J., 144
Boyd, J., 103
British Aircraft Corporation, 42, 68
British Airways, 36, 38, 49, 51, 54, 62, 67, 115-117
British Broadcasting Corporation, 9, 13, 18, 20, 23, 24n, 26, 37, 71-72, 84-86, 108, 118n, 136-138, 142, 145
British Film Institute, 138
British Leyland Motor Corporation, 31, 40, 42, 45n, 49, 52, 54-62, 67-68, 93-107, 121-123, 139
British Medical Association, 52
British Rail, 36, 37, 38, 39, 45n, 49, 51, 54, 57, 68, 143
British Steel Corporation, 113-115
Broadcasting Act, 1981, 25n

Campaign for Press and Broadcasting Freedom, 17
Castle, B., 56
Chadburn, R., 5
Chandler, Sir Geoffrey, 75
Channel Four, 11, 128, 144-145
Chemical Industry, 29
Chrysler, 102-106
Cine & Television Technicians, Association of, 8
Civil Servants, 41, 48, 49, 51, 54, 62-63, 68, 143
Clydeside, 83, 91
Coal Strike 1974, 7
Coal Strike 1984-85, 5, 78, 82n, 131n, 132n, 134, 140
Confederation of British Industry, 71-72
Conservative Party, 6, 17, 42, 52
Construction Industry, 29, 36
Consultants, 27, 36, 41, 49, 51, 54-55, 57, 62, 67
Consumers, 38, 39
Containerisation, 34, 35, 41, 49, 53-55, 65
Conti, 124
Cowley, 49, 51, 60, 64, 93-97, 102, 104, 107n

Cox, Sir Geoffrey, 9, 45n, 85
Curran, Sir Charles, 24n

Daily Mirror, 49, 51, 54, 61-62
Daily Telegraph, 122
Darlington & Stockton Times, 138
Datsun, 103
Democracy, 24n, 134
Department of Employment, 28-32, 35-37, 43, 48n
Differentials, 33, 37, 56-57, 61, 83-84, 85-87, 91
Disputes, see Strikes
Distribution, 35, 36
Diverse Reports, 11
Dix, B., 109
Docks, 34, 35, 41, 49-51, 53-54, 56, 62-64, 66-67, 77, 79, 140
Donovan Commission, 148n
Dunlop, 72, 122-123
Dustcart drivers, 23, 41, 43, 48-49, 51, 54, 62-64, 79, 83-92, 143, 146
Dynes, Councillor, 87, 89-90

Ebbw Vale, 41, 42, 57, 113-115
Eldridge, J., 8
Electricians, 33-34
Ellesmere Port, 42, 58, 104-105
Employment, Secretary of State for, 41
Employers, 5-8, 15, 22, 34-35, 48, 52, 57-58, 61, 63, 65-66, 68, 70n, 71-75, 78-79, 81, 82n, 94, 102n, 112, 118n, 122-123, 139-140
Engineering Industry, 29, 133
Engineering Workers, Amalgamated Union of, 50, 52, 58, 77, 96, 103
Equal pay, 33-34
European Community, 42, 80
Evans, M., 104-105

Fairness, 24n, 128
Falkland Islands, 67
Financial News, 2
Finniston, Sir Monty, 114-115
Fleet Street, 8, 49, 52, 54, 62, 131n, 135
Foot, M., 42, 114-115
Ford, Motor Co. 35, 57, 68, 103-104, 118n
Foreign News, 27
Frames, inferential and dominant, 84-85, 88, 102, 119-121, 124-126, 129
Freedom of Information Act, 134, 134
Friday Alternative, 10

Gallup Poll, 7
Gans, H., 127
Gardner, C., 20-21
General & Municipal Workers, National Union of, 77
Gerbner, G., 16
Glasgow, 52, 68, 116-117, 122
Glasgow Corporation, 83-85, 87, 89-90, 92n
Glasgow dustcart drivers, 23, 41, 43, 48-49, 51, 54, 62-64 68, 79, 83-92, 146

Glasgow Trades Council, 90
Glasgow University Media Group, 8, 12, 15, 21, 23, 28-33, 35, 37, 42-44, 47, 59-61, 63, 65-66, 68, 71, 74-76, 81, 85-88, 90, 99-100, 104, 113, 116, 119, 122, 125, 134, 139
Goffman, I., 43
Gormley, J., 81
Gouldner, A., 127
Graphic & Allied Trades, Society of, 35, 38, 49, 51, 54, 61-62
Gray, Sir William, 89
Green, M., 54, 111-112
Greene, Sir Hugh, 24n
Guardian newspaper, 35, 95

Hall, S., 16, 18, 24n, 124, 126, 133
Hartmann, P., 140
Hatfield, K., 50, 102, 114, 121-122
Healey, D., 17
Heath, E., 6, 8, 42
Hegemony, 18, 19, 123, 126-127
Heysham, 38, 57
Hilton, F., 90
Hobbs, L., 6, 10-11, 82n
Hoggart, R., 84
Holmes, D., 107n, 147n
Holloway, C., 63
Hood, A., 90
Hospital Consultants' and Specialists' Association, 52, 55
House of Commons, 41, 99, 141
HTV, 57
Huckfield, L., 95
Hull, 35, 53, 57, 68, 111
Hunterstone, 114
Huyton, 94-96

Ideology, 10, 15-17, 19-20, 24n, 44, 48, 60, 69, 119-120, 123-127, 144, 146
Impartiality, 5, 8, 19, 25n, 128-130
Imperial Chemical Industries, 72
Imperial Typewriters, 42, 49, 51, 54, 57, 62-64, 68, 111-113
Independent Broadcasting Authority, 10, 24n
Independent Television News, 9, 12, 13n, 19-20, 23, 26-28, 33-39, 42-43, 46n, 48-52, 55-57, 59-62, 64, 67-69, 83-92n, 94-97, 99-101, 103-104, 106, 107n, 108, 110-113, 115-116, 122-123, 125, 137, 139, 141, 144
Industrial news, 11-12, 27, 47-48, 71, 75, 80, 126
Institute of Directors, 5
Iron & Steel Trades Confederation, 114

Jones, J., 7, 50, 57, 79
Jones, N., 77

Kee, R., 56, 64, 86, 102, 116
Kellner, D., 127, 131n
Kitson, A., 87, 89

Labour Government, 42, 52, 55, 89-90, 104, 112
Labour movement, 6, 10-11, 82n
Labour Party, 6, 9-10, 17, 87-88, 109, 136
Lazarsfeld, P., 136
Lewis, M., 58, 103
Leyshon, S., 57
Linwood, 102-104
Litton Industries, 68, 111-112
Liverpool, 48-49, 51, 54, 62-63, 91, 143
Lockouts, 26, 34, 45n, 55, 122
London, 34-35, 41-42, 49-51, 54, 62-67, 77, 79, 116-117, 140
London Transport, 41-42
Longbridge, 107n, 136
Lowry, P., 101, 103

Man Alive, 93, 147n
Management, see Employers
Marx, K., 18, 44
McDonald, T., 21-23, 99, 114
McGahey, M., 124
McGarry, E., 97, 99-100
McKee, P., 137, 139
McQuail, D., 72, 126, 135
Media studies, 8, 10, 23, 126, 128-130, 133-142
Media Studies Association, 135
Miliband, R., 126
Millam, B., 92n, 89
Miners, 5, 7, 21-23, 27-29, 35, 63, 66, 77, 94,, 124, 128-129, 131n
Mineworkers, National Union of, 66, 70n, 74, 77-78, 80-81, 131n, 134
Money Box, 72
Money Programme, 141
Morris, Jamie, 109-111, 140
Morris, John, 115
Morriston Hospital, 35, 49,˙51, 54, 62-63
Motor industry, 28-29, 33, 36, 39-40, 49-50, 57-58, 93-107
Murray, L., 79

National & Local Government Officers Association, 77, 80-81, 110
National Board for Prices and Incomes, 89
National Coal Board, 23, 70n, 74, 131n, 132n
National Graphical Association, 34, 49, 51, 54, 56, 62
National Health Service, 41, 49, 51, 54, 56, 62, 108-109
National Joint Council for Civil Air Transport, 117
Naturalism, 19, 43
Neutrality, 19, 20, 25n, 48
Newsnight, 77, 144
News at One, 145
Newspaper Publishers' Association, 34, 38, 56

Paisley, I., 111
Panorama, 144
Parkin, L., 56
Pay and strikes, 36-37, 51-53, 55, 61, 64, 68, 83-88, 91, 96

Pay beds, 41, 50, 55, 61, 79, 108-111
Philo, G., 9, 11, 21, 93
Pluralism, 126-127
Political news, 27
Port of London, 35
Powell, E., 111
Prescott, J., 107n
Prices, 6, 35, 52
Prior, J., 32, 96
Prominent Stoppages, 32-34, 36-37, 101
Protheroe, A., 71-72, 74
Public Employees, National Union of, 77, 79-80, 108-111, 118n

Railwaymen, National Union of, 39, 51
Railway Signalmen, Union of, 39, 51, 64
Ramidge, T., 59
Rank-and-file, 47, 50, 63-69, 88-89
Reality, 30-44, 62, 68, 75, 120, 129
'Red Robbo', 136
Reporting Scotland, 88
Robinson, M., 142
Rose, D., 99
Ross, W., 88
Ryder, Sir Don, 97-98, 100

Scanlon, H., 7, 96
Scargill, A., 5, 66, 74, 78, 81, 111, 132n
Schlesinger, P., 43, 135
Science, 21, 26, 48, 71, 139, 147n
Scotland, 49, 103, 114
Scotland Today, 88
Scottish Trades Union Congress, 88, 90
Sealink, 38
Sheppard, J., 20-21
Shipbuilding, 31, 33, 36, 45n
Shop floor view, see Rank-and-file
Shop stewards, 58, 64-65, 72, 90, 97, 99, 103, 107n, 115, 118n, 124, 140
Short-time working, 30, 37, 58, 102-104
Shrewsbury pickets, 140
Signalmen, 31, 36, 39, 49, 51, 54, 60, 62
Sissons, P., 97-99, 137, 139
Sit-ins, 35, 41-42, 57-58, 68, 111-115
Skinner, D., 95
Smith, A., 136
Smith, G., 95, 97, 115-116
Social Contract, 75, 82n, 83-84, 120

Social Science Research Council, 8
Solsgirth Colliery, 21-22, 140
Steel, D., 17
Steelworkers, 57
Stewart, Prof. G., 86, 89
Stokes, Lord, 103-104
Stoppages, see Strikes
Strikes, as proportion of news, 26-27, 45n
Strikes, causes, 37, 47-48, 53-69, 70n, 85-87, 91, 96, 112, 115-116
Strikes, official, 47, 52, 84, 86
Strikes, prominence in news, 27-28
Strikes, statistics of, 23, 28-32, 35, 43, 60-62, 70n, 100-101, 122, 148
Strikes, unofficial, 47, 52, 63-64, 86-87
Sun newspaper, 122, 135
Swan-Hunter, 30
Swann, Sir Michael, 137, 148n

Tate, C., 112
Theedon, D., 51
Thirkettle, J., 103
Thomas, T., 116
Thurber, I., 133
Times newspaper, 35, 95
Torode, J., 78, 131n
Tracey M., 135
Trade Union World, 11
Trades Union Congress, 7, 10, 44, 71, 77, 79, 109
Transport industry, 36, 39, 57, 83
Transport & General Workers' Union, 7, 50, 57-58, 64, 77-79, 84, 86-87, 91, 104, 112-113, 117
Tuners, 49, 51, 54, 60, 62, 93, 95-97, 107n, 139
Tunstall, J., 131n
TV Eye, 144

Union World, 141

Vauxhall, 42, 58, 104-105

Ward, G., 140
Westminster Hospital, 49, 50, 51, 54-55, 57, 62-63, 79, 108-111
Williams, R., 123
Wilson, H., 8, 39, 93-95, 98-99, 102, 114
Wintour, P., 78
Workshop Supervisors (BR), 49, 51, 54, 62, 68,
Work-to-contract, 26, 41, 67